Proceedings of the North East Linguistic Society 34

Stony Brook University

Volume Two

Edited by
Keir Moulton and Matthew Wolf

ii

Published by
GLSA
(Graduate Linguistic Student Association)
Department of Linguistics
South College
University of Massachusetts
Amherst, MA 01003-7130
U.S.A.

glsa@linguist.umass.edu

Cover design: Jan Anderssen

ISBN: 1-59457-571-1 (Volume 2)

Contents

Volume Two

Locality in Echo Epenthesis: Comparison with Reduplication 295
Shigeto Kawahara

Foot Structure in Nuu-chah-nulth: Reconsidering Foot Typology within OT 311
Eun-Sook Kim

The Feature [Tense] Revisited: The Case of Korean Consonants 319
Hyunsoon Kim

Internally-Headed Relatives Instantiate Situation Subordination 333
Min-Joo Kim

The Case for Null Subject-Verb Agreement Morphology in Bantu 345
Kasangati K. W. Kinyalolo

Chain Resolution in Hebrew V(P)-fronting 357
Idan Landau

Syntax and Semantics of Focus Particles: Scope and the Mirror Principle 373
Youngjoo Lee

C-locality and the Interaction of Reflexives and Ditransitives 389
Jeffrey Lidz and Alexander Williams

Scope marking with adjunct clauses: new arguments for Dayal's approach 405
Anikó Lipták

Causatives Without Causers and Burzio's Generalization 425
Vita G. Markman

Processing Relative Clauses in Japanese with Two Attachment Sites 441
Edson T. Miyamoto, Michiko Nakamura, and Shoichi Takahashi

Two Constructions with *Most* and their Semantic Properties 453
Kimiko Nakanishi and Maribel Romero

On the Present Perfect Puzzle 469
Roumyana Pancheva and Arnim von Stechow

Nonlocal Reduplication 485
Jason Riggle

The Influence of Binding Theory on the On-line Reference Resolution of Pronouns 497
Jeffrey T. Runner, Rachel S. Sussman, and Michael K. Tanenhaus

A Silent Noun in Partitives 505
Uli Sauerland and Kazuko Yatsushiro

Presuppositon & Root Transforms in Adjunct Clauses 517
Miyuki Sawada and Richard K. Larson

Preverbal Negative Polarity Items in Cantonese 529
Scott Shank

Two Types of Multiple Accusative Constructions in Korean: 541
Inalienable Possession Type and Set Relation Type
Chang-Yong Sim

Event Decomposition and the Syntax and Semantics of *–kan* in Standard Indonesian 555
Minjeong Son and Peter Cole

Pseudogapping and Cyclic Linearization 571
Shoichi Takahashi

Prosody as a Diagonalization of Syntax. Evidence from Complex Predicates 587
Michael Wagner

Demonstratives, Definiteness, and Determined Reference 603
Lynsey Wolter

Reduplication in English Homeric Infixation 619
Alan C. L. Yu

Locality in Echo Epenthesis: Comparison with Reduplication[*]

Shigeto Kawahara

University of Massachusetts, Amherst

1.   Introduction

In echo epenthesis the quality of epenthetic vowels is determined by a neighboring vowel. This is illustrated by the examples from Kolami given in (1):

(1) Kolami echo epenthesis (Zou 1991: 463)

/ayk+t/ →	[ay<u>a</u>kt]	'swept away' cf.	/ayk/	→	[ayk]
/erk+t/ →	[er<u>e</u>kt]	'lit (fire)' cf.	/erk/	→	[erk]

In the data above, one underlying vowel is realized twice in the output, and one of the realizations serves as an epenthetic vowel to break up triconsonantal clusters.

Echo epenthesis involves repetition of one underlying segment and in this sense superficially resembles reduplication, exemplified below in (2) by the Agta plural. Again, a single underlying string of segments surfaces twice.

(2) Agta reduplication (Marantz 1982: 447)

/takki/	→	[<u>tak</u>-takki]	'leg(s)'
/uffu/	→	[<u>uf</u>-uffu]	'thigh(s)'

This similarity might lead one to think that that echo epenthesis and reduplication are fundamentally the same phenomenon; in fact, Kitto and de Lacy (1999) propose to treat them both under the general rubric of copying by way of correspondence (McCarthy and Prince 1995).

This paper, however, points out one major difference between echo epenthesis and reduplication. In terms of locality, echo epenthesis is subject to a stricter restriction than is reduplication: reduplication can copy a distant segment to satisfy a higher ranked

[*] I would like to acknowledge the support that I received from the following people: Michael Becker, Kathryn Flack, Nancy Hall, Beth Hume, Nicole Nelson, Hajime Ono, Chris Potts, Adam Werle, Cheryl Zoll, the members of UMass Phonology Reading Group and the audience at NELS 34 at SUNY, Stony Brook. John McCarthy and Joe Pater deserve special thanks for constant advice and encouragement. Remaining errors are mine.

constraint, but echo epenthesis never copies a distant vowel. To capture this difference, I propose that echo epenthesis and reduplication involve different mechanisms: echo epenthesis, which is inherently phonological, is always achieved by spreading of a V-place node, while reduplication is achieved by correspondence-based copying. To derive this asymmetry, I propose a restriction that copying is available only for morphological operations like reduplication, but not for phonological operations like echo epenthesis, which is driven by phonotactics. This position is, within the current framework of Optimality Theory (Prince and Smolensky 1993), a defense of Prince's (1987) claim that "copying [...] is fundamentally obliged to morphology" (507).

The rest of this paper is organized as follows. In §2, I illustrate the difference in locality between echo epenthesis and reduplication, and propose a way to account for the difference. §3 further discusses locality in echo epenthesis in more detail and also considers predictions of the proposed theory. In §4, I present several cases of nonlocal reduplication which contrast with known cases of echo epenthesis. §5 discusses theoretical implications for current phonological theory, mainly focusing on the role of copying and spreading in phonology.

2.   The difference and proposal illustrated

Consider the hypothetical pattern in (3). With the standard sonority scale (low vowels are the most sonorous; high vowels are the least; and mid vowels are inbetween), the hypothetical examples in (3) illustrate a pattern in which echo epenthesis targets the most sonorous vowel in the underlying form, skipping the closer vowel that could be potentially repeated ([e] in (a) and [i] in (b)). The main finding of this paper is that such sonority-based echo epenthesis is not attested. This is based on my survey of 55 cases of echo epenthesis.[1] The absence of such cases indicates that echo epenthesis is subject to a strict locality requirement.

(3) Sonority-based echo epenthesis (unattested)
    a.   /tametk/   →   [tametak]
    b.   /temitk/   →   [temitek]

The absence of such a pattern is all the more striking given that a parallel pattern is possible in reduplication. For example, in Nakanai, the most sonorous vowel in the base is copied as a reduplicative vowel (Johnston 1980; Spaelti 1997 among others) regardless of the distance between the corresponding segments. Some data are given in (4). As shown in (4ab), reduplication targets V_1 when V_1 is more sonorous than or equally sonorous to V_2. However, when V_2 is more sonorous than V_1, as in (4c-e), then V_2 is copied. The data in (4a) and (4c) constitute a minimal pair in this regard.

---

[1] The survey only includes echo epenthesis driven by phonotactic reasons such as cluster resolution or coda avoidance, excluding what has been treated as "morphemes with unspecified timing slots" (a.k.a. harmonizing affixes). It also excludes languages that have vowel harmony like Turkish. Due to space limitations, the entire list of these patterns and references are omitted from this version of the paper. See Kawahara (2004).

(4) Sonority-based reduplication

a.	/RED-taro/	$\rightarrow$	[ta-taro]	'away'
b.	/RED-buli/	$\rightarrow$	[bu-buli]	'roll'
c.	/RED-mota/	$\rightarrow$	[ma-mota]	'vines'
d.	/RED-kusa/	$\rightarrow$	[ka-kusa]	'wet'
e.	/RED-biso/	$\rightarrow$	[bo-biso]	'two by two'

Therefore, it seems that echo epenthesis is subject to a more strict locality requirement. To account for this difference, I propose that echo epenthesis always involves spreading a V-place node (see Clements 1989 *et seq* for V-place in feature organization) as in (5) whereas reduplication is achieved by correspondence-based copying (McCarthy and Prince 1995; also Marantz 1982; Steriade 1988), as illustrated in (6) (the numerical subscripts represent a correspondence relationship).

(5) Echo epenthesis as spreading of a V-place   (6) Reduplication as copying by correspondence

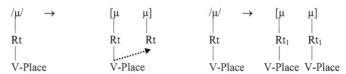

Given the uncontroversial assumption that spreading affects intervening segments while correspondence copying does not, the difference between echo epenthesis and reduplication follows naturally. Spreading can be viewed as the extension of articulatory gestures across a time domain to encompass more than one segment; therefore, spreading necessarily affects intervening segments. This is why spreading of a V-place node across another vowel, as depicted in (7), is impossible. (See below for some concrete proposals regarding the source of ungrammaticality of (7).) Correspondence, on the other hand, is nothing more than a relationship between two segments (McCarthy and Prince 1995), and it does not affect intervening segments at all. Therefore copying one vowel across a different vowel without affecting the latter is possible, as illustrated in (8).

(7) Skipping impossible for spreading   (8) Skipping possible for copying

To guarantee that echo epenthesis is always achieved by spreading rather than copying, we need to impose a restriction on assignment on correspondence. More concretely, because echo epenthesis should never be achieved by correspondence, we need to limit correspondence to morphological operations, despite some recent claims to the contrary. Two mechanisms have been proposed for non-reduplicative copying, which are both illustrated below in (9) ("S" stands for a segment; arrows represent correspondence relationships):

(9) Two ways to achieve copying outside of reduplication

(a) $/...S.../$ (b) $/....S.../$

         [...S...S]$_{morph}$ [S...S]$_{morph}$

    via surface-to-surface correspondence   *via multiple-IO mapping*

(9a) achieves copying by way of surface-to-surface correspondence just like reduplication, but without any reduplicative morpheme (see Kitto and de Lacy 1999; Rose and Walker 2001; Zuraw 2003 among others). (9b) involves (long distance) splitting, and achieves copying by having two output correspondents of one input segment (Ussishkin 2000; Nelson 2003 and others).

   As I have argued above, allowing such mappings predicts an unattested echo epenthesis pattern that potentially skips an intervening vowel. Thus we need to rule these out. Meanwhile, copying should be possible for reduplication, i.e., where an independent morpheme, which is usually taken to be a phonologically empty morpheme RED, is involved. Therefore, the correspondence relation depicted in (10) should be possible:

(10) $/...S...+ RED/$

             [...S...] [...S...]

To differentiate (9a) and (9b) from (10), the crucial observation is that the difference lies in the fact that in (9a) and (9b), multiple correspondents of one underlying segment are in a single morpheme, while in (10) they are in different morphemes.

   More formally, to rule out (9a) and (9b) while allowing (10), I propose to impose a restriction on correspondence, relying on the notion of *exponence* and *Morpheme Associate* in McCarthy and Prince (1995: 312):

   A morpheme stands in a primitive relation of *exponence* with some structure
   of segments or autosegments. Typically, this is given by the lexical entry of the
   morpheme, but in the case of reduplicative morphemes, their only content is
   what's in the output, and this is then their exponence.

The exponents of underlying nonempty morphemes are their segments found in the input. However, the exponents of reduplicative morphemes, which by definition lack underlying content, are their output segments. McCarthy and Prince (1995:312) further define a more general notion of morphemic content, *Morpheme Associate*, which is preserved under correspondence:

(11)   Morpheme Associate:
       A segment (autosegment) x is an associate of morpheme M if x or some
       correspondent of x is an exponent of M.

Given this definition, in both (9a) and (9b) the multiple correspondents of S are
output morpheme associates of S in the input. Now consider the diagram below which
summarizes exponence and output morpheme associates in (9a), (9b) and (10)
(Morpheme Associates in the input are ignored as they are irrelevant for the discussion):

(12)   exponence of morph M1

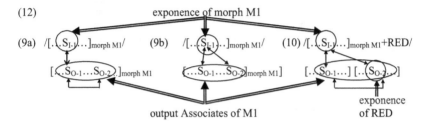

       output Associates of M1   exponence
                                                            of RED

One critical observation is that having multiple Associates in the output (S_{O-1} and S_{O-2}) of
one underlying segment in morpheme M1 ($=S_{I-1}$) is allowed iff one of the Associates is
also exponent of another morpheme. I thus propose the following restriction:

(13)   Let S be elements in the Input and Output where
            $S_I \in$ Input
            $S_o \in$ Output
       S_{O-1} and S_{O-2} cannot be output Associates of a morpheme M1 for S_{I-1} unless S_{O-2}
       is also an exponent of morpheme M2 (where M1 ≠ M2).

As a corollary of this proposal, multiple correspondents of one underlying segment,
whether generated by (9a) or (9b), are not allowed within one morpheme.[2] It then
follows that a phonological operation like echo epenthesis cannot be achieved by (9a) or
(9b), as it would violate (13).

3.   Locality in Echo Epenthesis

This section discusses how to rule out the unattested pattern in (3) under the
current proposal. Given (13), copying is inherently limited to morphological operations.
As a consequence, copying, which can potentially skip intervening segments (see §4),
cannot be used for echo epenthesis. The only way to achieve echo epenthesis, therefore,
is to resort to spreading. However, spreading cannot skip a potential target for the reason
detailed below.

---

[2] This has consequences for a correspondence-based analysis of fission and other phenomena
(such as an analysis of Semitic biconsonantal roots). See §5 for some discussion.

For the sake of illustration, I assume locality of spreading, which basically prohibits skipping in spreading.[3] It does not matter whether we use strict locality, which requires segment-level locality (Gafos 1996; Ní Chiosáin and Padgett 1997 and others) or tier-dependent locality which requires spreading of V-place to be local at the level of the V-place tier (Archangeli and Pulleyblank 1994 among others). I take the former view here for illustration, which follows from the conception of spreading as extending the temporal span of articulatory gestures to encompass more than one segmental root node. However, nothing hinges upon this choice.

Schematically, suppose that underlying $/C_1V_1C_2V_2C_3C_4/$ attempts to resolve the word-final consonantal cluster via spreading of V_1. In order for V_1 to be realized between C_3 and C_4, the V-Place of V_1 must also spread onto V_2 (recall that skipping is impossible). Total spreading of V_1 changes V_2 into V_1, since one vowel cannot simultaneously bear two V-Place specifications.[4] This is illustrated in the diagram (14), using /tametk/ as an example, which results in [tam<u>a</u>t<u>a</u>k], not [tamet<u>a</u>k]:

(14)

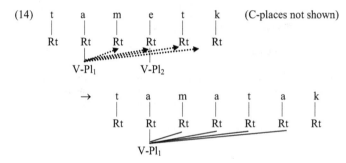

In short, the reason why echo epenthesis cannot map underlying /tametk/ onto [tametak] is that, given locality of spreading, it must instead result in [tamatak].[5]

To complete the discussion on locality of echo epenthesis, there is one more point to address. Although echo epenthesis is subject to a very strict locality restriction, there is one case where we find variation in terms of which segment is targeted for echo epenthesis.[6] The variation arises in case where a glide is closer to the target position than a vowel. In such a configuration, some languages chose the intervening glide as the echoed segment, but other languages allow such intervening glides to be transparent. For

---

[3] In theories that do not assume such strict locality, a representation like (5) is ruled out by prohibition on line crossing (see Goldsmith 1976; Clements and Hume 1995).

[4] A V-place node may be imposed on consonants; this means that the vocalic gesture is coarticulated with the consonantal gestures. In some recent proposals, such structures are claimed to be marked and penalized by a various set of constraints. See e.g. Gafos and Lombardi (1999).

[5] The issue of vowel transparency in vowel harmony remains as a problem for a theory that assumes locality of spreading. The question - why spreading of the entire V-Place (in echo epenthesis) does not exhibit transparency - is an interesting question, but to solve this problem is beyond the scope of this paper. Bakovic (2000: 263-268) provides a nice overview of several approaches for relevant problems.

[6] This observation has already been made by Kitto and de Lacy (1999), though their analysis is based on morphemes with unspecified timing slots.

example, given an input like /twa/, two outputs are possible cross-linguistically: [tuwa] and [tawa]. This variation is illustrated by the following examples from Fula and Winnebago:

(15) Fula Borrowing from French (Paradis 1996: 516)

a. [CC(≠G)V]: echo a vowel

French	Fula	
[plas]	[pa̱las]	'place'
[traktœr]	[ta̱raktɔr]	'tractor'

b. [CGV]: echo of a glide

French	Fula	
[bwasõ]	[bu̱wasɔŋ]	'drink'
[kwafe]	[ku̱wa:f-a:-dɛ]	'coif'

(16) Winnebago epenthesis (Miner 1992)

a. [CC(≠G)V]: echo a vowel

/ʃroʃ/	[ʃo̱roʃ]	'deep'
/xrutʃ/	[xu̱rutʃ]	'inch long'

b. [CGV]: echo a vowel

/kwe/	[ke̱we]	NO GLOSS
/ʃ+waʃi/	[ʃawaʃi]	'dance 2nd'

Glides in Winnebgao are transparent to echo epenthesis, while glides in Fula are opaque. This ambiguous behavior of glides is independently observed in the context of vowel harmony: some glides are transparent while other glides are opaque to vowel harmony, which is arguably another kind of operation which spreads vocalic features (Clements 1977 *et seq*). Following Herman (1994) and Hume (1995), this dual behavior of glides can be captured as resulting from the dual status of glides: some glides are consonantal, having C-place specifications, while other glides are vocalic and therefore have V-place specifications instead.[7]

Glides in Fula, therefore, have V-place values, and thus echo epenthesis cannot spread across these glides. This can either be achieved by a prohibition on line crossing (Goldsmith 1976; Clements and Hume 1995) or, if we assume strict locality, can be derived from the impossibility of two contradictory V-place specifications on a single segment. Either way, as a result, echo epenthesis must be initiated by the intervening glides because spreading across these vowels is impossible.[8] Glides in Winnebago, on the other hand, have only C-place specifications, and therefore it is possible for V-place to spread through them just like vowel harmony can rather freely permeate consonants.

In summary, I have pointed out two generalizations concerning the locality of echo epenthesis:

(17) (i)   Echo epenthesis never targets a distant vowel.
      (ii) Echo epenthesis can target a vowel when a closer glide is available.

---

[7] Another way to account for glides' variation between vocalic and consonantal is to assume that glides can either be true onsets or be incorporated in nucleus thereby functioning as nuclear onglides (see Smith (2002: 146-158) and references cited therein). I do not attempt to apply this line approach to the problem of variable transparency of glides here.

[8] In some languages, once spreading is blocked, a default vowel is epenthesized. See the Japanese foreign word epenthesis case discussed below.

I have argued that if echo epenthesis is always achieved by spreading, the first local property of echo epenthesis follows. The second property can be captured by assuming that the status of place specifications for glides is cross-linguistically variable.

Finally, to close this section, I discuss some more predictions of the proposal in (13) for echo epenthesis. Due to space limitations, I can only briefly discuss each of the predictions; see Kawahara (2004) for further discussion on these points. The predictions are:

(18)   (i)   There is no long-distance consonantal echo epenthesis across vowels.
       (ii)   Echo epenthesis can be blocked by intervening segments.
       (iii)   Length is never transferred.

First, it has been observed that major C-place does not spread across vowels (Clements and Hume 1995; Gafos 1996; Ní Chiosáin and Padgett 1997 *inter alia*); therefore the proposed theory, which prohibits non-reduplicative copying, predicts that there should be no language that has consonantal echo epenthesis across vowels. This prediction seems to be borne out, since, for example, no language is reported to supply a consonant to onsetless syllables by long-distance consonantal echo epenthesis; there are no cases like /ata/ → [tata], /aka/ → [kaka].[9]

Second, spreading is known to sometimes be blocked by a particular set of segments, so echo epenthesis should also sometimes be blocked when certain segments would intervene between the echoed vowels. Japanese loanword epenthesis provides an example: echo epenthesis takes place only across [h]. Echo epenthesis takes place across [h] as in [bahha] 'Bach' or [gohho] 'Gogh', but a default [ɯ] is inserted instead if an oral consonant intervenes, as in [sokkɯsɯ] 'socks'. This sort of laryngeal transparency is one well-known property of spreading (Steriade 1987).

Finally, since length not a property of segments, it cannot be transmitted when a segment spreads ("length harmony" is not attested; see Hyman and Udoh 2002 for recent discussion). This predicts that even when a long vowel initiates echo epenthesis, the result is always a short vowel because of the effect of *LONGVOWEL (no faithfulness constraint could require an echoed vowel to preserve the length of the trigger vowel). On the other hand, if echo epenthesis could be achieved by correspondence-based copying, IDENT-BR(μ) could produce long epenthetic echo vowels. Note that in reduplication, length of the base is sometimes transferred to the reduplicants. In Kihehe reduplication, for example, as seen in /mi-doodo+RED/ → [mi-doodo-doodo] 'fairly little', the long vowel reduplicates as long and the short vowel as short (Odden and Odden 1985). In my survey, the prediction in (18c) is also borne out, although there are admittedly not many cases where echo epenthesis is triggered by long vowels.

4.   Locality in reduplication

In §3, I discussed the locality requirement on echo epenthesis. In this section, I

---

[9] Kawu (2000) argues that such a case exists in Yoruba, but the pattern he discusses is inherently morphological, which is likely to involve reduplication. See Marantz (1982) and Alderete et al. (1999) for an analysis of this case as reduplication.

show that even though reduplication too is subject to a locality requirement, the requirement here is less stringent. I first provide illustrative cases of nonlocal reduplication. Next, adopting the position that locality of corresponding segments is governed by violable constraints (Hogoboom 2003; Kitto and de Lacy 1999; Nelson 2003; Riggle this volume), I provide an analysis of these cases. This assumes that reduplication is achieved by a mechanism different from spreading; namely, by correspondence-based copying, a standard position in the generative literature (McCarthy and Prince 1995; Marantz 1982; Steriade 1988).[10]

4.1.   Examples

The fact that the locality requirement in reduplication is violable is clearly illustrated by reduplication in Nakanai. The data are repeated below:

(19) Sonority based reduplication

a.	/RED-taro/	→	[ta-taro]	'away'
b.	/RED-buli/	→	[bu-buli]	'roll'
c.	/RED-mota/	→	[ma-mota]	'vines'
d.	/RED-kusa/	→	[ka-kusa]	'wet'
e.	/RED-biso/	→	[bo-biso]	'two by two'

As seen in (c-e), when V_2 is more sonorous than V_1, V_2 is reduplicated. Nakanai is not an isolated example; a similar example is found in Tawala, where a CV_1V_2 base reduplicates as CV_2-CV_1V_2, as in *ge-gae* 'go up' (Ezard 1997: 43) in which V_1 is never copied.[11] Efik (Cook 1987) provides yet another example where, if the base has [-ATR] vowel followed by [+ATR] vowel, the second vowel is copied; /RED+tika/ → [a-tika] 'kick'.[12]

Yoruba ideophone reduplication shows a parallel sonority-driven copying pattern, but for consonants (Nelson 2003: 174-185 and references cited therein).[13] Yoruba expands three-syllable ideophones to four syllables by copying one syllable to express emphasis or increased intensity. The distinct behavior of phonological two types of

---

[10] When reduplicative copying is impossible for independent reasons, other strategies can be used to assign exponence to reduplicants. In Igbo and Lushootseed, for example, epenthesis is used when copying is made impossible by higher ranked constraints (Alderete et al. 1999). Similarly, in Fe?Fe? Bemileke, spreading is necessitated when copying is impossible, and further epenthesis is observed when spreading is blocked. See Kawahara (2004) for an analysis of Fe?Fe? Bemileke.

[11] Given that V_2 is always less sonorous than V_1 and thus is shorter than V_1, it might be that reduplicative vowels are required to be as short as possible (see Kirchner 1996; Alderete et al. 1999).

[12] This reduplication fails to copy a consonant, but it is a general property of this language that prefixes begin with a vowel.

[13] Nelson (2003) in fact argues that (20) is not a case of morphological reduplication but rather of phonological augmentation to a four-syllable template, arguing that a morphological analysis cannot explain the difference between (a) and (b) in (20). However, a simple analysis is possible as discussed below. Moreover, since this process accompanies a change in meaning, it casts doubt on an analysis that augmentation is purely phonological. Also, as Nelson admits, there are some cases where the same process creates an output larger than four syllables; if this echo were the result of purely a phonological requirement to be four syllables, this pattern remains unexplained. Hence, I take the data in (20) as a genuine case of morphological reduplication.

ideophones is of some interest here: when the third syllable has an [r] onset, the target of reduplication is either the third or second syllable; otherwise, it is always the third syllable that is targeted. Some examples are provided in (20):

(20) Yoruba ideophone reduplication

    a. CVCVrV → CVC$_i$V$_j$rVC$_i$V$_j$ or CVCVrVrV

    pepere → pepere-pe ~ pepere-re   'of being very cute and robust'
    gègèrè → gègèrè-gè ~ gègèrè-rè   'of being very stout and bulky'
    gogoro → gogoro-go ~ gogoro-ro   'loftiness'

    b. CVCVC(≠r)V → CVCVC$_i$V$_j$C$_i$V$_j$

    rogodo → rogodo-do   'of being very round and small'
    lɔkɔtĭ → lɔkɔtĭ-tĭ   'of being very sticky'
    lɔ́kósán → lɔ́kósán-sán   'of being very slim and agile'

As seen in (20a), syllables with an onset [r] can be skipped in reduplicative copying. The variation in (20a) follows from avoiding [r] onsets in reduplicants; [r] is a sonorous segment and hence is avoided as an onset consonant. Such avoidance of onset [r] is in fact independently motivated in the phonology of Yoruba, which manifests itself through the optional deletion of intervocalic [r] (see Akinlabi 1993).

Finally, so-called opposite-edge reduplication constitutes another example of reduplication that skips potential local targets. Even though some recent proposals, notably Nelson (2003), argue that such cases are nonexistent, Creek provides one convincing case of opposite-edge reduplication (Riggle this volume):

(21) Creek reduplication

          Base   Reduplicated
    a.   polo:k-i: polo:-po-k-i: 'round'
    b.   holwak-i: holwa:ho-k-i: 'ugly'

Descriptively speaking, the stem-initial CV is copied and infixed before the root-final consonant. Notice again that potentially closer targets are skipped for reduplicative copying: [l] in (21a), and [l] and [w] in (21b).

In summary, there is a set of cases where reduplication skips potential targets that are closer than segments which are actually copied. This contrasts with echo epenthesis, where such skipping is not allowed, as discussed in §3.

4.2. Analyses

This difference between echo epenthesis and reduplication can be derived from the difference in the mechanisms involved: as shown in §3, if echo epenthesis is always achieved via spreading, its strict locality condition follows on the assumption that spreading affects each intervening segment. On the other hand, if reduplication involves copying by way of correspondence, then the weaker locality condition on reduplication follows if such locality is governed by violable constraints. It then follows that skipping is possible in reduplication because correspondence-based copying does not affect intervening segments, unlike spreading.

Exactly how locality of correspondence should be formalized in terms of constraints is a topic for current research, but this issue is orthogonal to the concerns of this paper (see Hogoboom 2003; Kitto and de Lacy 1999; Nelson 2003; Riggle this volume for relevant discussion and different proposals). For current purposes, all that is required is that the adjacency requirement on corresponding segments be violable. To provide a concrete analysis, I adopt from Kitto and de Lacy (1999) the following constraint that requires that correspondents be as close as possible:

(22)   ADJACENCY: Corresponding segments must be adjacent. Assign one violation
         mark for each segment that stands between corresponding segments.

The violation of this constraint is calculated gradiently to capture the fact that in reduplication total adjacency is rarely achieved, yet copying usually results in such a way that adjacency is maximally respected (though cf. McCarthy 2004).

In Nakanai, the markedness requirement that vocalic nuclei be as sonorous as possible overrides the locality requirement in reduplication. Following Prince and Smolensky (1993) and other subsequent work, I adopt the family of *X/NUC constraints with the fixed ranking given in (23). Assuming that a nuclear low vowel is entirely not marked, I leave out the constraint *LOWVOWEL/NUC (see Gouskova 2003).

(23)   *X/NUC: X cannot be in the nucleus of the syllable
         *HIGHVOWEL/NUC » *MIDVOWEL/NUC

In Nakanai, these constraints dominate ADJACENCY. The tableaux below illustrate the interaction of these constraints. For simplicity's sake, violation marks of ADJACENCY and *X/NUC are shown only when they are incurred by the reduplicative vowel:

(24)

/RED+buli/		*HIV/NUC	*MIDV/NUC	ADJACENCY
a. ☞	[b_1u_2-$b_1u_2l_3i_4$]	*		*
b.	[b_1i_2-$b_1u_2l_3i_4$]	*		**!*

(25)

/RED+beta/		*HIV/NUC	*MIDV/NUC	ADJACENCY
a.	[b_1e_2-$b_1e_2t_3a_4$]		*!	*
b. ☞	[b_1a_4-$b_1e_2t_3a_4$]			***

As seen in the first tableau, when the two vowels are equal in sonority, ADJACENCY exerts its effect, requiring the closer base vowel to be copied. On the other hand, when V_2

is more sonorous than V_1, reduplication targets the more sonorous vowel, disregarding the distance between the corresponding segments.

To express tendency to avoid an onset [r] in Yoruba, I employ the markedness constraint *r/ONSET. If this constraint is crucially unranked with respect to ADJACENCY (see e.g., Anttila and Cho 1998 for unranked constraints), a specific ranking between them is chosen at each evaluation time, as in (26) and (27) below. As a result, the variation arises:

(26)

/pepere+RED/	ADJACENCY	*r/ONSET
a. ☞ [$p_1e_2p_3e_4r_5e_6$-r_5e_6]	*/*	**
b. [$p_1e_2p_3e_4r_5e_6$-p_3e_4]	***!/***	*

(27)

/pepere+RED/	*r/ONSET	ADJACENCY
a. [$p_1e_2p_3e_4r_5e_6$-r_5e_6]	**!	*/*
b. ☞ [$p_1e_2p_3e_4r_5e_6$-p_3e_4]	*	***/***

Finally, for the case of Creek, the requirement to copy the initial segments of the base, which is either expressed as ANCHOR-L or MAX-BR$_{\sigma 1}$, takes precedence over locality requirement on correspondence segments. See Riggle (this volume) for a more detailed analysis.

5. Discussion: Copying and Spreading

In the discussion above, I have argued that the difference in locality requirements between echo epenthesis and reduplication follows naturally if the former involves spreading and the latter involves copying. The independently motivated characteristics - spreading affects intervening segments while reduplication does not - derives the difference in their locality requirements. What is particularly important is that correspondence-based copying can never derive echo epenthesis. Otherwise, we would lose the explanation of why echo epenthesis cannot skip a potential target vowel, while reduplication can. Recall that in my analysis, echo epenthesis cannot skip an intervening target because skipping is inherently a property of correspondence, but correspondence does not trigger echo epenthesis.

My proposal limits multiple correspondents of one underlying segment where each of the surface correspondents is an exponent of a different morpheme. With this modification added to the original Correspondence Theory of McCarthy and Prince (1995), purely phonological copying is in principle ruled out.

There are two major theoretical consequences of the view advanced in this paper. First, it provides support for the thesis that copying and spreading are distinct mechanisms: some recent works have cast doubt on the existence of autosegmental spreading in Optimality Theory (Bakovic 2000; Krämer 1999; Kitto and de Lacy 1999). The analysis presented here suggests that autosegmental spreading still plays a vital role in phonological theory, contrary to such claims.

Second, the proposal in (13) runs counter to some recent proposals that utilize the mechanism of phonological copying (Krämer 1999; Kitto and de Lacy 1999; Nelson 2003; Rose and Walker 2001; Zuraw 2003 among others). To the extent that this paper's conclusion is on the right track, it suggests reexamination of any analysis that relies on non-reduplicative copying.

Here, I will provide a brief reanalysis of some of such representative cases that have been analyzed in terms of non-reduplicative copying. Due to space limitations, I can only provide an outline of possible line of reanalyses. See Kawahara (2004) for more discussion.

First, fission (a.k.a. breaking or diphthongization) has been analyzed as a process that involves one-to-many correspondence (Keer 1999); this is rendered impossible by (13). One possible reanalysis is to treat fission as an insertion of a new root node (in violation of DEP) with concomitant redistribution of underlying features.

Second, Rose and Walker (2001) analyze long-distance assimilation as the effect of word-internal correspondence (see Zuraw 2003 for a similar approach); however, such cases can instead be analyzed as the effect of AGREE (or other co-occurrence constraints) on a large domain (e.g., stem or root). However, we need to make sure that it is impossible to achieve the unattested pattern in (3) by AGREE; this is guaranteed if there are no AGREE(PLACE) constraints. In fact, the absence of such a constraint is supported by the fact that there is no long-distance place assimilation.

Finally, a famous mapping of underlyingly biconsonantal Semitic roots (/sm/ → [smm]) has been analyzed as non-reduplicative copying (Ussishkin 2000). This can be perhaps reanalyzed by either (i) regarding the mapping as inherently morphological and thus involving a RED morpheme or (ii) assuming that underlyingly biconsonantal roots undergo default consonant epenthesis rather than copying to satisfy templatic requirements (see Gafos 2003 for such a view).

6. Conclusion

In this paper, I have proposed a modification to Correspondence Theory so as to limit correspondence-based copying to morphological operations like reduplication. From this proposal, it follows that echo epenthesis is always achieved by spreading of V-place, and never by copying. This explains the strict locality requirement on echo epenthesis, where skipping a closer target is absolutely banned. Reduplication, on the other hand, in principle involves copying via correspondence, unless copying is blocked by higher-ranked constraints (see footnote 10). As the locality requirement on corresponding segments is inherently governed by violable constraints, reduplication exhibits a looser locality requirement.

To the extent that this analysis is on the right track, it shows that spreading and copying are distinct mechanisms, even though both of them result in repetition of underlying single segments. My proposal further suggests that correspondence cannot be established without limit; rather, copying is fundamentally limited to morphological operations.

References

Akinlabi, Akinbiyi. 1993. Underspecification and the phonology of Yoruba /r/. *Linguistic Inquiry* 24, 139-160.

Alderete, John, Jill Beckman, Laura Benua, Amalia Gnanadesikan, John McCarthy, and Suzanne Urbanczyk. 1999. Reduplication with fixed segmentism. *Linguistic Inquiry* 30, 327-64.

Archangeli, Diana and Douglas Pulleyblank. 1994. *Grounded Phonology*. Cambridge: MIT Press.

Anttila, Arto and Young-mee, Cho. 1998. Variation and change in Optimality Theory. *Lingua* 104, 31-56.

Bakovic, Eric. 2000. *Harmony, Dominance, and Control*. PhD dissertation, Rutgers University.

Clements, Nick. 1977. The autosegmental treatment of vowel harmony. *Phonologica 1976*, 111-119.

Clements, Nick. 1989. Place of articulation in consonants and vowels: A unified theory. *Working Papers of the Cornell Phonetics Laboratory* 5, 77-123.

Cook, T. L. (1987) The chameleonic vowel in the harmonizing prefixes of Efik. In Koen. Bogers, Harry van der Hulst and Maarten Mous (eds.), *The Phonological Representation of Suprasegmentals*. Dordrecht: Foris Publications. pp. 209-232.

Ezard, Bryan. 1997. *A Grammar of Tawala, an Austronesian Language of the Milne Bay Area, Papua New Guinea*. Canberra: The Australian National University.

Gafos, Adamantios. 1996. *The Articulatory Basis of Locality in Phonology*. PhD dissertation, Johns Hopkins University.

Gafos, Adamantios. 2003. Greenberg's asymmetry in Arabic: A consequence of stems in paradigms. *Language* 79, 317-355.

Gafos, Adamantios, and Linda Lombardi. 1999. Consonant transparency and vowel echo. *Proceedings of North East Linguistic Society* 29, 81-95.

Goldsmith, John. 1976. *Autosegmental Phonology*. PhD dissertation, MIT.

Gouskova, Maria. 2003. *Deriving Economy: Syncope in Optimality Theory*. PhD dissertation, University of Massachusetts, Amherst.

Herman, Rebecca. 1994. The status of [w] in Karuk. *Studies in the Linguistic Sciences* 24, 233-244.

Hogoboom, Anya (2003) Marantz's generalization in OT: Accounting for locality effects in reduplication. Ms., University of California, Santa Cruz.

Hume, Elizabeth. 1995. Representing the duality of glides. In G. Tsouls and L. Nash (eds). *Les Actes du Congrés: Langues et Grammaire 1*. Université Paris-8.

Hyman, Larry and Imelda Udoh. 2002. Lenth hamony in Leggbó: A counter-universal? *Proceedings of the Workshop on the Phonology of African Languages*.

Kawahara, Shigeto. 2004. Copying and spreading in phonological theory: Evidence from echo epenthesis. Ms. University of Massachusetts, Amherst.

Kawu, Ahmadu. 2000. Structural markedness and non-reduplicative copying. *Proceedings of North East Linguistic Society* 20, 377-388.

Keer, Edward (1999) *Geminates, the OCP and the Nature of CON*. PhD dissertation, Rutgers University.

Kirchner, Robert (1996) Synchronic chain shifts in Optimality Theory. *Linguistic Inquiry*

27, 341-50.

Kitto, Catherine and de Lacy, Paul. 1999. Correspondence and epenthetic quality. *Proceedings of the Austronesian Formal Linguistics Association* 4, 181-200

Krämer, Martin. 1999. A correspondence approach to vowel harmony and disharmony. Ms. Heinrich-Heine-Universität Düsseldorf.

Marantz, Alec. 1982. Re Reduplication. *Linguistic Inquiry* 13, 483-545.

McCarthy, John. 2004. OT constraints are categorical. *Phonology* 20, 75-138.

McCarthy, John and Alan Prince (1995) Faithfulness and reduplicative identity. *University of Massachusetts Occasional Papers in Linguistics 18*, 249-384.

Miner, Kenneth. 1992. Winnebago accent: The rest of the data. In *Indiana University Linguistics Club Twenty-fifth Anniversary Volume,* 28-53.

Nelson, Nicole. 2003. *Asymmetric Anchoring.* PhD dissertation, Rutgers University.

Ní Chiosáin, Máire and Jaye Padgett. 1997. Markedness, segment realization, and locality in spreading. Report LRC-97-01, Linguistics Research Center, UCSC.

Odden, David, and Mary Odden. 1985. Ordered reduplication in Kihehe. *Linguistic Inquiry* 16, 497-503.

Paradis, Carole. 1996. The inadequacy of filters and faithfulness in loanword adaptation. In Jacques Durand and Bernard Laks (eds.), *Current Trends in Phonology: Models and Methods.* Salford: ESRI. pp. 509–534.

Prince, Alan. 1987. Planes and copying. *Linguistic Inquiry* 18, 491-509.

Prince, Alan and Paul Smolensky. 1993. Optimality Theory: Constraint interaction in generative grammar. Report no. RuCCS-TR-2. New Brunswick, NJ: Rutgers University Center for Cognitive Science.

Riggle, Jason. this volume. Nonlocal reduplication.

Rose, Sharon and Rachel Walker. 2001. A typology of consonant agreement as correspondence. Ms. University of California, San Diego and University of Southern California.

Smith, Jennifer. 2002. *Phonological Augmentation in Strong Positions.* PhD dissertation, University of Massachusetts, Amherst.

Spaelti, Philip. 1997. *Dimensions of Variation in Multi-pattern Reduplication.* PhD dissertation, University of California, Santa Cruz.

Steriade, Donca. 1987. Locality conditions and feature geometry. *Proceedings of North East Linguistics Society* 17, 595-618.

Steriade, Donca. 1988. Reduplication and syllable transfer in Sanskrit and elsewhere. *Phonology* 5, 73-155.

Zou, K. 1991. Assimilation as spreading in Kolami. *1990 Mid-America Linguistics Conference Papers*, 461-475.

Zuraw, Kie. 2003. Aggressive reduplication. *Phonology* 19, 395-439.

Department of Linguistics
South College
University of Massachusetts, Amherst
Amherst, MA 01003

kawahara@linguist.umass.edu
http://www.people.umass.edu/kawahara/

Foot Structure in Nuu-chah-nulth: Reconsidering Foot Typology within OT[*]

Eun-Sook Kim

University of British Columbia

1.   Introduction

No full consensus has been reached on what kind of foot forms are possible cross-linguistically, and what the complete list of metrical parameters is, despite developments in metrical theory (Hayes 1985, 1987, 1989, 1995; McCarthy and Prince 1986, 1990; Halle & Vergnaud 1978, 1987; van der Hulst 1984, 1999; Crowhurst 1990, 1991; Kager 1993).   Nevertheless, the mainstream with respect to foot typology is that the foot inventory can be reduced to one foot-type, either trochaic or iambic, excluding a single language with free variation in foot structure (Hayes 1995 and van der Hulst 1999).   In this paper, I claim that Nuu-chah-nulth foot structure poses interesting problems for Parametric Theory (Hayes 1995) both theoretically and typologically, and I show how to solve the problems using two diagnostics -stress and variable vowels- within Optimality Theory (OT).

2.   Data

In order to uncover Nuu-chah-nulth foot structure, we need to examine stress.   In particular, Nuu-chah-nulth stress can be diagnostic for locating the head of the foot.   As seen in (1), stress falls on the 1st syllable of the word, unless it is light and the 2nd is heavy, in which case stress falls on the 2nd syllable; there is no secondary stress; codas are non-moraic (Wilson 1986, Stonham 1994, Fraser & Howe 1996, Kim 2003b).[1]

---

[*] Nuu-chah-nulth (nuučaańuɬ), along with Ditidaht and Makah, constitutes the Southern Wakashan branch of the Wakashan language family.   It is spoken on the west coast of Vancouver Island, from Barkley Sound north to Quatsino Sound. The data in the paper are from Ahousaht (ʕaaḥuusʔatḥ), one of the 12 dialects. I would like to thank my language consultants Mary Jane Dick, Sarah Webster, and Katie Fraser for sharing their language with me and for their enthusiasm and patience. I am also very grateful to Doug Pulleyblank, Pat Shaw, Joe Stemberger, and John Stonham for their insightful suggestions and corrections. My fieldwork for this research was supported by the Jacobs Research Fund and the Phillips Fund for Native American Research. All errors of fact or interpretation are my own responsibility.
[1] Wilson (1986), Stonham (1994) provide some Tseshaht data where coda can be moraic when the coda consonant is sonorant. However, I have not found any strong examples supporting their arguments in the Ahousaht dialect.

Keir Moulton and Matthew Wolf (eds.): Proceedings of NELS 34,
Stony Brook University: 311 – 318. GLSA, Amherst.

(1) a. mú.wač 'deer'
    → both syllables are light (Trochee)

    b. súu.tiɬ 'somebody referring to you [you (obj.)-ESK]'
       → the 1st syllable is heavy and the 2nd is light (Trochee)

    c. míitx.miit.xʷa 'turning around and around '
       → both syllables are heavy (Trochee)

    d. ča.píis 'unmarried woman'
       → the 1st syllable is light and the 2nd is heavy (**Iamb**)

(Fraser & Howe 1996)

3.   Problems and Proposals

The data we saw in section 2 raise the following question: what kind of parameter has Nuu-chah-nulth employed under previous approaches: iambic, trochaic or both? One might suggest that Nuu-chah-nulth is a trochaic language and make use of extrametricality to treat cases such as (1d), which is apparently iambic. This treatment would exclude the possibility of the existence of an iambic system in the language, following previous studies (Hayes 1995, van der Hulst 1999). However, the following examples provide evidence that Nuu-chah-nulth is a language with BOTH iambic and trochaic foot structures.

      The first piece of evidence is from variable vowels, a diagnostic for presence/absence of the foot. They are called variable, since their length depends on location in a word.

(2) a. naʔ/**u(u)**/k-ʔiš   →   naʔ[**uu**]k_φ ʔiš   (*naʔ[**u**]kʔiš)
       going along-3sg/IND   'S/he went (along with s.o.)'

    b. na-naʔ/**u(u)**/k-ʔiik   →   nanaʔ[**u**]_φ k̓iik   (*nanaʔ[**uu**]kʔiš)
       RED-to accompany-s.o. who is always 's.o. who goes always along (with another)'

(3) a. wik-s/**i(i)**/š   hiixʷatḥi   →   wiks[**ii**]š_φ   hiixʷtḥi   (*wiks[**i**]š ...)
       not-1sg/IND angry   'I am not angry.'

    b. ʔu-kɬaa-s/**i(i)**/š   John   →   ʔukɬaa_φ s[**i**]š   John   (*ʔukɬaas[**ii**]š)
       it-to be called-1sg/IND   'I am John.'

(4) a. čuš-ʔ/**a(a)**/p-ʔiš   →   čuš?[**aa**]p?iš
       new-to buy-3sg/IND   'S/he bought s.t. new'

    b. šuwis-ʔ/**a(a)**/p-skʷii-ʔiš   →   šuwiy̓[**a**]pskʷiʔiš
       shoes-to buy-must be-3sg/IND   'it must be that s/he bought shoes.'

Variable vowels are long within the foot, which is defined over the first two syllables, as in (2a), (3a) and (4a), and short outside the foot as in (2b), (3b), and (4b) (φ indicates foot.). If the 1st syllable is extrametrical and thus the 2nd syllable is the head of the foot, then we would expect each vowel /u/ in (2b), /i/ in (3b), /a/ in (4b) to be long, since it would be inside the foot. However, the vowel appears short on the surface, revealing that it is outside the foot. This means that the 1st syllable is within the foot rather than extrametrical, constituting an iambic foot.[2] Given this assumption, data in (1) support the claim that a single language can have both iambic and trochaic foot structures. (Also see Erwin 1994 for Yidiny and Kondo 2001 for Guahibo: these languages are reported to have both foot structures.)

The second problem with respect to foot structure is related to the presence of a foot with two heavy syllables. Most previous work does not accept the existence of such a foot structure. However, Nuu-chah-nulth provides evidence that such a foot exists. (Also see Ishihara 1990, Hammond 1990 for arguments for such a foot form in Lenakel and in Okinawan Japanese, respectively.)

As seen in (5a), if the 1st heavy syllable itself constitutes a foot, then the variable vowel /i/ would be shortened, since it would be outside the foot, but it appears long on the surface. Also, as seen in (6), even when a lengthening suffix is attached to a stem and thus the 1st syllable is lengthened, the variable vowel /a/ still stands within the foot, surfacing as a long vowel.

(5) a. ʔuuc-skʷ/i(i)/   →   ʔuucskʷ[ii]$_\varphi$ (*ʔuuc$_\varphi$ skʷ[i])
    to belong-must have been   'it must be that (it) belongs to (her/him)'

   b. šuwis-ʔaap-skʷ/i(i)/   →   šuwis$_\varphi$ ʔapskʷ[i]   (*šuwisʔapskʷ[ii])
    shoes-to buy-must...   'it must be that (s/he) bought shoes'

(6) naʔ/u(u)/k-panač   →   naaʔ[uu]k$_\varphi$ panač   (*naaʔ[u]kpanač)
    to accompany-moving around [L]   'accompanying s.o. everywhere'

   cf. na-naʔ/u(u)/k-ʔiik   →   nana$_\varphi$ ʔ[u]k̓iik
    RED-to accompany-s.o. who is always 's.o. who goes always along (with another)'

Interestingly, these metrical patterns are also observed in reduplication triggered by suffixes (Kim 2003a). Nuu-chah-nulth has 7 types of reduplication (see (7); in particular, with class IV suffixes, both the first syllable (RED) and the second syllable (BASE) must be heavy, and with class VII suffixes, the first syllable must be light and the second syllable heavy as seen in (8). (See Kim 2003a,b for a detailed discussion where multiple patterns of reduplication are treated by metrical requirements specified for each triggering suffix.)

---

[2]In order to disallow extrametricality at the left edge of the Prosodic Word, we can make use of the following constraint:

ALIGN(PW, L, Ft, L): the left edge of the Prosodic Word coincides with the left edge of a foot.

(7) Patterns of reduplication in Nuu-chah-nulth (Kim 2003b: 194 (8))

Type	RED-BASE	Foot Form
Class I	CV(V)-CV(V)]$_\varphi$	Trochee
Class II	CVV-CV(V)]$_\varphi$	Trochee
Class III	CV-CV(V)]$_\varphi$	Trochee or Iamb
Class IV	**CVV-CVV**]$_\varphi$	Trochee
Class V	CV-CV]$_\varphi$	Trochee
Class VI	CVV-CV]$_\varphi$	Trochee
Class VII	**CV-CVV**]$_\varphi$	**Iamb**

(8) a. ẇaaẇaasaqaʔiš
    RED-ẇasaq-(y)a-ʔiš
    RED-to cough-continuously-3sg/IND
    'She is continuously coughing.'

        cf. ẇasaqitʔiš 'S/he coughed'

   b. cuuccuucaʔiš
    RED-cuc-(y)a-ʔiš
    RED-to scratch-continuously-3sg/IND
    'S/he is continuously scratching.'

        cf. cucaa 'scratching'

     In sum, the consequence of Nuu-chah-nulth metrical patterns is that it provides another piece of evidence that a language can have i) a foot with two heavy syllables and ii) both iambic and trochaic foot structures.

5.   Foot Typology within OT

I argue that we can solve the parametrical problems presented above within OT by using universal constraints, (9), and their language specific ranking, and by allowing highly articulated feet inventories including a foot with two heavy syllables.

(9) a. Weight-to-Stress Principle (WSP):
    Heavy syllables are prominent in foot structure.

b. FT-BIN: Feet must be binary under syllabic or moraic analysis.

c. HeadLeft (Trochaic): The left edge of the Prosodic Word is the head of the Prosodic Word.

d. HeadRight (Iambic): The right edge of the Prosodic Word is the head of the Prosodic Word.

The constraints and their different ranking status derive the following possible language groups as seen in (10).

(10) Factorial typology

a. languages with both iambic and trochaic foot structures

WSP, FtBin >> HeadLeft (Trochaic) >> HeadRight (Iambic)

b. languages with iambic foot structures only

FtBin >> HeadRight (Iambic) >> HeadLeft (Trochaic), WSP

c. languages with trochaic foot structures only

FtBin >> HeadLeft (Trochaic) >> HeadRight (Iambic), WSP

Nuu-chah-nulth is a case of (10a): Nuu-chah-nulth has trochaic foot structures except when only the second syllable of a foot is heavy. The ranking in (10a) drives languages where both iambic and trochaic foot structures are allowed, although major foot forms are trochaic. If some languages allows only one type of foot structure, their grammar in terms of metrical structures will be either (10b) or (10c).

The following tableaux illustrate how (10a) drives both iambic and trochaic foot structures in Nuu-chah-nulth.

(11) súu.tiɬ 'somebody referring to you' (Trochee)

(12) Tableau

suu.tiɬ	WSP	FtBin(Syll)	HeadLeft	HeadRight
☞a. súu.tiɬ]φ				*
b. suu.tíɬ]φ	*!		*	
c. súu]φtiɬ		*!		

In (11), the first syllable is heavy and the second is light.   In this context, (10a) causes
trochaic foot structure as seen in tableau (12).   Candidate a only observes the highly-
ranked constraints, WSP and FtBin.

(13) mú.wač 'deer' (Trochee)

(14) Tableau

mu.wač	WSP	FtBin(Syll)	HeadLeft	HeadRight
☞a. mú.wač]φ				*
b. mu.wáč]φ			*!	
c. mú]φwač		*!		

(13) is the case where both syllables are light.   (10a) causes the first syllable to be
stressed.   As seen with candidate b in (14), if the second syllable is stressed, it will
violate HeadLeft constraint, which is higher-ranked than HeadRight in Nuu-chah-nulth.
Candidate c is ruled out, since although the first syllable is a head of the foot, the foot is
not binary.   Therefore, as in candidate a, the first syllable must be stressed.

(15) a. ča.píis 'unmarried woman' (Iamb)

b. Tableau

ča.piis	WSP	FtBin(Syll)	HeadLeft	HeadRight
☞a. ča.píis]ᵩ			*	
b. čá.piis]ᵩ	*!			*
c. ča[píis]ᵩ		*!		

(15) is the case where the first syllable is light and the second syllable is heavy. In this case, the second syllable is stressed and it results from (10a). If the first syllable is a head, then, as seen with candidate b, the output form will violate WSP. The constraint prevents a light syllable is a head of the foot. Candidate c violates FtBin, since the constituents of the foot is not binary. Therefore, candidate a is selected as an optimal output form.

5.   Implications and Conclusion

This analysis of Nuu-chah-nulth foot structure can explain both the cross-linguistically unmarked status of trochaic over iambic feet (cf. de Lacy 2002), and the presence of both foot structures in a single language. Furthermore, we can treat cross-linguistic variation simply by the different ranking status of the constraints. This study also provides another chance to examine possible foot forms: in particular, a foot with two heavy syllables.

References

Crowhurst, Megan. 1990. On morphological and metrical feet in Tubatulabal. *Proceedings of Western Conference on Linguistics* 20.
Crowhurst, Megan. 1991. *Minimality and Foot Structure in Metrical Phonology and Prosodic Morphology*. Ph.D. dissertation. University of Arizona, Tucson.
De Lacy, Paul. 2002. *The Formal Expression of Markedness*. Ph.D. dissertation. UMass.
Erwin, Sean J. 1994. Stress lapse in Yidiny: a metrical reanalysis. *Linguistic Notes from La Jolla* 17, 78-96.
Fraser, Katherine & Darin Howe. 1996. *Introduction to Nuu-chah-nulth Phonology*. MS., University of British Columbia.
Halle, Morris & Jean-Roger Vergnaud. 1978. Metrical structures in phonology. Ms., MIT.
Halle, Morris & Jean-Roger Vergnaud. 1987. An Essay on Stress. Cambridge, MA: MIT Press.

Hammond, Michael. 1990. Metrical theory and learnability. MS. University of Arizona, Tucson.

Hayes, Bruce. 1985. *A Metrical Theory of Stress Rules*. New York: Garland Publishing.

Hayes, Bruce. 1987. A revised parametric theory. *Proceedings of NELS 17.*

Hayes, Bruce. 1989. Compensatory lengthening in moraic phonology. *Linguistic Inquiry* 20, 253-306.

Hayes, Bruce. 1995. *A Metrical Theory of Stress: Principles and Case Studies*. Chicago, Illinois: University of Chicago Press.

Hulst, Harry van der. 1984. *Syllable Structure and Stress in Dutch*. Dordrecht: Foris.

Hulst, Harry van der. 1999. Issues in foot typology. In Hannahs, S.J. & M. Davenport (eds.), *Issues in Phonological Structure*. Amsterdam: John Benjamins.

Ishihara, M. 1990. Hypocoristic formation in Okinawan Japanese: evidence from heavy feet in morphology. Ms. University of Arizona.

Kager, René. 1993. Alternatives to the iambic-trochaic law. *NLLT* 2, 381-432.

Kim, Eun-Sook. 2003a. Patterns of Reduplication in Nuu-chah-nulth. *Proceedings of NELS 33*. Kadowaki, M. & S. Kawahara (eds.). 127-146. University of Massachusetts, Amherst.

Kim, Eun-Sook. 2003b. *Theoretical Issues in Nuu-chah-nulth Phonology and Morphology*. Ph.D. dissertation. University of British Columbia.

Kondo, Riena. 2001. Guahibo stress: both trochaic and iambic. *IJAL* 67-2, 136-166.

McCarthy, John and Alan Prince. 1986. Prosodic morphology. Ms. UMass, Amherst, and Brandeis University, Waltham, Mass.

McCarthy, John and Alan Prince 1990. Foot and word in Prosodic Morphology: the Arabic broken plural. *NLLT* 8, 209-283.

Stonham, John. 1994. *Combinatorial Morphology*. Amsterdam: John Benjamins.

Wilson, Stephen A. 1986. Metrical structure in Wakashan phonology. In Nikiforidou, V., Vanclay, M, Niepokuj, M., Feder, D. (eds.), *Proceedings of BLS* 17. UC Berkeley: Berkeley Linguistics Society. 284-291.

Department of Linguistics
University of British Columbia
Buchanan E 270-1866 Main Mall
Vancouver, B.C.
Canada V6T 1Z1

vanabba@yahoo.ca

The Feature [Tense] Revisited:
The Case of Korean Consonants*

Hyunsoon Kim

Hongik University, Seoul Korea

1. Introduction

Korean stop consonants, which are all voiceless, are in a three-series laryngeal system: lenis, aspirated and fortis in labial, coronal and dorsal place of articulation: /p, t, ts, k/, /p^h, t^h, ts^h, k^h/ and /p', t', ts', k'/. The three-way phonation contrast has been discussed a lot in the literature, as for how they are represented in terms of features. In particular, C.-W. Kim (1965) suggested that they should be classified in terms of tenseness primarily, such that fortis and aspirated consonants are classified as tense with the two series consonants being distinguished secondarily by their different aspiration duration, whereas lenis ones as lax. C.-W. Kim's proposal is based on the Jakobsonian view of tenseness such as "tense phonemes are articulated with greater distinctness and pressure than the corresponding lax phonemes" (Jakobson, Fant & Halle 1952:38). In his articulatory, aerodynamic and acoustic data of the plosive consonants /p, p^h, p', t, t^h, t', k, k^h, k'/, the fortis and aspirated consonants were observed to be longer in palatal contact, closure duration, higher in air pressure as well as in burst and energy distribution after release and larger in airflow than their lenis counterparts. As for aspiration duration, however, it is much longer in the aspirated consonants than in their fortis counterparts with no overlapping, which is in line with Lisker & Abramson (1964).

Since C.-W. Kim (1965), the notion of tenseness has rarely been used in the representation of Korean three-way laryngeal contrast in the literature. For example, given their four binary *articulator-bound* features -- [±stiff vocal cords], [±slack vocal cords], [±constricted glottis] and [±spread glottis] (henceforth, [±stiff], [±slack], [±c.g.] and [±s.g.], respectively) based on two dimensions of laryngeal control: the stiffness-slackness of the vocal cords and their spread-constricted positioning, Halle & Stevens (1971) classified Korean fortis consonants as [+c.g., -s.g.] in glottal width and [+stiff, -slack] in the state of the vocal cords, aspirated as [+s.g., -c.g.] and [+stiff, -slack] and lenis as [+s.g., -c.g.] and [-stiff, -slack]. It was due to the fact that Korean lenis consonants are "moderately aspirated"(e.g., C.-W. Kim 1970) that they assigned Korean lenis consonants with [+s.g.]. In line with Halle & Stevens (1971), however, Iverson (1983) proposed, on the basis of Kagaya's (1974) fiberscopic study of Korean word-

© 2003 Hyunsoon Kim
Keir Moulton and Matthew Wolf (eds.): Proceedings of NELS 34,
Stony Brook University: 319 – 332. GLSA, Amherst.

initial consonants whose glottal width varies from small to large in the order of fortis, lenis and aspirated consonants, that fortis consonants are represented by [+c.g.], aspirated ones by [+s.g.], lenis ones by [-c.g., -s.g.]. On the other hand, since the laryngeal features [c.g.] and [s.g.] are assumed to be privative (i.e. unary) in recent studies (e.g., Lombardi 1991, 1995), the three-way phonation contrast is proposed to be represented by [c.g.] for fortis consonants, [s.g.] for aspirated ones and no specification for lenis ones.

In the present study we will consider how the three-way laryngeal contrast in Korean consonants can be represented. For this purpose, we are to examine our cine MRI data (in section 2), discuss the terms of tenseness based on the experimental data and propose that the feature [±tense] should be employed in Korean, in support of C.-W. Kim (1965) (in section 3) and provide the sound patterns of Korean consonants in sound symbolism and foreign loans in favor of the proposed feature (in section 4). A brief conclusion is in section 5.

2. A stroboscopic-cine MRI study of Kim, Honda and Maeda (2002)

In order to see how the vocal tract and the larynx are involved during the production of the Korean consonants /t, tʰ, t', ts, tsʰ, ts'/, we can refer to a stroboscopic-cine MRI study of Kim, Honda & Maeda (2002). In the experiments where two native speakers (one male and one female) commanding the Seoul dialect (standard Korean) participated in, we measured the tongue movement (i.e. apex (i) and blade (ii)) in (a), glottal height from the hard palate (i) to the center of the thyroid cartilage (ii) in (b) and glottal opening in transverse data (c) and in coronal data (d), as shown in Figure 1. The target consonants were put in the contexts /ma_a/ in (a), (b) and (c), and in /#_a_a/ in (d) in Figure 1.

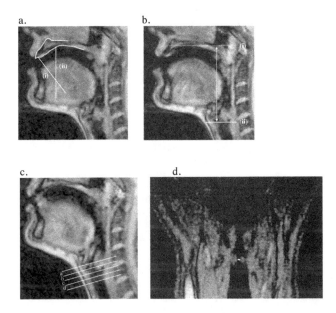

Figure 1. The measurements of the tongue apex (i) and blade (ii) (a), the glottal height from the hard palate (i) to the center of the thyroid cartilage (ii) (b), the glottal width in transverse data (c) and in coronal data (d).

The results of our MRI experiments showed that two systematic variations occur in the production of the consonants / t, t^h, t', ts, ts^h, ts'/. First, as shown in Tables I, II and III, linguopalatal contacts and closure duration tend to vary from short to long in the order of lenis, aspirated and fortis consonants and both tongue movement and glottal height are also likely to vary from low to high in the same order.[1]

---

[1] More closure duration caused by the higher tongue position with more linguopalatal contact in MRI data was also confirmed in our acoustic study of ten native speakers from Seoul, wherein the closure duration of /t', ts'/ and /t^h, ts^h/ were almost twice as long as that of their lenis counterparts in /a_a/ and /#_a/, though the aspirated consonants were less long than their fortis ones (H. Kim 2002).

Table I. Linguopalatal contact of the consonants / t, t^h, t', ts, ts^h, ts'/ when it was the most extended.

	a. Female speaker	b. Male speaker
/t/	apico-dental	apico-dental
/t^h/	apico-lamino-postalveolar	apico-lamino-postalveolar
/t'/	apico-lamino-postalveolar	apico-lamino-postalveolar
/ts/	lamino-alveolar	lamino-alveolar
/ts^h/	lamino-postalveolar	lamino-alveolar
/ts'/	lamino-postalveolar	lamino-alveolar

Table II. Tongue blade position in terms of the distance from the mouth roof (unit: mm) at the maximally raised instance during consonantal oral closure and its duration (unit: ms). All the consonants are embedded in /ma_a/.

	a. tongue movement		b. closure duration	
	F	M	F	M
/t/	7.7	6.2	83.5	83.5
/t^h/	2.8	3.9	133.6	100.2
/t'/	0.7	3.1	167	167
/ts/	2.8	3.9	83.5	100.2
/ts^h/	1.4	3.9	116.9	150.3
/ts'/	0.7	3.1	167	167

Table III. Glottal position (height) (a) in terms of the distance (unit: mm) from the hard palate to the "center" of the thyroid cartilage at most raised instances during the oral closure. The duration (b) refers to how long the glottis maintains the maximal height (unit: ms).

	a. Glottal position		b. Duration	
	F	M	F	M
/t/	88.2	93.9	100.2	66.8
/t^h/	83.9	89.6	33.4	66.8
/t'/	82.5	89.6	16.7	133.6
/ts/	85.3	93.9	100.2	183.7
/ts^h/	83.9	91	66.8	66.8
/ts'/	82.5	89.6	16.7	50.1

However, glottal opening varies differently from the movement of the tongue blade, linguopalatal contact, closure duration and the vertical laryngeal movement. In our transverse data, we have noted a wide glottal opening of the aspirated consonants but the comparison of the lenis and fortis ones was hard to make, as shown in Figure 2.

/t/   /tʰ/   /t'/

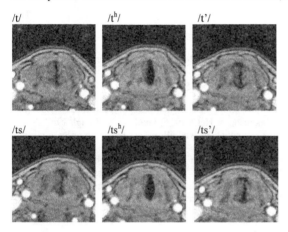

/ts/   /tsʰ/   /ts'/

Figure 2. The glottal width of /t, tʰ, t'/ and / ts, tsʰ, ts'/ of the female subject just before oral release in the context /ma_a/.

Similar to the transverse data, our coronal data also showed that the aspirated type always has much wider glottal width than the other two types both word-medially and word-initially, as shown in Table IV. Between the fortis and lenis consonants, the glottal width is narrower in the latter word-medially, predumablly due to the intervocalic voicing, and in the former word-initially.

Table IV. The glottal width during the oral closure of the target consonants in the word-medial position /a_a/ and in the word-initial position /#_a/.

	a. word-medially (mm)	b. word-initially (mm)
/t/	0.4	5.2
/tʰ/	5.6	10.1
/t'/	1.1	2.0
/ts/	0.9	6.4
/tsʰ/	6.3	9.4
/ts'/	1.2	3.8

Given the MRI data, Kim, Honda & Maeda (2002) have suggested that the two independent systematic patterns -(a) the tongue and vertical laryngeal movements and (b) glottal opening- characterize the three-way phonation contrast.

3. Proposal

What is of interest in the above MRI data is that both fortis and aspirated consonants are likely to be longer in closure duration than their lenis counterparts, across contexts (Table II b) and that they also tend to be longer in linguopalatal contact and higher in the tongue movement and glottal position than lenis ones (Tables I, II, III), though the fortis consonants are a little longer or higher in those phonetic properties than aspirated ones, as in closure duration. Given this, we adopt the term *tenseness* in the Jakobsian view (e.g. Jakobson, Fant & Halle 1952; Jakobson & Halle 1956; Jakobson & Waugh 1987; Jessen 1998) with some modifications of its scope, as we will discuss below, in order to classify Korean consonants.

To be specific, the vertical larynx movement, that is, glottal position is associated with glottal tension (e.g., Honda 1995, 1999). As shown in Figure 3, vertical larynx movements have an effect on vocal fold length: when the larynx moves up, the vocal folds get longer since the thyroid and cricoid cartilage tend to follow the curvature, so called the lordosis, of the cervical spine.

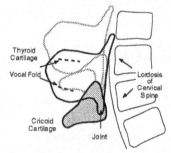

Figure 3.   Effect of vertical laryngeal movements on vocal fold length
(Honda 1995)

A lengthening of the vocal folds in turn stiffens the vocal folds, which results in higher intrinsic F0 of vowels. For example, Honda, Hirai, Masaki & Shimada (1999) have noted in their MRI data that, in the production of the Japanese vowel /a/, the larynx moves higher when F0 is in high (262 Hz to 165 Hz) than in low (147 Hz to 87 Hz) ranges. In relation to this, we can refer to previous studies of Korean consonants which have shown that the stiffness of the vocal folds before release is the highest in fortis consonants which is followed by aspirated and then by lenis ones (e.g., Hirose *et al.* 1974, 1983; Hong *et al.* 1991). Hence, the onset value of F0 of a vowel is highest after fortis, lowest after lenis and intermediate after aspirated ones with the difference in F0 after fortis and aspirated ones being often very slight (e.g., C.-W. Kim, 1965, 1970; Han &

Weitzman, 1970; Hardcastle, 1973; Kagaya 1974; Ahn, 1999; Cho, Jun & Ladefoged 2002).

Our MRI data are also in agreement with the previous studies in that glottal position varies from low to high in the order of the lenis, aspirated and fortis consonants with the latter two series being higher than the former in glottal position. In that closure duration, linguopalatal contact and tongue movement show the same variation in parallel to glottal position associated with glottal tension (and stiffness of the vocal folds) in the production of Korean consonants, we suggest that these phonetic properties including glottal position should be all related to tenseness, that is, tension of articulation in Korean three-series laryngeal contrast. Thus longer closure duration and linguopalatal contact (Tables I and II b), higher tongue and vertical laryngeal movements (Tables II a and III) in fortis and aspirated consonants than in lenis ones, can be attributed to the tenseness of the fortis and aspirated in comparison with their lenis ones which are lax.

As for aspiration duration which has been considered as one of phonetic correlates of tenseness in the Jakobsonian view, the MRI data lead us to suggest that it should be a phonetic correlate of glottal opening, the other systematic pattern independent of the concomitant tongue and larynx movements in the production of Korean consonants. For illustration, Figure 4 is taken from Kim *et al.* (2002) wherein the timing of the glottal opening/closing and the oral closing/opening in the consonants /t, t^h, t'/ is presented in the context /a_a/.

a.   b.   c.

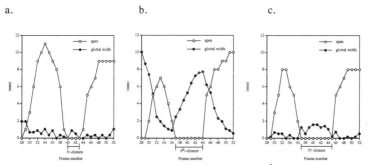

Figure 4. The glottal width and the apex movement of /t, t^h, t'/ in /a_a/ as a function of time (Kim *et al.* 2002).

In the case of the aspirated consonant /t^h/, the glottis opens the largest during its oral closure among the three-series plosives, with the widest glottal opening just at the oral release (at frame 44). Even after the oral release (from frames 44 through 45), the glottis is more open than the oral release, where frication could be expected, and it gets narrower as the oral opening is made more from frame 46 through 52 (corresponding to about 100 ms), during which aspiration could arise. The delay of the glottal closure for voicing beyond the oral release in the aspirated consonant can be understood in terms of articulatory coordination: the glottis opens the largest, in order to maintain the highest airflow that is needed to create the aspiration noise, one of relevant cues for the aspirated consonant type. In contrast, during the oral closure of the lenis plosive /t/, the glottis is open the smallest and immediately after the consonantal release it closes for the voicing of the vowel /a/. The glottal width of the fortis plosive, which is larger than that of the lenis one during oral closure, reaches almost zero at frame 45 and the glottis closes at frame 47, where aspiration could occur between the frames, although the duration would be very short. Given that aspiration results from the articulatory coordination of the glottis (that is, glottal opening/closing) and oral (constriction) closing/opening, we can attribute it to glottal opening, not to tenseness associated with the tongue and larynx movements in Korean consonants.

Based on the experimental data, we can now ask ourselves how the three-way laryngeal contrast in Korean consonants are represented in the grammar. We propose that glottal opening and the tongue and larynx movements should be phonologically incorporated as the features [±s.g.] and [±tense], respectively, under the view that distinctive features are defined in phonetically concrete terms and that they have one or more invariant phonetic properties across different conditions (Jakobson, Fant & Halle 1952; Jakobson & Waugh 1987; Stevens & Blumstein 1981; Stevens *et al.* 1986; Stevens & Keyser 1989). That is, as for glottal opening, we suggest that the Halle & Stevens' (1971) articulator-bound feature [±s.g.] should be phonetically motivated as a common denominator of glottal opening in Korean, such that aspirated consonants are specified for [+s.g.] and non-aspirated ones, that is, fortis and lenis ones for [-s.g.]. As for the tongue and larynx movements we have attributed to tenseness, we use the Jakobsonian feature [±tense] with some modifications of its scope, as discussed in the above, such that fortis and aspirated consonants are specified for [+tense] and their lenis counterparts for [-tense]. Hence, in our proposal, lenis consonants are specified for [-s.g., -tense], fortis ones for [-s.g., +tense], aspirated ones for [+s.g., +tense], as shown in (1).

(1)   Lenis   Fortis   Aspirated

          [s.g.]   -   -   +
          [tense]   -   +   +

Our proposed feature representation of Korean consonants in (1) is, to some extent, in agreement with C.-W. Kim's (1965), according to which fortis and aspirated consonants are proposed to be tense with the two series consonants being distinguished by their different degree of aspiration. But, different from C.-W. Kim (1965), we have suggested that aspiration should be a phonetic correlate of glottal opening. As for this, it would be noteworthy that Korean three-way phonation contrast has been reported to be overlapped in aspiration duration, that is, voice onset time (VOT) in the literature (e.g., Lisker & Abramson 1964; C.-W. Kim 1965; Han & Weitzman 1970; Cho *et al.* 2002): VOT of fortis and lenis consonants and/or of lenis and aspirated ones can be overlapped. However, such an overlap does not occur in glottal opening between aspirated and non-aspirated consonants, as in the above MRI data (Table IV and Figure 4). In this aspect, glottal opening is more straightforward than aspiration in characterizing Korean three-way laryngeal contrast.

Another difference lies in our claim that glottal opening and the tongue and larynx movements associated with tenseness are two independent control parameters in the three-way phonation contrast. C.-W. Kim (1965) proposed that tenseness should be primary and aspiration duration secondary in characterizing Korean consonants, in that lenis consonants are opposed against both aspirated and fortis consonants, not in VOT but intensity such that they can be either voiced (negative VOT) or voiceless (positive VOT). Yet, as we will discuss below, lenis consonants can alternate with fortis ones in opposition to aspirated ones in the Korean grammar, which indicates that the feature [±s.g.] encoding glottal opening plays a distinctive role as equally as [±tense] encoding tenseness does.

4. Phonological data

From the feature representation of Korean three-way phonation contrast in (1), we can expect the following two sound patterns in Korean: (a) fortis and aspirated consonants group together in opposition to lenis ones by virtue of the feature [tense] and (b) aspirated consonants pattern in opposition to lenis and fortis ones by virtue of the feature [s.g.]. Korean sound symbolism and French loanwords can be referred to as the sound pattern (a). For example, in Korean reduplication, intensified expressions are conveyed by fortis and aspirated consonants, not by lenis ones. As shown in (2), intensified expression in Korean can be represented either by fortis (2a) or aspirated (2b) or by both fortis and aspirated consonants (2c), as first pointed out by C.-W. Kim (1965).[2]

(2)

a.	kəmin	'black'	k'əmin	'pitch black'
	pants'ak	'glittering'	p'ants'ak	'glittering very brightly'
	tal.tal.	'memorizing'	t'al.t'al.	'memorizing thoroughly'
	tsil.kim.tsil.k im	'weeping'	ts'il.k'im.ts'il.kim	'weeping hard'

b.	pələŋ	'waving'		pʰələŋ	'fluttering'
	toŋtoŋ	'stamping one's feet'		tʰoŋtʰoŋ	'stamping one's feet hard'
	tsəltsəl	'overflowing'		tsʰəltsʰəl	'overflowing much'

c.	piŋpiŋ	~	pʰiŋpʰiŋ	~	p'iŋp'iŋ	'round and round'
	(slowly)		(fast and roughly)		(fast and tightly)	
	tæntæŋ	~	tʰæŋtʰæŋ	~	t'æŋt'æŋ	'ding-dong'
	tsoltsol	~	tsʰoltsʰol	~	ts'olts'ol	'trickling'

French loans also provide evidence for the sound pattern of fortis and aspirated consonants, as a natural class, in opposition to lenis ones. As shown in (3), when voiceless French stop consonants are borrowed into Korean, they are adapted as aspirated or fortis ones (a) across the board, whereas voiced ones into lenis ones (b).[3]

---

[2] C.-W. Kim (1965) suggests that when intensified expressions are used with both aspirated and fortis consonants, there is no difference in meaning between the two intensified expressions. In contrast, Kim-Renaud (1974) suggests that aspirated and fortis consonants in sound symbolism, have a little different intensified connotation, which we follow, as in (2c).

[3] Not only French loans but also Japanese loans show the same adaptation. See H. Kim (2003).

(3)

a. /pa.ri/   pʰa.li   ~   p'a.li   'Paris'

    /prɛ̃tã/   pʰi.lɛŋ.tʰaŋ ~ p'i.lɛŋ.t'aŋ   'Printemps'

    /mitɛʀã/   mi.tʰɛ.laŋ   ~   mi.t'ɛ.laŋ   'Mitterrand'

    /kan/   kʰan.nɨ   ~   k'an.nɨ   'Cannes'

b. /bagɛt/   pa.kɛ.tʰɨ   *pʰa.kɛ.tʰɨ, *p'a.kɛ.hʰɨ   'baguette'

    /deʒa/   tɛ.tsa   *tʰɛ.tsa, *t'ɛ.tsa   'déja↓'

    /gijɥtin/   ki.lo.tʰin * kʰi.lo.tʰin, * k'i.lo.tʰin   'guillotine'

French loans (3) as well as Korean sound symbolism in (2) clearly show that fortis and aspirated consonants pattern together in opposition to their lenis counterparts. The binary feature [±tense] can straightforwardly account for this sound pattern. The fortis and aspirated consonants which are [+tense] are expected to group together as a natural class in opposition to lenis ones which are lax, that is, [-tense].

On the other hand, the feature [±s.g.] in the representation of Korean three-way phonation contrast predicts that aspirated consonants ([+s.g.]) pattern in opposition to lenis and fortis ones ([-s.g.]), which is supported by English loans in Korean. As shown in (4), English voiceless stop consonants are borrowed as aspirated ones, while English voiced stop consonants as lenis ones. Word- or syllable-initial voiceless consonants are adapted as aspirated consonants and word-final voiceless consonants are also borrowed as aspirated counterparts with the epenthesis of the vowel /ɨ/ as in (4a i). The English voiceless stop consonants /p, t, k/, which are rarely aspirated after the word-initial fricative /s/ in English, are also substituted as the aspirated counterparts [pʰ, tʰ, kʰ], respectively, as in (4a ii). In contrast, English voiced consonants are borrowed as lenis consonants, as shown in (4b).

(4)

a.

i.   tʰa.i.pʰɨ   'type'   tʰɨ.wi.sɨ.tʰɨ   'twist'

     pʰa.i.pʰɨ   'pipe'   pʰiŋ.kʰɨ   'pink'

     kʰəm.pʰu.tʰə   'computer'   kʰæ.pʰi.tʰal   'capital'

     tsʰip   'chip'   kʰo.kʰa.kʰo.la   'coca cola'

ii. sɨ.tʰim   'steam'   sɨ.pʰi.kʰə   'speaker'

     sɨ.tʰɨ.la.i.kʰɨ   'strike'   sɨ.pʰɨ.le.i   'spray'

     sɨ.tʰa.kʰiŋ   'stocking'   sɨ.kʰa.i   'sky'

b.   ti.swi   'dish'   ti.tsa.in   'design'

     ti.lim   'dream'   pæn.tɨ   'band(age)'

     pi.ə   'beer'   pa.i.ə   'buyer'

     pæ.i.sɨ.pol   'baseball'   kɨ.lil   'grill'

     ka.i.tɨ   'guide'   tsəm.po   'jumbo'

Furthermore, some English loans, whose word-initial consonants are voiceless, have the alternation of lenis and fortis consonants when they are emphasized for intensified expression, as in (5).

(5)
pæk	~	p'æk	*pʰæk	'bag'
pə.sɨ	~	p'ə.sɨ	* pʰə.sɨ	'bus'
tæn.sɨ	~	t'æn.sɨ	* tʰæn.sɨ	'dance'
tsæm	~	ts'æm	* tsʰæm	'jam'
kæŋ	~	k'æŋ	* kʰæŋ	'gang'
ka.sɨ	~	k'a.sɨ	* kʰa.sɨ	'gas'

From the English loans in (4) and (5), it is evident that Korean aspirated consonants pattern in opposition to their lenis and fortis counterparts. The sound pattern in (4) can be accounted for straightforwardly on the assumption that the binary feature [±s.g.] is as distinctive as [±tense] in Korean consonants. The voiceless consonants in the source language are borrowed as aspirated consonants which are specified for [+s.g.], and voiced ones as lenis ones which are specified for [-s.g., -tense]. The alternation of lenis and fortis consonants to the exclusion of aspirated ones in (5) can be explained by the natural class of the non-aspirated consonants which are specified for [-s.g.] but different in the feature [tense]: lenis ones are lax ([-tense]) and fortis ones tense ([+tense]).

What is noteworthy here is that the feature [c.g.] is not phonologically motivated in Korean, no matter whether it is binary or privative. The sound pattern of fortis consonants together with aspirated ones, as a natural class, in the Korean sound symbolism (2) and in French loanwords (3) as well as that of fortis and lenis consonants in English loans (5) cannot be explained by the feature [c.g.]. On the assumption that lenis consonants are lexically specified for [-tense, -s.g.] in opposition to their aspirated and fortis ones which are specified for [+tense, +s.g.] and [+tense, -s.g.], respectively, can we explain the sound pattern in a straightforward fashion. In addition, the feature [c.g.] is not phonetically grounded for the representation of Korean fortis consonants, either. We have already noted that fortis and lenis consonants are hard to differentiate word-medially in terms of glottal width per se in our transverse data (Figure 2) and that their glottal width is much narrower than that of aspirated consonants in our coronal data (Table IV). Now that glottal closing is not appropriate to describe fortis consonants across contexts and that the feature [c.g.] cannot capture the phonological sound pattern of fortis consonants together with aspirated or lenis ones, we can say that the feature [c.g.] is neither phonetically nor phonologically motivated in Korean.

5. Conclusion

In this paper, we have first looked into the MRI study of Kim *et al.* (2002) and then considered its empirical consequences, for the representation of the three-way laryngeal contrast in Korean consonants. We have suggested, on the basis of the MRI data, that not only closure duration but also linguopalatal contact, tongue movement and glottal position associated with glottal tension should be phonetic correlates of tenseness and that aspiration be referred to glottal opening, the other independent systematic control parameter in characterizing Korean consonants. Given this, we have proposed that glottal opening and the tongue and larynx movements should be phonologically incorporated into the features [±s.g.] and [±tense], respectively, and that Korean fortis consonants should be specified for [+tense, -s.g.], aspirated ones for [+tense, +s.g.] and lenis ones for [-tense, -s.g.]. Korean sound symbolism and loanwords from French and English have been provided in support of the proposed feature representation of Korean consonants.

Some theoretical implications of the present study can be made. One of them is that the articulator-bound feature [s.g.] is binary, not privative, in Korean, providing further evidence that laryngeal features such as [voice] are binary, in support of Wetzels & Mascaró (2001). The examination of English loanwords has shown that the feature value [-s.g.] is phonologically active in a fashion parallel to [+s.g.]. This paper also suggests that the feature [c.g.] is not active in Korean. Not only our MRI data on glottal width but also the sound pattern of Korean sound symbolism and foreign loans supports that the feature [±tense], not [c.g.] is both phonetically and phonologically motivated in Korean, in favor of C.-W. Kim's (1965) insight that *tenseness* plays a distinctive role in Korean consonants. Another implication is that Korean fortis consonants are singletons, not geminates. In recent studies, fortis consonants have been proposed to be geminates because the closure duration of the consonants is twice as long as that of lenis ones (e.g., Silva 1992, Han 1996). But as already shown in Table II (b), the closure duration of fortis consonants almost doubles that of their lenis counterparts in our two subjects and that of aspirated ones is also much longer than the lenis ones.[4] In addition, in the geminate analyses of Korean fortis consonants, neither the sound pattern of fortis and lenis consonants in the English loans in (4) and (5) nor that of fortis and aspirated ones in French loans (3) as well as in Korean sound symbolism in (2) can be accounted for. Rather the sound patterns of Korean consonants provide phonological evidence that the proposed features, not timing units such as singletons and geminates, are concerned in the three-way phonation contrast in Korean consonants.

*A longer version of this paper will appear in *The internal organization of phonological segments* edited by Marc van Oostendorp and Jeroen van de Weijer, Berlin: Mouton de Gruyter.

References

Avery, Peter and William J. Idsardi. 2001. Laryngeal dimensions, completion and enhancement. In *Phonology and Phonetics*, ed. T. Alan Hall, 41-70. Berlin: Mouton de Gruyter.
Cho, Tae-hong, Sun-Ah Jun, and Peter Ladefoged. 2002. Acoustic and aerodynamic correlates of Korean stops and fricatives. *Journal of Phonetics* 30: 193-228.

---

[4] See H. Kim (2002, 2004) as well as Cho & Inkelas (1992, 1995), Cho & Iverson (1997) and Davis & Lee (1996) for a literature review as well as phonological, morphological arguments and phonetic data in relation to the issue of whether Korean fortis consonants are geminates or singletons.

Cho, Young-Mee and Sharon Inkelas. 1992.   Geminate Inalterability and Structure Preservation. Paper presented at the Chicago Linguistics Society meeting.
Cho, Young-Mee and Sharon Inkelas. 1995. Post-Obstruent Tensification in Korean and Geminate Inalterability. In *Theoretical Issues in Korean Linguistics*, ed. Young-Key Kim-Renaud , 45-60. Stanford University: CSLI.
Cho, Young-Mee and Gregory K. Iverson. 1997. Korean Phonology in the late twentieth century. *Language Research* 33 (4): 687-735. Seoul: Seoul National University.
Davis, Stuart and Jin-Seong Lee. 1996.   Korean partial reduplication reconsidered. *Lingua* 99: 85-105.
Halle, Morris and Kenneth N. Stevens. 1971. A note on laryngeal features. *Research Laboratory of Electronics Quarterly progress report* 101: 198-212. Cambridge, MA: MIT.
Han, Jeong-Im. 1996. The phonetics and phonology of tense and plain consonants in Korean. Doctoral dissertation, Cornell University, Ithaca, N.Y.
Hirose, Hajime, C. Y. Lee, and Ushijima, T. 1974. Laryngeal control in Korean stop production. *Journal of Phonetics* 2: 145-152.
Hirose, Hajime, Hea-Suk Park, and Masayuki Sawashima. 1983.   Activity of the thyroarytenoid muscle in the production of Korean stops and fricatives. *Ann. Bull. RILP* 17: 73-81.
Honda, Kiyoshi. 1995. Laryngeal and extralaryngeal mechanisms of F0 control. In *Producing speech: Contemporary issues*, ed. F. Bell-Berti and J. H. Abbs, 215-232. New York: American Institute of Physics.
Honda, Kiyoshi. 1999. Interactions between vowel articulation and F0 control.   In *Proceedings of LP'98* , ed. O. Fujimura, B.D. Joseph and B. Palek, 517-527. Prague: Charles University.
Honda, Kiyoshi, Hiroyuki Hirai, Shinobu Masaki and Yasuhiro Shimada. 1999. Role of vertical larynx movement and cervical lordosis in F0 control. *Language and Speech* 42 (4): 401-411.
Hong, Kihwan, Seiji Niimi, and Hajime Hirose. 1991. Laryngeal adjustments for Korean stops, affricates and fricatives – an electromyographic study. *Ann. Bull. RILP* 25: 17-31.
Iverson, Gregory K. 1983. On glottal width features. *Lingua* 60: 331-339.
Jakobson, Roman, Gunnar Fant and Morris Halle. 1952.   *Preliminaries to Speech Analysis*. Cambridge, Mass.: MIT Press.
Jakobson, Roman and Linda. R Waugh. 1987. *The Sound Shape of Language*. Berlin: Mouton de Gruyter.
Jessen, Michael. 1998. *Phonetics and phonology of tense and lax obstruents in German*. Amsterdam: Benjamins.
Kagaya, Ryohei. 1974.   A Fiberscopic and Acoustic Study of the Korean Stops, Affricates and Fricatives. *Journal of Phonetics* 2: 161-180.
Kim, Chin-W. 1965. On the Autonomy of the Tensity Feature in Stop Classification (with the Special Reference to Korean Stops). *Word* 21: 339-359.
Kim, Chin-W. 1970. A theory of aspiration. *Phonetica* 21: 107-16.
Kim, Hyunsoon. 2002. Korean tense consonants as singletons. In *Proceedings of CLS 38: Main Session*, 329-344.

Kim, Hyunsoon. 2003. The representation of the three-way laryngeal contrast in Korean consonants. To appear in *The internal organization of phonological segments*, ed. Marc van Oostendorp and Jeroen van de Weijer. Berlin: Mouton de Gruyter.

Kim, Hyunsoon. 2004. The singleton analysis of Korean fortis consonants. Ms., Hongik University, Seoul, Korea.

Kim, Hyunsoon, Kiyoshi Honda, and Shinji Maeda. 2002. Stroboscopic-cine MRI study on the phasing between the tongue and the larynx in Korean three-way phonation consonants. A final version will appear in *Journal of Phonetics*.

Kim-Renaud, Young-Key. 1974. Korean Consonantal Phonology. Doctoral dissertation, University of Hawaii.

Lisker, Leigh and Arthur S. Abramson. 1964. Cross-language study of voicing in initial stops: Acoustical measurements. *Word* 20: 384-422.

Lombardi, Linda. 1991. Laryngeal features and laryngeal neutralization. Doctoral dissertation, Unviersity of Massachusetts, Amherst.

Lombardi, Linda. 1995. Laryngeal features and privativity. *The Linguistic Review* 12: 35-59.

Silva, David. 1992 The phonetics and phonology of stop lenition in Korean. Doctoral dissertation, Cornell University, Ithaca, N.Y.

Stevens, Kenneth N. 1999. *Acoustic Phonetics*. Cambridge, Mass.: MIT Press.

Stevens, Kenneth N. and Sheila E. Blumstein. 1981. The search for invariant acoustic correlates of phonetic features. In *Perspectives in the study of speech*, ed. Eimas, P.D. & Miller, J.L. Hillsdale: Lawrence Erlbaum. 1-39.

Stevens, Kenneth N., S. Jay Keyser, and Haruko Kawasaki. 1986. Toward a phonetic and phonologoical theory of redundant features. In *Invariance and variability in speech processes*, ed. Joseph S. Perkell and Dennis H. Klatt, 426-449. Hillsdale, NJ: Lawrence Erlbaum Associates.

Stevens, Kenneth N. and S. Jay Keyser. 1989. Primary features and their enhancement in consonants. *Language* 65: 81-106.

Wetzels, W. Leo and Joan Mascaró. 2001 The typology of voicing and devoicing. *Language* 77(2): 207-244.

Internally-Headed Relatives Instantiate Situation Subordination[*]

Min-Joo Kim

University of Massachusetts at Amherst

1.   Introduction

Korean is one of the languages that have the Internally Headed Relative Clause (IHRC) construction, in addition to the more familiar Externally Headed Relative Clause (EHRC) construction.[1] IHRCs in Korean are gapless, as the semantic head noun is contained inside, and they are always followed by the grammatical element *kes*, which is best analyzed as a pronoun (see C. Chan and J. Kim 2003, M. Kim to appear, among others). Compare (1) and (2) ('e' below indicates an empty category or a gap).[2]

(1)   EHRC construction:
       John-un   [DP [e_i   tomangka]-nun   totwuk_i]-ul   cap-ess-ta
       J.-top   [[___   run.away]-rel.imprf thief]-acc   catch-pst-decl
       'John caught a/the thief who was running away.'

(2)   IHRC construction:
       John-un   [DP [totwuk_i-i tomangka]-nun   kes_i]-ul   cap-ess-ta
       J.-top   [[thief-nom run.away]-rel.imprf kes]-acc   catch-pst-decl
       'John caught a/the thief, who was running away.'

The IHRC construction in Korean provides us with a unique opportunity to investigate the principles that govern the mapping between syntax and semantics, as there

---

[*] This work benefited greatly from discussions with Chris Barker, Kyle Johnson, Makoto Kadowaki, Chisato Kitagawa, Angelika Kratzer, Chris Potts, Peggy Speas, Uli Sauerland, and Ellen Woolford. I am of course solely responsible for any remaining errors.
    [1] The IHRC construction is found in languages such as Japanese, Quechua, Lakhota, Navajo, Yuman languages which tend to be head-final. See, among others, Cole 1987, Williamson 1987, Culy 1990, Basilico 1996, Grosu and Landman 1998.
    [2] For the transcription of the Korean data, the following abbreviations are used:
acc: accusative; cl: classifier; comp: complementizer; conj: conjunction; cop: copular verb; dat: dative case; decl: declarative sentence ending; fut: future tense; gen: genitive case; imprf: imperfective aspect; inst: instrumental case; loc: locative; nom: nominative case; pass: past tense; prst: present tense; prf: perfective aspect; prg: progressive aspect; rel: relative marker; top: topic.

appear to be discrepancies between its form and meaning (Ohara 1993, Y. Kim 2002). First, although an IHRC is located inside a DP, it is interpreted like an independent sentence, as the English translation for (2) suggests. Second, the semantic head is buried inside the IHRC, but it is interpreted in such a way that it seems to serve as an argument of the embedding predicate; for example, in (2), what John caught was a thief.

In this paper, I propose a way of resolving these syntax-semantics mismatches. I account for the mismatch exhibited by an IHRC by motivating an LF movement of the IHRC: I propose that the RC is a generalized quantifier that operates in the eventuality domain and hence is interpreted in a position higher than its surface position by combining with an event-level denotation of the embedding clause. To solve the other mismatch problem, I propose that the semantic head appears to function as an argument of the embedding predicate because it is indirectly but formally linked to the pronoun *kes*.

2.   The semantic properties of the IHRC construction in Korean[3]

The IHRC construction in Korean is distinguished from the EHRC construction by a variety of properties. These properties prove challenging to describe.

First, whereas an EHRC restricts the denotation of the semantic head, as illustrated in (3), an IHRC does not, as illustrated in (4) (Jung 1995, Hoshi 1996).

(3)   John-un   [[e_i tomangka]-nun   sey   myeng-uy   totwuk$_i$]-ul
      J.-top   [[___   run.away]-rel.imprf   three   cl-gen   thief]-acc
      cap-ess-ta
      catch-pst-decl
      'John caught three thieves who were running away.'

(4)   John-un   [[sey myeng-uy   totwuk$_i$-i   tomangka]-nun
      J.-top   [[three cl-gen   thief-nom   run.away]-rel.imprf
      kes$_i$]-ul   cap-ess-ta
      kes]-acc   catch-pst-decl
      'John caught three thieves, who were running away.'

Since an EHRC reduces the set denoted by the head noun, (3) will be felicitous in a context where there were five thieves running away from the bank and John caught only three of them. But (4) will be false in such a context; it will be true if and only if there were only three thieves running away and John caught all of them. In other words, the content of the IHRC+*kes* string in (4) denotes the maximal entity that satisfies the description of the semantic head (see Shimoyama 1999 for Japanese).

Next, unlike an EHRC, the content of an IHRC restricts the eventuality described by the embedding clause (Kuroda 1976, 1992, Ohara 1993, Y. Kim 2002). To illustrate, compare (5) and (6). These sentences show that an IHRC's content can restrict the time of the eventuality described by the embedding clause but an EHRC's content cannot.

---

[3] Our discussion will be limited to Korean, but it is assumed that the core part of the proposal carries over to the Japanese IHRC construction.

(5) John-un   [e$_i$ tel   ik]-un   sayngsen$_i$-ul   mek-ess-ta
     J.-top   [___   yet   cook]-rel.prst   fish-acc   eat-pst-decl
     'John ate the fish which was not cooked.'

(6) John-un   [sayngsen-i   tel   ik]-un   kes-ul
     J.-top   [fish-nom   yet   cooked]-rel.prst   kes-acc
     mek-ess-ta
     eat-pst-decl
     'John ate the fish <u>when</u> it was not cooked.'

Sentence (5), which illustrates the EHRC construction, will be felicitous in a context where the discourse participants are talking about a particular fish which was uncooked at some point in the past but which got fully cooked at the time when John ate it. But (6) will be true if and only if the fish was uncooked at the time when John ate it.

Consider now (7) and (8). This paradigm shows that unlike an EHRC, the content of an IHRC can stand in a causal relation to the content of the embedding clause.

(7) John-un   [e$_i$ kangaci-lul   ttayli]-n   Mary$_i$-lul   yatanchi-ess-ta
     J.-top   [___   puppy-acc   hit]-rel.prf   M.-acc   scold-pst-decl
     'John scolded Mary, who hit a puppy.'

(8) John-un   [Mary-ka   kangaci-lul   ttayli]-n   kes-ul
     J.-top   [M.-nom   puppy-acc   hit]-rel.prf   kes-acc
     yatanchi-ess-ta
     scold-pst-decl
     'John scolded Mary <u>because</u> she hit a puppy.'

(7) will be true even if John scolded Mary for not doing her homework. But, for (8) to be true, it must be the case that John scolded Mary because she hit a puppy.

Another notable property of the IHRC construction is that the semantic head varies depending on the context (Kuroda 1992: 153, C. Chung and J. Kim 2003). This property is illustrated by (9), which can be ambiguous in three ways.

(9) John-un   **[koyangi-ka cwi-lul**   coch-ko   iss]-nun   kes-ul
     J.-top   **[cat-nom   mouse-acc**   chase-comp   cop]-rel.imprf   kes-acc
     cap-ess-ta
     catch-pst-decl
     'A cat was chasing a mouse and John caught <u>the cat</u>.'
     'A cat was chasing a mouse and John caught <u>the mouse</u>.'
     'A cat was chasing a mouse and John caught <u>the cat and the mouse</u>.'

The ambiguity of the above sentence shows that the semantic head of an IHRC is intrinsically indeterminate and hence must be determined by the context in conjunction with the embedding predicate's semantics.

To summarize, in this section, we saw that the IHRC construction in Korean differs semantically from the corresponding EHRC construction. In the next section, I propose an analysis which accounts for these distinct properties of the IHRC construction and the two mismatch problems addressed at the outset of the paper.

3.   Analysis

We begin this section with the semantics of an IHRC, i.e. the embedded clause, and turn to the semantics of *kes*, i.e. the pronoun that follows an IHRC.

3.1.   The semantics of an IHRC

In recent literature, the semantics of IHRCs has been studied by several authors. Although the details of these studies differ from each other, they point towards the same direction: IHRCs are quantificational.

First, Strivastav (1991) claims that IHRCs have the same semantics as correlatives: they are generalized quantifiers that denote a function from properties to truth-values. According to Strivastav, correlatives are base-generated adjoined to the embedding clause but they undergo a type-shifting operation where they are converted from entity-denoting terms to generalized quantifiers over the entity domain (p. 661-662).[4]

Second, Fuji (1998) argues that IHRCs in Japanese have the semantics of temporal connectives such as *as soon as* or *immediately after* in English. Within a framework of Discourse Representation Theory (Kamp and Reyle 1993), Fuji posits that the morpheme *no*, which corresponds to *kes* in Korean, is a temporal operator. He proposes that the entire IHRC+*no* string raises at LF to a position higher than the root clause. The two clauses are combined with each other via dynamic conjunction.

Third, Simoyama (1999) claims that IHRCs in Japanese are interpreted like appositives in Demirdache's (1991) system: an IHRC undergoes LF-raising and adjoins to the embedding clause. In this position, the IHRC combines with the embedding clause via a logical connective.

There is no doubt that these quantificational analyses of IHRCs provide genuine insight into the semantics of IHRCs. As they stand, however, they cannot be applied to the semantics of IHRCs in Korean; neither generalized quantifiers that operate in the entity domain (e.g. *every boy*) nor appositive clauses restrict the eventuality described by the embedding clause (see the English translation for (7)). And although the temporal adverbial analysis of IHRCs captures the temporal modifier-like meaning of IHRCs, it fails to account for the cases where the embedded clause bears a causal relation to the embedding clause as we saw in (8).

I offer a new quantificational account of IHRCs which keeps the basic insights of previous research intact but which accommodates the event-restricting semantics of IHRCs in Korean. I claim that the event-restricting semantics of IHRCs in Korean is due to the quantificational semantics of the relative operator (REL). I propose that REL denotes a higher order relation between two sets of eventualities. That is, it is a function that takes a set of eventualities and returns a function that maps another set of eventualities onto truth-values, as given in (10).

---

[4] But Strivastav does not make it explicit whether IHRCs have an identical surface structure as correlatives.

(10) $[[REL]] = \lambda f_{<s,t>}.\lambda g_{<s,t>}$.there is an eventuality s such that $f(s) =1$ and $g(s) =1$, where s ranges over eventualities (undefined if there is no x such that $f(x) =1$).

As will be shown below in Section 3.3., I posit that the first argument of REL is saturated by the denotation of the embedded clause and its second argument is saturated by an event-level denotation of the embedding clause. Hence, the IHRC, which consists of the embedded clause and REL, has the semantics of a generalized quantifier over the eventuality domain (compare Strivastav 1991).

3.2.   The semantics of *kes*

In recent literature, it has been claimed that the IHRC construction in Korean employs an E-type pronoun strategy (M. Kim to appear; see Hoji 1996, Shimoyama 1999, Matsuda 2002 for Japanese). Under an analysis that treats *kes* as a pronoun, what this means is that *kes* denotes a function that takes a salient property recovered from context and returns the unique, maximal entity that has that property.

Treating *kes* as an E-type pronoun captures both the maximality effect and the context-dependency of its value we saw in (4) and (9), respectively. But it turns out that this analysis is too unconstrained: it predicts that the descriptive content of *kes* can be provided by any salient property in the discourse context, but this property can come only from the content of the embedded clause. To illustrate, consider (11) (see Shimoyama 2002: 130 for Japanese).

(11)   Context: John and Mary are married. Mary does all the shopping for the house and John arranges things when she comes back from shopping.

a.
Onul	Mary-ka	John-uy	os-ul	sa-e	o-ess-ta
Today	M.-nom	J.-gen	clothes-acc	buy-comp	come-pst-decl

'Today Mary bought and brought home John's clothes.'

b.
John-un	Mary-ka	shinpal		ttohan	sa-e
J.-top	M.-nom	shoes		also	buy-comp
o-n	kes-ul	os-cang-ey		neh-ess-ta	
o-n	kes-acc	clothes-robe-loc		put-pst-decl	

'John put the shoes that Mary also bought and brought home in the closet.'

In the above discourse, uttering the first sentence makes the clothes that Mary bought for John salient. Furthermore, our world knowledge tells us that it is plausible for one to put clothes in the closet. Hence, under the existing E-type pronoun analysis of *kes*, it is entirely possible that the *kes* in (11b) refers to the clothes for John or the plural entity that consists of the clothes and the shoes that Mary bought and brought home. But the pronoun can refer only to the singular entity that consists of the shoes.

I overcome this difficulty by minimally amending the existing E-type pronoun analyses. I propose that *kes* denotes a function that takes an eventuality and returns a

Min-Joo Kim

maximal individual that has a salient property in that eventuality[5] (compare Hoshi 1996, Shimoyama 1999). A formalization of this idea is given in (12).

(12) $[[kes]] = \lambda s.\sigma x[x$ has a property P in s], where σ is a sum operator and s ranges over eventuality variables, x over entity variables and P over predicates of individuals.[6]

I maintain that the semantics of *kes* is reflected in its syntax. *Kes* spells out a definite article which optionally takes an elided NP sister.[7] In other words, it means something like 'the NP' (compare Hoshi 1996, Shimoyama 1999). Here, the definite article contributes the maximality component in (13), and its elided NP sister, which corresponds to the semantic head in our terms, contributes the free property variable P.

As will be shown in the next section, this proposal captures the intuition that *kes* means something like 'the maximal entity that has a salient property in the eventuality described by the embedded clause.' It thus ensures that the descriptive content of *kes* will come only from the content of the embedded clause.

3.3. The composition scheme

Let us now put together the proposals made thus far and derive the semantics of the IHRC construction in a compositional manner.

To begin with the overt syntactic structure of the construction, I assume that the IHRC is base-generated as an argument of *kes* and the entire IHRC+*kes* string is base-generated as an argument of the embedding predicate (see C. Chung and J. Kim 2003 for evidence).

Turning now to the semantics, I assume that the embedded clause denotes a set of eventualities (M. Kim 2004, to appear). In addition, I posit that due to a semantic type-mismatch between the IHRC and *kes*, the IHRC raises at LF to a position where it can combine with an event-level denotation of the embedding clause (compare Fuji 1998, and Shimoyama 1999, M. Kim to appear).

Given the Principle of Compositionality, the trace of the raised IHRC is interpreted as an eventuality variable. This variable combines with the denotation of *kes*, saturating its eventuality argument, thereby making it formally linked to the content of the IHRC (compare Hoji 1996, Fuji 1998, Shimoyama 1999).

Following Heim and Kratzer (1998), I assume that movement creates an index node which introduces a lambda operator that binds the trace of the moved material. Since the trace of the raised IHRC denotes an eventuality variable, the node that dominates the index will denote a set of eventualities. This combines with the denotation of the IHRC (or the RelP in (13b) below), yielding a truth-value.

When we apply the proposed system to an actual sentence (13a), we obtain (13b) as its LF structure and (13c) as its truth-conditions.

---

[5] Heim (1990) also posits that the denotation of an E-type pronoun contains a situation argument.

[6] The sum operator in (12) can be replaced by an iota operator as long as it can capture the maximality effect exhibited by *kes* (see Shimoyama 1999 for Japanese IHRCs).

[7] See Elbourne 2002 for arguments for treating pronouns this way.

(13)   a.   John-un [[totwuk-i   tomangka]-nun   kes]-ul   capessta
                J.-top   [[thief-nom run.away]-rel.imprf kes]-acc   caught
                'John caught the thief when he (= the thief) was running away.'

b.

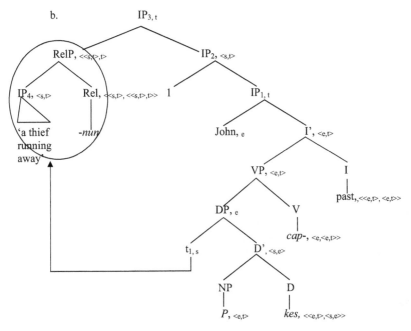

c. There is an eventuality s_1 such that it is an event of a thief running away and there is an eventuality s_2 such that it is an event of John catching the maximal individual x such that x has the property of being a thief in eventuality s_1 (undefined if there is no eventuality s_1).

Derivation of (13c):

$[[DP]]^g = [[kes]]^g([[t_1]]^g) = \lambda s.\sigma x[x$ has the salient property P in event s$]([[t_1]]^g) = \sigma x[x$ has the salient property P in $[[t_1]]^g]$
(via function application).

$[[catch]]^g = \lambda x \lambda y \lambda s[catch(x)(y)(s)]$.

$[[VP]]^g = [[catch]]^g([[DP]]^g) = \lambda y \lambda s[catch(\sigma x[x$ has the salient property P in $[[t_1]]]^g)(y)(s)]$.

$[[IP_1]]^g$ = $[[VP]]^g([[John]]^g)$ = $\lambda s[catch(\sigma x[x$ has the salient property P in $[[t_1]]^g])(John)(s)]$.

$[[IP_2]]^g = \lambda s'[\lambda s[catch(\sigma x[x$ has the salient property P in $[[t_1]]^g])(John)(s)]$
(via predicate abstraction).

$[[IP_2]]^{[1 \to s']} = \lambda s'[\lambda s[catch(\sigma x[x$ has the salient property P in s'])(John)(s)]$
(via variable assignment).

$[[IP_4]]^g = \lambda s[run.away(a$ thief)(s)]$.

$[[-nun]]^g = \lambda f_{<st>}.\lambda g_{<st>}.$there is an eventuality s such that $f(s) = 1$ and $g(s) = 1$ (undefined
if there is no x such that $f(x) = 1$).

$[[RelP]]^g = [[-nun]]^g([[IP_4]]^g) = \lambda g_{<st>}.$there is an eventuality s'' such that run.away(a
thief)(s'') = 1$ and $g(s'') = 1$.

$[IP_3]]^g = [[RelP]]^g([[IP_2]]^g) =$ there is an eventuality s'' such that run.away(a thief)(s'') = 1
and $\lambda s[catch(\sigma x[x$ has the salient property P in s''])(John)(s)] = 1$
(saturating the free variable P).

= there is an eventuality s'' such that run.away(a thief)(s'') = 1 and there is an eventuality
s such that $catch(\sigma x[x$ is a thief in s''])(John)(s) = 1$
(via existential quantification over eventualities).

These truth-conditions we derived for (13a) seem to match native speakers' intuitions
about the meaning of the sentence. It is thus concluded that the proposed analysis derives
the correct semantics of the IHRC construction in Korean.

3.4.   Evaluation of the present proposal

Let us now see how the proposed analysis squares with the problems that concern us in
this paper, namely the two syntax-semantics mismatch problems and the distinct
properties of the IHRC construction.

    First, the LF-raising of an IHRC above the root clause explains why it is interpreted
like an independent sentence although it is inside a DP in its surface structure.

    Second, the proposed semantics of *kes* explains how the semantic head inside the
IHRC is accessed by the matrix predicate.

    Third, the quantificational semantics of the IHRC explains why the content of the
embedded clause restricts the content of the embedding clause, rather than that of the
head noun.

    Finally, the sum operator inside the denotation of *kes*, which is contributed by the
definite article, explains why it exhibits a maximality effect. On the other hand, the free
property variable inside the denotation of *kes*, which is contributed by an elided NP,
explains why its value varies depending on the context.

4.   Welcome results of the present proposal

The present proposal has several welcome results. First, as noted in M. Kim 2004, the truth of a sentence containing an IHRC entails the truth of the embedded clause. To illustrate, consider (14).

(14) John-un   Mary-ka   ppang-ul   mantu-n   kes-ul
      J.-top   M.-nom   bread-acc   make-rel.prf   kes-acc
      chac-ko   iss-ta
      look.for-comp   cop-decl
      'John is looking for the bread, which Mary made.'

In (14), although the embedding predicate is intensional, the embedded clause's content is extensional. In other words, the sentence entails that the event of Mary making bread actually happened. So if the sentence is followed by the speaker's denial of the existence of the embedded event, the discourse becomes contradictory, as shown in (15).

(15) John-un   Mary-ka   ppang-ul   mantu-n   kes-ul
      J.-top   M.-nom   bread-acc   make-rel.prf   kes-acc
      chac-ko   iss-ta
      look.for-comp   cop-decl
      'John is looking for the bread, which Mary made.'

      #Kulentay,   Mary-ka   ppang-ul   **mantul-ci**   **an-h-ess-ta**
      But,   M.-nom   bread-acc   **make-ci**   **neg-do-pst-decl**
      'But, Mary didn't make bread.'

Under the present proposal, this property of the IHRC construction is expected; it has been independently proposed by several authors that in order for the semantic computation to work, the quantification domain of a strong quantifier should not be empty (Strawson 1952, von Fintel 1994, Heim and Kratzer 1998). In the proposed system, the quantification domain for REL is provided by the denotation of the embedded clause. It thus follows that uttering the entire sentence entails the truth of the embedded clause.

Another welcome result of the present analysis concerns the parallel between the IHRC construction in Korean and the correlative construction in Hindi illustrated in (16).

(16) [[jo   laRkii   khaRii   ha]   vo   lambii hai
      [[REL   girl   standing   is]   DEM   tall   is
      'The girl who is standing is tall.'   (from Dwivedi 1994:115, (2))

The two constructions are parallel in that (i) they are both head internal, (ii) the content of the RC is presupposed (Strivastav 1991, M. Kim 2004), and (iii) they contain an E-type pronoun which is linked to the content of the RC (Dayal 1995, M. Kim in progress; see also Hoshi 1996, Shimoyama 1999 for Japanese).

Under the present analysis, this parallel is a natural consequence, because the LF structure of the IHRC construction proposed in this paper is identical to the overt syntactic structure of correlatives in the standard analysis (Strivastav 1991), as schematically represented in (17).

(17)   [$_{IP}$ [$_{RelP}$ [... DP$_i$ ...V]] [$_{IP}$ DP$_i$... V]]

Given this, the IHRC construction and the correlative construction seem to differ from each other merely in where the structure in (17) is represented: in the former, it occurs in covert syntax and in the latter, in overt syntax.

Finally, the present analysis accounts for why IHRCs in Korean parallel direct perceptual reports in Korean and participial small clauses in other languages, as noted by M. Kim (to appear): that is, (i) why in all these constructions, the embedded eventuality temporally overlaps with the embedding eventuality, (ii) the embedded clause tends to contain only stage-level predicates in the sense of Carlson (1977), and (iii) the embedded clause is syntactically smaller than a full clause.

In view of the present analysis, these parallels are also expected; they pattern together, because their semantics all involve connecting two sets of eventualities.

5.   Remaining issue: adding a temporal element

The proposed analysis carves out an important semantic condition on the interpretability of the IHRC construction in Korean. A descriptive generalization of the phenomenon is that, in order for a sentence containing an IHRC to be interpreted, the embedded clause must describe an eventuality which temporally intersects with the eventuality in the description of the embedding clause.

To see this, compare (21) and (22) below. Suppose that these sentences were uttered in a context where John and Mary had a fight, and John lost it, so he did something to get his revenge on Mary. Notice that, although it seems felicitous to say either (21) or (22) in the given context, only the latter is grammatical (or acceptable).[8]

(21)   *John-un   Mary-ka   ecey   cangnankam-ul   kaci-ko
        J.-top   M.-nom   yesterday   toy-acc   have-comp
        no-n   kes-ul   peliessta
        play-rel.prf   kes-acc   threw.away
        Intended: 'John threw away the toy that Mary played with yesterday'

---

[8] When the embedded aspect is progressive, the contrast between (21) and (22) disappears, as shown in (i) and (ii), because, in this case, the embedded event time and the embedding event time intersect.

(i)   John-un   Mary-ka   cangnankam-ul   kaciko   **nol-ko**
        J.-top   M.-nom   toy-acc   with   **play-comp**
        iss-nun   kes-ul   (ppassa-se)   peliessta
        cop-rel.imprf kes-acc   (took.away-conj)   threw.away
        'John threw away the toy that Mary was playing with a toy (by taking it from her).'
(ii)   John-un   Mary-ka   cangnankam-ul   senmwul-lo   **pat-ko**
        J.-top   M.-nom   toy-acc   present-as   **receive-comp**
        iss-nun   kes-ul   (ppassa-se)   peliessta
        cop-rel.imprf kes-acc   (took.away-conj)   threw.away
        'John threw away the toy that Mary was receiving as a present (by taking it from her).'

(22) John-un   Mary-ka   ecey   cangnankam-ul
      J.-top   M.-nom   yesterday   toy-acc
      senmwul-lo   pat-un   kes-ul   peliessta
      present-inst   receive-rel.prf   kes-acc   threw.away
      'John threw away the toy that Mary received as a present yesterday.'

What is responsible for the difference between the two sentences? I suggest that this contrast is due to the fact that the embedded predicate of (21) is atelic whereas that of (22) is telic. When embedded predicate is atelic, the IHRC does not describe an eventuality that temporally intersects with the embedding event. When the embedded predicate is telic, however, the IHRC describes a target state, i.e. a state that results from the culmination of the event described by the embedded predicate, and this state temporally intersects with the embedding event.

This analysis, if correct, suggests that we need to add a temporal element to the present system, thereby making the two sets of eventualities described by the embedded clause and the embedding clause temporally intersect (see M. Kim in progress).

6.   Conclusion

In this paper, I accounted for the discrepancies between the syntax and semantics of the IHRC construction in Korean, which have been longstanding problems in the literature. I proposed that the semantics of the relative operator quantifies over sets of eventualities and that *kes* is a pronominal definite description which contains an eventuality variable. The proposed analysis suggests that the semantics of relative clauses is more flexible and varied than has been assumed in the literature. It also suggests a strong parallel between relative operators and determiners.

References

Basilico, David. 1996. Head position and internally headed relative clauses. *Language* 72: 498-532.
Carlson, Gregory N. 1977. Reference to Kinds in English, UMass-Amherst: Doctoral dissertation. Published and distributed by GLSA.
Chung, Chan and Jong-Bok Kim. 2003. Differences between externally and internally headed relative clause constructions, in J.-B. Kim ed., *On-line Proceedings of HPSG 2002*, 3-25.
Cole, Peter. 1987. The structure of internally headed relative clauses. *Natural Language and Linguistic Theory* 5: 277-302.
Culy, C. Douglas. 1990. The syntax and semantics of internally headed relative clauses, Stanford University: Doctoral Dissertation.
Demirdache, Hamida. 1991. Resumptive chains in restrictive relatives, appositives, and dislocation structure. MIT: Doctoral dissertation.
Dwivedi, Veena. 1994. Syntactic dependencies and relative phrases in Hindi. UMass-Amherst: Doctoral dissertation. Published and distributed by GLSA.

Elbourne, Paul. 2002. E-type anaphora as NP-deletion. *Natural Language Semantics* 9: 241-288.

von Fintel, Kai 1994. Restrictions on Quantifier Domains. UMass-Amherst: Doctoral dissertation. Published and distributed by GLSA.

Fuji, Masaaki. 1998. Temporal interpretation of internally headed relative clauses in Japanese. *Working Papers from Rutgers University* 1: 75-91.

Grosu, Alexander and Fred Landman 1998. Strange relatives of the third kind. *Natural Language Semantics* 6:125-170.

Heim, Irene. 1990. E-type pronouns and donkey-anaphora. *Linguistics and Philosophy* 13: 137-177.

Heim, Irene and Angelika Kratzer. 1998. *Semantics in Generative Grammar*. Malden, MA: Blackwell.

Hoshi, Koji. 1996. Structural and interpretive aspects of head-internal and head-external relative clauses, University of Rochester: Doctoral dissertation.

Jung, Yunsun. 1995. Internally headed relative clauses in Korean. In *Harvard Studies in Korean Linguistics*, eds. Kuno et al., 235-248. Seoul, Korea: Hanshin.

Kamp, Hans and Uwe Reyle. 1993. *From Discourse to Logic*. Dordrecht: Kluwer.

Kim, Min-Joo. 2004. Three types of *kes*-nominalization in Korean. Lee, I.-H. et al. eds., *Harvard Studies in Korean Linguistics 10*, 479-492, Seoul: Hanshin.

Kim, Min-Joo. To appear. Internally-headed relatives parallel direct perception complements. E. Hudson et al. eds., *Japanese/Korean Linguistics 13*.

Kim, Min-Joo. In progress. Internally-headed relatives, eventualities, and definite descriptions. UMass-Amherst: Doctoral dissertation.

Kim, Yong-Beom. 2002. Relevancy in internally headed relative clauses in Korean. *Lingua* 112: 541-559.

Kuroda, Shige-yuki. 1992. *Japanese Syntax and Semantics*. Dortrecht: Kluwer.

Matsuda, Yuki. 2002. Event sensitivity of head-internal relatives in Japanese. *Japanese/Korean Linguistics* 10: 629-643. Stanford: CSLI.

Ohara, H. Kyoko. 1993. On Japanese internally headed relative clauses. *Proceedings of BLS 18*, Buszard-Wechsler et al. eds., 100-109.

Shimoyama, Junko. 1999. Internally headed relative clauses in Japanese and E-type anaphora. *Journal of East Asian Linguistics* 8: 147-182.

Shimoyama, Junko. 2002. Wh-constructions in Japanese, UMass-Amherst: Doctoral dissertation.

Strawson, Peter. F. 1952. *Introduction to Logical Theory*, London: Methuen.

Strivastav, Veneeta. 1991. The syntax and semantics of correlatives, *Natural Language and Linguistic Theory* 9: 637-686.

Williamson, Janis. 1987. An indefiniteness restriction on relative clauses in Lakhota. In *The Representation of (In)definites*, eds. E. Reuland and A.G.B. ter Meulen, 168-190. Cambridge, MA: the MIT press.

Department of Linguistics
South College, University of Massachusetts
Amherst, MA 01003

minjoo@linguist.umass.edu

The Case for Null Subject-Verb Agreement Morphology in Bantu

Kasangati K. W. Kinyalolo

SUNY Stony Brook, Stony Brook

1.   Introduction

Meeussen (1967, 1971a), Takizala (1972), Bokamba (1976), Kimenyi (1980), Nsuka (1982), among others, establish that though Bantu languages are considered SVO, they nevertheless exhibit XVS word order. In the latter case, V cannot show agreement with the post-verbal S. Where relevant data are available, the post-verbal subject precedes other constituents of the VP. Examples (1)-(3) from KiLega (D25) illustrate the core cases, i.e., subject-object reversal (SOR)[1], locative inversion, and a *wh*-construction.

(1)   a.   *kabánga   **ká** – na – ly –á   mwǎmí túgú.*
           12sp. of pangolin 12SM-POT-eat-FV 1mwami only
           'Only a member of the *bwǎmí* association can eat pangolin meat.'

      b.   ***bw** – á –ténd–ag - a   nǎzí, bú – b – o* ?
           14SM-A-say-HAB-FV 1who 14RED-14NBR-D
           'Who used to say that?'

(2)   a.   *ku maswá **kú** – kw – end – ág -á bǎna tondo.*
           17 6farm   17SM-PROG-go-HAB-FV 2child also
           'To the farms go children also.'

      b.   *tw – ǐk - á   mu kyumo ky - á   ngulube líno;*
           1PL:A-arrive-FV 18 7village 7AGR-AM 9warthog now

---

[1] Restrictions on SOR involve *freezing effects* when SUBJ & OBJ belong to the same class. Such is not the case in a *wh*-construction, however, arguing that the two constructions involve different types of movement (Kinyalolo 1991). In (1b) and similar sentences, the post-verbal *wh*-phrase has both echo and non-echo interpretations.

ta - **mú** – *ku* - *ténd* – *ag* -*a*   *mwăna*.
NEG-18SM-A-speak-HAB-FV 1child
'We've now arrived in Ngulube's village; *no child* utters a word in it.'

(3)   *b-á-ly-á*   *ku mupunga* **ú** – (*á*) – *ku* - *yik–íl-á*   *Kubóta basábuki*.
         2SM-A-eat-FV 17 3rice   3RM-1SM-PROG-cook-APPL-FV K   2fisherman
         'They ate some of the rice that Kubota is cooking for the fishermen.'

When SUBJ is *wh*-extracted, SM cannot appear alongside RM (4a). In contrast, when SUBJ is pronominal, SM occurs alongside RM (4b).

(4)   a.   *mwăna* **ú** - (*á*) - *ku* - *yan* - *ág* - *á*   *n'*   *isé*   -   *ngúlú*...
            1child 1RM-(*1SM)-PROG-joke-HAB-FV with 1father:IIISG:POSS great
            'the child who usually jokes with his / her grand-father...'

      b.   *b–á -ly-á*   *ku magomá* *ma* – *bá* - *ku* – *yik* – *íl* - *á*   *basábuki*.
            2SM-A-eat-FV 17 6plantain 6RM-2SM-PROG-cook-APPL-FV 2fisherman
            'They ate some of the plantains that they are cooking for the fishermen.'

LFG and Minimalism contain two representative views of the nature of SM. For Bresnan and Mchombo (1987), SM is ambiguous between pronominal clitic (which may be bound to a topic NP) and SVA morphology[2]. In Minimalism, two camps are clearly identifiable. For the first camp, SM is SVA morphology with SpecTP, irrespective of the phonetic contents of the element that sits in it. For the second (e.g., Baker 2003), SM is a SVA marker tailored to identifying *pro*. Baker argues that an overt nominal is never in the specifier of an agreeing head: it is in a dislocated, adjunct position.

In this paper, building on the old claim that SM is a pronominal, I argue that SMs and RMs are neither agreement morphology between YP in Spec XP and X^o (where X^o is Asp^o, T^o or C^o), nor X^o or a feature that drives movement of YP (phonetically null or not) into SpecXP. Rather, they are clitics [DP_{CLITIC} and $OP(erator)_{CLITIC}$] which merge in θ-positions the way lexical DPs do.

(5)

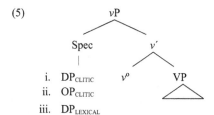

          i. DP_{CLITIC}
          ii. OP_{CLITIC}
          iii. $DP_{LEXICAL}$

Turning to licensing, I assume that a lexical SUBJ is licensed in Spec*v*P (1, 3a)[3]. It is immaterial whether it is nominative (Kinyalolo 1991), or ergative (following Bittner &

---

[2] See Gregersen (1967) for a review of some of the earlier views on prefixes and pronouns in Bantu.
[3] Given that the counterpart argument of an unaccusative verb in Romance can occur in a *na*-phrase (i.e., *by*-phrase) in the passive in KiLega, I hold the view that there are no unaccusative verbs in KiLega.

Hale 1996; or Woolford 1997).

The paper is organized as follows. Section 2 introduces the observations on which the proposal is based. Section 3 shows that movement of a DP$_{\text{CLITIC}}$ into SpecTP does not correlate with overt SVA, contra the *Agreement Parameter*. Section 4 shows that other principles of grammar may conspire to enforce the V-S order. Section 5 claims that a clitic enters into a binding relation with a lexical XP merged in the left periphery.

2.   SMs and RMs as Clitics

2.1.   Zero Copula

In the present tense, the copula may be null, and a SM or RM from any class stand alone in the affirmative[4]. (6a-b) show 1st, 2nd person plural markers. (6c-d) are a minimal pair; in (6c) *mutíma* 'heart' is the complement of P, i.e., *ku*; in (6d), a relative clause, it is the subject while *kú* corresponds to *where*. (6e-f) shows the presence of RM in *wh*-questions.

(6)   a.   *ééé băna b - á Lega, **tu** munt' ú - mozi.*
          2child 2AGR-AM L   IPL 1person 1AGR-one
          'Eh Lega, we're one person.'

     b.   *ámbu **mu** băna   b - á   mitamba z - a   mu kí – ki - nó   kyumo?*
          EV   IIPL 2child 2AGR-AM 4lady   4AGR-AM 18 7RED-7NBR-D 7village
          'Is it true, as rumored, that you were born to ladies from this village?'

     c.   *ikozí   ly – á   kw' ibúngu   lí – tik – y - é   mĩlí ku mutíma.*
          5stone 5agr-AM 17 5shore   5SM-come out-CAUS-SUBJ 6crab 17 3heart
          'A stone on the shore should give up hope on crabs [burrowing under it].'

     d.   *ikozí   ly – á   kw' ibúngu   lí – tik – y - é   mĩlí **kú**   mutíma.*
          5stone 5agr-AM 17 5shore   5SM-come out-CAUS-SUBJ 6crab 17RM 3heart
          'A stone on the shore should bring crabs from where the heart is.'

     e.   *kúní   **kú**   bí – by - o   bipúká?*   f.   *năzí **ú**   mu numbá?*
          17where 17RM   8RED-8NBR-D 8giant   1who 1RM 18   9house
          'Where are those giants?'   'who is in the house?'

If, and when, it has a phonetic representation, the copula surfaces as *–li*. For similar facts in other languages, see Doron (1986) on PRON in Hebrew, bearing in mind that there are differences between Hebrew and KiLega wrt the distribution of SM and PRON.

What is the account of the facts? There are empirical problems for the view that they may be heads with some XP in their Spec. On the other hand, if they are elements attached to a host, a rule would have to delete the said head and its complement, while paradoxically leaving behind the element said to attach to it. As far as I know, Agr

---

[4] In the negative, RM occurs to the left of NEG and SM to its right, the way they would do if a verb were phonetically present. If NEG merges with TP (cf. Belletti 1990), this order follows naturally.

markers do not stand alone. In contrast, pronouns do. As such, they could stand alone in the specifier of a null head. In this paper, I proceed from the claim that SMs and RMs are clitics and thus independent lexical entries and not unvalued features of some head, as would be expected from the assumptions of the Agree relation. What will have to be accounted for therefore is whether they are deficient in some syntactic projections (Cardinaletti & Starke 1999).

2.2.   *ín(y)ĕné* 'alone'

A consideration of the partial paradigm in (7) of the adverbial use of *ín(y)ĕné* 'alone' found in sentences of the format 'XP$_i$ VERB ALONE$_i$' provides more support to our claim.

(7)   Singular   Plural[5]

   a. i. *in 'ín(y)ĕné*   ii. *tu   b 'ín(y)ĕné*
           ISG-alone   IPL 2NBR-alone

   b. i. *u(g)w 'ín(y)ĕné*   ii. *mu   b 'ín(y)ĕné*
           IISG-alone   IIPL 2NBR-alone

   c. i. *(g)w 'ín(y)ĕné*   ii. *b - ó   b 'ín(y)ĕné*
           IIISG-alone   2NBR-D 2NBR-alone

   d. i. *k - ó   k̲- 'ín(y)ĕné*   ii. *t - ó   tw 'ín(y)ĕné*
           12NBR-D 12NBR-alone   13NBR-D 13NBR-alone

The construction consists of three elements: (i) a strong pronoun indicating the person of the subject DP (7ai, 7bi, 7c, 7d), or the exponent thereof for 1st and 2nd persons plural, viz., *tu* (7aii) and *mu* (7bii); (ii) the exponents of the class and number of the subject; and (iii) *ín(y)ĕné* 'alone,' as illustrated in (8). I assume that in class 1, the exponent of class and number is null (7ai, 7bi, 7ci):

(8)   a.   **PERSON** + [CL & NBR] + ín(y)ĕné   [cl 1:1st-3rd; cl 2:1st-2nd]
       b.   [[CL & NBR] + D] + [CL & NBR] + ín(y)ĕné   [cl 2:3rd & onward]

Elsewhere, *tu* is SM or OM; *mu* only SM. The question that arises therefore concerns the treatment of *tu* and *mu* in (7) in the absence of T, *v* or V which are claimed to host them. Assuming that (8) is a small clause whose subject is the pronoun, the simplest solution comes from the hypothesis that as DPs, *tu* and *mu* enter the numeration as independent lexical entries.

2.3.   Operators & Pronouns

Another argument for treating SMs as pronouns is theory-internal. This is a constraint

---

[5] One also finds strong pronouns for 1st and 2nd persons plural.

barring a pronoun from being locally (A-bar) bound by an operator as found in Jaeggli (1986: 40) (also see, among others, Rizzi 1986, Cinque 1990, Ouhalla 1993):

(9)   A pronominal must be Operator free.

Except in instances of extraction out of PP, this constraint appears to hold in KiLega. Extending (9) to KiLega therefore has immediate advantages if RM is an operator and SM a pronominal. Recall that in *wh*-extraction of SUBJ in KiLega, RM cannot co-occur with SM, as seen in (4a) repeated below:

(4)   a.   *mwăna* **ú** - (***á***) - *ku* - *yan* - *ág* - *á*   *n'* *isé*   -   *ngúlú*...
             1child 1RM-(*1SM)-PROG-joke-HAB-FV with 1father:IIISG:POSS great
             'the child who usually jokes with his / her grand-father...'

Since in (4a), RM (OP_{CLITIC}) in SpecCP would be A-bar binding SM (DP_{CLITIC}) in SpecTP, the sentence would be ruled out. Another possible analysis comes from Chomsky's (1995: 347) claim that "an argument with no θ-role is not a legitimate object [since] it violates FI and causes a derivation to crash." Consider (5). For SM and SUBJ, or SM and RM to co-occur in V-S order, they would have to originate in (or compete for) the same position, i.e., Spec*v*P. As seen, one naturally derives the complementary distribution of SM (DP_{CLITIC}) and SUBJ ($DP_{LEXICAL}$) in V-S order (cf. (3)) as well as that of SM and RM (OP_{CLITIC}) in *wh*-extraction of SUBJ.

3.   Agree (Probe, Goal), internal Merge and Clitics

In line with the research on clitics initiated in Kayne (1975), a dominant account of them is that they are DPs that merge in θ-positions and move as XPs before adjoining to their host by head-movement (cf. Chomsky 1995, among others). As has been noted, though, the last part of clitic movement pertains to morphology and/or phonology.

    In Chomsky (2001), the claim is made that all instances of internal Merge require the Agree relation. In short, the unvalued φ-features of the Probe are valued by the Goal; and the EPP-feature of T is satisfied by raising the agreed-with Goal into SpecTP. As is known, however, in IE languages like English, SVA is possible between the Probe and the Goal under c-command and without internal Merge:

(10)   There were many philologists in the garden.

In (10), *are* agrees with the post-verbal noun *many philologists*; on the other hand, *there* in SpecTP satisfies the EPP-feature of T. Based on SOR, locative inversion, etc., it is now claimed that agreement is obligatorily accompanied with internal Merge in Bantu. To capture this difference between Bantu and other languages, Baker (2003) proposes the following parameter, the *Agreement Parameter*:

(11)   a.   Tense agrees with the nominative NP in Indo-European.
        b.   Tense agrees with its specifier in Bantu.

See Carstens (2003) for a different statement of the said parameter. Central to this view is the fact that agreement does not correlate with Case-deletion (see Carstens 2001).

With this in mind, let us consider (1b) under the claim that SMs are DP$_{CLITIC}$s:

(1)   b.   *bw – á –ténd–ag - a   năzí, bú – b – o* ?
           14SM-A-say-HAB-FV 1who 14RED-14NBR-D
           'Who used to say that?'

Assuming that SOR involves movement of OBJ into SpecTP (Collins 1997; Ndayiragije 1999; Ura 2000; Carstens 2003; e.g.), we expect movement of DP$_{CLITIC}$ into SpecTP to correlate with overt SVA morphology. That this is not the case is illustrated by (12):

(12)   *   *bu - bw – á –ténd–ag - a   năzí, bú – b – o* ?

Since there are languages where clitics and lexical subject DPs trigger overt SVA, and since under the *Agreement Parameter* assumptions, T overtly agrees with SpecTP in Bantu, one needs to explain why suddenly T cannot do so with the raised DP$_{CLITIC}$. While a ban on a sequence of two identical phonetic elements with the same referent may account for why (12) is ruled out, one still has to explain why RM and SM cannot co-occur (see (4a)). A recent attempt to do so is Carstens (2003). For Carstens, "the EPP-feature which raises Kilega subjects is a property not of T itself but of the features comprising subject agreement." Faced with the fact that a *wh*-operator that goes through SpecTP does not trigger SVA, Carstens (paradoxically) writes, *"Kilega T agrees silently with the operator."*

4.   Agree, NPI & *DP túgú* 'only DP'

This section identifies two constructions that show that an account of word order that relies on the Agree relation falls short of a sound explanation of the facts. As will be seen, other principles of grammar conspire to derive the V-S order while bleeding, or blocking, as it were, the Agree relation.

The first construction involves the licensing of negative polarity items (NPIs). An inherently negative sensitive item like *kámpa* is licensed by NEG under c-command. This requirement is met in (13a), but not in (13b) where NEG is absent, nor in (13c) where *kámpa* precedes NEG:

(13)   a.   *basábuki   ta – b – á – món - in - e kámpa*   *ku Lwĭndí.*
            2fisherman NEG-2SM-A-see-PERF-FV 12some/anything 17 L
            'The fishermen caught nothing at the Lwindi (river).'

       b.   *? *basábuki b–á-món-in-e kámpa ku Lwĭndí.*

       c.   *   *kámpa   ta – k – á – món – w - a   ku Lwĭndí.*
            Some/anything NEG-12SM-A-see-PASS-FV 17 L
            'Nothing was caught at the Lwindi (river).'

I take these facts to suggest that NEG does not undergo (covert) raising, on the one hand, and that **kámpa** does not reconstruct, on the other. Under the copy theory of movement, it must be explained why this reading is unavailable.

For a non-inherently negative noun to be interpreted as an NPI, it too must be under the scope of NEG at Spell-out. To see this, consider (2b), repeated below, and (14). Unlike in (14), the subject DP is c-commanded by NEG in (2b). Note that in (14), the DP *mwăna* is specific and cannot be understood as '*no N*:'

(2b)   *tw – ĭk - á   mu kyumo   ky - á   ngulube   líno*;
       IPL:A-arrive-FV 18   7village 7AGR-AM 9warthog now

       *ta - **mú** – ku - ténd – ag -a   mwăna.*
       NEG-18SM-PROG-speak-HAB-FV 1child
       'We have now arrived in Ngulube's village; *no child* utters a word in it.'

(14)   *mwăna t – á –ku - ténd – ag – a   mu kyumo ky - á   ngulube.*   .
       1child NEG-1SM-PROG-speak-HAB-FV 18 7village 7AGR-AM 9warthog
       '*The child* does not utter a word in Ngulube's village.' / * '*No child*…'

Given the restriction on c-command by NEG, SUBJ cannot raise from SpecvP, whether T values its φ-features or not. Now, to be "frozen in place," SUBJ in SpecvP must have its Case-feature probed by T (cf. Chomsky 2001). Therefore, the only solution for the derivation of (6) to converge is for some other constituent to raise to Spec TP, yielding locative inversion. What is important to note is the failure for the locative DP$_{CLITIC}$ to trigger "subject agreement" on the verb. I claim that the presence of the locative DP$_{CLITIC}$ in Spec TP reflects the need to satisfy the requirement that SpecTP be filled by Spell-out more than anything having to do with the Agree relation.

The second construction involves SUBJ modified by *túgú* 'only.' For space reasons, suffice it to note that *túgú* takes scope over various constituents. In (15a), the scope is over VP; in (15b), it is over OBJ:

(15)   a.   *nti   mw – ínún - á   túgú* mízŏngú.
            EVID IIPL:A-take out of water-FV only 4cassava root
            'You should only take the cassava roots out of the water.'

       b.   *nti   mw – ínún - á   mízŏngú   túgú.*
            EVID IIPL:A-take out of water-FV 4cassava root only
            'You should take only the cassava roots out of the water.'

I suggest that in (16a), *túgú* adjoins to VP; and that in (16b), *mízŏngú* is in Spec of *túgú*[6]:

(16)   a.   V [$_{VP}$ [$_{QP}$ túgú [$_{VP}$ [t_v]]]   b.   [$_{QP}$ DP [$_{Q'}$ túgú [$_{DP}$ t_{DP}]]]

---

[6] See Kayne (1998) for a different approach to the syntax of *only*.

For the present discussion, I assume that *XP túgú* is identificational focus (cf. Kiss 1998). Let us now consider (17), where the post-verbal SUBJ is modified by *túgú*:

(17) a. *kabánga   ká – na – ly –á   mwǎmí túgú.*
          12sp. pangolin 12SM-POT-eat-FV 1mwami only
          'Only a member of the *bwǎmí* association can eat pangolin meat.'

      b. *ku bwalí   kú – kw – end – ág -á   balúme túgú.*
          17 14circumcision rites 17SM-PROG-go-HAB-FV 2male   only
          'Only males go to / attend the circumcision rites.'

The *Agreement Parameter* predicts that *DP túgú* should be able to occur in SpecTP, which would entail the presence of SM. This prediction is not borne out:

(18) a. *mwǎmí   (*túgú) á – na – ly –á   kabánga.*
          1mwami (*only) 1SM-POT-eat-FV 12sp. of pangolin
          '(*Only) A member of the *bwǎmí* association can eat pangolin meat.'

      b. *balúme (*túgú) bá – kw – end – ág - á ku bwalí.*
          2male   (*only) 2SM-PROG-go-HAB-FV 17 14circumcision rites
          '(*Only) Males go to / attend the circumcision rites.'

If one invokes the lexical ambiguity of SM as in Bresnan & Mchombo (1987), it is not clear why *DP túgú* Agr-V is ruled out. There is no such constraint in English, as (19) clearly shows:

(19) It seems that only the old philologists will enjoy historical linguistics.

This restriction on SM could follow from (20), presumably a representational constraint:

(20) SM is incompatible with *XP túgú*.

If *XP túgú* is an operator, (20) falls under the contraint that bans a pronominal from being locally A-bar bound by an operator.
    For *DP túgú* to occur preverbally, KiLega resorts to the construction in (21)[7]:

(21) a. *mwǎmí túgú ú   ú – (*á) - na – ly –á   kabánga.*
          1mwami only PTCL 1RM-1SM-POT-eat-FV 12sp. pangolin
          'Only a member of the *bwǎmí* association can eat pangolin meat.'

---

[7] In Meeussen (1971b), this *ú* (or *í*) is considered to be a copula. If correct, *ú* (or *í*) would be the only irregular verb in the language not to bear any inflectional markers. On this view, the question is why NEG appears as the first element of the clause as in *Tǎ Bútangá ú mwǎna mutó* 'Butanga is not the youngest child' (cf. 22b). I suggest that *ú* (or *í*) is a marker of assertion. Its properties are to be investigated further.

b. *balúme túgú ú* **bá** *– (*bá) - kw - end – ág - á ku bwalí.*
2male only PTCL 2RM-2SM-PROG-go-HAB-FV   17 14circumcision rites
'Only males attend the circumcision rites.'

This construction mediates between syntax and the property of exhaustivity, as can be seen in (22). In (22a), the predicate '*first born*' can only be exhausted by one subject. The only way to convey this information is through the use of *ú*, as seen by the impossibility for the copula *-li* to appear. In (22b), two different relations obtain between the subject and the predicate. The choice of the copula *–li* or the particle *ú* is done accordingly.

(22) a. *Bwăto ú*   / ** á - li*   *nkúla*   *z – ă - né.*
B   PTCL / 1SM-COP 9first born 9agr-AM-ISG
'(It is) Bwato (who) is my first born.'

Bútangá ú   / *á – li*   *mwăna mu – tó.*
B   PTCL / 1SM-COP 1child 1agr-young
b. '(It is) Butanga (that) is the youngest child.'
c. 'Butanga is a young child.'

Note that while (21) could extend to *wh*-extraction of SUBJ as well as a question *wh*-word like *năzí* or *běnyí* 'who', it would say nothing about *Bwăto* and *Bútangá* in (22).

To return to (18) *vs* (20), I would like to sketch the lines of research that will be pursued to explain why the sequence *DP túgú SM-V* is ruled out in KiLega. Hajičová, Partee & Sgall (1998: 32) argue that *only* is a focus-sensitive operator 'targeted' to a particular constituent. Hajičová, Partee & Sgall (1998) further argue that the semantics of *only* is such that it explicitly declares 'exhaustivity' with respect to targeted constituents, presupposing the truth-condition of the corresponding non-exhaustive proposition. Also, like quantifiers, *only* effects a tripartite structure of a clause into an operator, a restrictor and a nuclear scope.

Supposing that KiLega *túgú* corresponds to English *only*, what the above implies for (18) is that the sequence *DP túgú SM-V* does not lend itself to the tripartite partition that is required for its interpretation --- which would imply that SOR easily lends itself to such a division. So, while the said tripartite division must hold at LF in English, it seems to be the case that in KiLega, overt syntax must be as close as possible to the syntax of LF-movement. So, let us assume that the subject *DP túgú* is not in an operator position in (18). In contrast, in (21), it must be in an operator position from which it can bind a variable. The role of RM in mediating this relation is now obvious. This fact also argues that movement of the identificational focus constituent to Spec FocusP (see Kiss 1998) is not necessary. In sum, on the assumption that RM is an operator, *DP túgú* must merge in the left periphery while entering a binding relationship with OP$_{CLITIC}$. There is evidence from the behavior of the universally quantified noun that this view is correct.

5. The Left Periphery

Beghelli and Stowell (1997) identify five major classes of QP-types. They also argue that
each QP-type has its feature checked in a designated specifier. For instance, a universally
quantified phrase (DQP) occurs in the specifier of a Distr(ibutive) head. I want to suggest
that in KiLega, the DPQ is merged in SpecDistP and enters a binding relation with
OP$_{CLITIC}$ in SpecCP.

The facts about DQP are as follows. A noun (singular or plural) preceded by *na*
translates the English *every / each N*. Note that a pronoun may also be preceded by *na*:

(23) a.   *na   mwăna*   b.   *na   băna*
           every 1child   every 2child
           'every / each child'   'every / each group of children'

      c.   *na   (g)wé*   d.   *na   ky - ó*
           every IIISG   every 7NBR-D
           'every / each one'   'every / each one'

The DPQ occurs at the beginning of a sentence, as seen in (24). Notice that the DPQ is
followed by *na*. Moreover, like OP$_{CLITIC}$, not only is it incompatible with SM, it also
requires the presence of RM:

(24)   *na   mwăna na   w - á – túnd - á   nina.*
           Every 1child DIST 1RM:A-love-FV   mother:POSS:IIISG
      a.   'Every child loves his / her mother.'
      b.   'His / her mother loves every child.'

      c. * *na   mwăna n'   á – túnd - á   nina.*
           Every 1child DIST 1SM:A-love-FV   mother:POSS:IIISG
           'Every child loves his / her mother.'

Following Beghelli and Stowell (1997), I assume that the second *na* is the head of DistrP.
Unlike in Beghelli & Stowell (1997) where DistrP is lower than AgrSP, I claim that in
KiLega, *na* merges with, among others, a CP (25). This is based on the fact that the
"verbal complex" may contain RM as well as SM.

(25) [$_{DISTRP}$ *na mwăna* [$_{DISTR'}$ na [$_{CP}$ OP$_{CLITIC}$ ... [[$_{vP}$ *t*OPCLITIC ...]]]]]

We saw that in VS order, S may be a *wh*-phrase. If a DPQ merges in Spec*v*P, the
prediction is that it too should be able to surface there. However, this is not the case:

(26) * *ku maswá kw – énd – il - e   na   (g)wé.*
           17 6farm 17SM:A-go-PERF-FV every IIISG
           'Every one went to the farms.'

One possible way to account for (26) would be to stipulate that a DPQ must always raise out of Spec$v$P. I would like to propose that what raises is the OP$_{CLITIC}$. This clearly makes this stipulation unecessary. Clitics will always raise. Thus, an OP$_{CLITIC}$ (RM) that merges in Spec$v$P or with V will move to SpecCP, subsequently entering into a chain with the DQP external-merged in SpecDistP.

This line of analysis opens the possibility for a question *wh*-phrase to external-merge in the left periphery while entering a binding relation with RM. Similarly for the nominal occurring with SM. It is telling that in complex inversion in French, a lexical DP may co-occur with the clitic when a *wh*-word cannot:

(27)   Paul / (*Qui) a-t-il déjà lu *L'Etranger* par A. Camus?
         'Has Paul / (*Who) has already read *L'Etranger* by A. Camus?'

The general idea is that if a lexical SUBJ can be licensed in Spec$v$P on the one hand, and if it can relate to a clitic in SpecTP from a position higher in the left periphery on the other hand, then on the assumption that DP$_{CLITIC}$ merges in Spec$v$P, an apparent optional rule of lexical SUBJ raising will be eliminated from the grammar of KiLega.

6.   Conclusion

I have proposed that SMs and RMs are clitics, rather than agreement markers. I have shown that there is no relationship between movement and agreement. To the extent that the major facts follow without any stipulation while they cannot under the Agree relation, I have provided an argument against the latter in KiLega.

Selected References

Baker, M.   2003. Agreement, dislocation, and partial configurationality. In *Formal Approaches to Function in Grammar*, eds. A. Carnie, H. Harley, E. Jelinek, and M. Willie. Philadelphia: John Benjamins.

Beghelli, F. T. Stowell. 1997. Distributivity and Negation: The Syntax of Each and Every. In A. Szabolcsi (ed.), Ways of Scope Taking.   Dordrecht: Kluwer Academic Publishers.

Bittner, M. & K. Hale. 1996. Ergativity: Toward a Theory of a Heterogeneous Class. *Linguistic Inquiry* 27.4: 1-68.

Bokamba, E. G. 1976. *Question Formation in Some Bantu Languages*. Unpublished PhD Dissertation. Bloomington, IN: Indiana University.

Bresnan, J. W. & S. A. Mchombo 1987. Topic, pronoun and agreement in Chichewa. *Lge* 63.4: 741-782.

Cardinaletti, A. & M. Starke. 1999. The Typology of Structural Deficiency: A Case Study of the Three Classes of Pronouns. In H. van Riemsdijk (ed.), *Clitics in the Languages of Europe*. Berlin: Mouton de Gruyter.

Carstens, V. 2003. *Agree and EPP in Bantu*. ms, University of Missouri, Columbia.

Chomsky, N. 1995. *The Minimalist Program*. Cambridge, MA: The MIT Press.

Chomsky, N. 2001. *Beyond Explanatory Adequacy*. ms, MIT.

Cinque, G. 1990. *Types of A-Bar Dependencies*. Cambridge, MA: The MIT Press.

Collins, C. 1997. *Local Economy*. Cambridge, MA: MIT Press.

Doron, E. 1986. The Pronominal "Copula" as Agreement Clitic. In Borer, H. (ed.) *The Syntax of Pronominal Clitics*. 313-332. New York: Academic Press.

Gregersen, E. A. 1967. Prefix and Pronoun in Bantu. *International Journal of American Linguistics*, Vol. 33: 3.

Hajičová, E., B. H. Partee & P. Sgall 1998. *Topic-Focus Articulation, Tripartite Structures, and Semantic Content*. Dordrecht: Kluwer Academic Press.

Jaeggli, O. 1986. Three Issues in the theory of clitics: Case, Doubled NPs, and Extraction. In Borer, H. (ed.) *The Syntax of Pronominal Clitics*. 15-42. New York: Academic Press.

Kayne, R. S. 1998. Overt vs. Covert Movements. *Syntax* 1.2: 128-191.

Kimenyi, A. 1980. *A Relational Grammar of Kinyarwanda*. Los Angeles: UC Press.

Kinyalolo, K. K. W. 1991. *Syntactic Dependencies and the SPEC-HEAD Agreement Hypothesis in KiLega*. Unpublished PhD dissertation. Los Angeles, CA: UCLA.

Kiss, K. É. 1998. Identificational Focus versus Information Focus. *Lge* 74.2: 245-273.

Meeussen, A. E. 1967. Bantu Grammatical Reconstructions. *Africana Linguistica* 3: 80-121.

Meeussen, A. E. 1971a. Relative clauses in Bantu. *Studies in African Linguistics*, Supplement 2: 3-10.

Meeussen, A. E. 1971b. *Eléments de grammaire Lega*. Tervuren: Musée Royal de l'Afrique Centrale.

Nsuka, N. F. 1982. *Les Structures Fondamentales du Relatif dans les Langues Bantoues*. Tervuren: Musée Royal de l'Afrique Centrale.

Rizzi, L. 1997. The Fine Structure of the Left Periphery. In Haegeman, L. (ed.). *Elements of Grammar. Handbook in Generative Syntax*. Dordrecht: Kluwer Academic Publishers.

Takizala, A. 1972. Focus and Relativization in Kihung'an. In J.P. Kimball (ed.), *Syntax and Semantics*, vol. 2. New York: Academic Press.

Ura, H. 2000. *Checking Theory and Grammatical Functions in Universal Grammar*. New York: Oxford University Press.

Woolford, E. 1997. Four Way Case Systems: Ergative, Nominative, Objective and Accusative. *Natural Language & Linguistic Theory* 15.1: 181-227.

P.O. Box 346
Miller Place, NY 11764-0346

kkinyalolo@optonline.net

Chain Resolution in Hebrew V(P)-fronting

Idan Landau

Ben Gurion University

1. Introduction

This article is an attempt to deepen our understanding of a domain where the shift to "interface-driven syntax" has already made some non-trivial progress: The resolution of chains at the interfaces.

Chomsky's (1995) proposal that chains are formed by copying an element, merging the new copy in a higher position and deleting the redundant copy, provided a new framework for looking at various syntactic phenomena. Another guiding intuition is that when possible, maximal explanatory burden should be shifted to the interfaces. Consider in this light the question of chain resolution: which copy gets to be interpreted at LF, and which to be pronounced at PF. It is conceivable that "narrow syntax" has a say on these matters; that syntactic operations affect, or even determine, how chains are pronounced and interpreted. Yet clearly this state of affairs would be suboptimal from a minimalist point of view, and should be avoided, if possible. Let us state this desideratum as follows.

(1) *Post-Syntactic Chain Resolution (PSCR)*
     The decision which chain copy to pronounce or interpret is solely determined
     at the interfaces.

On the PF side, the PSCR is explicitly defended in Pesetsky (1998), Franks (1998, 1999), Bošković (2001), Bobaljik (2002) and others.

The PSCR leaves open the question of how the PF/LF interfaces decide which copy to pronounce/interpret. Here there are many proposals, yet again, general constraints may be pursued. One natural question is – how autonomous are the interfaces in resolving chains? In particular, is the choice at the PF side affected by the choice on the LF side, and vice versa? Notice that such cross-interface dependence is at odds with a central tenet of modern cognitive science, namely, the *modularity* hypothesis. Again, if possible, it should be avoided, a desideratum we can state as follows.

© 2003 Idan Landau
Keir Moulton and Matthew Wolf (eds.): Proceedings of NELS 34,
Stony Brook University: 357 – 371. GLSA, Amherst.

(2)   *Modular Chain Resolution (MCR)*
       The decision which chain copy to pronounce/interpret is locally determined
       at PF/LF, respectively.

The MCR is a stronger version of PSCR, entailing but not entailed by the latter. Unlike the
PSCR, the MCR is not explicitly upheld by many authors, although, as mentioned, it
accords well with current understanding of cognitive systems.

There are obvious challenges to MCR within current research. One important
challenge is the constraint on recoverability of deletion (RoD), which appears to make PF
deletion contingent on LF recoverability. Notice that such a statement is at odds with the
MCR. Allowing LF information to be accessible to PF choices is precisely what it barred
by MCR. I believe that the undeniably correct intuition behind RoD constraints can be
given an MCR-compatible form (by restating them as interpretive constraints), although I
will not attempt this in this paper.

A second challenge to MCR has to do with preference principles favoring identical
choices at PF and LF. Two recent formulations are given below.

(3)   a.   *ParseScope* (Fanselow & Ćavar 2001)
             If α has scope over β then the phonetic matrix of α c-commands the
             phonetic matrix of β.

       b.   *Minimize Mismatch* (Bobaljik 2002)
             (To the extent possible) privilege the same copy at PF and LF.

These preference principles have an obvious functionalist rationale: they guarantee that
semantic scope relations will be read off surface structures – whenever possible. However,
this preference can be overridden to avoid a violation of a PF requirement, resulting in
non-transparent scope. Again, we may accept this rationale as a design feature of the
computational system, while denying its causal role in specific derivations. Notice that
Minimize Mismatch principles presuppose a syntax-external "scanner", capable of
comparing the positions of the PF-copy and the LF-copy, and in fact backfeeding into the
algorithm selecting those copies. This is clearly inconsistent with the MCR, so the
question arises again – can the empirical results of these principles be captured by an
alternative, MCR-compatible account?

The phenomenon studied in this paper is VP-fronting in Hebrew. This construction
offers particular insight into issues of chain resolution due to the fact that two chain
positions are visible at PF: The verb is doubled, occurring both in the base position and in
the fronted one. Thus, the construction invites an investigation of the factors requiring,
allowing or excluding the phonetic expression of chain copies.

The structure of this paper is as follows. Section 2 provides a general description of
the VP-fronting construction – morphology, syntax and pragmatics. Section 3
demonstrates that the dependency between the fronted and the base verbal copies is island-
sensitive, hence formed by movement. Section 4 investigates more closely the properties
of the doubled verb. Section 4.1 shows that the copied element is already a verb (light v +
root), while section 4.2 argues that when stranding its arguments, the fronted category is a
bare V (rather than a remnant VP). Section 5 develops a PF-algorithm for chain resolution,

consisting of a P(honological)-recoverability constraint, interacting with economy preferences. The algorithm is consistent with the MCR and accounts for the obligatory spellout of the two verbal copies. Section 6 concludes the paper.

2.   General Description of V(P)-fronting in Hebrew

Unlike in English, Hebrew has no *do*-support strategy to spell out tense and agreement features when the VP is moved (or elided). Instead, the verb is spelled out both in T^0 and in the fronted VP, giving rise to V-copying. While the low verbal copy is fully inflected, the higher one is an infinitive.[1] An internal argument may either front with the verb or be stranded. I will call the former option Phrasal-Infinitive fronting (*PI-fronting*) and the latter one Bare-Infinitive fronting (*BI-fronting*).

(4)   *PI-fronting*
          a.   liknot et   ha-praxim, hi kanta.
                   to-buy ACC. the-flowers, she bought
          BI-fronting
          b.   liknot, hi kanta et   ha-praxim.
                   to-buy she bought ACC. the-flowers
                   'Buy the flowers, she did'

The alternation between the two fronting options is pragmatic (see below). I will assume that the fronted category occupies some topic position.[2]

     The identity of the fronted category in BI-fronting is a matter of some debate; for now I put it aside and return to the issue in section 4.2.. As to PI-fronting, despite the infinitival morphology, which might suggest a clausal projection, it can be shown that the initial infinitive is a bare VP. Negation and sentential adverbs are strictly forbidden in the initial position (see also Ziv 1997, Doron 1999):

(5)   a.   le'horid et   ha-maym, Gil lo   tamid morid.
                   to-flush ACC. the-water   Gil not always flushes
                   'Flush the toilet, Gil not always does'

          b.   (*lo) (*tamid) le'horid et   ha-maym, Gil morid.
                   (*not) (*always) to-flush ACC. the-water   Gil flushes

Thus, the initial infinitive in (6) is a bare VP (we return in section 4.1 to the source of the infinitival morphology), which may contain only the verb and its arguments.

     As to the phonology of the construction, the relevant aspect is intonation. Here I will limit myself to the most basic observations. The most salient intonational feature of VP-fronting is the high pitch accent on the stressed syllable of the (infinitival) fronted

---

[1] Many languages employ V-copying in VP-fronting, e.g., Haitian, Vata, Yoruba, Brazilian Portuguese, Yiddish and Russian. The last three, like Hebrew, realize the higher V-copy as an infinitive.

[2] In this paper I ignore more complex options available with ditransitive verbs, e.g., fronting one argument and stranding the other one; see Landau (2004).

verb. In normal circumstances (when nothing else inside the fronted VP is focused), this high tone will be followed by a plateau of a low phrase accent. If the fronted VP forms its own intonational phrase (i.e., when separated from the sentence by a perceptible pause), it will end with a high boundary tone; otherwise, the low plateau will stretch into the sentence. This is roughly illustrated below.

(7)   H* L⁻   (H%)
          likRO et   ha-sefer, Gil kara.
          to-read ACC. the-book Gil read
          'Read the book, Gil did'

The infinitival verb must coincide with the left boundary of its intonational phrase. Left-adjoined VP-adverbs, even when monosyllabic and destressed, may not front with the VP.

(8)   (*kvar) lištof   et   ha-kelim hu (kvar) šataf.
          (*already) to-wash ACC. the-dishes he (already) washed.
          'Wash the dishes, he already did'

For Hebrew, then, the following requirement holds at PF.

(9)   In Hebrew VP-fronting, the fronted (infinitival) verb bears high pitch accent (on its stressed syllable) and coincides with the left boundary of its intonational phrase.

Pragmatically, V-copying constructions across languages seem to fall into two categories: Topicalization and cleft. The predicate cleft construction, attested in African and Caribbean Creole languages, is consistently associated with a contrastive focus interpretation. The topicalization construction, attested in Hebrew, Yiddish and Portuguese, is pragmatically more open, allowing simple topic and (possibly, in Hebrew) a focus interpretation. This pragmatic difference correlates with a syntactic one – the predicate cleft construction is biclausal (constructed with a copula) whereas the topicalization construction is monoclausal.

Most commonly, VP-fronting in Hebrew marks a Topic or contrastive Focus. The new information could be either a certain constituent in the clause, or the affirmation/negation of that clause.[3] Stress placement serves to mark that information.

(10)   a.   le-Rina yeš   xuš humor, aval licxok hi coxeket rak al axeRIM.
              to-Rina there-is sense humor but to-laugh she laughs only on others
              'Rina has a sense of humor, but she will only laugh at *others*'

       b.   le-Rina yeš   xuš humor, aval licxok   al acma hi LO ticxak.
              to-Rina there-is sense humor but   to-laugh on herself she not will-laugh
              'Rina has a sense of humor, but laugh at herself – she *won't*'

---

[3] The pragmatics of the construction is very similar in Yiddish (Källgren & Prince 1989) and Russian (Abels 2001).

In both (10a,b), the fronted infinitive is interpreted contrastively (the occurrence of *aval* 'but' before VP-fronting is very common). In (10a) *axerim* 'others' is in focus while in (10b) the entire negative proposition *hi lo ticxak* 'she won't laugh' is focused. Notice that the contrastive focus is 'to laugh' in (10a) but 'to laugh at herself' in (10b). In other words, the choice between BI- and PI-fronting crucially affects the topic/contrastive focus of the sentence. In fact – as I will argue below, this pragmatic effect is the *only* aspect of meaning which distinguishes the two constructions.

BI-fronting is ruled out with auxiliary verbs, a fact observed in all languages with V(P)-topicalization or predicate cleft. I follow Davis & Prince (1986) in tracing this restriction to the requirement that the Topic bear semantic content. Although the lower copy of the auxiliary verb is associated with Tense, the higher copy is not, given that the fronted category is V(P). The result of topicalizing an auxiliary verb is pragmatically uninterpretable.

(11) a.   lihyot zamin,   Gil lo tamid   haya.
            to-be available Gil not always was

      b.   *lihyot, Gil lo   tamid haya zamin.
            to-be Gil not always was available
            'To be available, Gil wasn't always'

3.   Evidence for A-bar movement

We have already seen that the initial infinitive heads a category no bigger than a VP. In this section I will show that the relation between the higher and the lower VP positions is formed by A-bar movement. Importantly, the characteristics of A-bar movement show up regardless of whether the initial infinitive is phrasal or bare.

First, observe that the dependency is unbounded, and in particular, can cross finite clause boundaries, a hallmark of A-bar dependencies:

(12) a.   la'azor, eyn   li   safek še-Gil hivtiax   še-hu ya'azor le-Rina.
            to-help there-isn't to-me doubt that-Gil promised that-he will-help to-Rina
            'Help Rina, I have no doubt that Gil promised he will'

      b.   lenakot et   ha-xacer, nidme li   še-Rina amra še-Gil kvar   nika.
            to-clean ACC. the-yard seems to-me that-Rina said that-Gil already cleaned
            'Clean the yard, it seems to me that Rina said that Gil already had'

However, the dependency is island sensitive.

(13) *Wh-island*
      a.   ?? likro,   ša'alti   matay Gil kvar   kara et   ha-sefer.
            to-read asked.1sg when   Gil already read ACC. the-book
            'Read the book, I asked when Gil already had'

Complex NP island

b.   * likro   et   ha-sefer, Gil daxa   et   ha-te'ana še-hu kvar   kara.
       to-read ACC. the-book Gil rejected ACC. the-claim that-he already read
       'Read the book, Gil rejected the claim that he already had'

Subject island

c.   * likro   et   ha-sefer, še-yevakšu   me-Gil še-yikra   ze ma'aliv.
       to-read ACC. the-book that-will-ask.3pl from-Gil that-will-read.3sg it insulting
       'Read the book, that they would ask Gil to is insulting'

Adjunct island

d.   *likro, nifgašnu axarey še-kulam   kar'u   et ha-sefer.
       to-read met.1pl after   that-everybody read.3pl ACC. the-book
       'Read the book, we have met after everybody did'

The data in of (12)-(13) clearly indicate that the dependency between the initial (infinitival) VP and its copy downstairs is formed by A-bar movement. In other words, we are looking at an instance of *VP-fronting*.[4]

4.   Doubling V

A question naturally arises at this point: Why are two phonological copies of the verb spelled out? Normal cases of movement are known to leave unpronounced copies ("traces"). Furthermore, why does the fronted copy show up as an infinitive, and not as an identical, inflected verb? A third puzzle is raised by (12a), where the fronted element appears to be the bare verb. If appearance is reliable, the initial infinitive in these examples is a syntactic head; yet the data suggest that this head is related to its lower copy by A-bar movement. How can movement of a head, which is supposed to be subject to strict locality, apply in an unbounded fashion? Let us address the second question first – the infinitival morphology on the fronted verb – and then turn to the other two questions.

4.1.   Root or Category Copying?

Following recent work, I will assume that the predicate phrase is headed by a light v. On this view, lexical verbs are the product of a syntactic fusion (following head-to-head movement) between some "core" or root V ($\sqrt{V}$) and a functional light v, the latter encoding properties like voice, transitivity and agentivity (Hale & Keyser 1993, Chomsky 1995, Kratzer 1996, Marantz 1997, Doron 2003). I will also adopt the stronger thesis, put forward in Marantz (1997) and subsequent work in Distributed Morphology, that the root is category neutral, and light v provides the categorial feature [+V].

    If $\sqrt{V}$ and v project distinct syntactic categories, the question immediately arises which of these categories is targeted in the PI-fronting construction.[5] Considerations

---

[4] These data refute the view of Ziv (1997) and Doron (1999) that the infinitive in the Hebrew construction is base-generated in the initial position.

[5] I return below to BI-fronting.

internal to the grammar of Modern Hebrew suggest that VP-topicalization is really vP-topicalization. The verbal system in Hebrew (like all Semitic languages) is based on consonantal roots, which map onto seven paradigms, called *binyanim*, each with its own particular morphological template. Although the mapping is not entirely systematic, each *binyan* is associated, in the usual case, with a prototypical set of grammatical/semantic properties. These properties include a voice distinction (active vs. passive), transitivity, reflexivity and causativity. Inspired by Distributed Morphology, recent research has argued that the Hebrew verb is derived by merging the root with a light v, where the light v encodes the verbal paradigm, the *binyan* (Arad 1999, Doron 2003).

Now, it is a significant fact that Hebrew infinitival verbs are derived by adding the prefix *li-/le-/la-* to an absolute form already in the relevant *binyan*, and not directly to the root.[6] In other words, the infinitival verb is already fixed in a specific *binyan*, as can be seen below.

(14)   Infinitival verbs from the root [s,r,k]

     a.   *li-srok* – 'to scan'
     b.   *le-hisarek* – 'to be scanned'
     c.   *le-sarek* – 'to comb'
     d.   *le-histarek* – 'to comb oneself'

Given the discussion above, this means that the Hebrew infinitival verb is (minimally) a complex [$\sqrt{V}$+v], where $\sqrt{V}$ is the root and v contributes the *binyan* template. It follows that PI-fronting targets the vP category. Since no tense/agreement features are present on the head [$\sqrt{V}$+v], it is assigned a default spellout of an infinitive.

On this view, the morphological discrepancy between the two verbal copies does not undermine the movement analysis (based on Copy and Delete); what is copied is, strictly speaking, a feature matrix that is only paired with phonological expression at the point of Spellout, following all syntactic operations (up to the phase level). Thus, we find here an argument for "Late Insertion" in the sense of Distributed Morphology.

In fact, this division of labor between syntax and morphology finds striking support in an example where the two verbal copies differ not only in inflection but in their actual root. The roots [y,g,d] and [ʔ,m,r] both mean 'tell' (in different *binyanim*), yet the former's morphological paradigm is defective in modern Hebrew, lacking all past and present forms; only the future and infinitive forms can be derived from [y,g,d]. There is reason to believe that in the missing tenses, inflected forms of [ʔ,m,r] are inserted as suppletive forms for [y,g,d]. In this light, consider the following contrast (to facilitate reading, I label defective and regular verbs as 'D' and 'R', respectively).

(15)   Rina omnam nista le'hašpia   alay, aval ...
       Rina although tried to-influence on-me, but...
       'Although Rina tried to influence me...

---

[6] Two passive *binyanim* (*pu'al* and *huf'al*) do not have synthetic infinitives.

a.   ... le'hagid$_D$ li ma   la'asot, hi lo amra$_R$.
     to-tell   me what to-do   she not told
     '... tell me what to do, she didn't'

b.   *... lomar$_R$ li ma   la'asot, hi lo tagid$_D$.
     to-tell   me what to-do   she not will-tell
     '... tell me what to do, she won't'

In both examples the defective root $[y,g,d]$ is inserted under $\sqrt{V}$. After merging with v and T, the lower copy is spelled out using the suppletive form in (15a), due to the past tense. Nonetheless, it is the *original* root which is copied with the entire vP, as is evident from the fact that it is this root which projects the fronted, infinitival copy. Since $[y,g,d]$ does have an infinitival form, $[?,m,r]$ cannot substitute for the higher copy in (15b), explaining the asymmetry.[7]

The minimal pair in (15) confirms three important points. First, the fronted vP is indeed (copied and) moved to its surface position, and not generated there (otherwise, (15a) and (15b) would have been *both* good, or *both* bad, but not contrasting in a way that suggests asymmetrical copying). Second, it is vP and not any higher inflectional category that is copied and fronted (otherwise, the defective root would not have surfaced in the fronted copy in (15a)). Third, syntax maneuvers abstract feature bundles, not actual phonological matrices (otherwise, copy mismatches such as those in (15) would have been impossible).

We may ask whether the choice of the copied head – root or category – differs across languages. In particular, are there languages in which it is the root, rather than the category V, which is copied in predicate fronting? Evidence for this choice would be i) loss of the morphological template on the fronted verb, or ii) ban on argument fronting with the verb (no counterpart to PI-fronting). Both features are displayed by predicate clefts in Biblical Hebrew, while the latter characterizes the construction in Vata and Haiti (Harbour 1999, 2002, Koopman 1984). It is reasonable to localize the parameter in the possible host of the [+Top/Foc] feature: light v in Modern Hebrew (as well as Brazilian Portuguese, see Bastos 2002), $\sqrt{V}$ in Biblical Hebrew, Haitian and Vata.

4.2.   Head or Phrasal Movement?

In the previous section we have established that PI-fronting, as in (16a), involves vP-Copying. We now turn to BI-fronting, as in (16b), and ask – what category is fronted?

---

[7] Example (i), predicted to be ungrammatical, is judged marginal by some speakers:

i.   ?% le'hagid$_D$ li   ma la'asot, hi lo tomar$_R$.
     to-tell   me what to-do   she not will-tell
     'Tell me what to do, she won't'

Speakers who accept such examples might substitute suppletive $[?,m,r]$ forms for future forms of $[y,g,d]$ as well.

(16)   a.   [$_{vP}$ likro   et   ha-sefer], hu kara.
               to-read ACC. the-book   he read
        b.   [$_\alpha$ likro],   hu kara et   ha-sefer.
               to-read he   read ACC. the-book
              'Read the book, he did'

Logically, there are two possibilities. If α=V in (16b), then V-fronting is a non-standard case of long head movement. If α=vP, then it must contain a trace of the stranded object ("remnant movement"). Both positions were explored in the literature on VP-topicalization and predicate clefts in other languages. Long head movement of V has been proposed, among others, by Koopman (1984), Larson & Lefebvre (1991), Holmberg (1999), Harbour (2002) and Fanselow (2002). Remnant VP-movement has been proposed, among others, by den Besten & Webelhuth (1990), Koopman (1997), Müller (1998), Takano (2000), Abels (2001) and Hinterhölzl (2002).

For the Hebrew case, I will adopt the long V-movement analysis. Two sets of considerations point to this analysis. First, mounting positive evidence against the remnant VP-movement approach, even in scrambling languages like German (see Fanselow 2002); and second, the recent dissipation of the traditional argument against long V-movement.

The remnant movement analysis posits some scrambling operation of the stranded argument, prior to VP-fronting. However, Hebrew has no scrambling rule. Perhaps one could argue that the movement vacating VP need not be scrambling, for example, it could be movement for licensing purposes (Hinterhölzl 2002). The problem is that such movement is never attested *without* VP-fronting (Hebrew lacking overt Object Shift), and furthermore, there seems to be no restriction whatsoever on the type of elements that can be stranded in VP-fronting (PPs, secondary predicates, etc.). Re-labelling "scrambling" as "licensing movement" does not advance our understanding of the construction.

Consider then the alternative analysis, in which long V-movement is allowed. The traditional objection to this idea rests on the dichotomy between the strict locality of head movement and the unbounded nature of (A-bar) XP-movement. However, all the terms in this dichotomy – head, XP, A-bar – have lost much of their independent "essence" in recent research. The distinction between X^0 and XP, under bare phrase structure, is partly reduced to contextual relations: a non-projecting head is simultaneously an X^0 and an XP. The distinction between A- and A-bar positions is decomposed into smaller distinctions between case/agreement and operator features. Most importantly, within the minimalist framework, there is no theoretical link between the bar-level of an item (not even a detectable property, according to Chomsky 1995) and the scope of its potential movement.

Conversely, the alleged head nature of V-movement may be an artifact of constraints on affixation (e.g., T^0 may not attach to units bigger than a word). This approach leaves open the possibility that when nothing rules it out, long V-movement will be possible. My claim is that this is precisely what we observe in (16b) and, plausibly, in many other languages exhibiting parallel constructions.

To review, we have analysed PI-fronting as vP-fronting and BI-fronting as V-fronting (no remnant involved). We have answered two of the three questions posed at the beginning of section 4: Why is the fronted verb spelled out as an infinitive, and why is it allowed to undergo A-bar movement. Let us turn to the remaining question - Why is it that two copies of the verb are phonologically realized in VP-fronting?

5.   P-Recoverability and Economy of Pronunciation

Recall that chain resolution is constrained by the MCR.

(17)   *Modular Chain Resolution (MCR)*
        The decision which chain copy to pronounce/interpret is locally determined
        at PF/LF, respectively.

Theories meeting this condition on the PF side generally converge on two conclusions.

(18)   a.   PF copies that are demanded by PF requirements cannot not deleted.
        b.   PF copies that are excluded by PF requirements must be deleted.

Recent proposals appeal to (18b) in order to sanction PF-deletion of high copies in special
circumstances (Franks 1998, 1999, Bobaljik 2002). But what forces pronunciation of the
lower copy in these cases? Presumably, low pronunciation results from some notion of
semantic recoverability: deleting both the higher copy (for PF reasons) and the lower one
(for no particular reason) would make the semantic content of the item unrecoverable.
        However, it was noted in section 1 that this line of reasoning runs afoul of the ban
on PF-LF interactions (viz à viz chain resolution) implied by the MCR: PF has no way of
"knowing" what copy, if any, is interpreted at LF, hence cannot use such information in
deciding which copy to pronounce. Suppose instead that we restrict attention to
recoverability of phonological features, call it *P-recoverability*. One can place a lower
bound on pronunciation, which must be accepted on trivial grounds.

(19)   *P-Recoverability*
        In a chain $<X_1, ... X_i ... X_n>$, where some X_i is associated with phonetic content,
        X_i must be pronounced.

(19) implies that null chains can be formed only from null elements (*pro*, PRO, Op); PF
does not tolerate unrecoverable phonological deletion, irrespective of its semantic
repercussions. We understand "associated with phonetic content" as either having intrinsic
phonetic content or occurring in a position specified with one (e.g., suporting an affix). P-
recoverability places a lower bound on pronunciation in a chain: At least those copies must
be pronounced which are associated with phonetic content.
        An important aspect of (19), distinguishing it from the traditional formulations of
recoverability, is that it does not assume any kind of contact between PF and LF. Thus, it
is not because of the semantic content of X that at least one of its copies must be
pronounced; indeed, (19) holds even if X is semantically vacuous, as long as X is
associated with some phonetic content. A case in point is expletive chains (if they exist),
where the top link must be pronounced, despite of being semantically empty.
        While (19) places a lower bound on chain pronunciation, it places no upper bound.
Obviously, such a bound is needed, or else chain copies will never fail to be pronounced. I
suggest that economy is the source of this bound.

(20)   *Economy of Pronunciation*
        Delete all chain copies at PF up to P-recoverability.

The qualification "up to P-recoverability" in (20) serves as an permanent "ranking mark", indicating that P-recoverability *always* overrides economy. The universality of this ranking suggests that it is not part of some optimality-theoretic algorithm for chain resolution (where the relevant constraints are expected to be re-ranked in different constructions or languages). V(P)-fronting in Hebrew is a case where the overriding effect of P-recoverability is strikingly visible. Consider a typical example. The structure of (21a), in fact, contains three copies of V, only two of which are pronounced (21b).

(21)   a.   lirkod,   hu rakad.
              to-dance, he danced
              'Dance, he did'

        b.

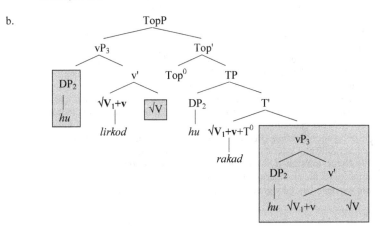

PF-deletion applies to the shaded constituents. Let us refer to [√V+v] simply as V. V raises to T, leaving a copy inside vP, and the subject raises to [Spec,TP]. The remnant vP then raises to the Topic position. Of the three V-copies, two are pronounced (boldfaced in (21b)): The V-copy adjoined to T, and the V-copy heading the fronted vP. The lower vP-copy is deleted at PF, together with its V-copy head.

        Observe now that the pronunciation of the two copies in (21b) is required by P-recoverability. The T^0-adjoined copy is associated with the phonological requirement of T^0 – namely, the need to spell out tense and agreement features (Hebrew lacks *do*-support). The fronted V-copy is associated with a phonological requirement imposed by Top^0, namely, the characteristic intonation of fronted VPs. This requirement, stated in (9), is crucially imposed on V, the head of the fronted VP. Failure to pronounce any of these two

V-copies would violate (19). By contrast, the lowest V-copy is not associated with any phonological requirement, hence the economy condition (20) demands its deletion.[8]

This analysis solves a major puzzle – the double pronunciation of V in V(P)-fronting. Far from being an exception to general conditions on syntactic chains, the phenomenon of V-copying provides striking confirmation to these conditions, which cannot be gleaned from more familiar cases of movement.

Further evidence that it is a purely phonological requirement that forces pronunciation of the lower V-copy comes from minimal pairs like the following.

(22)   a.   le'ho'il   la-proyekt   šelanu hu lo *(ho'il)   af-pa'am.
            to-be-useful to-the-project our   he not *(be-useful.V) never

       b.   lihyot mo'il la-proyekt   šelanu hu lo haya (*mo'il)   af-pa'am.
            to-be useful to-the-project our   he not was (*useful.A) never
            'Useful to our project, he never was'

(22a,b) are semantically indistinguishable; they differ only in that the predicate is a synthetic verb in (22a) but an [Aux+Adj] complex in (22b). Crucially, the lower V-copy must be pronounced in the former, but deleted in the latter. The contrast follows from the fact that it is the lexical V itself that raises to T in (22a), spelling out tense/agreement features. By contrast, in (22b) it is Aux, not Adj., that raises to T to spell out those features; the lower A-copy must be deleted on economy grounds. It is hard to see how a semantic/pragmatic approach to chain pronunciation would deal with this contrast.[9]

More generally, P-recoverability improves over proposals that separate the cause of obligatory *deletion* (PF-constraints) from the cause of obligatory *pronunciation* (LF-recoverability). Under the present analysis, both follow from PF-constraints. The only non-PF factor implicated in deletion is economy, an overarching principle that does not impinge on the modularity of the system. Ideally, no principle beyond (19) and (20), which are warranted by very general considerations, should affect pronunciation of chain copies.

---

[8] See Davis & Prince (1986), Dekydspotter (1992) and Abels (2001) for analyses that motivate pronunciation of the lower V-copy in VP-fronting along the same lines (namely, spelling out the p-features of T). Abels (2001) further argues that pronunciation of the higher V-copy is forced by recoverability of the focus interpretation (See Koopman 1997 for the analogous claim for Vata predicate cleft). The latter proposal is incompatible with the idea that PF-decisions are impenetrable to LF considerations (the MCR; see section 1).

[9] Abels (2001) cites a parallel contrast in Russian:

i.   Čitat' (-to) on čitatet, no ...
        to-read (PRT) he reads, but ...
        'He does read, but ...'

ii.   Čitat' (-to) on budet (*čitat'),   no ...
        to-read (PRT) he will (*to-read), but ...
        'He will read, but ...'

The synthetic present tense verb in (i) is spelled out to support the features of T. By contrast, in the analytic future tense (ii) it is the auxiliary verb that serves this function, hence the lower (infinitival) V-copy must be deleted.

6. Conclusion

The view of chain resolution developed in this article has clear consequences for current syntactic theory. Perhaps the most robust empirical finding is the existence of copying operations in syntax. Throughout the discussion, we accumulated evidence that chains are formed by an operation *copying*, rather than *removing*, phonological and morphological information. The fate of that information – expression or deletion – is decided at PF.

Schematically, we analyzed two varieties of VP-fronting in Hebrew.

(23)   a.   *PI-fronting*

$[_{TopP} [_{VP} \text{SUB} [_{V'} V_i \text{ ARG}]]_j \text{ Top}^0 [_{TP} \text{SUB } V_i+T [_{VP} \text{SUB V ARG}]_j]]]$

       b.   *BI-fronting*

$[_{TopP} V_i \text{ Top}^0 [_{TP} \text{SUB } V_i+T [_{VP} \text{SUB } V_i \text{ ARG }]]]$

After establishing the movement relation between the two VP copies, we posed three questions: (i) Why is V pronounced twice? (ii) Why is the higher V-copy spelled out as an infinitive? (iii) What is the size of the fronted category in BI-fronting?

The answer to (i) rested on the notion of P-recoverability (19). It was argued that both the low position of V (adjoined to T) and the high position (Spec,Top) are associated with specific phonological requirements; failing to satisfy these requirements would result in a PF crash. In such special circumstances, the economy condition (20), normally deleting all copies but one, permits double pronunciation. Various independent arguments, both internal to Hebrew and crosslinguistic, support the claim that it is PF considerations *alone* that determine copy pronunciation. This result accords well with the MCR.

(24)   *Modular Chain Resolution (MCR)*
      The decision which chain copy to pronounce/interpret is locally determined
      at PF/LF, respectively.

The answer to (ii) rested on the notion of Late Insertion of p-features. I argued that the V node moved in the syntax is not specified for actual p-features, but rather those are inserted at the end of the syntactic phase. Lacking any tense/agreement features, the fronted V is spelled out as the default infinitival form (as seen in Hebrew, Yiddish, Russian and Brazilian Portuguese). In answering (iii) I rejected the remnant-VP analysis for (23b) and argued instead for a bare V-fronting analysis, no longer inconsistent with current conceptions of phrase structure.

One desirable consequence of the analysis is that it brings closer our notions of PF deletion and pronunciation. There is a tendency to attribute obligatory deletion to PF factors but obligatory pronunciation to recoverability constraints. The picture advocated here is more uniform, insofar as PF is endowed with the power to force either deletion or pronunciation in a given chain position. Residual instances of recoverability, I suggested, may be better viewed as constraints on possible interpretations rather than on possible deletions.

References

Abels, Klaus. 2001. The Predicate Cleft Construction in Russian. In: Franks, Steven, Tracy H. King and Michael Yadroff (eds.), *Proceedings of FASL 9*, Ann Arbor: Michigan Slavic Publications, 1-18.

Alexiadou, Artemis, Elena Anagnostopoulou, Sjef Barbiers and Hans-Martin Gaertner. 2002. *Dimensions of Movement: From Features to Remnants*. Amsterdam: Johns Benjamins.

Arad, Maya. 1999. On 'Little v'. In: Arregi, Karlos, Ben Bruening, Cornelia Krause and Vivian Lin (eds.), *Papers in Morphology and Syntax, Cycle One*, MITWPL 33, 1-26.

Bastos, Ana Cláudia P. 2002. Three Types of V-topicalization in Brazilian Portuguese. Ms., Universidade Federal do Pará.

Bobaljik, Jonathan D. 2002. A-Chains at the PF-Interface: Copies and 'Covert' Movement. *NLLT* 20, 197-267.

Bošković, Željko. 2001. *On the Nature of the Syntax-Phonology Interface: Cliticization and Related Phenomena*. North-Holland Linguistics Series: Linguistic Variations, Elsevier Science, Oxford.

Chomsky, Noam. 1995. *The Minimalist Program*. MIT Press, Cambridge Mass.

Davis, Lori J. and Ellen F. Prince. 1986. Yiddish Verb-topicalization and the Notion 'Lexical Integrity'. In: Farley, Anne M., Peter T. Farley and Karl-Eric McCullough (eds.), *Proceedings of CLS* 22, University of Chicago, 90-97.

Dekydspotter, Laurent P. 1992. The Syntax of Predicate Clefts. In Broderick, K. (ed.), *Proceedings of NELS* 22, GLSA, Amherst, MA, 119-133.

den Besten, Hans and Gerth Webelhuth. 1990. Stranding. In: Grewendorf, Günther and Wolfgang Sternefeld (eds.), *Scrambling and Barriers*, Amsterdam: Benjamins, 77-92.

Doron, Edit. 1999. V-movement and VP-ellipsis. In: Benmamoun, Elabbas and Shalom Lappin (eds.), *Fragments: Studies in Ellipsis and Gapping*, Oxford: Oxford University Press, 124-140.

Doron, Edit. 2003. Agency and Voice: The Semantics of the Semitic Templates. *Natural Language Semantics* 11, 1-67.

Fanselow, Gisbert. 2002. Against Remnant VP-Movement. In: Alexiadou et. al. (eds.), 91-125.

Fanselow, Gisbert, and Damir Ćavar. 2001. Remarks on the Economy of Pronunciation. In: *Competition in Syntax*, ed. by Müller, Gereon and Wolfgang Sternfeld, Mouton de Gruyter, Berlin and New York, 107-150.

Franks, Steven. 1998. Clitics in Slavic. Position paper in the conference on "Comparative Slavic Morphosyntax", Indiana University.

Franks, Steven. 1999. Optimality Theory and Clitics at PF. In: Dziwirek, Katarzyna, Herbert Coats and Cynthia M. Vakareliyska (eds.), *Proceedings of FASL 7*, Ann Arbor: Michigan Slavic Publications, 101-116.

Hale, Ken and Samuel Jay Keyser, 1993. On Argument Structure and The Lexical Expression of Syntactic Relations. In: Hale, Ken and Samuel Jay Keyser (eds.), *The View From Building 20*, MIT Press, Cambridge, MA, 53-109.

Harbour, Daniel. 1999. The Two Types of Predicate Clefts: Classical Hebrew and Beyond. In: Lin, Vivian, Cornelia Krause, Benjamin Bruening and Karlos Arregi (eds.), *Papers in Morphology and Syntax, Cycle Two*, MITWPL 34, 159-176.

Harbour, Daniel. 2002. Klivaj Predika or Predicate Clefts in Haitian. To appear in *Journal of Pidgin and Creole Languages*.

Hinterhölzl, Roland. 2002. Remnant Movement and Partial Deletion. In: Alexiadou et. al. (eds.), 127-149.

Holmberg, Andres. 1999. Remarks on Holmberg's Generalization. *Studia Linguistica* 53, 1-39.

Källgren, Gunnel and Ellen F. Prince. 1989. Swedish VP-topicalization and Yiddish Verb-topicalization. *Nordic Journal of Linguistics* 12, 47-58.

Koopman, Hilda. 1984. *The Syntax of Verbs: From Verb Movement Rules in the Kru Languages to Universal Grammar*. Dordrecht: Foris.

Koopman, Hilda. 1997. Unifying Predicate Cleft Constructions. In: Moore, K. (ed.), *Proceedings of BLS 23, Special Session on Syntax and Semantics in Africa*, University of Berkeley.

Kratzer, Angelika, 1996. Severing the External Argument From Its Verb. In Rooryck, Johan and Laurie Zaring (eds.), *Phrase Structure and the Lexicon*, Dordrecht: Kluwer, 109-137.

Landau, Idan. 2004. Constraints on Partial VP-fronting. Ms., Ben Gurion University.

Larson, Richard and Claire Lefebvre. 1991. Predicate Cleft in Haitian Creole. In Sherer, Tim, Joseph Bayer and Jaklin Kornflit (eds.), *Proceedings of NELS 21*, GLSA, Umass, Amherst MA, 247-261.

Marantz, Alec. 1997. No Escape From Syntax: Don't Try Morphological Analysis in the Privacy of Your Lexicon. In: *UPENN Working Papers in Linguistics* 4.2, University of Pennsylvania.

Müller, Gereon. 1998. *Incomplete Category Fronting: A Derivational Approach to Remnant Movement in German*. Dordrecht: Kluwer Academic Publishers.

Pesetsky, David. 1998. Some Optimality Principles of Sentence Pronunciation. In: *Is the Best Good Enough?*, ed. by Pilar Barbosa, Danny Fox, Paul Haegstrom, Martha McGinnis and David Pesetsky, MIT Press and MITWPL, Cambridge MA, 337-383.

Takano, Yuji. 2000. Illicit Remnant Movement: An Argument for Feature-Driven Movement. *Linguistic Inquiry* 31, 141-156.

Ziv, Yael. 1997. Infinitives Initially: Theme/Topic/Focus. In: Connolly, John H., Roel M. Vismans, Christopher S. Butler and Richard A. Gatward (eds.), *Discourse and Pragmatics in Functional Grammar*, Berlin: Mouton de Gruyter, 163-175.

Department of Foreign Literatures & Linguistics
Ben Gurion University
P.O. Box 653
Beer Sheva 84105
Israel

idanl@bgumail.bgu.ac.il

Syntax and Semantics of Focus Particles: Scope and the Mirror Principle*

Youngjoo Lee

Massachusetts Institute of Technology

1.   Introduction

The focus particle *man* 'only' in Korean shows different scopal behavior depending upon the syntactic environment it appears in. Interestingly, the scope of a *man*-phrase varies with its morphological marking.[1] If a *man*-phrase is case-marked, its scope is fixed to its case position no matter where it appears in the sentence. By contrast, if it is marked by a postposition, its surface position affects scope relations.

I first show that this non-uniform scope pattern cannot be accounted for if the particle is a scope-bearing element. I, then, argue that, despite appearances, the particle *man* is not a scope-bearing element. Specifically, I argue that the particle *man* is actually an agreement morpheme that indicates the presence of a null head ONLY. This null head carries the exhaustive meaning of English *only*, and the particle has no meaning of its own. I also argue for a strong correlation between syntax and morphology, as claimed by Baker (1985) in the name of the Mirror Principle. Due to this correlation, we can infer the position of the ONLY head from the order of nominal affixes. The proposed analysis accounts for the peculiar scope patterns without making special stipulations about *man*-phrases, unlike the commonly held view that takes the particle to be a quantificational element.

This paper is organized as follows. After presenting the scope puzzle in section 2, I put forward the main proposal and analysis in section 3. Section 4 enumerates and confirms predictions of the null head analysis. Finally, section 5 concludes the paper.

2.   The Scope Puzzle

This section presents the scopal behavior of *man*-phrases in scrambling contexts. The discussion will lead to the conclusion that we cannot account for the scope pattern of *man*-phrases if the particle *man* is a scope-bearing element.

---

* I would like to thank Danny Fox and Irene Heim for valuable suggestions and discussion. I am also grateful to Noam Chomsky, Kai von Fintel, Jon Gajewski, Sabine Iatridou, Alec Marantz, Shigeru Miyagawa, David Pesetsky, Shoich Takahashi, and the audience at NELS 34 for questions and comments.
    [1] Throughout the paper, the term '*man*-phrase' refers to an XP that is accompanied by *man*.

Keir Moulton and Matthew Wolf (eds.): Proceedings of NELS 34,
Stony Brook University: 373 – 387. GLSA, Amherst.

Let us start with case-marked *man*-phrases. Case-marked *man*-phrases appear to obligatorily reconstruct when scrambled clause-internally. That is, clause-internal scrambling does not induce ambiguity. The relevant examples are illustrated below.

(1)   a.   **Motun**-salam-i   John-**man-ul**   salanghanta.
             every-person-NOM   John-only- ACC   love
             'Everyone loves only John.'
             (i) Everyone loves John and no one else.   (every > only)
             (ii) *John is the only one whom everyone loves.   (*only > every)
       b.   John-**man-ul**$_1$ [**motun**-salam-i   t$_1$ salanghanta].
             John-only-ACC   every-person-NOM   love
             'Only John, everyone loves *t*.'
             (i) Everyone loves John and no one else.   (every > only)
             (ii) *John is the only one whom everyone loves.   (*only > every)

The sequence of a universal quantifier and a *man*-phrase in (1a) only allows a surface scope reading whereby *everyone* takes scope over *only John*. So (1a) is true iff each person loves John and no one else. The other reading, where John is the only one whom everyone loves, is not available. In (1b), the *man*-phrase is scrambled across the subject quantifier *everyone*. Here the scope relation remains the same as in (1a); wide scope for *man* is still not possible.[2] Notice that the particle *man* precedes the case marker.

    Now we turn to *man*-phrases marked by a postposition. Postposition-marked *man*-phrases show different scopal behavior from case-marked ones. The scrambled PP-*man* phrase can take scope in the surface position, thus creating ambiguity, as shown in (2).

(2)   a.   **Motun**-salam-i   John-**hako-man**   akswuhayssta.
             every-person-NOM   John-with-only   shook_hands
             'Everyone shook hands only with John.'
             (i) Everyone shook hands with John and with no one else.   (every > only)
             (ii) *John is the only one with whom everyone shook hands. (*only > every)
       b.   John-**hako-man**$_1$ [**motun**-salam-i   t$_1$ akswuhayssta].
             John-with-only   every-person-NOM   shook_hands]
             'Only with John, everyone shook hands *t*.'
             (i) Everyone shook hands with John and with no one else.   (every > only)
             (ii) John is the only one with whom everyone shook hands. (only > every)

_____

    [2] In order for the *man*-phrase to take scope over the subject QP, the *man*-phrase must appear in the sentence initial position without any case marker, as shown in (i). The sentence also has the narrow scope reading of the *man*-phrase, thus allowing ambiguity. In the interest of space, I leave the analysis of (i) for another occasion, and interested readers are referred to Lee (2003) for further discussion.

(i)   John-**man**$_i$ [**motun**-salam-i   e$_i$ salanghanta].
       John-only   every-person-Nom   love
       'Only John, everyone loves *e*.'
       a. Everyone loves John and no one else.   (every > only)
       b. John is the only one whom everyone loves.   (only > every)

Without scrambling, the base order between the two elements determines the scope relation, as in (2a). If the PP is scrambled as in (2b), however, the *man*-phrase can take scope over the subject quantifier. Note also that the particle follows the postposition.

This non-uniform behavior of *man*-phrases contrasts with the scopal behavior of quantifier phrases (QPs). It is well known that scrambled QPs optionally reconstruct and induce ambiguity in so-called scope-rigid languages (See Hoji 1985 for Japanese, Ahn 1990 for Korean, among many others). The sentences in (3) exemplify the relevant facts for Korean.

(3)　　a.　　**Nwukwunka-ka**　　**manhun-**salam-ul　　　salanghanta.
　　　　　　　someone-NOM　　　many-person-ACC　　　love
　　　　　　　'Someone loves many people.'
　　　　　　　(i) There is someone who loves many people.　　　(some > many)
　　　　　　　(ii) *There are many people who are loved by someone. (*many > some)

　　　　b.　　**Manhun-**salam-ul$_1$　　[**nwukwunka-ka**　　　t$_1$　　salanghanta].
　　　　　　　many-person-ACC　　　someone-NOM　　　　　　　love
　　　　　　　'Many people, someone loves *t*.'
　　　　　　　(i) There is someone who loves many people.　　　(some > many).
　　　　　　　(ii) There are many people who are loved by someone.　(many > some).

When two quantifiers are in their base positions, as in (3a), the surface word order determines the scope relation between the two. When there is scrambling, however, the wide scope reading of the object QP becomes available, as in (3b). The scrambled QP can but need not undergo reconstruction, thus the sentence is ambiguous.[3] A schematic summary of the scope patterns is given in (4). The solid line indicates obligatory reconstruction, and the dotted line optional reconstruction.

(4)　　a.　　[$_{TP}$ **DP-man-Acc$_i$**　　[$_{TP}$　　QP　　t$_i$　　verb]]　　　(unambiguous: 1b)

　　　　b.　　[$_{TP}$ **PP-man$_i$**　　[$_{TP}$　　QP　　t$_i$　　verb]]　　　(ambiguous: 2b)

　　　　c.　　[$_{TP}$　　**QP$_i$**　　[$_{TP}$　　QP　　t$_i$　　verb]]　　　(ambiguous: 3b)

Suppose that the *man*-phrase is a QP of type <et, t>, that is, the set of properties that no one other than John has (J.-W. Choe 1998). Then, the non-ambiguity in (4a) is puzzling. Apparently, it undergoes obligatory reconstruction when scrambled, unlike QPs. To solve this, one might stipulate that the *man*-phrase must reconstruct, e.g. that it is a special QP that can only undergo PF scrambling (Aoun and Benmamoun 1998, Sauerland and Elbourne 2002). However, this account lacks reasonable motivation, and faces empirical problems once we consider (4b). We would need another stipulation to distinguish the

---

[3] When the *man*-phrase occurs in the subject position and a QP occupies an object position (e.g. *Only Mary loves everyone*), scrambling of the object QP induces an ambiguity. This is because what moves is a QP, not a *man*-phrase, and the scrambled QP can optionally reconstruct as shown in (3). For this reason, all the *man*-phrases in this paper are accusative-marked.

two cases. Any account that treats the *man*-phrase as a QP without further assumptions would fail to account for both the non-ambiguity of (4a) and the ambiguity of (4b).

3.   Proposal and Analysis

3.1.   Proposal: *Man* is an Agreement Morpheme

This section proposes that the particle *man* is an agreement morpheme. As the Nominative marker is an indication of the T(ense) head under standard assumptions, *man* is an indication of a null ONLY head. Under this proposal, the null ONLY head, rather than the particle, carries the exhaustive meaning of English *only*. Therefore, the position of the null head, not the surface position of the particle, determines the scope relation.[4] [5]

I propose (5) as the lexical entry for the head ONLY, where ALT is the set of alternatives created by focus marking. It is the result of replacing the focused element by contextually plausible alternatives (see Rooth 1985).

(5) $[\![\text{ONLY}]\!] = \lambda P_{<e,t>}.\lambda x_e.P(x) = 1 \ \& \ \forall z_e \in \text{ALT}(x): P(z) = 1 \rightarrow z = x$

The ONLY head takes two arguments (a predicate and an individual), and asserts that the individual argument is the only element that satisfies the predicate argument. Since the individual argument is focused, ALT(x) is a set of individuals. Basically, it is a covert *only* (cf. Horn 1969).

I also claim that the ONLY head can occur in several distinct positions in the clause, as long as the semantic conditions imposed by (5) are satisfied. That is, there is no one fixed position for the null head. It can be above TP (high ONLY-P) or below TP (low ONLY-P). Now that the ONLY head can appear in various positions and it is phonologically null, a crucial task is to detect the position of this head. I argue that the position of ONLY can be detected, thanks to the strong correlation between morphology and syntax (Baker's (1985) Mirror Principle). Specifically, I argue that the relative order among the focus particle, case marker, and postposition reflects the hierarchy of the corresponding functional heads.[6] Take for example *John-man-i* 'John-only-Nom'. Since the particle *man* precedes the case marker, we conclude by the Mirror Principle that the ONLY head is lower than the Nominative case checking/assigning head, namely T (since Korean is a head-final language).

Having said this, let us move to see how this works in interpreting sentences containing a *man*-phrase. We start with the simple sentence in (6).

(6)   John-**man-i**   oassta.
        John-only-NOM   came
        'Only John came.'

---

[4] For the role of abstract heads in semantics literature, see Karttunen (1977) for question, and Laka (1990), Ladusaw (1992), von Stechow (1993), Beck & Kim (1997), Kelepir (2001), and Ovalle & Guerzoni (2002) for negation.

[5] I will continue to gloss *man* as 'only' for the sake of convenience.

[6] This idea was suggested to me by Danny Fox.

In (6), the particle precedes the nominative marker, and the Mirror Principle tells us that ONLY-P is lower than TP. I claim that the subject, which is generated VP-internally, moves first to [Spec, ONLY-P], and then undergoes a second movement to [Spec, TP] to check the Nominative feature (Chomsky 1995, S. Cho 2000). The DP picks up the affixes through derivation, and the order of the affixes reflects the derivational steps. The derivation is illustrated in (7a) along with the semantic composition in (7b). As one can verify, the tree correctly derives the compositional meaning of the sentence.[7]

(7) a.

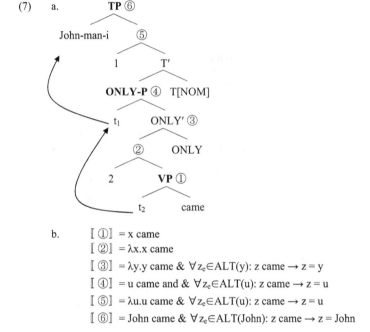

b. $[\![①]\!]$ = x came

$[\![②]\!]$ = λx.x came

$[\![③]\!]$ = λy.y came & $\forall z_e \in$ ALT(y): z came → z = y

$[\![④]\!]$ = u came and & $\forall z_e \in$ ALT(u): z came → z = u

$[\![⑤]\!]$ = λu.u came & $\forall z_e \in$ ALT(u): z came → z = u

$[\![⑥]\!]$ = John came & $\forall z_e \in$ ALT(John): z came → z = John

The focused phrase *John* undergoes focus movement to [Spec, ONLY-P], creating a lambda-predicate.[8] This predicate is the first argument of ONLY, and the focused phrase in [Spec, ONLY-P] becomes the second argument of the ONLY head. This movement is obligatory although it sometimes applies string-vacuously, and thus has no effect on word order. One might wonder at this point why we complicate the system by introducing the

---

[7] Throughout this paper, I adopt Heim & Kratzer's (1998) framework for semantic representation, e.g. numerical index as the variable binder. I also assume for convenience that case heads (T and Agro) are semantically vacuous.

[8] The lambda-abstractor in the first movement in (7) is in an unusual place, not directly under the moved element, as also pointed out by von Fintel (2001). There are other possible implementations that do not involve this choice (e.g. late merge of the ONLY head or movement to the sister node of the ONLY head), but the analysis does not hinge on the choice on this issue.

abstract ONLY head. When we look at simple cases like this, the motivation is not clear. Yet, this approach offers a non-stipulative account for the scope puzzle, as will be shown in the next section.

3.2.   Deriving the Compositional Meaning

Let us first discuss case-marked *man*-phrases, and then turn to PP-*man* cases. The scope pattern of the case-marked *man*-phrase is repeated in (8). The point here is that clause-internal scrambling of the *man*-phrase does not affect scope interpretation; (8b) is not ambiguous.

(8)   a.   **Motun**-salam-i   John-**man-ul**   salanghanta.
                every-person-NOM   John-only-ACC   love
                'Everyone loves only John.'
                (i) Everyone loves John and no one else.   (every > only)
                (ii) *John is the only one whom everyone loves.   (*only > every)
        b.   John-**man-ul**₁   [**motun**-salam-i   t₁   salanghanta].
                John-only-ACC   every-person-NOM   love
                'Only John, everyone loves *t*.'
                (i) Everyone loves John and no one else.   (every > only)
                (ii) *John is the only one whom everyone loves.   (*only > every)

Let us start with (8a). From the order *man-ul* 'man-acc', we conclude by the Mirror Principle that ONLY-P is lower than AgroP where Accusative is assigned/checked. The AgroP is in turn below TP that contains the universal quantifier in its spec position. Therefore, the universal quantifier takes scope over the ONLY head. The structure of (8a) is given in (9a) along with the semantic value of the top node in (9b).

The reading in (9b) is the meaning we want: each person has the property of loving John and no one else. Note also that we must not allow reconstruction of the subject QP to its θ-position (*t₁*), since it will produce the unattested reading (*only > every*). This is independently justified from the behavior of QPs in the scope-rigid languages. If the reconstruction were possible, sentences in the base order would be ambiguous, as in English (cf. (3a)).

(9)   a.

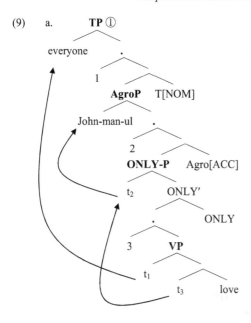

b.   ⟦ ① ⟧ = For each person x, x loves John & ∀wₑ∈ALT(John):
           x loves w → w = John

Next, consider (8b) where *John-man-ul* 'John-only-Acc' is scrambled to the sentence initial position. Since *man* is a mere agreement morpheme, the *man*-phrase is a referential expression, not a QP. Given this, it is natural that scrambling of the *man*-phrase does not affect meaning, as is the case with referential expressions. The structure of (8b) is given in (10a) in the next page, where the clausal structure remains the same as in (9a), except that the *man*-phrase is adjoined to TP via scrambling. The semantic value of the top node is given in (10b).

Compare the semantic values of (9b) and (10b). They are the same: each person loves no one other than John. Even though *John* is interpreted in the scrambled position in (10a), the same reading results since the ONLY head is still below AgroP. This explains the apparent "reconstruction" effect, although there is no reconstruction of a QP in the real sense. What determines the scope relation is not the surface position of the particle, but the position of the ONLY head.

One might ask at this point why ONLY-P should be below AgroP and if there is any principled reason to rule out ONLY-P above AgroP. In principle, the present analysis does not rule out such a configuration. What it rules out, however, is the form where the particle is preceded by an overt case marker, for example *Mary-lul-man. We assume that the case marker is realized as a zero variant when it is followed by the particle *man* and some other particles such as *to* 'also', which disallows case marking in any position.

Therefore, when case marking is covert, *DP-man* can be a spell-out of *DP-Case-man* or *DP-man-Case*. This means, then, that if *DP-man* appears without case marking in the S-initial position, it does not guarantee the low ONLY-P and thus ambiguity is expected. This is indeed the case (see fn. 3).

(10)   a.

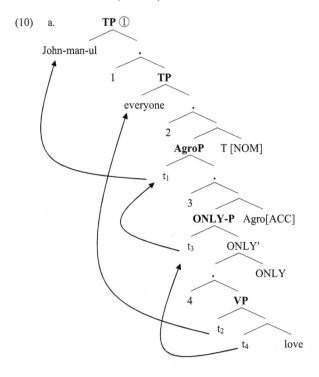

b.   ⟦ ① ⟧ = For each person x, x loves John & $\forall w_e \in ALT(John)$:
        x loves w → w = John

    Now we turn to the scope pattern of PP-*man* case. The *man*-phrase marked by a postposition does not have a fixed scope, unlike the case-marked one. Its scope seems to be affected by its surface structure. The data is repeated in (11).

(11)   a.   **Motun**-salam-i   John-**hako-man**   akswuhayssta.
              every-person-NOM   John-with-only   shook_hands
              'Everyone shook hands only with John.'
              (i) Everyone shook hands with John and with no one else.   (every > only)
              (ii) *John is the only one with whom everyone shook hands. (*only > every)

b.   John-**hako-man**₁   [**motun**-salam-i   t₁   akswuhayssta].
    John-with-only   every-person-NOM   shook_hands]
    'Only with John, everyone shook hands *t*.'
    (i) Everyone shook hands with John and with no one else. (every > only)
    (ii) John is the only one with whom everyone shook hands. (only > every)

Why are postpositions different from case markers? The ordering among affixes provides an answer to this question. Postpositions precede the particle *man*; this shows that ONLY-P is higher than VP, where PP is generated. But it does not tell us whether ONLY-P is higher than TP or lower than TP, whose spec position is occupied by the subject QP. By contrast, case markers explicitly specify that ONLY-P is lower than AgroP or TP since they always follow the particle.

With this contrast in mind, we derive the scope patterns in (11). First, in (11a), ONLY-P is positioned above VP (as inferred from the morpheme order *hako-man* 'with-only') but below TP. If the ONLY-P were located above TP, we expect the *man*-phrase to occur to the left of the subject QP since focused phrases move overtly to [Spec, ONLY-P]. The structure of (11a) is represented in (12).

(12)   [$_{TP}$ **everyone** λx [$_{ONLY-P}$ with_John [λy [$_{VP}$ x y shake_hands]] $_{ONLY}$] $_T$]

                Focus Movement

Since the subject QP is above ONLY-P in (12), the scope relation follows from this syntactic configuration: for each person x, x shook hands with John, and for all alternatives z to John, if x shook hands with z, z is John.[9]

Let us next see the case of the ambiguous sentence in (11b). I argue that the two readings are due to different positions of ONLY-P, not to the reconstruction of the *man*-phrase as a QP. On the first reading, where *everyone* takes scope over the *man*-phrase, ONLY-P is still below TP. The *man*-phrase undergoes scrambling after focus movement. Thus, the clausal structure is the same as the one in (12) except that the PP is adjoined to TP. The same interpretation obtains, even though the *man*-phrase is interpreted in the scrambled position.

(13)   [$_{TP}$ with_John λz [$_{TP}$ **everyone** λx [$_{ONLY-P}$ z[λy [$_{VP}$ x y shake_hands]] $_{ONLY}$] $_T$]]

          Scrambling   Focus Mvt.

On the second reading of (11b) (*only > every*), the ONLY head takes scope over the subject QP. That is, ONLY-P is positioned above TP. The S-initial appearance of the *man*-phrase is due to focus movement, not to scrambling. The structure is represented in (14).

---

[9] I assume that the postposition moves along with the focused element in the overt syntax, but reconstructs at LF for semantic interpretation. Under this assumption, there is no need to adjust the entry of ONLY for the PP case. Thanks to Irene Heim for suggesting this possibility.

(14)   [$_{ONLY-P}$ with_John [λy [$_{TP}$ **everyone** λx [$_{VP}$ x y shake_hands] $_T$]] $_{ONLY}$]

Focus Movement

Thus, the S-initial appearance of a *PP-man* could either be due to scrambling as in (13) or to focus movement as in (14), whereas that of a case-marked *man*-phrase could only be due to scrambling. The order of the postposition and the focus particle is compatible with both positions of ONLY-P (high ONLY-P above TP and low ONLY-P below TP), and the surface position does not distinguish focus movement from scrambling. This is why postpositions behave differently from case markers. Overt case marking rules out the high ONLY-P, and thus brings about the scope-fixing effect.

This section showed how the current proposal accounts for the scope patterns of the *man*-phrase. I showed that the apparent reconstruction of the *man*-phrase is not the reconstruction of a QP, and that the scope is determined by the position of the ONLY head. The scopal difference between case-marked and postposition-marked *man*-phrases is correlated with the distribution of the particle with respect to case markers and postpositions. The current proposal derives this correlation without stipulations, unlike the QP approach under which the *man*-phrase is a QP that shows a non-uniform behavior.

4.   Further Predictions on Scope

This section introduces further predictions of the null head analysis, and shows that each prediction is borne out. The result provides further support to the proposed analysis.

4.1.   Multiple Occurrences

The first prediction is that multiple occurrences of the particle *man* would be able to indicate the presence of a single instance of the ONLY head. Suppose that the ONLY head can host more than one focused phrase in its spec position. Then, the number of particles in a sentence would not necessarily match the number of ONLY heads in the syntactic tree. Interpretation would depend on the number of ONLY heads, not on the number of particles.[10]

This prediction is borne out. When the particle occurs twice in a sentence, the sentence is ambiguous between one ONLY and two ONLY's, as illustrated in (15).

(15)   John-**man**   sakwa-**man**   mekesse.
        John-only   apple-only   ate
        'Only John ate only apples.'
        (i) John is the only one who ate only apples. Others ate other fruits as wells as apples.
        (ii) John is the only one who ate something, and John ate only apples (not other fruits).

The first reading involves two ONLY heads. It says John is the only one who has the property of eating only apples. By contrast, the second reading involves just one ONLY

---

[10] Thanks to Kai von Fintel and Danny Fox for bringing this prediction to my attention.

head, and says that the pair <John, apples> is the only element that satisfies the eating relation.[11] If it were the particle *man* that carried the exclusive meaning, the second reading would not arise. This lends further support to the claim that *man* is a mere agreement morpheme.[12]

4.2. Scope Splitting

The second prediction is that if the scrambled *man*-phrase contains a scope-bearing element, the scope of the new scope-bearing element can be dissociated from the ONLY head. This is so because the new scope-bearing element, contained in the *man*-phrase, can be interpreted in the scrambled position, while the ONLY head still can be lower than TP. Suppose there is a subject QP intervening between the scrambled *man*-phrase and the low ONLY head. Then, the subject QP would be able to take scope between the new scope-bearing element and the ONLY head. The present analysis predicts this dissociation to be possible, and this section confirms this prediction.[13]

For this, we introduce a conjoined DP as a new scope element. Consider the following sentences, where a *man*-phrase contains a conjoined DP.

(16) a. **Nwukwunka-ka**   John-**kwa**-Bill-**man**-ul   salanghanta.
          someone-NOM   John-and-Bill-only-ACC   love
          'Someone loves only John and Bill.'
          (i) There is someone who loves only John and Bill. (some > only >and)
          (ii) *There is someone who loves only John and someone who loves only Bill.
                                                               (*and > some > only)

      b. John-**kwa**-Bill-**man**-ul$_1$ [**nwukwunka**-ka   t$_1$ salanhanta].
          John-and-Bill-only-ACCc   someone-NOM   love
          'Only John and Bill, someone loves *t*.'
          (i) There is someone who loves only John and Bill. (some > only > and)
          (ii) There is someone who loves only John and someone who loves only Bill.
                                                               (and > some > only)

---

[11] Here the ONLY head takes a relation (of type <e, et>) and two individuals as arguments. The new entry would be the following:

(i) $[\![$ ONLY $]\!]$ $= \lambda R_{<e,<e,t>>}.\lambda x_e.\lambda y_e.R(x)(y) =1$ & $\forall z_e \in ALT(x) \forall w_e \in ALT(y): R(z)(w) = 1 \rightarrow$
                  $z = x$ & $w = y$

[12] One can think of this in parallel to negation in negative concord languages, where multiple occurrences of negation can contribute a single instance of negation. For instance, in the following English and Italian sentences, the two negations do not cancel each other out. The interpretation involves only one negation.

(i)   a.   Maria **didn't** say **nothing** to **nobody**.   (Nonstandard English)
       b.   Mario **non** ha parlato di **niente** con **nessuno**.   (Italian)
             'Mario hasn't spoken with anyone about anything.' (Ladusaw 1992:237)

[13] I thank Danny Fox and Sabine Iatridou for bringing this question and prediction to my attention.

Sentence (16a) is not ambiguous. It only allows a surface scope reading. For this reading to be true, there should be someone who loves John and Bill and loves no one else. Sentence (16b), by contrast, has two readings. In one reading, one and the same person loves only John and Bill, as in (16a). In the other reading, there must be two different people involved such that one person loves only John, and the other person loves only Bill.

The ambiguity of (16b) is interesting since scrambling of case-marked *man*-phrases has not induced ambiguity so far. This ambiguity, however, does not make a counterexample to our analysis. Compare the scope relations in the two readings. In (16a) and in the first reading of (16b), the subject QP takes scope over both the conjunction and the ONLY head. In the second reading of (16b), the conjunction takes scope over the subject QP, which in turn takes scope over the ONLY head. In both cases, the scope relation between the subject QP and the ONLY head remains the same. The former takes scope over the latter. What differentiates the two cases is where the conjoined DP is interpreted. If the conjoined DP is interpreted in the scrambled position, the scope of the conjunction is split from the ONLY head (*and > some > only*).

Let me spell out how this reading is derived. In the interest of space, we focus on the scrambled sentence, but the interpretation of the non-scrambling case should be straightforward. Based on the morpheme order *man-ul* 'only-acc', we conclude that the ONLY head is positioned lower than Agro. Next, in order to interpret the conjunction, we introduce a D(istributivity) operator. Following Link 1983, Roberts 1987, and Beck 2000 among others, I assume the following lexical entry for the D-operator.

(17) $[\![D]\!] = \lambda f_{<e,t>}. \lambda X_e. \forall x \in X: f(x) = 1$

The D-operator takes two arguments, a predicate and a group individual, which is marked by a capital letter to be distinguished from an atomic individual. It asserts that the property *f* holds for all the atomic individuals that are parts of the group individual X.

The structure of (16b) is illustrated in (18) in the next page, where the scrambling of the conjoined DP *John & Bill* creates a new position for the D operator to apply. In this structure, the readings diverge depending upon whether we apply the D-operator. Without the D-operator, the first reading in (16b) obtains (*some > only > and*). For this reading to be true, there should be someone who loves only John and Bill. That person does not love Tom, for example. The reading we are interested in (*and > some > only*) arises when the D-operator is present. In this reading the one who loves only John does not love Bill and the one who loves only Bill does not love John. The two values of the top node are given in (19). The one in (19a) is without the D-operator, and the one in (19b) is with the D-operator in the tree.

(18)

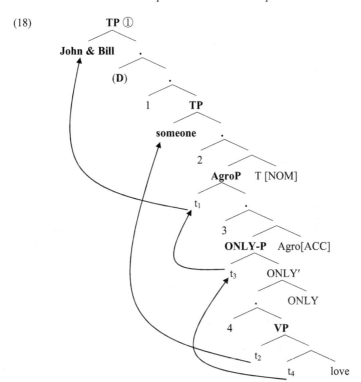

(19) a.   ⟦ ① ⟧ = There is someone x such that x loves John and Bill &

$\forall w_e \in$ ALT(J&B): x loves w → w ∈ J & B[14]

b.   ⟦ ① ⟧ = $\forall z \in$ J&B: There is someone who loves only z, i.e. there is
someone who loves only John and there is someone who loves
only Bill.

---

[14] I assume that the set of alternatives to a group individual still includes atomic individuals (for
reasons that I cannot discuss here in the interest of space). Under this assumption, we need to adjust the
entry so that we do not wrongly rule out some elements from the set of alternatives:

(i)   ⟦ ONLY ⟧ = $\lambda P_{<e,t>}.\lambda x_e.P(x) = 1$ & $\forall z_e \in$ ALT(x): P(z) = 1 → [P(x) ⇒ P(z)] (cf. von Fintel 1997)

The new entry says that if some alternative satisfies the predicate, the resulting proposition *P(z)* is entailed
by the presupposed proposition *P(x)*. With respect to our example, this means that if x loves w among the
alternatives, w is a part of *J&B*. That is, w is John, Bill, or John & Bill. I thank Danny Fox and Irene Heim
for pointing this out to me.

The existence of this reading confirms our second prediction. The scope of a scope-bearing element within the *man*-phrase can be split from the scope of the ONLY head.

5.   Concluding Remarks

This paper presented a theory of the scope-taking properties of the Korean focus particle *man* 'only'. I argued that the particle is an agreement morpheme rather than a scope-bearing element. The particle merely indicates the presence of a head ONLY, which carries the quantificational meaning. I claimed that this null head can appear at various points in the tree, therefore its position (not that of the particle itself) determines the scope relation with respect to other quantificational elements. I also argued for a new correlation between the order of nominal affixes and the scope of focus particles, thus supporting Baker's Mirror Principle in a new area outside the verbal domain. Specifically I argued that the relative order among the particle, case marker, and postposition reflects the hierarchy of functional heads, which played a crucial role in identifying the position of the ONLY head. The proposed analysis accounted for the puzzling scope facts without stipulations, and also derived the correlation between the particle's distributional properties and its scopal behavior.

References

Ahn, S.-H. 1990. *Korean Quantification and Universal Grammar*. Doctoral dissertation, University of Connecticut, Storrs.

Aoun, J. and E. Benmamoun. 1998. Minimality, Reconstruction, and PF movement. *Linguistic Inquiry* 29, 569-597.

Baker, M. 1985. The Mirror Principle and Morphosyntactic Explanation. *Linguistic Inquiry* 16, 373-415.

Beck, S. 2000. Star Operators* Episode 1: Defense of the Double Star. In *University of Massachusetts occasional papers in linguistics 23: Issues in semantics*, 1-23. Department of Linguistics, University of Massachusetts, Amherst.

Beck, S. and S.-S. Kim. 1997. On *wh*- and Operator Scope in Korean. *Journal of East Asian Linguistics* 6, 339-384.

Büring, D. and K. Hartmann. 2001. The Syntax and Semantics of Focus-Sensitive Particles in German. *Natural Language and Linguistic Theory* 19, 229-281.

Cho, S. 2000. *Three Forms of Case Agreement in Korean*. Doctoral dissertation, State University of New York, Stony Brook.

Choe, H. S. 1995. Focus and Topic Movement in Korean and Licensing. In *Discourse Configurational Languages*, ed. K. Kiss, 269-334. Oxford: Oxford University Press.

Choe, J.-W. 1998. The Formal Analysis of the Particle *man* (in Korean). *Korean Semantics* 3, 41-65.

Chomsky, N. 1995. *The Minimalist Program*. Cambridge, Mass.: MIT Press.

von Fintel, K. 1997. Bare Plurals, Bare Conditionals, and *Only*. *Journal of Semantics* 14, 1-56.

von Fintel, K. 2001. Why Focus Movement is Weird. Lecture Notes, MIT, Cambridge, Mass.

Heim, I. and A. Kratzer. 1998. *Semantics in generative grammar*. Oxford: Blackwell.

Hoji, H. 1985. *Logical Form Constraints and Configurational Structures in Japanese*. Doctoral dissertation, University of Washington, Seattle.

Horn, L. 1969. A Presuppositional Analysis of Only and Even. In *Papers from the 5th Regional Meeting, Chicago Linguistic Society*, 98-107. Chicago Linguistic Society, University of Chicago, Chicago, Ill.

Karttunen, L.1977. Syntax and Semantics of Questions. *Linguistics and Philosophy* 1, 3-44.

Kayne, R. 1998. Overt vs. Covert Movement. *Syntax* 1, 128-191.

Kelepir, M. 2001. *Topics in Turkish Syntax: Clausal Structure and Scope*. Doctoral dissertation, MIT, Cambridge, Mass.

Kiss, K. 1998. Identificational Focus versus Information Focus. *Language* 74, 245-273.

Ladusaw, W. 1992. Expressing Negation. In *Proceedings of Semantics And Linguistic Theory 2*, 220-229. CLC Publications, Cornell University, Ithaca, NY.

Laka, I. 1990. *Negation in Syntax: On the Nature of Functional Categories and Projections*. Doctoral dissertation, MIT, Cambridge, Mass.

Lee, Y. 2003. *Only*, Scope, and the Mirror Principle. Ms., MIT, Cambridge, Mass.

Link, G. 1983. The Logical Analysis of Plurals and Mass Terms: a Lattice-Theoretical Approach. In *Meaning, use, and interpretation of language*, ed. R. Bauerle, C. Schwarze, and A. von Stechow, 302-323. Berlin: De Gruyter.

Ovalle, L. and E. Guerzoni. 2002. Double Negation, Negative Concord, and Metalinguistic Negation. Paper presented at the 38th Chicago Linguistic Society, University of Chicago, Chicago, Ill., April. 2002.

Rizzi, L. 1997. The Fine Structure of the Left Periphery. In *Elements of Grammar*, ed. L. Haegeman, 281-337. Dordrecht: Kluwer.

Robert, C. 1987. *Modal Subordination, Anaphora, and Distributivity*. Doctoral dissertation. University of Massachusetts, Amherst.

Rooth, M. 1985. *Association with Focus*. Doctoral dissertation. University of Massachusetts, Amherst.

Sauerland, U. 1998. Plurals, Derived Predicates and Reciprocals. In *MIT working papers in linguistics 25: The interpretive tract*, 177-204. Department of Linguistics and Philosophy, MIT, Cambridge, Mass.

Sauerland, U. and P. Elbourne. 2002. Total Reconstruction, PF Movement, and Derivational Order. *Linguistic Inquiry* 33, 283-319.

von Stechow, A. 1993. Die Aufgaben der Syntax. In *Syntax – Ein internationals Handbuch zeitgenössischer Forschung*, ed. J. Jacobs, A. von Stechow, W. Sternefeld, and T. Vennemann, 1-88. Berlin: De Gruyter.

Department of Linguistics and Philosophy
Massachusetts Institute of Technology
77 Massachusetts Avenue, 32-D808
Cambridge, MA 02139-4307

youngjoo@mit.edu

C-locality and the Interaction of Reflexives and Ditransitives

Jeffrey Lidz and Alexander Williams

Northwestern University and University of Pennsylvania

1. Introduction

In Kannada, ditransitives with benefactive morphology cannot have a reflexive indirect object, or have reflexive marking on the verb. This paper seeks to explain why. We argue that the benefactive structure, when its indirect object is a locally bound anaphor, is subject to two conflicting requirements. The anaphor must be local to its antecedent, and the direct object must be local to its Case licenser, but these conditions cannot be met in the same derivation. Thus reflexive benefactives are syntactically underivable. As the crucial conflict follows from the theory of object licensing introduced in Lidz and Williams 2002, our explanation provides additional support for that framework.

The primary data are presented in (1-4). In (1) we see the two types of ditransitive found in Kannada: the plain ditransitive (1a) and the benefactive ditransitive (1b). (1b) includes the benefactive auxiliary *koDu*, which attaches to the main verb in its past participle form and bears the tense and agreement inflection.

(1) a.   Hari Rashmi-ge   pustaka-vannu kalis-id-a
          Hari Rashmi-DAT book-ACC   send-PST-3SM
          'Hari sent a book to Rashmi.'

     b.   Hari Rashmi-ge pustaka-vannu kalisi-**koTT**-a
          Hari Rashmi-DAT book-ACC   send-**BEN.PST**-3SM
          'Hari sent a book to Rashmi.'

In (2) we make the indirect object a reflexive anaphor: *tann* 'self'. (2a) has the verbal reflexive morpheme *koLLu* (VRM), and this is grammatical. But adding the benefactive morpheme is impossible, (2b), either with or without the verbal reflexive.

(2) a.   Hari tann-age pustaka-vannu kalisi-**koND**-a
         Hari self-DAT book-ACC   send-**VRM.PST**-3SM
         'Hari sent a book to himself.'

   b.   * Hari tann-age pustaka-vannu kalisi-**(koNDu)-koTT**-a
       Hari self-DAT book-ACC   send-**(VRM)-BEN.PST**-3SM

The word order of (2a) is also important.[1] Generally, the order of the dative and accusative arguments in a ditransitive is free, as shown in (3).

  (3) a.   Hari Rashmi-ge pustaka-vannu kalisi-(koTT)-a
          Hari Rashmi-DAT book-ACC   send-(BEN.PST)-3SM
          'Hari sent a book to Rashmi.'

      b.   Hari pustaka-vannu Rashmi-ge kalisi-(koTT)-a
          Hari book-ACC   Rashmi-DAT send-(BEN.PST)-3SM
          'Hari sent a book to Rashmi.'

However, when the dative argument is a locally bound anaphor, as in (4), the dative must precede the accusative.

  (4) a.   Hari tann-age pustaka-vannu kalisi-koND-a
         Hari self-DAT book-ACC   send-VRM.PST-3SM
         'Hari sent a book to himself.'

      b.   * Hari pustaka-vannu tann-age kalisi-koND-a
         Hari book-ACC   self-DAT send-VRM.PST-3SM

We propose a syntactic explanation of the facts in (1-2),[2] relying on three points. First, we establish the basic hierarchical structure of the Kannada benefactive. Second, we observe the minimality properties of anaphor chains in Kannada, based on the word order fact in (4). Finally, we introduce the relation of c-locality and the theory of DP-licensing that uses this relation (Lidz and Williams 2002). Putting the pieces together, we will show that, given the structure of the benefactive, a dative anaphor cannot be local to its antecedent at the same time as an accusative object is local to its licenser. Simply put, reflexive benefactives are syntactically underivable.

---

[1] Speakers generally find ditransitives with accusative anaphors, such as (i-ii), odd to varying degrees, making it very difficult to determine whether these are even grammatical and if so, what structure they might have:

  (i)   % Hari bangalor-ige tann-annu kalisi-koND-a
       Hari Bangalore-DAT self-ACC send-VRM.PST-3SM
       'Hari sent himself to Bangalore.'

  (ii)   % Hari tann-annu bangalor-ige kalisi-koND-a
       Hari self-ACC Bangalore-DAT send-VRM.PST-3SM
       'Hari sent himself to Bangalore.'

[2] The ungrammaticality of (2b) has traditionally been treated as due simply to the *meaning* of the benefactive morpheme. For example, Bhat (1979) says, "*koDu* indicates that the action referred to was carried out for the benefit of a person other than the agent himself" (see also Sridhar 1990). While this description is accurate, it is just that. If the lack of reflexive benefactives can be derived from independently motivated properties of the syntax, then we will have moved beyond description and achieved something of an explanation. Additionally, we will have preserved a simpler meaning for the benefactive morpheme.

2.   Two structures for Kannada ditransitives

Lidz 2002 shows that benefactive and nonbenefactive ditransitives are distinct both in meaning and in structure.

Semantically, the Kannada benefactives imply a transfer of possession, like double object constructions in English (Green 1974, Oerhle 1976, Harley 2000, among others). The person named by the dative is understood to receive the object named by the accusative. Thus (5a) cannot felicitously be followed by (5b).

(5)   a.   nannu rashmi-ge   keek-annu suTT-u-**koTT**-e
               I   rashmi-DAT cake-ACC   prepare-PP-**BEN.PST**-1S
               'I made rashmi a cake...'

        b.   ?? adare ad-annu nann-a taayi-ge   koTT-e
               but   it-ACC   I-GEN mother-DAT give.PST-1S
               '...but I gave it to my mother.'

In a nonbenefactive ditransitive, however, like (6a), there is no implication of transfer. So in this case the follow-up sentence, (6b), is acceptable.

(6)   a.   nannu rashmi-ge   keek-annu suTT-e
               I   rashmi-DAT cake-ACC prepare.PST-1S
               'I made a cake for Rashmi...'

        b.   adare ad-annu nann-a taayi-ge   koTT-e
               but   it-ACC   I-GEN mother-DAT give.PST-1S
               '...but I gave it to my mother.'

Syntactically, we can see that the two ditransitives also differ in the hierarchical placement of their arguments. The distinct underlying structures can be determined by examining patterns of quantifier-variable binding (Barss and Lasnik 1986, Harley 2000, Bleam 2001).

In (7-8) we see the possible bindings between dative and accusative arguments in nonbenefactive ditransitives. Here, an accusative quantifier can bind into the dative regardless of whether it precedes the dative or follows it.

(7)   a.   sampaadaka pratiyondu lekhana-vannu adar-a lekhan-ige kaLisida
               editor   every   article-ACC   it-GEN author-DAT send-PST-3SM
               'The editor sent every article to its author.'   (ACC > DAT)

        b.   sampaadaka adar-a lekhan-ige   pratiyondu lekhana-vannu kaLis-id-a
               editor   it-GEN author-DAT every   article-ACC   send-PST-3SM
               'The editor sent every article to its author.'   (DAT < ACC)

But a dative quantifier can bind into an accusative only if the dative comes first.

(8) a. sampaadaka pratiyobba lekhan-ige avaL-a lekhana-vannu kaLis-id-a
         editor   every   author-dat she-GEN article-ACC   send-PST-3SM
         'The editor sent every author her article.'   (DAT > ACC)

     b. * sampaadaka avaLa lekhanavannu pratiyobba lekhanige kaLis-id-a
          editor   she-GEN article-ACC every   author-DAT send-PST-3SM
          'The editor sent every author her article.'   (* ACC < DAT)

These facts indicate that the accusative argument is higher than the dative in underlying structure, as in (9).

(9)

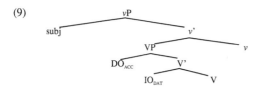

When the dative precedes the accusative, the surface order must be derived by moving the dative above the accusative, as in (10).

(10)

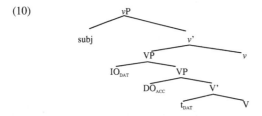

Because this movement creates new binding possibilities, we conclude that it must be A-movement (Mahajan 1990).

Benefactive ditransitives, however, show the opposite pattern, as shown in (11-12). Here the dative can bind into the accusative, independent of word order.

(11) a. sampaadaka pratiyondu lekhana-vannu adara lekhan-ige kaLis-i-**koTT**-a
          editor   every   article-ACC   it-GEN author-DAT send-PP-**BEN.PST**-3SM
          'The editor sent every article to its author.'   (ACC > DAT)

      b. * sampaadaka adar-a lekhan-ige pratiyondu lekhana-vannu kaLis-i-**koTT**-a
           editor   it-GEN author-DAT every   article-ACC send-PP-**BEN.PST**-3SM
           'The editor sent every article to its author.'   (* DAT < ACC)

But the accusative can bind into Dative only when the accusative comes first:

(12) a.   sampaadaka pratiyobba lekhan-ige avaL-a   lekhana-vannu kaLis-i-**koTT**-a
          editor   every   author-DAT she-GEN article-ACC send-PP-**BEN.PST**-3SM
          'The editor sent every author her article.'   (DAT > ACC)

   b.   sampaadaka avaL-a lekhana-vannu pratiyobba lekhan-ige kaLis-i-**koTT**-a
          editor   she-GEN article-ACC   every   author-DAT send-PP-BEN.PST-3SM
          'The editor sent every author her article.'   (ACC < DAT)

So, for the benefactive, the dative must be higher than the accusative in the underlying structure, (13), with the accusative-dative order derived by A-movement, (14).[3]

(13)
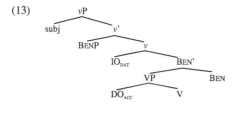

(14)
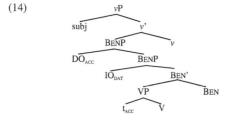

3.   Which structure does the reflexive ditransitive have?

Recall now the reflexive ditransitive (2a), repeated here as (15).

(15)   Hari tann-age pustaka-vannu kalisi-**koND**-a
         Hari self-DAT book-ACC   send-**VRM.PST**-3SM
         'Hari sent a book to himself.'

Here there is no benefactive morpheme, suggesting a nonbenefactive structure. But the dative precedes the accusative, suggesting a benefactive structure. So which is it?

---

[3] It would make no difference to the claims in this paper if we assigned Kannada benefactives the structure Pylkkänen (2002) gives her "low applicatives": [vP V [BenP IO [Ben' DO Ben]]]. According to Pylkkänen's diagnostics, the Kannada benefactive does count as a "low applicative" semantically, since it cannot apply to unergatives or statives. But Pylkkänen's syntax implies incorrectly that the BEN morpheme should precede the verb in Kannada, a head-final language. Hence we do not adopt it here.

The binding tests cannot be run for two reasons. First, the Kannada anaphor *tann-* is subject oriented and so cannot be bound by an accusative quantifier independent of the word order. In addition, because anaphors are full DPs by themselves, they cannot contain an additional (non-subject oriented) anaphor to be bound by an accusative quantifier. The semantic test, however, indicates that the reflexive ditransitives do not have a benefactive structure. (16a), for example, does not entail that Rashmi herself receives the cake that she makes. She may make it for herself but give it to her mother, as in (16b).

(16) a.   Rashmi tann-age keek-annu suTTu-koND-aLu
           Rashmi self-DAT cake-ACC prepare-VRM.PST-3SF
           'Rashmi made a cake for herself...'

     b.   adare ad-annu tann-a   taayi-ge   koTT-aLu
           but   it-ACC she-GEN mother-DAT give.PST-3SF
           '...but she gave it to her mother.'

We can therefore conclude that reflexive ditransitives have the plain ditransitive structure (9) and that the dative-accusative order of internal arguments is derived by A-movement of the dative to a higher position.

This now leaves us with the following question: Why can't there be a reflexive benefactive? Given that reflexive ditransitives are nonbenefactive, we need to determine what blocks locally bound anaphors from occurring in a benefactive structure. Before answering this question, however, we must first take three short digressions examining (a) the word-order of reflexive ditransitives; (b) the distrubtion of VRM; and, (c) the theory of DP-licensing developed in Lidz and Williams 2002.

4.   Word-order in reflexive ditransitives

As noted above, word-order is flexible in ditransitives but not in reflexive ditransitives. If the dative argument is a locally bound anaphor, the dative must precede the accusative, as in (17).

(17) a.   Hari tann-age pustaka-vannu kalisi-koND-a
           Hari self-DAT book-ACC   send-VRM.PST-3SM
           'Hari sent a book to himself.'

     b.   * Hari pustaka-vannu tann-age kalis (-koND / -id / -koTT) -a
           Hari book-ACC   self-DAT send (-VRM.PST / -PST / -BEN.PST) -3SM
           intended: 'Hari sent a book to himself.'

Having just concluded that (17a) is a plain ditransitive, we know it has the underlying structure (18), where the dative is lower than the accusative.

(18)

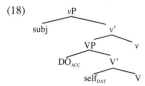

Evidently this configuration is ill-formed, since the dative anaphor cannot remain *in situ* and follow the accusative. Instead, raising is required, yielding the surface structure (19).

(19)

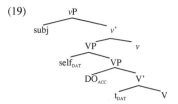

On the assumption that the anaphor-antecedent relation is an A-chain (Rizzi 1986, Reinhart and Reuland 1993, Lidz and Idsardi 1997, Lidz 1998, 2003), we infer that the anaphor-antecedent chain in (18) is ill-formed. By creating an A-chain that crosses an argument NP, minimality is violated. The anaphor-antecedent chain in (19), on the other hand, is well-formed, apparently because the dative anaphor adjoins to the same node that the accusative argument is attached to. The chain <subj, self$_{DAT}$> is well-formed because there are no arguments intervening between these links. Similarly, the chain <self$_{DAT}$, t$_{DAT}$> is well-formed because this chain does not *cross* the accusative DP. That is, the dative argument is adjoined to VP where it and the accusative DP are equidistant from the trace of the dative (May 1985, Chomsky 1986). In short, the obligatory dative-accusative order in reflexives follows from minimality considerations. The dative has to raise in order to avoid violating relativized minimality (Rizzi 1990). This locality property of anaphora chains will ultimately, in section 7, play a large role in explaining the incompatibility of reflexive and benefactive structures.

5.   VRM

Although the theory of VRM plays only a small role in this paper, it is important to specify precisely what this theory is. Descriptively speaking, VRM occurs on reflexive clauses (20) and also on certain anticausatives, such as (21).

(20) a.   Hari tann-annu hogaLi-**koLL**-utt-aane
          Hari self-ACC   praise-**VRM**-NPST-3SM
          'Hari praises himself.'

    b. *   Hari tann-annu hogaL-utt-aane
          Hari self-ACC   praise-NPST-3SM

(21) a.   gaali-ge   baagilu tere-du-**koND**-itu
             wind-DAT door   open-PP-**VRM.PST**-3SN
             'Because of the wind, the door opened'

      b.   (*gaali-ge)   baagil-u   terey-i-tu
             (*wind-DAT) door-NOM open-PST-3SN

When VRM occurs on anticausatives, it implies that the event had an external agent, even though no agent DP is present. Following this lead, Lidz (1998, 2003) proposes that VRM is licensed just when there is no DP in the specifier of agentive little-v, as indicated in (22) (cf. Embick 1998).

(22) VRM ⟷   there is no DP in a specifier of vP.

Reflexives are assimilated to this case through the theory of chain-formation. In effect, only the head and tail of an A-chain are visible to the morphological component. Consequently, when a raised subject is linked by chain to an anaphor, the trace of the subject in [spec, vP] is deleted, as in (23b).

(23) a.   [$_{TP}$ hari [$_{vP}$ ~~hari~~ [$_{VP}$ saw rashmi]]]   Chain: <hari, ~~hari~~>
      b.   [$_{TP}$ hari [$_{vP}$ [$_{VP}$ saw himself]]]   Chain <hari, himself>

[Spec, vP] is therefore empty, and VRM is licensed. This theory has been defended extensively in Lidz 1998, 2003 and interested readers are referred to these papers.

6.   C-locality and the licensing of DPs

In Lidz and Williams 2002, we introduced the relation of c-locality in (24).

(24) Y is <u>c-local</u> to X iff
         i) Y c-commands X
         ii) Every Z, such that Z c-commands X, and Z does not c-command Y, is a
             function over its sister.

C-locality can be understood in terms of function composability. When X is c-local to Y, then what intervenes between X and Y is a cascade of composable functions. The nodes c-commanding X, up to Y, are functions that could be composed, in consecutive hierarchical order, to form a single complex function over X.[4]

To get a feel for where c-locality will and will not obtain, compare the two trees in (25), where each node is paired with its semantic type. Arrows point from functions that c-command A to their arguments, and dotted lines connect functions that are composable.

---

[4] F can compose with G iff the range of G is the domain of F. By definition: COMPOSE (f,g) ≡ λx. f(g(x)).

(25) a.

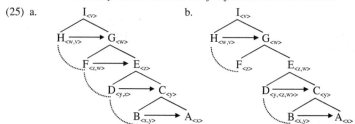

The two trees differ just in the types of the nodes F and D. F is a function over its sister in (25a) but not in (25b). In (25b), F is an argument of its sister, owing to the fact that D here is a two-place predicate.

As a result, node A enjoys broader c-locality relations in (25a) than in (25b). Every node that c-commands A in (25a) is a function over its sister, hence here A is c-local to all its c-commanders. This is not true in (25b). Here A is again c-local to B, D and F; but then c-locality is interrupted by F. Node A is not c-local to anything above F, i.e., it is not c-local to H, since F is not a function over its sister.

We use c-locality to define the domain of *in situ* Case licensing. We assume that Case is licensed *in situ* by the AGREE relation, which operates only over a c-local domain, as in (26):

(26)   Case by AGREE: X has Case in its base position iff X is c-local to a head Y and Y assigns Case.

Assuming that agentive little-*v* (v_{AG}) assigns accusative Case (Chomsky 1995), accusative case is licensed *in situ* just when the object DP is c-local to v_{AG}. DPs that are not c-local to v_{AG} are not licensed *in situ*, and must instead move to a specifier of a case assigning head (27).

(27)   Case by MOVE: X has Case if X is in a specifier of Y and Y assigns Case.

This movement is subject to Last Resort (Chomsky 1995), stated in (28), which permits Case-driven movement only for those DPs that would not have Case *in situ*. Importantly, we assume that A-movement is not bounded by c-locality, but rather by familiar conditions on A-movement, which are slightly looser.

(28)   Last Resort: X moves to check a feature iff failure to move would leave the feature unchecked.

6.1   Motivations for c-locality

The relation of c-locality provides a natural way to link syntactic licensing to the elementary relation of function to argument, even in a theory where objects are syntactically licensed not by their verb, but by some higher functional head. The original motivation for this relation, however, was not conceptual but empirical. In Lidz and Williams 2002, we showed that c-locality makes exactly the right distinction between resultatives and other constructions which are superficially similar. In particular, we showed that c-locality distinguishes resultatives from simple causatives and ECM constructions with respect to VRM. While VRM is possible in simple causatives and ECM constructions, it is not possible in reflexive resultatives:

(29) a.   Hari tann-annu chappatey-isi-koND-a
           Hari self-ACC flat-CAUS-VRM.PST-3SM
           'Hari flattened himself.'

     b.   Hari tann-annu puNyavantanendu nambi-koLL-utt-aane
           Hari self-ACC wealthy   believe-VRM-NPST-3SM
           'Hari believes himself to be wealthy.'

     c. * Hari tann-annu chappatey-aagi taTTi-koND-a
           Hari self-ACC flat-ADVL   hammer-VRM.PST-3SM
           Intended: 'Hari hammered himself flat.'

     d.   Hari tann-annu chappatey-aagi taTT-id-a
           Hari self-ACC flat-ADVL   hammer-PST-3SM
           'Hari hammered himself flat.'

We argued that this difference follows directly from the theory of Case just described, in which *in situ* case-licensing is possible only when the DP is c-local to its Case assigner. In simple causatives and ECM constructions, the accusative DP is c-local to its Case assigner, as illustrated in (30), where arrows point from functions that c-command the object DP to their arguments:[5]

(30) a.   causative:

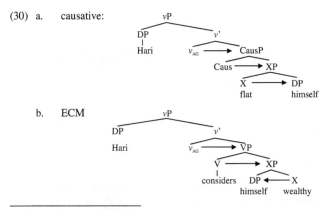

     b.   ECM

---

[5] Here we take v_{AG} to denote a function over its sister: $\lambda P\lambda x\lambda e.[AG(e)=x \ \& \ P(e)]$. Adopting the more conventional view—that v_{AG} combines with VP by "Event Identification" (Kratzer 1996), rather than Function Application—would have no effect on the present discussion.

c.   Resultatives

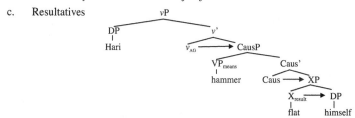

What distinguishes the object in (30c) from the objects in (30a-b) is c-locality. Whereas the DP objects in (30a-b) are c-local to v_{AG}, and so can get case *in situ*, the DP object in (30c) is not c-local to v_{AG} because the means predicate, *hammer*, is not a function over its sister. It is an argument of Caus', rather, since Caus denotes a two-place relation between the means and result predicates. Failure of c-locality forces this DP to raise in order to get Case. Now, given that VRM is licensed only when [spec, vP] is empty and given that raising of an object DP is forced in a resultative, it follows that VRM could never be licensed in a reflexive resultative. In order to check its Case feature, the reflexive object necessarily raises to [spec, vP], bleeding the environment for the insertion of VRM in v. See Lidz and Williams 2002 for further detail.

7.   Putting it all together

We are now in a position to answer the question of why reflexive benefactives are impossible. Recall that benefactives have the structure in (31).

(31)

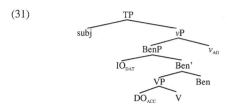

Here, the dative argument is introduced below v_{AG} but above the accusative argument. The dative c-commands the accusative but is not a function over its sister. Consequently, the accusative is not c-local to v_{AG}, its licenser, and so must move to [spec, vP] for Case, as in (32).

(32)

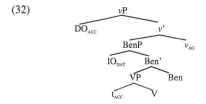

One consequence of this movement is that VRM will not be licensed, because [spec, vP] is now filled. So we can conclude that a benefactive structure could not possibly be morphologically marked with VRM. Yet what we learned above is not just that VRM is morphologically impossible in a benefactive but, more strictly, that local anaphora is incompatible with a benefactive structure.

This incompability also follows from the derivation in (31-32). Raising the direct object to [spec, vP] for Case creates precisely the configuration that, as we learned in section 4, makes the anaphora chain ill-formed. When the accusative argument raises, it interrupts the chain between the dative anaphor and its subject antecedent. As we saw with regard to examples (17a-b), we know that no DP can intervene between an anaphor and a clausemate antecedent without creating a minimality violating configuration (compare (32) to (18)). Thus, the requirement that the direct object receive Case by movement, a consequence of c-locality, cannot be satisfied if the indirect object is an anaphor. Movement for Case creates a minimality-violating configuration for the anaphor. In essence, reflexive benefactives are ungrammatical for precisely the same reason that a dative anaphor must precede the accusative argument in a nonbenefactive ditransitive.

8.   Conclusions

Finally, then, we have solved the complementarity puzzle. A reflexive benefactive structure is subject to two requirements that cannot be met at the same time. A dative anaphor must be able to form a minimal chain with its antecedent in subject position. But because of the c-locality condition on *in situ* Case assigment, the accusative argument, which originates below the dative, must raise in order to get Case. This raising induces a minimality violation in the anaphora chain. Thus, no benefactive structure with a dative anaphor can be derived. The complementarity between reflexive and benefactive morphology is simply a reflection of the fact that reflexive benefactives are underivable.

More generally, the analysis presented here provides further support for the framework of locality and Case developed in Lidz and Williams 2002. The licensing of DPs *in situ* is constrained by the c-locality relation, which is defined not strictly in syntactic terms but rather on the basis of function-argument relations. The link this theory posits between the function-argument relation and syntactic licensing is its central attraction. At the same time, it poses a clear challenge to the strict modularity of syntax and semantics often assumed in generative syntax.

9.   Residual complications

In this section, we consider two potential problems with the proposed (non)derivations of reflexive ditransitives. We show however that these are only apparent problems, leaving our analysis unaffected.

First, our explanation of the impossiblity of reflexive benefactives was based on the observation that the derivation (31-32) is impossible. This derivation fails due to the ill-formedness of the anaphora chain in (32), which is analogous to that in (18). But recall that (18) was saved by further movement of the anaphor, as in (19). This raises the question of whether the minimality violation in (32) could be averted by moving the dative anaphor past the raised direct object, yielding (33). This derivation would yield a structure in which the anaphor is local to its binder, and there is no VRM because [spec, *v*P] is filled. In this structure, the direct object would receive Case by movement, as before, but the minimality violation in (32) would be averted by moving the anaphor into the same domain as the raised object.

(33)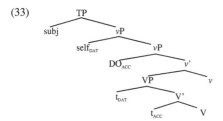

We suggest that this derivation is problematic because the subject starts out in [spec, *v*P], as shown in (34). Moving the anaphor, as proposed in (33/34), would therefore involve moving the anaphor past the trace of its antecedent, the subject. This move creates an environment of "Lethal Ambiguity" (McGinnis, to appear), essentially a violation of Rizzi's (1986) Chain Condition, and the derivation is ruled out. Thus, the minimality violation in (32) cannot be averted by subsequent movement of the anaphor, as this movement is also blocked.[6] So our conclusion remains safe: a reflexive benefactive has no grammatical derivation.

(34)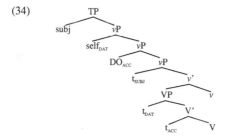

A second potential concern centers on the question of what counts as an intervener for the c-locality relation in an adjunction structure. Recall that to derive the obligatory dative-accusative word-order in reflexive (nonbenefactive) ditransitives, like (17a), we

---

[6] It is not difficult to think of cases of anaphors raising past (traces of) their antecedents, as in (i):

(i) Himself, John seems to like; but his wife, he clearly doesn't.

Such examples, however, involve topicalization, which, unlike the movement proposed here, is A-bar movement, and is therefore expected to show different properties. Moreover, the problem with (34) is not just moving the anaphor past the trace of its antecedent, but into the same XP. Thus, any other examples of anaphors raising past (traces of) their antecedents would have to be examined closely to determine whether they represent actual counterexamples to the claims made here.

required the dative anaphor to adjoin to VP in order to avert a potential minimality violation, as in (19), repeated here as (35). One might suppose that this adjunction would
therefore disrupt the c-locality relation between v_{AG} and the accusative DO, forcing
movement of the DO to [spec, vP], and thus—so it may seem—inducing a new minimality violation.

(35)

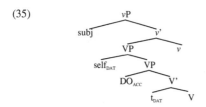

But this worry is dispelled by attention to our definition of c-locality, repeated here.

(36)   Y is <u>c-local</u> to X iff
        i) Y c-commands X
        ii) Every Z, such that Z c-commands X and Z does not c-command Y, is a
            function over its sister.

Crucially, Z is an intervener only if it does not c-command the higher element in the c-
locality relation. That is, if Y and Z in (36) are in a mutual c-command relation, then Z
does not intervene between Y and other things that Y c-commands (cf. May 1985, Chomsky 1986, Frank and Vijayshanker 2001, Bobaljik 2002). In the structure in (35), the first
branching node dominating the dative argument is v' (only one segment of VP dominates
the dative and so VP does not dominate it). Consequently v_{AG} and the dative argument are
in a mutual c-command relation and so the latter does not intervene between v_{AG} and the
direcct object. Thus, v_{AG} is c-local to the direct object, and the direct object can therefore
check Case *in situ*.

References

Barss, A. and H. Lasnik. 1986. A note on anaphora and the double object construction.
        Linguistic Inquiry 17: 347–354.
Bhat, D.N.S. 1979. Vectors in Kannada. *International Journal of Dravidian Linguistics*
        8.2: 300–309.
Bleam, T. 2001. Properties of the double object construction in Spanish. *Proceedings of
        LSRL* 31.
Bobaljik, J.D. 2002. A-chains at the PF-interface: Copies and "covert" movement. *Natu-
        ral Language and Linguistic Theory* 20(2): 197–267.
Chomsky, N. 1986. *Barriers*. Cambridge, MA: MIT Press.
Chomsky, N. 1995. *The Minimalist Program*. Cambridge, MA: MIT Press.
Embick, D. 1998. *Voice and the Interfaces of Syntax*. Ph.D. dissertation, University of

Pennsylvania.

Frank, R. and K. Vijay-shanker, 2001. Primitive C-command. *Syntax* 4(3): 164–204.

Green, G. 1974. *Semantics and Syntactic Regularity*. Bloomington: Indiana University Press.

Harley, H. 2000. Possession and the double object construction. Unpublished ms. University of Pennsylvania.

Kratzer, A. 1996. Severing the External Argument from its Verb. In J. Rooryk and L. Zaring (eds.), *Phrase Structure and the Lexicon*, 109–138. Dordrecht: Kluwer.

Lidz, J. 1998. Valency in Kannada: Evidence for Interpretive Morphology. *U.Penn Working Papers in Linguistics* 5.2: 37–63.

Lidz, J. 2002. Two Structures for Kannada Ditransitives. Paper presented at *South Asian Languages Analysis Roundtable* 22.

Lidz, J. 2003. Causation and Reflexivity in Kannada. In V. Dayal and A. Mahajan (eds.), *Clause Structure in South Asian Languages*, 93–130. Dordecht: Kluwer.

Lidz, J. and W. Idsardi. 1998. Chains and Phono-Logical Form. *U.Penn Working Papers in Linguistics* 5.1: 109–125.

Lidz, J. and A. Williams. 2002. Reflexivity and Resultatives. In L. Mikkelsen and C. Potts (eds.), *WCCFL 21 Proceedings*, 250–263. Somerville, MA: Cascadilla Press.

Mahajan, A. 1990. *The A/A-bar Distinction and Movement Theory*. Ph.D. Dissertation, MIT.

May, R. 1985. *Logical Form*. Cambridge, MA: MIT Press.

McGinnis, M. to appear. Lethal Ambiguity. *Linguistic Inquiry*.

Oerhle, R. 1976. *The grammatical status of the English dative alternation*. Ph.D. Dissertation, MIT.

Pylkkänen, L. 2002. *Introducing Arguments*. Ph.D. Dissertation, MIT.

Reinhart, T. and E. Reuland. 1993. Reflexivity. *Linguistic Inquiry* 24: 657–720.

Rizzi, L. 1986. On chain formation. In H. Borer (ed.), *The syntax of pronominal clitics: Syntax and Semantics 19*, 65–95. New York: Academic Press.

Rizzi, L. 1990. *Relativized Minimality*. Cambridge, MA: MIT Press.

Sridhar, S.N. 1990. *Kannada*. London: Routledge.

Jeffrey Lidz
Northwestern University
Department of Linguistics
2016 Sheridan Rd
Evanston, IL 60208

jlidz@northwestern.edu

Alexander Williams
University of Pennsylvania
Department of Linguistics
619 Williams Hall
Philadelphia, PA 19104

alexand3@ling.upenn.edu

Scope marking with adjunct clauses: new arguments for Dayal's approach

Anikó Lipták

ULCL, Leiden University

1. Introduction

Since the early 1980's, scope marking (or *partial wh-movement*) is on the generative research agenda for many languages, including German (van Riemsdijk 1983), Romani (McDaniel 1989), Hindi (Mahajan 1990), Hungarian (Marácz 1990, Horvath 1995), just to mention the most well-studied ones. In this paper I present new data from the realm of scope marking constructions in a couple of languages, first of all, Hungarian.[1] The data to be presented here have high theoretical significance, as they provide primary and unambiguous evidence of Dayal's (1994, 2000) *indirect dependency* analysis for scope marking.

The empirical novelty supporting Dayal's treatment of scope marking constructions comes from constructions involving embedded adjunct clauses: relative and noun-associate clauses, which, similarly to well-studied cases of argumental embedded clauses in languages with scope marking, can license embedded *wh*-items with matrix interpretation. It will be shown that unlike argumental embedded clauses, which in principle can lend themselves to various analyses, the newly discovered adjunct scope marking can only be analysed along the lines of Dayal's proposal.

The article is structured in the following way. Section 2 introduces scope marking constructions from a bird's eye view and lists the characteristic properties of these constructions, with a section on Hungarian scope marking in particular. The novel data will be introduced on the basis of Hungarian in section 3. Section 4 provides a brief crosslinguistic overview on the availability of similar data in other languages. The theoretical impact as well as the subsequent analysis of adjunct scope marking data will be handled

---

[1] The research reported here was financed by NWO (*Netherlands Organisation for Scientific Research*), whose support is greatly acknowledged. I owe gratitude to Malte Zimmermann for his help with the semantics part (section 5), and to Crit Cremers, Veneeta Dayal, István Kenesei for their comments on previous versions of this paper, as well as to Chris Reingtes for stylistic remarks. All remaining errors are mine. For a more detailed version of this paper, see Lipták (to appear).

Keir Moulton and Matthew Wolf (eds.): Proceedings of NELS 34,
Stony Brook University: 405 – 423. GLSA, Amherst.

in section 5. It will be shown that no existing account apart from Dayal (1994, 2000) could account for these data. Section 6 summarizes the findings.

2.   Scope marking phenomena: properties and explananda

2.1.   Properties of scope marking

As illustration of scope marking, consider a run-of-the-mill example for this sentence type from German together with the answer it triggers:

(1)   **Was**$_1$ denkt   sie   [*wen*$_1$ Fritz t$_1$ eingeladen   hat]?
        what   thinks   she   whom   Fritz   invited   has
        'Who does she think Fritz invited?'
(1A)   Anna.
        'Anna.'

As (1) illustrates, scope marking involves a bi-clausal structure, with one *wh*-item in each clause. The *wh*-item in the matrix clause is referred to as the *scope marker* (represented in bold), and the one in the embedded clause as the contentful *wh*-phrase (in italics).

A question like (1) is at first sight equivalent to a question with long *wh*-extraction (as the translation also indicates), which shows that in the particular example in (1), the matrix *wh*-item (*was*) is a placeholder element, while the embedded *wh*-item (*wen*) is what the question is about.[2] Looking at scope marking constructions crosslinguistically, the following properties appear to characterize them:

(2)   *Characteristic properties of scope marking constructions*

(i)   There is a scope marker *wh*-item in the superordinate clause.
(ii)   Any *wh*-item can occur in the embedded *wh*-position (*who, why, which concept, how many unripe coconuts*, etc).
(iii)   The answer given to a scope marking question specifies the embedded *wh*-item (cf. ex. (1A)).
(iv)   Scope marking is unbounded; scope markers are usually spelled out in every intermediate clause, as illustrated in (3):

(3)   **Was** denkt sie   [**was** Hans gesagt hat   [*wen* Fritz eingeladen hat]]?
        what thinks she   what Hans said has   whom Fritz invited has
        'Who does she think Hans said Fritz has invited?'

---

[2] More detailed investigation (Herburger 1994, Lahiri 2002) shows that the parallel with long extraction is not absolute.

(v)   The embedded clause hosting the contentful *wh*-item cannot be a *selected* question (matrix predicates like *ask* are not allowed), cf. (4):

(4)   ***Was** fragt sie [$_{<+wh>}$ *wen* Fritz eingeladen hat]?
        what asks she   whom Fritz invited has
        (lit.) 'Who does she ask Fritz invited?'

Properties (i)-(v) will come handy in section 3, where new instances of scope marking constructions will be identified with the help of these.[3]

Scope marking phenomena present theoretically interesting puzzles that are not easy to explain. The most important one of these concerns the syntactic and interpretive relation between the scope marker and the embedded question word. Under the general assumption that only *wh*-items with matrix scope get answered, the fact that the embedded *wh*-item in scope marking constructions is filled in by the answer suggests that the embedded *wh*-item has matrix scope. However, its overt position does not reflect this: it is found in the embedded clause. Various solutions have been proposed to resolve this issue, arguing either for LF-raising of the embedded *wh*-item or the whole embedded clause (via expletive replacement) or for an underlying semantic mechanism that ensures matrix scope for the embedded question. The details of the various proposals will be spelled out in section 5.

2.2. Hungarian scope marking: the standard data

Hungarian scope marking constructions fall into two basic types: *sequential* and *subordinated* scope marking constructions. Sequential scope marking is the most frequently occurring type of scope marking among native speakers. According to my survey, about 25% of Hungarian speakers prefer these constructions to subordinated ones. Sequential scope marking involves two juxtaposed, prosodically and syntactically autonomous clauses, whose order is freely reversible. For illustration, see (5a) and (5b):

(5) a. **Mit**   gondolsz?   *Ki*   nyeri   a versenyt?
         what-ACC   think-2SG   who   win-3SG   the competition-ACC
     b. *Ki*   nyeri   a versenyt?   **Mit**   gondolsz?
         who   win-3SG   the competition-ACC   what-ACC   think-2SG
         'What do you think? Who will win the competition?'

---

[3] Other properties that characterize scope marking constructions, which I do not further discuss in this paper, are subject to variation across languages. In German or Hungarian, for example, the scope marker *wh*-item is overtly fronted, while in Hindi, it can also stay in-situ. Similarly, yes/no questions are fine in the embedded clause in Hindi, but not in German or Hungarian. Factive verbs can be matrix predicates in Hindi and to some extent in Hungarian, but never in German.

The most frequent predicates ocurring in the "matrix" clause of these constructions are: *gondol* "think", *tud* "know", *hall* "hear", *mond* "say", *szeretne* "would like", *akar* "want", *számít* "count on", *ajánl* "recommend", *javasol* "advise", *jósol* "predict".

Subordinated scope marking differs from non-subordinated ones in that it clearly involves syntactic subordination. In Hungarian embedded argumental clauses subordination is indicated by the presence of *hogy* "that", a finite complementizer (available both in indicative and interrogative clauses). As expected, the order of the clauses is not reversible in this case:

(6)   a.   **Mitől**   fél   Mari, hogy *ki*   lesz   az igazgató?
           what-FROM   fear-3SG Mari that   who   be-FUT.3SG the director
           (lit.) 'What does Mari fear that who will be the director?'
      b.   *Hogy *ki*   lesz   az igazgató,   **mitől** fél   Mari?
           that   who   be-FUT.3SG the director   what-FROM fear-3SG Mari

A typical answer to the scope marking question in (6a) is (6A):

(6A) **Attól**,   hogy   Péter.
      that-FROM   that   Péter-NOM
      '(Mari fears that it will be) Péter.'

The characteristic intonation pattern of (6a) is shown in (6'):

(6') | 'Mitől fél Mari | □ hogy `ki` lesz az igazgató? |[4]

Unlike in sequential scope marking, yes/no questions are not allowed in subordinated scope marking. The matrix clause can be negated to some extent, subject to individual variation and choice of the predicate. Subordinated scope marking can occur in many environments. Both response-stance and non-stance predicates can take part in this pattern: *elfelejt* "forget", *emlékezik* "remember", *észrevesz* "notice", *rájön* "find out", *megbán* "regret", *említ* "mention", *fél* "fear", *megesküszik* "swear", *megakadályoz* "block", *(meg)jósol* "predict", *kihirdet* "make public". Similarly, predicates taking subject clauses: *zavar* "bother", *kiderül* "turn out" occur with this pattern.

Hungarian scope marking constructions as noted by Horváth (1995, 1997, 1998, 2000) occur both with argumental (object and subject) embedded clauses as well as with adverbial ones. Subject and adverbial clauses are illustrated in (7) and (8):

(7)   **Mi**   zavarta   Marit   [hogy *kinek*   telefonáltál]?
      what   bothered-3SG Mari-ACC   that   who-DAT   phoned-2SG

---

[4] Symbols are taken from Varga (2002): | = edge of intonational phrase; □ = pause; ` = full fall major stress; ' = half-fall major stress

(lit.) 'What bothered Mari that you phoned whom?'

(7A)   **Az,**   hogy Péternek.
        that   that Péter-DAT
        'That I phoned Péter.'

(7') | **'Mi** zavarta Marit | □ hogy `kinek telefonáltál | ?

(8)   **Miért** vagy   dühös   [mert   *kivel*   találkoztál]?
       what-FOR be-2SG   angry   because who-WITH   met-2SG
       (lit.) 'Why are you angry because you met whom?'

(8A)   **Azért,**   mert Péterrel.
        that-FOR   because Péter-WITH
        'Because I met Péter.'

(8') | **'Miért** vagy dühös | □ mert `kivel találkoztál | ?

The common property characterizing both argumental and adverbial embedded clauses in scope marking constructions is the occurrence of a pronominal associate *az* "that" in declarative contexts (i.e. the answer pattern) and *mi* "what" in interrogative contexts, the latter functioning as the scope marker.

3.   New cases of scope marking: adjunct clauses embedded under NP/DPs in Hungarian

The previous section concerned itself with the various types of scope marking constructions that have hitherto been mentioned in the previous literature. The present section shows that subordinate scope marking has a much wider empirical base than previously recognized: it occurs with relative and noun-associate clauses as well, which have NP/DP scope markers. These will be introduced in sections 3.1. and 3.2. in turn.

3.1.   Scope marking with relative clauses

Relative clauses in Hungarian can be headed relatives or free relatives. The type of relative clauses that are important for purposes of illustrating scope marking data are the headed restrictive relatives, which can be either headed by a pronominal *az* "that" as in (9) or by a full NP/DP as in (10). Note that both relatives are extraposed, which is indicated by coindexation:

(9)   [$_{DP}$ **Az** [t$_i$]]   megy át   a vizsgán   [aki   20 pontot   szerez]$_i$.
      that   go-3SG PV   the exam-ON   who-REL 20 point-ACC score-3SG
      'The person who scores 20 points passes the exam.'

(10)   [$_{DP}$ **Az a**   **diák** [t$_i$]]   megy át   a vizsgán
       that   the   student   go-3SG PV   the exam-ON
       [aki   20 pontot   szerez]$_i$.
       who-REL   20 point-ACC   score-3SG
       'The student who scores 20 points passes the exam.'

When scope marking occurs with relative clauses, we find two *wh*-elements: the embedded relative clause contains a *wh*-item and the head of the relative clause must be or must
contain a *wh*-phrase. In these examples we are dealing with two questions: the matrix
question ranges over individuals (*ki* "who" or *melyik diák* "which student") and the embedded question ranges over the number of points (*hány pontot* "how many points-ACC").
For illustration, consider the following examples with their corresponding answers.

(11)   [DP **Ki** [t$_i$]]   megy át a vizsgán   [aki   *hány pontot*   szerez]$_i$?
       who   go-3SG PV the exam-ON who-REL how many point-ACC score-3SG
       (lit.) 'Who$_i$, who$_i$ scores how many points, passes the exam?'
       (intended) 'How many points does one have to score to pass the exam?'
(11A) [DP **Az** [t$_i$]]   [aki   *20 pontot*   szerez]$_i$.   /*Mari.
       that   who-REL 20 point-ACC score-3SG   /Mari
       'Who(ever) scores 20.'   /'Mari.'
(12)   [DP **Melyik diák** [t$_i$]] megy   át   a vizsgán
       which student   go-3SG PV   the exam-ON
       [aki   *hány pontot*   szerez]$_i$?
       who-REL   how many point-ACC   score-3SG
       (lit.) 'Which student$_i$, who$_i$ scores how many points, passes the exam?'
       (intended) 'How many points does a student have to score to pass the exam?'
(12A) [DP **Az a diák** [t$_i$]]   [aki   20 pontot szerez]$_i$.   /*Mari.
       that the student   who-REL   20 point-ACC score-3SG   / Mari
       'The student who scores 20 points.'   / 'Mari.'

As we can see, the interpretation of these questions is clearly reflected by the particular
answers they trigger: the answer necessarily has to specify the embedded question, i.e.
the number of points that need to be scored for passing the exam. An answer naming particular individuals who pass the exam is not satisfactory.

The intonation contour (at least one of the possible intonation contours) of these complex constructions is parallel to that of argumental subordinated scope marking constructions, as was illustrated in (6'/7'/8') above:

(11'/12') | '**Melyik diák/'ki** megy át a vizsgán, | □ aki `*hány pontot* szerez? |

The constructions in (11)-(12) comply with all criteria we identified in (2) as defining
properties of scope marking. There is a scope marker (*ki, melyik diák*; property (i)); the
choice of the embedded *wh*-phrase is free (property (ii)); the question is answered by
providing a value for the embedded *wh*-item (property (iii), cf. (11A),(12A)). The relation is unbounded, it can involve multiple layers of embedding (property iv):

(13)   **Melyik diák**   megy át   a vizsgán,   [aki   *milyen könyvből* tanul

which student go-3SG PV   the exam-ON who-REL what book-FROM study-3SG
[amit   *ki*   írt]]?
what-REL.ACC who   wrote-3SG
(lit.) 'Which student$_i$, who$_i$ studies from what kind of book$_j$, that$_j$ who wrote,
passes the exam?'

The ban on selected interrogative subclauses (property (v)) is satisfied vacuously, since
relative clauses are never selected to be interrogative. In fact, they can never contain a
wh-item in any construction except in the construction under investigation here. If the
matrix clause was not an interrogative clause, the relative clause would fail to license a
question:

(14) ***Az** megy   át   a vizsgán   [aki   *hány pontot*   szerez]?
      that go-3SG   PV   the exam   who-REL how many point-ACC score-3SG
      (lit.) 'Who(ever) scores how many points, passes the exam.'

The matrix interrogative clause has to comply with one requirement: the *wh*-phrase in it
has to either correspond to the *head* of the embedded relative clause or ask for a property
that is also spelled out in the relative clause. The following two examples illustrate these
points:

(15) ***Hány diák$_i$**   megy át   a vizsgán
      how many student   go-3SG PV   the exam-ON
      [aki$_i$ *hány pontot*   szerez]?
      who-REL   how many point-ACC   get-3SG
      (lit.) 'How many students$_i$, who$_i$ score how many points, pass the exam?'
(16) **Kinek$_i$**   a   **diákja**   megy át   a vizsgán,
      who-DAT   the student-POSS.3SG   go-3SG PV   the exam-ON
      [aki$_i$ *hány pontot*   szerez]?
      who-REL   how many point-ACC   get-3SG
      (lit.) 'Whose$_i$ student$_j$, who$_{i/*j}$ scores how many points, passes the exam?'
      (intended) 'How many points does a teacher have to score to pass a student?'
      /'*How many points does a student have to score to pass the exam?'

In (15) we see that although the matrix and the embedded *wh*-phrases are identical in
meaning (*hány* "how many"), the sentence fails to be interpretable, because the relative
clause is not construed as a numeral modifier of students. In (16), the relative clause has
to be interpreted as a modifier over the smallest *wh*-phrase, *kinek* "who-DAT", and not the
larger phrase *kinek a diákja* "whose student-NOM", even though the resulting meaning is
pragmatically unlikely. This shows that in case the matrix *wh*-phrase can be found in a
referentially independent larger NP/DP, the relative clause in scope marking has to associate with the smallest *wh*-phrase possible, as a scope marker.

To summarize, this section showed beyond doubt that the constructions in (11)-(12) instantiate an example of scope marking, namely scope marking with an adjunct embedded clause. The semantic and intonational properties of these clauses are exactly parallel to well-established cases of scope marking with argumental embedded clauses. The scope marker is (or is found within) the head of relativization, and the embedded clause is contained inside the relative clause. The answer necessarily has to fill in the embedded *wh*-variable.

3.2. Scope marking with noun-associate clauses

In Hungarian, the behaviour of relative clauses in scope marking is fully paralleled by adjunct noun-associate clauses in Hungarian. Noun-embedded clauses have been argued to be of two kinds: arguments or adjuncts (Kenesei 1992). Scope marking with adjunct noun-associate clauses are grammatical for all speakers of Hungarian, while argumental embedded clauses show some variation: many informants found them just as good as adjunct embedded clauses; several of them, however, found them degraded or ungrammatical. Therefore, in the following I concentrate on adjunct noun-associate clauses only.

Scope marking with noun-associate adjunct clauses is exemplified in (17):

(17)   **Milyen üzenetet**ᵢ   kapott Péter   [hogy *hova*   kell   mennie]ᵢ?
        what   message-ACC   got-3SG Péter   that   where need go-INF-3SG
        (lit.) 'What message, that he has to go where, did Péter get?'

(17A) Péter **azt   az   üzenetet**ᵢ   kapta
       Péter that   the   message-ACC   got-3SG
       [hogy a rendőrségre   kell   mennie]ᵢ
       that   the police-TO   need   go-INF-3SG
       'Péter got a message that he has to go to the police force.'

Just like with relative clauses, the matrix *wh*-phrase is a "what kind" question that asks for the same kind of property that is also expressed by the embedded clause. As far as intonation is concerned, these sentences are most frequently pronounced with the same intonation contour as argumental or relative clauses above:

(17') |'**Milyen üzenetet** kapott Péter | □ hogy `*hova* kell mennie? |

(17) also complies with all criteria for scope marking listed in (2) above: namely (i) there is a scope marker (*milyen üzenetet* "what message-ACC"); (ii) the choice of the embedded *wh*-phrase is free; (iii) the required answer specifies the embedded *wh*-phrase. The unbounded nature of the construction (property iv) is illustrated in (18):

(18)   **Milyen üzenetet**   kaptál, [hogy *melyik állítást*   ellenőrizzük

what message-ACC got-2SG   that   which claim-ACC   check-IMP-1PL
[hogy *melyik üzem*   nyereséges]]?
that   which factory profitable
(lit.) 'What message, that we should check which claim, that which factory is
profitable, did you get?'

The nominal with which the embedded clauses are associated has to be a "what kind" *wh*-phrase in each clause. The ban on selected <+wh>-clauses (property v) is complied with as well. If the embedding noun requires a question, like the noun *kérdés* 'question', scope marking is unavailable:

(19)   **Milyen kérdéssel** foglalkoztak [$_{CP+wh}$hogy *mire* kell a pénz]?
        what question-WITH dealt-3PL   that what-ON need the money
        (lit.) 'What question, that they need the money for what, did they discuss?'

It appears then that adjunct noun-associate clauses, just like relative clauses, are capable of hosting a *wh*-phrase with matrix interpretation as long as the nominal they are associated with is a "what kind" *wh*-expression. In other words, these constructions show the same properties as standard cases of scope marking, and therefore should be considered as such.

4.   The crosslinguistic scene of adjunct scope marking

The adjunct scope marking data presented in the previous section are not unique to Hungarian. My initial investigations about a small set of other languages, among which both languages with and without scope marking revealed that adjunct-type scope marking constructions are found in a *subset* of the languages that have standard argumental scope marking constructions.

The languages under investigation were Moroccan Arabic, Bavarian, Mandarin Chinese, Danish, Dutch, English, Finnish, Flemish, Frisian, German, Greek, Hindi, Italian, Japanese, Serbian, Slovenian, Spanish. Out of these languages, adjunct scope marking constructions parallel to the Hungarian facts occur in Frisian and in some Slavic languages (Serbian and Slovenian).[5,6] These languages are known to have subordinate scope

---

[5] An exception to this generalizaiton is Japanese, which does not exhibit standard scope marking constructions, but still allows for *wh*-items in relative clauses and noun-associate clauses (Naoki Fukui, Akira Watanabe, pc.) of the scope marking type discussed in this paper:

(i)   anata-wa   [$_{NP}$[doko-ni ikeba ii ka]   to-yuu doo-yuu messeezi]-o uketorimasita-ka?
       you-top   where-to go should Q   that   which   message-ACC received Q
       'Which/what kind of message did you get, where do you have to go?'

Note, however, that at least to some speakers, (i) sounds "redundant", compared to the more natural (ii), in which an in-situ *wh*-expression is found in an CNP island, a grammatical stategy for arguments (Lasnik and Saito 1984):

(ii)   anata-wa [$_{NP}$[doko-ni ikeba ii ka] to-yuu   messeezi]-o uketorimasita-ka?
       you-top where-to go should Q   that   message-ACC received   Q

marking (see Hiemstra 1986 for Frisian, and Golden 1995, Stepanov 2000 for Slavic). The following two examples illustrate noun-associate clauses in Frisian (20) and Slovenian (21) respectively:

(20)   **Wat** boadskip hast   krigen, *wêr*'tst   hinne moatst?
       what message have-2SG   got   where-that-2SG   to   must
       (lit.) 'What message, where do you have to appear, did you get?'
(21)   **Kakšno sporočilo** si   dobil, *kam* da   moraš iti   jutri?
       what message   aux   get-PTC where that   must   go   tomorrow
       (lit.) 'What message, where do you have to appear, did you get?'

Scope marking with relative clauses is illustrated in the following examples. (22) is a Frisian and (23) is a Slovenian case. It is also visible in these examples that while the examples above with noun-associate clauses involve overt *wh*-movement to Spec,CP, the *wh*-phrases in relative clauses stay in situ:

(22)   ?**Hokker studint** komt dertroch,   dy't   *hoefolle punten* hat?
       which student comes through   REL-that   how-many points has
       (lit.) 'Which student, who scores how many points, passes the exam?'
(23)   **Koji student** prolazi ispit,   koji dobije   *koliko poena*?
       which student passes exam   which gets   how many points?
       (lit.) 'Which student, who scores how many points, passes the exam?'

   Unlike Frisian and Slovenian, German and Hindi do not seem to have adjunct scope marking (ex. (24/25) and (26/27) respectively):[7,8]

(24)   *****Welcher Student** besteht die Prüfung,   der *wieviele Punkte* erzielt?
       which   student passes the exam   who how many points achieves
       (lit.) 'Which student, who scores how many points, passes the exam?'
(25)   *****Was für eine Nachricht** hast du bekommen, *wo* du erscheinen musst?
       what for   a message have you   got   where you appear-INF must
       (lit.) 'What message, where do you have to appear, did you get?'

'Did you receive a message as to where you should go?'
   [6] The Frisian data are based on the judgements of Siebren Dijk, Willem Visser and Henk Wolf; the Slovenian ones on the judgements of Franc Marušič, Tatjana Marvin and Rok Žaucer.
   [7] While adjunct scope marking is clearly ungrammatical in Hindi, German has noun-associate adjunct scope marking constructions which are quite acceptable for some speakers:
(i)   ?Was ist dein Rat,   wen wir um Hilfe bitten sollten?
       what is your advice   who we for help ask   should
       (lit.) 'What is your advice, whom should we ask for help?'
   [8] The German examples are due to Anne Breitbarth, Agnes Jäger, Peter Gallmann, Kleanthes Grohmann, Martin Salzmann, Chris Reingtes, Kristina Riedel, Kathrin Würth; the Hindi ones to Rajesh Bhatt and Veneeta Dayal.

(26) ***kaun-saa chaatra**   [jo kitne points haasil kar-egaa] prize jiit-egaa?
      which   student   REL how-many   achieve do-Fut win-FUT
      (lit.) 'Which student, who scores how many points, will win the prize?'
(27) ***unhone**   kaun-sii afvaah failaa dii   [ki *kaun* garbhvati hai].
      they   which rumor spread   that who pregnant is
      (lit.) 'Which rumour, who is pregnant, did they spread?'

Even languages in which adjunct scope marking is ruled out as an ordinary interrogative allow for these constructions to be used in special contexts, most frequently as echo questions or in the special context of quiz-questions, like the following English example:

(28) Which actor, who was nominated for Oscar for which film in 1965, died in 1980?

Adjunct scope marking therefore seems to be a crosslinguistically well-attested phenomenon.

5. The analysis of adjunct scope marking

Scope marking constructions have been analysed along the lines of two general apporaches: the *direct* and the *indirect* dependency approaches. The two approaches differ in the kind of relationship they ascribe to the embedded *wh*-item and the matrix scope marker. In the direct dependency, the embedded *wh*-item directly replaces the scope marker at LF, thereby gaining matrix scope. The indirect dependency approaches argue that there is no direct link between the scope marker and the embedded *wh*-expression, but there is a *syntactic* or a *semantic* link between the scope marker and the embedded clause. In this section I briefly sketch each approach and show whether or not it suits the newly discovered cases of Hungarian scope marking. As it turns out, the direct dependency approach or the indirect syntactic dependency approach cannot account for these. The only feasible account is the *semantic indirect* dependency account. I conclude this section by sketching the analysis of adjunct scope marking, extending Dayal's analysis.

5.1. Direct dependency approach

According to the advocates of the *direct dependency* approach (van Riemsdijk 1983, McDaniel 1989, Cheng 2000, among others) the embedded *wh*-item is directly linked to the matrix *wh*-item in the syntax and semantics, via LF-expletive replacement of the sort well-known from *there*-expletive constructions. The scope marker is an expletival place-holder for the embedded *wh*-item in the main clause:

(29) S-str [$_{CP+wh}$ **was**   [$_{CP-wh}$ *wh-phrase*   [$_{IP}$ ... t$_i$ ...]]]
      LF   [$_{CP+wh}$ *wh-phrase*   [$_{CP-wh}$ t$_i$ [$_{IP}$ ... t$_i$ ...]]]

The general unavailability of this approach to the cases of Hungarian scope mark-ing under discussion can easily be seen from the fact that these constructions constitute islands for extraction (CNPC):

(30)   *Hány pontot$_i$ megy   át   a vizsgán   [aki t$_i$ szerez]?
        how many points-ACC go-3SG PV   the exam-ON   who-REL score-3SG
        (intended) 'How many points does one have to score to pass the exam?'

The same has been noticed about subject clauses and adverbial clauses as well (Horvath 1995): scope marking, unlike long extraction, is possible across subject and adjunct is-lands (CED-effects). This militates against an analysis in terms of LF-long extraction.

5.2.   The syntactic indirect dependency approach

In contrast to the direct dependency approach, the *indirect dependency* approaches posit an indirect relationship between the *wh*-items: it is argued that the scope marker is di-rectly linked to the whole embedded clause.

There are two types of ideas about what provides the link between the scope marker and the embedded clause: in some analyses the link is syntactic, in others it is semantic in nature. In this section I briefly review the syntactic accounts. Apart from Mahajan (1990) and Fanselow & Mahajan (2000), the extant analysis of Hungarian, Horvath (1995, 1997, 1998, 2000), belongs to this type of approach as well. In the following short exposition, I am only concerned with Horvath's analysis.

In Horvath's analysis, the scope marker is a (*wh*-)pronominal anticipatory pro-noun, generated in A-position (AgrP in Horvath 1997); associated with the embedded CP proposition, bearing the case that is assigned to the CP and which the CP cannot carry due to the case resistance principle (Stowell 1981). In scope marking constructions, just as in any case of clausal subordination, the subordinated CP needs to "meet" its case be-fore the end of the derivation (to satisfy Full Interpretation). To achieve this, the CP has to adjoin the sentential pronominal at LF:

(31)   [$_{CP}$ [$_{FocP}$ *mi*$_{+case}$ [$_{AgrP}$ t$_j$ [$_{CP}$ [$_{FocP}$ *wh-phrase$_i$*   [$_{IP}$... t$_i$ ...]]]]]]

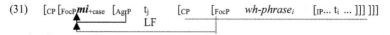

The LF movement step of clausal pied-piping is futher restricted to cases where the em-bedded CP and the sentential expletive *match* in *wh*-features.[9]

---

[9] The scope marker is a <+wh> item, which then requires the embedded clause to have a matching <+wh> feature as well. This <+wh> feature will have to come from the embedded *wh*-item (through perco-lation), since in scope marking constructions the embedded clause is never selected to be a question (see (4) above), and consequently it does not possess any inherent <+wh>-feature. After <+wh>-feature transmission from the *wh*-item onto the embedded CP, the *wh*-item looses its *wh*-hood, and its operator nature. As a "disarmed" *wh*-item, it does not cause any violation of the *Wh*-criterion.

The right interpretation of scope marking constructions (i.e. a meaning similar to long *wh*-questions) comes about due to the LF CP-movement step to the matrix explative, the result of which is that the whole embedded CP, and in that the embedded *wh*-item acquires matrix scope:

(32) $[_{CP+wh} [_{CP+wh} wh_{i+wh} [_{C'} C_{-wh} [_{IP} ... t_i ...]]]$-**mi** $[_{AgrP} t_j ...]]$

Although other syntactic indirect approaches are slightly different in their techni-cal apparatus, the treatment of the matrix *wh*-element as a sentential explative is inherent and crucial to all of them.

This is also the very reason why these accounts do not suit the newly presented data of adjunct scope marking. Adjunct scope marking does not lend itself to any analysis along the syntactic indirect dependency line of approach. As these accounts are crucially based on an *expletive replacement* step, they need to assume that the scope markers are *expletives*. While this is certainly an a priori possible stand for the analysis of embedded clauses that combine with a uniform pronoun *mi* "what", it is not an option for relative and noun-associate clauses for the simple fact that these are *never* associated with exple-tival elements. The scope markers in these constructions are not (*wh*-)expletives, but full-blown argument NP/DPs, with a lexical meaning of their own. Therefore, an analysis in terms of expletive replacement by the embedded CP at LF is not tenable:

(33) $[_{CP}$ $[_{Focp}$***melyik diák***$_i$ $[_{DP} t_i [_{CP-wh}$ aki $[_{Focp}$*hány pontot*$_j$ $[_{IP}... t_i ...]]]]]]$
LF

Note that this is true even if expletive replacement is taken to be *adjunction* of the em-bedded CP to the matrix pronominal. Such an adjunction step would be totally unmoti-vated in the case of relative and noun-associated embedded clauses, as these clauses, be-ing adjuncts, are not in need of case.

In the next section I turn to the only account that can handle the newly found cases scope marking: Dayal's (1994, 2000) indirect dependency.

5.3.   The semantic indirect dependency approach (Dayal 1994, 2000)

The *semantic* type of *indirect dependency* approach (Dayal 1994, 2000), argues for an underlying *semantic* link between the scope marker and the embedded clause.[10] The scope marker in this account is a standard argumental *wh*-phrase, which quantifies over

---

[10] Allowing for the option that there is also a *syntactic* link between them as well. The syntactic relation between the matrix *wh*-item and the embedded clause can range from a loose juxtaposition to a real syntactic dependency. Crucial to this analysis is the treatment of sentential pronominals as full arguments, which follows the spirit of a number of syntactic proposals (Rosenbaum 1967, Bennis 1986, É.Kiss 1987, Torrego & Uriagereka 1989, Müller 1995, Moro 1997, Stepanov 2000) and the analysis of the embedded clause as a syntactic adjunct, a semantic *restrictor* over the matrix argument nominal.

propositions. The embedded clause, a full-blown question, restricts the domain of propositions that the scope marker quantifies over.

In the presice semantics, Dayal follows Hamblin (1973) in taking questions to denote the set of possible answers to them. *Wh*-expressions are existential quantifiers whose restriction is either implicit or provided by some overt restriction. The matrix propositional variable *wh*-expression can only be restricted by a question (due to their semantic type). For illustration, consider the example in (34):

(34) **Mitől** fél   Mari,   hogy *ki*   lesz   az igazgató?
      what-FROM fear-3SG Mari   that who   be-FUT.3SG   the director
      (lit.) 'What does Mari fear that who will be the director?'

This question has the following logical representation: $\lambda p \exists q[p$ a proposition & $p=^\wedge fear(Mari,q)]$. Dayal assumes that quantification is always restricted in natural languages, thus also with quantification over propositions. The overt or covert restrictor of the matrix propositional quantifier can be represented by a variable T: $\lambda p \exists q[T(q)$ & $p=^\wedge fear(Mari,q)]$. The meaning of the embedded clause is $\lambda p \exists x$ $[p= {}^\wedge will\text{-}be\text{-}director$ $(x)]$, which can be made the restrictor T in the interpretation of the matrix question. The end result is: $\lambda p \exists q[\exists x$ $[q= {}^\wedge will\text{-}be\text{-}director$ $(x)]$ & $p=^\wedge fear(Mari,q)]$. In an informal paraphrase, (34) denotes the following question: "what proposition p, such that p is a possible answer to 'who will be the director?' is such that Mari fears p?" Possible answers to the question "who will be the director" are propositions like *Péter will be the director; Anna will be the director; Hugo will be the director*. From this set of propositions, (34) asks for the one that Mari fears.

The above sketched analysis suits adjunct scope marking like a glove: as we have seen, in this language scope marking does not only occur with standard sentential subordination, but also with other types of embedding, where an expletive—associate relationship is completely out of the question, as relative and noun-associate clauses do not combine with expletives, but with lexical NPs/DPs. Furthermore, their role is exactly as described by Dayal's account: to provide a restriction over the NP/DP they modify. The next section spells this out in more detail.

5.4.   The analysis of adjunct scope marking constructions: extending Dayal's approach[11]

As the previous section has shown, Dayal's account can neatly accommodate the adjunct scope marking data due to its "unorthodox" view on standard scope marking data, which identifies the scope marker—embedded clause relationship as that between a restricted item and a restrictor. The full proposal, however, does not straightfowardly carry over to the adjunct scope marking data. To cover these data, in what follows I extend Dayal's

---

[11] This section heavily builds on help I received from Malte Zimmermann on the semantic representation of adjunct scope marking. Thanks also to Ede Zimmermann for illuminating discussion.

proposal in two directions. One being the type of question asked by the matrix *wh-*expression, the other being what specifications can be provided by the embedded *wh-*clause. In this section I briefly outline an extended Dayal-type semantic analysis for adjunct scope marking. The discussion will be kept at an informal level and is merely meant to sketch the outlines of a possible semantic analysis.

5.4.1. Relative clauses

In scope marking with relative clauses, an example of which is repeated here from above, the relative clause serves as a restriction on the matrix *wh-*phrase:

(35)   **Ki**$_i$ megy át   a vizsgán   [aki$_i$ *hány pontot*   szerez]?
       who go-3SG PV the exam-ON   who-REL how many point-ACC score-3SG
       (lit.) 'Who$_i$, who$_i$ scores how many points, passes the exam?'
       (intended) 'How many points does one have to score to pass the exam?'

The difference between these constructions and standard argumental scope marking as treated in Dayals' analysis (see previous section) is that in (35) the main question is not about propositions, but about *properties* of individuals. That is, the matrix question introduces existential quantification over properties. What kind of properties these are is specified by the relative clause, which denotes a *set* of properties under this account. In (35), the property is identified as a property that characterizes individuals in terms of how many points they score. For this analysis to go through we have to assume that the embedded question denotes a set of (individual) *properties*, and not the usual set of *propositions* (for a similar proposal concerning scope marking with adverb clauses (cf. (8) above), see Sternefeld 2002). With this assumption in mind, the meaning of the matrix question can be represented as in (36):

(36)   the set of properties Q such that there is a natural number n and Q is the property of an individual x scoring n points

Relative clauses in scope marking have the syntax of extraposed relatives. The head NP/DP and the relative clause are generated together in the base, followed by an extraposition step of the relative clause. Evidence for generating the relative next to its syntactic head comes from reconstructions facts:[12]

(37)   *Melyik embert vitték (ők$_i$) kórházba,   akit a fiúk$_i$ hol találtak?

---

[12] A further argument comes from the fact that their adjacency can be tolerated in overt syntax, too:
(i)   (?)?**Ki** [aki   *hány pontot*   szerez]   megy át a vizsgán?
      who   who-REL how many point-ACC score-3SG   go-3SG PV the exam-ON
      (lit.) 'Who, who scores how many points, passes the exam?'

which man took-3PL   they hospital-INTO REL-whom the boys where found-3PL
(lit.) 'Which man did the boys take into hospital, the one they found where?'

As we can see, BT-C is violated if the relative extraposed from objects position contains
an R-expression and the subject pronoun is coindexed with it. This provides unambiguous
evidence to the effect that the relative clause is base-generated together with the matrix *wh*-expression.

5.4.2. Noun-associate clauses

The semantics underlying adjunct scope marking with noun-associate clauses is slightly
different from that of relative clauses. Noun-associate clauses represent the intermediate
case between standard, argumental scope marking and that with relative clauses as
spelled out in the previous sections. As in the case of relative clauses, the questions is
about an (individual) property, namely a property of nouns with a *propositional* content.
The nouns occuring in these constructions (*message, claim, order* etc.) are nouns which
associate with propositions that spell out their *content*. The propositional property of the
given noun is specified by the denotation of the embedded question, which is, just like in
the standard case, is a set of propositions.
    Thus an example like (38) repeated from above has the following informal semantic representation:

(38)   **Milyen üzenetet**   kapott Péter   [hogy *hova*   kell mennie]?
        what   message-ACC   got-3SG Péter   that   where need go-INF-3SG
        (lit.) 'What message, that he has to go where, did Péter get?'
(39)   the set of propositions p such that there is a proposition q, with q element of the
        set of propositions of the kind 'Péter has to appear at x', and p = Péter got a a message with propositional content q

How the embedded proposition can be construed as a property of an entity is far from
trival. This, however, is not a problem that is specific to the analysis presented here. It
concerns all noun-associate clause relations with or without a *wh*-item in the associated
clause.
    The syntactic account of relative clauses in the previous section carries over in all
relevant respects to adjunct noun-associate clauses (base-generation together with the
noun, followed by an extraposition step). As noun-associate clauses have been argued to
be clausal adjuncts (Stowell 1981, Grimshaw 1990, Kenesei 1992, 1994), these can be
treated in the same way as relative clauses for our purposes.

6.   Summary

This paper introduced hitherto unidentified scope marking constructions from Hungarian,
Frisian, and Slovenian, and showed that these involve complex questions embedding ad-

junct clauses, namely noun-associate and relative clauses. It was shown that these constructions provide primary evidence for a Dayal-type indirect dependency analysis, and that a proposed extension of this analysis can account for these data in full.

References

Beck, S. & S. Berman. 2000. *Wh*-Scope Marking: Direct vs. Indirect Dependency. In Wh-*Scope Marking*, ed. U. Lutz, G. Müller and A. v. Stechow, 17-44. Amsterdam: John Benjamins.

Bennis, H. 1986. *Gaps and dummies*. Dordrecht: Foris.

Cheng, L. 2000. Moving just the feature. In Wh-*Scope Marking*, ed. U. Lutz, G. Müller and A. v. Stechow, 77-99. Amsterdam: John Benjamins.

Dayal, V. 1994. Scope Marking as Indirect *Wh* Dependency. *Natural Language Semantics* 2: 137-170.

Dayal, V. 1996. *Locality in* Wh *Quantification: Questions and Relative Clauses in Hindi*. Dordrecht: Kluwer.

Dayal, V. 2000. Scope Marking: Cross Linguistic Variation in Indirect Dependency. In Wh-*Scope Marking*, ed. U. Lutz, G. Müller and A. v. Stechow, 157-193. Amsterdam: John Benjamins.

Fanselow, G. & A. Mahajan. 2000. Towards a Minimalist Theory of *Wh*-expletives, Wh-Copying and Successive Cyclicity. In Wh-*Scope Marking*, ed. U. Lutz, G. Müller and A. v. Stechow, 195-230. Amsterdam: John Benjamins.

Golden, M. 1995. Interrogative Wh-movement in Slovene and English. *Acta Analytica* 14: 145-186.

Grimshaw, J. 1990. *Argument structure*. Cambridge, Mass.: MIT Press.

Hamblin, C. L. 1973. Questions in montague English. *Foundations of Language* 10: 41-53.

Herburger, E. 1994. A semantic difference between full and partial *Wh*-Movement in German. Paper presented at SLA, Boston.

Hiemstra, I. 1986. Some aspects of Wh-Questions in Frisian. *North-Western European Language Evolution* 8. 97-110.

Horvath, J. 1995. Partial *Wh*-Movement and the *Wh* "Scope-Markers". In *Approaches to Hungarian 5*, ed. I. Kenesei, 69-124. Szeged: Jate Press.

Horvath, J. 1997. The status of '*wh*-expletives' and the partial movement construction in Hungarian. *Natural Language and Linguistic Theory* 15, 509-572.

Horvath, J. 1998 Multiple *WH*-phrases and the *WH*-Scope-Marker strategy in Hungarian Interrogatives. *Acta Lingustica Hungarica* 45, 31-60.

Horvath, J. 2000 On the Syntax of "*Wh*-Scope Marker" Constructions: Some Comparative
     Evidence. In Wh-*Scope Marking*, ed. U. Lutz, G. Müller and A. v. Stechow, 271-
     316. Amsterdam: John Benjamins.
Kenesei, I. 1992. Az alárendelés. [Subordination.] In *Strukturális Magyar nyelvtan I,
     Mondattan* [Structural Hungarian Grammar I. Syntax.], ed. F. Kiefer, 529-714.
     Budapest: Akadémiai Kiadó.
Kenesei, I. 1994. Subordinate clauses. In *The syntactic Structure of Hungarian*, ed. F.
     Kiefer and K. É.Kiss, 275-354. San Diego: Academic Press.
É. Kiss, K. 1987. *Configurationality in Hungarian*. Budapest: Akadémiai Kiadó.
Lahiri, U. 2002. On the Proper Treatment of "Expletive *WH*" in Hindi. *Lingua* 112, 501-
     540.
Lasnik, H. & M. Saito. 1984. On the nature of proper government. *Linguistic Inquiry* 15,
     235-289.
Lipták, A. (to appear) Scope marking constructions in Dayal-type indirect dependency. In
     Proceedings of the 2002 workshop on Triggers, ed. A. Breitbarth and H. van
     Riemsdijk. Berlin: Mouton de Gruyter.
Lutz, U, G. Müller and A. v. Stechow, ed. 2000. Wh-*Scope Marking*. Amsterdam: John
     Benjamins.
Mahajan, A. 1990. The A/A-bar Distinction and Movement Theory. Doctoral disserta-
     tion, MIT, Cambridge, Mass.
Marácz, L. 1990. *Asymmetries in Hungarian*. Doctoral dissertation. University of
     Groningen.
McDaniel, D. 1989. Partial and multiple *Wh*-Movement. *Natural Language and Linguis-
     tic Theory* 7, 565-604.
Moro, A. 1997. *The raising of predicates. Predicative noun phrases and the theory of
     clause structure.* Cambridge: Cambridge University Press.
Müller, G. 1995. *A-bar syntax. The study of movement types.* New York, Mouton.
Riemsdijk, H. van. 1983. Correspondence Effects and the Empty Category Principle. In
     Studies in Generative Grammar and Language Acquisition, ed. Y. Otsu et al, 5-
     16. Tokio: ICU.
Rosenbaum, P. 1967. *The grammar of English predicate complement constructions*.
     Cambridge, Mass.
Stepanov, A. 2000. *Wh*-Scope Marking in Slavic. *Studia Linguistica* 54, 1-40.
Sternefeld, W. 2002. *Wh*-Expletives and Partial *Wh*-Movement: Two Non-Existing
     Concepts? In *Issues in Formal German(ic) Typology*, ed. W. Abraham and C.
     J-W. Zwart, 285-305. Amsterdam: John Benjamins.
Stowell, T. 1981. *Origins of Phrase Structure.* Cambridge, Mass.: MIT Press.
Torrego, E. & J. Uriagereka. 1989. Indicative dependence. Ms., University of
     Massachussetts, University of Maryland, Amherst.
Varga, L. 2002. *Intonation and Stress. Evidence from Hungarian.* New York: Palgrave
     Macmillan.

ULCL
Leiden University
P.O. Box 9515
2300 RA Leiden
The Netherlands

A.Liptak@let.leidenuniv.nl

Causatives without Causers and Burzio's Generalization[*]

Vita G. Markman

Rutgers University

1.   The Problem

The accidental construction in Russian given in (1) (also termed 'adversity impersonal' in Babby (1993a,b), Tsedryk (2003) and as 'accusative unaccusative' in Levin and Freidin 2001) presents a counterexample to Burzio's Generalization[1] (BG) (Burzio (1986), (2000: p.196)). The construction involves an internal argument marked with the accusative case but lacks an agent.

(1) a Bumag-u   sozhgl-o   b Dim-u   udaril-o   c Berez-u   svalil-o
         Paper-acc   burned-neut   Dima-acc hit-neut   Birch-acc make-fall-neut
         The paper got burned   Dima got hit   The birch was caused to fall

The NP in (1) has the accusative case, but there is no implicit agent in the construction. This is seen from 3 facts. First, the accidental construction does not allow control into purpose clauses as seen in (2):

(2)   Dom   sozhgl-o   (*chtob poluchit' strahovku)
          House-acc burn-neut   (*to   receive   insurance)
          The house got burned down (*to collect the insurance)

---

[*] I would like to thank Mark Baker, Ken Safir, and Viviane Deprez for their enormous help and support. I would also like to thank my friend and colleague S. Malamud as well as my fellow students at the Rutgers Linguistics department for their input and comments. Last, but not least, I thank the participants of NELS 2003 for their insightful comments and questions. All mistakes and shortcomings are of course, my own.
[1] I am assuming a version of BG that is a one-way implication:
Burzio's Generalization: Accusative case → *External argument* (Burzio (2000:p.196))

© 2003 Vita G. Markman
Keir Moulton and Matthew Wolf (eds.): Proceedings of NELS 34,
Stony Brook University: 425 – 439. GLSA, Amherst.

Second, the construction does not allow an agentive by-phrase, only a non-agentive one as seen in (3):

(3)   Vanj-u   udaril-o   (molni-ej)   /(*Dim-oj)
        Vanja-acc hit-neut   (lightning-inst) /(*Dima-inst)
        Vanja got hit   (by the lightning) / (*by Dima)

(4)   Berezu   svalil-o   (molni-ej)   /(*Dim-oj)
        Birch-acc fell-neut (lightning-inst) /(*Dima-inst)
        The birch got fallen down (by the lightning) / (*by Dima)

Third, the construction is incompatible with an agent-oriented adverbial such as "purposefully" as seen in (5):

(5)   Berezu   svalil-o   (*special'no)
        Birch-accfell-neut   (*purposefully)
        The birch got fallen down (*on purpose)

(6)   Dom   sozhgl-o   (*special'no)
        House-acc burn-neut (*purposefully)
        The house got burned down (*on purpose)

In this respect, the accidental construction is crucially different from the passive. The passive does inolve an implicit agent. It allows control into purpose clauses, is possible with an agentive by-phrase and agent –oriented adverbs[2] as shown in (7):

(7)   Dom   byl   sozhzhen Dimoj   special'no   chtob poluchit' strahovku
        House was   burned   Dima-instr purposefully   to   receive   insurance
        The house was burned down by Dima on purpose to collect the insurance

---

[2] Interestingly, in Ukrainian, a language closely related to Russian, the passive construction is compatible with the accusative case on the theme. [Thanks to John Bailyn for pointing it out]. However, the construction is crucially different from the accidental construction because in the Ukranian passive the implict agent is present as we can see in (i).

(i)   Cerkvu   bylo   sbudovano   robitnykami   special'no schob molytysja Bogu
        Church-acc was   built   workers-instr purposefully   to pray   God
        The church was built by the workers, purposefully to pray to God

The implicit agent in (i) is diagnozable via the addition of an agentive by-phrase, control into purpose clauses and agent-oriented adverbials. Consequently, this is not a violation of BG – the external argument is present underlyingly. The Ukranian passive and the accidental construction thus cannot be treated on a par. Since the passive construction is not the topic of this paper I will not dwell on it any longer and will not discuss the possibility of the accusative case on the theme in the Ukranian passive. For discussion see Baker, Johnson and Roberts 1989.

Further, unlike the passive, the accidental construction is only possible with those verbs whose meaning is compatible with inanimate causation (8a,b).

(8) a Knig-a   byl-a   prochitan-a   b * Knig-u   prochital-o
       Book-nom   was-fem   read-fem   Book-acc   read-neut
       The book was read   The book got read

While the above examples can lead us to say that BG is invalid, this conclusion would be premature since in English the analogue of the accidental construction is indeed impossible as seen in (9):

(9) a. *Him killed. = > something killed him
    b. *It[expletive] killed him

The story is thus more complicated than it may appear at first: BG is obeyed in some languages but not in all. The central question I address in this paper is what allows a language to violate BG?

2.   The Proposal.

2.1   Causatives without Causers

I argue that BG violations are related to the nature of causative heads that exist in a language where a causative head (Caus) licenses the accusative case. I crucially adopt a proposal in Pylkkanen (2002), who argues that causative constructions universally involve a head Caus that introduces a causing event. However, Pylkkanen argues that Caus can be spelled-out separately or together (bundled) with Voice – the head that introduces an agent (Kratzer 1996). Pylkkanen further claims that voice-bundling is subject to language variation. I argue that using Pylkkanen's idea, we can derive parametric variation with respect to BG as follows: *If Caus is not bundled with Voice, BG can be violated.*
       This claim raises two questions:
       1) What does it mean to be a causative without a causer?
       2) What is the evidence that the Russian is a non-voice-bundling language ?

To answer the first question let us consider the central idea presented in Pylkkanen (2002). Pylkkanen argues that a Caus head does not introduce a theta-role, but a causing event as shown below:

(i)

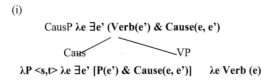

CausP λe ∃e' (**Verb(e') & Cause(e, e')**)

Caus   VP

λP <s,t> λe ∃e' [P(e') & Cause(e, e')]   λe Verb (e)

That is, causation is treated as a relationship between events, not between an event and an individual – a causer. Thus, in a sentence such as (10) causation is a relationship between the causing-to-melt event and the melting event.

(10)   John melted the ice-cream

In addition, the construction above contains a causer – the agent of melting – John. Crucially, the Agent (Causer) is a theta-role assigned by Voice (Kratzer 1996). Now if Caus is realized as a single head with Voice, then we get the following configuration:

(11) a.

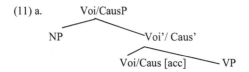

That is, in the above representation a single head carries two interpretable features that need to be processed in order. First the causing event is added to the VP, then the Causer (Agent) of the event is introduced by Voice[3].
Crucially, Caus can also be realized separately from Voice in some languages:

(11) b.

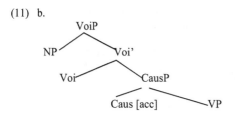

In this structure, we have two heads: Caus which introduces a causing event, and Voice which introduces a Causer (Agent) also via Event Identification (cf. ft3).
Briefly, the central motivation adduced by Pylkkanen 2002 for her claim that Voice and Caus can be separate heads comes from the fact that in some languages there are constructions that involve causation, but do not have external arguments. Pylkkanen argues that Japanese, Finnish, and Bemba are languages in which Caus and Voice are realized as different heads. In these languages, then, having a causing event is not the same as having a Causer (Agent). In the next section, I present evidence that Russian is also a non-voice-bundling language and argue that the accidental construction illustrates the fact that Voice and Caus realized as distinct heads in Russian.

---

[3] After the causing event is added, Voice adds a Causer (Agent) via Event Identification (Kratzer 1996). Event Identification: $<e, <s,t>> <s, t> \rightarrow <e, <s,t>>$. For further details see Kratzer (1996), Pylkkanen (2002: Ch.3).
    Note that I use 'Agent/Causer' to refer to the theta-role and 'agent/ causer' to refer to the individual that has the theta-role.

2.2   The Russian accidental construction: a causative without a causer

The evidence that the Russian accidental construction is a causative without a causer, i.e.
a construction that involves only a causing event, but no agent comes from three sources.
First, the accidental construction is a causative. This is indicated by the fact that external
causation is obligatory -- a modifier like "on its own" is impossible as seen in (12):

(12)   Dim-u   ubil-o /udarilo (* sam   / sam-o   po   sebe)
        Dima-acc   killed/hit-neut (*alone-masc / alone-neut by self)
        Dima got killed/hit   (*on his own/on its own)

As we can see from (12), the accidental construction is not compatible with a modifier
indicating that the individual caused the event by himself without any external
involvement. Another example illustrating the need for external causation is (13):

(13)   *. Dim-u   umertvilo   ubilo   ot starosti   ot raka   bolezn'ju
           Dima-acc die-caus-neut killed-neut from old age from cancer illness-instr
           Dima got killed by old age / by cancer /by illness

In (13), the accidental construction is impossible because there is no external cause of
death. Note that the accidental construction is different from the unaccusative in this
respect. The unaccusative does not require an external cause.

(14)   Dima upal   / umer   (sam po sebe)
        Dima fell down / died   (on his own)

In (14), the unaccusative verbs 'fall' and 'die' are compatible with the modifier "on its
own" in contrast with the accidental construction. Also unlike the accidental construction,
the unaccusative requires no external causation in a construction such as (15) (cf 13):

(15)   Vanja umer   ot   starosti /ot   raka
        Vanja died   from   old age /from   cancer
        Vanja died of old age/ cancer

Thus, the accidental construction is distinct from the unaccusative in requiring an
external cause.
        Second, that Caus is distinct from Voice in Russian is seen from the fact that it is
possible to attach an adverbial that modifies the causing event as long as the modifier is
not agentive. This is illustrated in (16):

(16)   a.Dub   svalil-o   (mgnovenno)   /(*special'no)
          Oak-acc fell-neut (instantaneously) /(*on purpose)
          The oak got fallen (instantaneously) / (*on purpose)

    b. Vanju   udaril-o (mgnovenno)   (*special'no)
       Vanja-acc hit-neut (instantaneously) (*on purpose)
       Vanja got hit (instantaneously) / (*on purpose)

In (16a), the modifier "instantaneously" modifies the causing event, but not necessarily
the falling event. The examples is compatible with a scenario in which the lightening
strikes the tree in an instant, however, the tree does not instantaneously fall down. Thus,
it is the causing event that is instantaneous, but the caused event may not occur in an
instant. In this respect, the accidental construction is again crucially different from an
unaccusative which involves only one event.

(17)   Dima upal   / prijexal mgnovenno
       Dima fell down / arrived instanteneosly

In (17) where the adverb "instantaneously" modifies "fall", the event of falling must be
instant. This is different from what we saw in (16) where the caused event need not be
instantaneous.
      Third, the Russian accidental construction is parallel to the Japanese adversity
lexical causative[4] argued by Pylkkanen 2002 to involve a Caus head but no external
argument. Like the Russian accidental construction[5], the adversity causative requires an
external cause as seen from the following data in (18):

(18) a.   Taro-ga   mukuko-o   (*katteni)   korob-ase-ta
         Taro-nom son-acc   (*by-self)   fall-caus-past
         Taro was adversely affected by his son falling down (*by himself)

     b.   # Taro-ga   titioya-o   sin-ase-ta
         Taro-nom father-acc   die-caus-past
         Taro was affected by his father dying

(18b) is impossible in the context where Taro's father passes away of natural causes.
(Pylkkanen 2002: Ch.3). However, the agent is not allowed as seen from the
impossibility of adding an agentive by-phrase:

(19)   Taro-ga   (*Hanako-ni-yotte) /(sensoo-ni-yotte) musuko-o sin-ase-ta
       Taro-nom (*Hanako-by)   /(war-by)   son-acc die-caus-past
       Taro's son was caused to die on him (*by Hanako) / (by war)

      Interestingly, the Japanese adversity causative also involves the accusative case in
the absence of an agent – a violation of BG. The accusative case is not possible with

---

    [4] Pylkkanen (2002: Ch3) further points out that the adversely affected argument, though marked
with the nominative case (Taro-ga) is not an agent. See Pylkkanen (2002: Ch.3 p.82) for details.
    [5] The Russian accidental construction does not involve an adversely affected argument. This
salient difference is irrelevant for the purposes of the current discussion.

mono-eventive unaccusative verbs such as "fall" and "die" (20a), but does appear on the adversity causative repeated in (20b):

(20) a. Taro-ga   /*Taro-o   sin-ta   b. Taro-ga   musuku-o   sin-ase-ta
          Taro-nom   /*Taro-acc   die-past   Taro-nom   son-acc   die-caus-past
          Taro died   Taro's son died on him

This supports the hypothesis that the licencer of the accusative case is Caus, as opposed to Voice.

Returning now to the Russian accidental construction, I propose the following configuration for it:

(21)   CausP

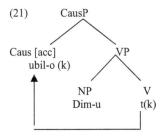

Caus [acc]   VP
   ubil-o (k)
                  NP   V
                  Dim-u   t(k)

In the above configuration, the accusative case on the NP is licensed by Caus, but the agent argument is absent. Instead, there is a causing event[6].

3.   More evidence that Russian is non-voice-bundling: Experiencer Unergatives[7]

3.1   Experiencer unergatives vs. agentive unergatives

In this section, I consider additional evidence for the claim that Russian is a language in which Caus is a head that is distinct from Voice. In Russian, there is a construction that involves an unergative verb with a causativized meaning, but the agent (causer) is absent.

---

[6] Unlike the Japanese lexical causative, the accidental construction in Russian does not involve an overt causative morpheme. Instead, the suppletive forms are used. For example, if an unaccusative verb such as 'fall' = 'upal' or 'die' = 'umer' is causativized in Russian, the V+Caus complex head is realized as a suppletive form 'dropped' = 'uronil' or 'umertvil' = 'made dead' is used instead. In some cases, the aspectual prefix is used to indicate causation:

(i) Dima smejal-sja   (ii) Vanja ras-smeshil   Dim-u
    Dima laughed-sja   Vanja perf-laughed Dima
    Dima laughed   Vanja made Dima laugh

[7] This construction is also discussed by Marušič and Žaucer [not appearing in this volume- *eds.*]. They present a different account, but a comparison would extend beyond the scope of this paper.

Instead, the construction involves an experiencer argument that is not a volitional participant of the event[8]. Consider the examples below:

(22)   Mne xorosho   bezhit-sja   / igraet-sja   / rabotaet-sja
        I-dat well   runs-sja   /plays-sja   / works-sja
        Running / playing / working goes well for me

While the English translation does not reflect it, the experiencer unergative[9] construction also involves a causing event, though it lacks an agent, much like what we saw in the accidental construction in (1-3). The non-agentivity is evidenced by the impossibility of both control into purpose clauses and agentive modification:

(23) a Mne xorosɬ igraet-sja (*chtoby vyigrat') / (*special'no)
        Me   well   plays-sja   (*to win)   / (*on purpose)
        Playing goes well for me   (*in order to win) / (*on purpose)/

     b Mne xorosho rabotaet-sja (*chtoby mnogo zarabotat'')   / (*special'no)
        Me   well   work-sja   (*to earn money)   / (*on purpose)
        Working goes well for me /feels well to me (*in order to earn money) / (*on purpose)

Yet, there is a clear sense that a causing/ facilitating event is present as seen from (24):

(24)   Mne xorosho igraet-sja / rabotaet-sja (*samo po sebe)/ (ok: iz-za pogody)
        Me   well   plays-sja /work-sja   (*alone by self) / (ok: due to weather)
        Playing/ Working goes well for me (*on my own) / (because of the weather)

The sentence in (24) is impossible with a modifier like "on its own" but is compatible with one asserting the presence of an external cause e.g. "because of the weather".
        Another example indicating that the experiencer unergative construction is impossible in a context that requires volitionality on the part of the individual is (25a):

(25) a. (#/* Posle dolgih usilij), mne   vspomnilsja   etot son
          (After   long   trials), me-dat remembered-sja this dream
          (After trying for a long time), the dream (finally) came back to me

The construction in (25a) is ungrammatical. Experiencer unergatives can only be used in a context where the dream comes back to me on its own or because something reminded me of it as we see in (25b):

---

    [8] The experiencer unergative construction is similar to the desiderative construction in Finish discussed in Pylkkanen 2002. For reasons of space I will not go into a comparison here and refer the reader to Pylkkanen 2002:ch3
    [9] A modifier like "well" or "easily" is obligatory if the sentence does not contain negation (e.g. *?* *Mne igraet-sja* = Me plays. When negated, the sentence does not require a modifier: *Mne ne igraet-sja* = Me not plays. The reasons for this are unclear at this point. I leave this issue for future research.

b. Posle prosmotra etogo fil'ma, mne   vspomnilsja   vcherashnij   son
    After viewing this movie, me-dat remembered-sja yesterday's   dream
    After seeing this movie, last night's dream came back to me

In (25b), seeing the movie reminds me of the dream. Crucially, no conscious effort or control on my part is being exercised here.

In contrast, an agentive unergative is compatible with control into purpose clauses and does not require causation of any kind (26):

(26) a. Ja xorosho igraju (chtoby vyigrat') / (sam po sebe)
          I   well   play   (to win)   / (on my own)
          I play well (in order to win) / (on my own) /

      b. Ja bystro begu (chtoby vyigrat') / (sam po sebe)
          I   fast   run   (to win)   / (on my own)
          I am running fast (in order to win) / (on my own)

The agentive unergative is also perfectly acceptable in the following construction:

      c. Posle dolgihusiliy, ja   vspomnil   etot   son
          After long Trials I-nom   remembered this   dream
          After trying for a long time, I finally remembered this dream.

Finally, the experiencer unergative construction can be used in a sluicing structure in (27) where the question 'why' refers to a cause of good running, not to the runner's intentions. (Pylkkanen uses a similar test to diagnose a causing event in the Finnish desiderative construction).

(27)   Mne xorosho bezhitsja no   ja ne   znaju pochemu
         I-dat well   run-sja   but I not   know   why
         Running goes well for me, but I don't know why

The above sentence cannot mean that I don't know my own reasons for running. It can only mean that I don't know the causes of my running well. In contrast, the salient reading[10] of the agentive unergative (28) is that I don't know the contents of my own mind – I am running but I have no idea what my purpose/ intention for running is.

(28)   Ja   xorosho begu   no   ja ne   znaju pochemu
         I-nom well   run-1st-sg but I not know why
         I run well, but I don't know why

---

[10] The sentence can also have the reading on which the person does not know of any external causes that make him run well. While the ambiguity in the agentive unergrative is interesting, what is crucial here is that the experiencer unergative construction (27) can never mean that the person is unaware of his own intentions for running. It is not ambiguous.

The experiencer unergative, on the other hand, crucially cannot have this meaning.

Thus, the above data indicates that the experiencer unergative unlike the agentive unergative cannot tolerate volitionality on the part of the individual involved. The event is beyond the person's control (Moore and Perlmutter 2000). From the above data, it is reasonable to conclude that the lack of control in these construction is attributable to the presence of a causing event[11].

The experiencer unergative construction, much like the accidental construction, also involves a causing event (albeit an internal one) but lacks an agent. The construction, therefore, provides further evidence that Caus and Voice in Russian are distinct heads. In the next section, I will show that the possibility of having the experiencer argument in this construction is also crucially dependant on Caus being a distinct head from Voice.

3.2.   Voice-bundling and the experiencer unergative construction

I propose that the experiencer unergative construction involves an NP embedded under a null preposition TO that assigns it an experiencer theta-role. I treat an experiencer as a recipient (see Emonds 1985, Baker 1997, and Landau 2003 for similar proposals, also Markman (in prep) for discussion). That is, crucially, the NP is not an argument of Caus, but of P [TO]. In other words, the individual in (29) is a recipient of a causing event[12].

(29)

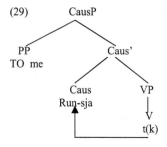

---

[11] Speaker's intuitions suggest that the causing event in the experiencer unergative may be internal to the individual. In other words, whatever makes the individual run or play well is internal to him/her as opposed to what we saw in the accidental construction where causation must be external. The term 'internal causation' employed here is similar to that in Pesetsky (1996: Ch4). However, internal causation is causation nonetheless, hence no volitionality on the part of the individual can be asserted as indicated by the agentivity tests above. Thus, Russian involves two different causative morphemes, both realized as separate heads from Voice, one referring to internal and one to external causation. For reasons of space, I will not disucss internal vs. external causation here and refer the interested reader to Pesetsky 1996.

[12] In the example above, TO relates an individual to a set of events of 'caused-running'. That is, the individual is *a recipient* of a caused-running.

Here I provisionally take the reflexive morpheme *–sja* as a spell out of the causative morpheme that denotes internal causation[13][14].

Crucially, the above construction can only be possible if Caus is not bundled with Voice. Otherwise, we would get a Theta-Criterion violation: the P theta-marks the NP embedded under it, leaving the agent theta-role of Voice unassigned. However, since Caus is not a theta-marking category -- it introduces an event, and not a theta-role --there is no conflict when we merge a PP into the spec of CausP. Thus, experiencer unergatives further indicate that Caus is distinct from Voice in Russian. Note that the above discussion implies that the possibility of BG violations and the possibility of the experiencer unergatives are related: both are linked to the voice-bundling-parameter (Pylkkanen 2002). This relationship is explored in detail in (Markman (in prep)).

4.   When BG must be obeyed.

I argue that in a BG-observing language such as English, Caus and Voice are realized as a single head: since Caus is the head licensing the accusative case, BG cannot be violated. While Pylkkanen does not provide extensive arguments to the effect that English is a voice-bundling language[15], I will take it as a null hypothesis that a language is voice-bundling, unless we have positive evidence that Caus and Voice are distinct heads. This view is plausible because it reduces the number of heads that need to be independently realized in a language[16]. Since English is a language that lacks any evidence of having Caus and Voice as distinct heads (e.g. it lacks not only the accidental construction but also any likeness of an experiencer unergative construction or a desiderative construction), I will assume with Pylkkanen 2002 that it is in fact a voice-bundling language. If so, the presence of the accusative case licensed by Caus necessitates the presence of the agent:

---

[13] In Russian, -sja has many meanings. I am not claiming that –sja is unambiguously a morpheme denoting an internal causing event. My claim is that it is merely one of its meanings. A similar view is taken by Pesetsky 1996: Ch.4.

[14] I am also provisionally assuming that –sja absorbs the accusative case here.

[15] Pylkkanen 2002 mentions another parameter that defines causative constructions – selection. She argues that the complement selected by the causative head can vary. Since this parameter is not relevant to the discussion here. I will refer the reader to Pylkkanen 2002:Ch.

[16] This position is similar to the one taken in Bobaljik and Thrainsson (1998) inter alia with respect to Agr projections. That is, the authors claim that unless we have evidence for an Agr projection, there is no reason to posit it. (A distinct view of UG is presented in Cinque 1999 who argues that if a particular functional head is present in one language it is present in all. I will not present further arguments for or against this view, however.)

(30)   VoiP/CausP

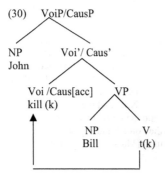

NP   Voi'/ Caus'
John

    Voi /Caus[acc]   VP
    kill (k)

               NP   V
               Bill   t(k)

Furthermore, since Caus is bundled with Voice, the experiencer unergatives are impossible (31):

(31)   *Me plays / runs/ works well.

(32)   *VoiP/CausP

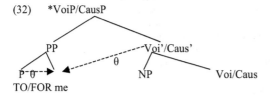

         PP   ----Voi'/Caus'
                 θ
  P θ   NP   Voi/Caus
TO/FOR me

Merging a PP into the spec of Voi/CausP is impossible in English since Voi is a theta-marker and so is the P. Hence, a Theta-Criterion violation results.

Before I close this section, I would like to make a brief note about the nature of the following English construction:

(33)   The wind broke the window.

In (33) there does not seem to be an agent, but this should be impossible given that the claim that Voice = Caus in English. To account for constructions such as (33) I will assume, in a slight departure from what was said above, that Voice assigns a Causer theta-role, rather than an Agent theta-role. A causer, unlike an agent, can be inanimate[17] as we see in (33). Crucially this is different from the accidental in Russian because a Causer is a theta-role that must be discharged to an NP in the spec of Voice. Hence, in English we cannot have:

---

[17] The reason you cannot use an agent-oriented adverb such as 'purposefully' in a construction involving an inanimate Causer is pragmatic – the wind is not the kind of thing that can break the window on purpose.

(34) a. * The window-acc broke = something broke the window
     b. *Him killed

In the absence of an overt Causer, the construction violates the Theta-Criterion. In contrast, nothing assigns a Causer theta-role to an NP in the accidental construction. There is no causer, just a causing event.

5.   Other accounts

Here I compare the current proposal with the one presented in Levine and Freidin (2001)[19]. Levine and Freidin (L&F) argue that the accidental construction (they refer to it as the 'accusative unaccusative' construction) results when the defective (phi-incomplete) T co-occurs in the same clause as a phi-complete light v. The phi-complete light v values the accusative case on the object NP. The object NP then moves to spec TP to satisfy the EPP – which they take to be an independent syntactic primitive (L & F, p.1). In other words, they claim that a T that lacks phi-features still has the EPP feature and is able to attract an NP into its spec. While interesting, their account faces a number of problems. First, the accusative object NP is not a subject – it does not appear in Spec, TP as evidenced by the fact that it cannot bind a subject-oriented anaphor, unlike the derived subject of the passive or the subject in a transitive construction:

(35) a. Dimu   ubilo   *svoim   /ego   ruzh'jem
          Dima-acc   killed-3rd-neut   *self's   /his   gun-instr
          Dima got killed by his own gun

      b. Dima   byl   ubit   svoim   ruzh'jem
          Dima-nom   was   killed self's gun-instr
          Dima got killed with his own gun

      a. Vanja(i)   ubil   Dimu(j)   iz   svoego(i/*j)   ruzh'ja
          Vanja-nom   killed Dima-acc   From   self's   gun
          Vanja killed Dima with his own gun

As seen from the contrasts in (35), the accusative NP in the accidental construction patterns with regular objects in the transitive constructions, and not with the subjects.
     L & F argue that the object in the accidental construction can bind the anaphor 'each other', but native speakers report that the examples are marginal. But more importantly, the anaphor 'each other' is not subject-oriented in contrast with 'self'.

---

[19] A different account of the accidental construction is presented in Babby 1993a, b. While interesting, this account is couched in a completely different theoretical framework which makes a comparison difficult. I therefore will not discuss this account here and refer the reader to Babby 1993a, b. Also a proposal of the accidental 'impersonal' construction is presented in Tsedryk 2003. Since the focus of this account is on case –agreement properties of this construction I will not be discussing it here.

Consequently, the argument from binding does not go through. This is seen from the following example where it is clear that the binder of 'each other' is an object.

(36)   Vanja   ubil   Dimu   i   Mishu   v   kvartirax   drug   druga
        Vanja-nom   killed   Dima-acc and   Misha'acc in   apartments   each   other-gen
        Vanja killed Dima and Misha in each other's apartments

Thus, evidence from anaphor-binding does not support the claim that the displaced object appears in spec TP[20].

        Second, L&F crucially assume the presence of light v (aka Voice) that carries phi-features and checks the accusative case on the object. However, it is unclear why the Agent / Causer theta-role that is ordinarily assigned to an NP by light v (Chomsky 1995) is missing here. Third, L&F have no principled account for why the accidental construction is absent in English while present in Russian. In fact, L&F attribute the absence of this to a lexical idiosyncrasy of the English verb 'be'. They argue that this verb 'has no finite form that lacks agreement morphology'(L& F p.11, ft.note 13). However, the accidental construction need not contain the verb 'be' (cf 1). Moreover, Russian also does not have a designated morpheme that is used solely to indicate non-agreeing forms -- it uses 3rd singular neuter. However, it does have the accidental construction. The lack of a designated non-agreeing verb form does not seem to bear on the presence/absence of the accidental construction in a language.

        In contrast, the account presented in this paper provides a principled reason why BG can be violated in Russian but not in English. Furthermore, since I assume that the accidental construction does not involve light v (Voice), (the accusative case is licensed by Caus), I can account for the fact that this construction does not require an overt causer while having a causing event.

6.   Conclusion

To sum up, I have proposed that Burzio's Generalization can be violated if Caus and Voice are realized as distinct heads (Pylkkanen 2002) where Caus is the head that licenses the accusative case and Voice introduces the agent. I have argued that in Russian Voice and Caus are distinct heads, while in English, Caus and Voice are realized as a single head. Consequently, BG violations can occur in Russian but not in English. The proposal, thus makes a testable crosslinguistic prediction: BG violations can occur only in non-voice-bundling languages. Crucially, the theory presented here accounts for the properties of the accidental construction without relinquishing BG completely. Furthermore, one can venture an even stronger claim: assume that BG should be re-phrased to state that the accusative case implies the existence of external causation, not necessarily an external argument. If so, then BG would be universal.[21]

---

[20] L & F present arguments from Weak Cross-Over and Focus that the displaced object is not in scrambled position (p.20 – 27). However, while the movement of the object may not be focus-driven scrambling, it is not enough to conclude that the object moves to an A position.

[21] Thanks to Ken Safir to bringing this point to my attention.

References

Babby, L.H (1989). "Subjectlessness, External Subcategorization, and the Projection Principle, Zbornik Matice Sprske za Filologiju i Lingvistiku XXXII/ 2, pp.7-40

Babby, L.H. (1993a). "A Theta-theoretic Analysis of Adversity Impersonal in Russian". *FASL 2: The MIT Meeting.*

Babby, L.H.(1993b). "Impersonal Forms of the Verb in Russian." Paper delivered at the 1993 AATSEEL Winter meeting (Toronto).

Baker, M., Johnson, K. and I. Roberts (1989) "Passive Arguments Raised" Linguistic Inquiry 20: 219 - 52

Baker, M. (1997). Thematic Roles and Syntactic Structure. In: Haegeman, Liliane (ed.), *Elements of Grammar: Handbook of Generative Syntax,* Dordrecht: Kluwer, 73 – 137.

Avrutin, S., Franks, S. and Progovac, L. (eds.) Ann Arbor: Michigan Slavic Publications

Bobalijk, J. and H. Thrainsson (1998). "Two Heads aren't Always Better than One." *Syntax* 1: 1 37 – 71.

Burzio, Luigi (1986). Italian Syntax: A Government-Binding Approach. Reidel.

Burzio, Luigi (2000). "Anatomy of a Generalization" in *Arguments and Case: Explaining Burzio's Generalization* ed. Eric Reuland.

Chomsky, N. (1995). *The Minimalist Program.* Cambridge: MIT Press.

Emonds, J (1985). *A Unified Theory of Syntactic Categories.* Foris, Dordrecht.

Kratzer, A.(1996). "Severing the External Argument from its Verb." In J. Rooryck and L. Zaring (eds.) *Phrase Structure and The Lexicon.* Dordrecht (Kluwer Academic Publishers).

Lavine, J. and R. Freidin (2001) "The subject of defective tense in Slavic". *Journal of Slavic Linguistics*

Landau, I.(2003). The Locative Syntax of Experiencers. Ben Gurion University, Ms.

Markman, V.G. (in prep). The Syntax of Case and Agreement: its relationship to morphology and argument structure. Dissertation in progress.

Marušič, Franc and Rok Žaucer "The intensional feel-like construction in Slovenian". Talk presented at NELS 34.

Moor and Perlmutter (2000). "What does it take to be a dative subject?", Natural Language and Linguistic Theory 18, 373 – 416.

Pylkkanen, L. (2002). *Introducing Arguments.* Ph.D. Thesis, MIT

Reuland, E.(2000). Arguments and Case: Explaining Burzio's Generalization, John Benjamins, Amsterdam.

Tsedryk, E.(2003). "Case and agreement in Russian adversity impersonal constructions". Presented at FASL 12, University of Ottawa.

Department of Linguistics
Rutgers University
New Brunswick, NJ 08901

markman@eden.rutgers.edu

Processing Relative Clauses in Japanese with Two Attachment Sites

Edson T. Miyamoto[1,2], Michiko Nakamura[2] and Shoichi Takahashi[3]

[1] U. Tsukuba   [2] NAIST   [3] MIT

1.   Introduction

Studies in various languages have been conducted to understand the processing of ambiguous relative clauses (RCs) like the following (from Cuetos & Mitchell, 1988).

(1)   the servant of the actress [$_{RC}$ who was on the balcony]

The RC can be associated with *servant* (the *high* noun in the tree structure) or *actress* (the *low* noun). Average preferences have been shown to vary across languages. For example, native speakers of English preferentially attach the RC to the low noun, whereas speakers of Dutch, French, Spanish among other languages prefer the high noun (Brysbaert & Mitchell, 1996; Cuetos & Mitchell, 1988; Zagar, Pynte & Rativeau, 1997; see http://www.lingua.tsukuba.ac.jp/etm/rc, for a more comprehensive list of languages tested).

The high preference in various languages goes against a large literature on locality preferences according to which the closest candidate site to the phrase being attached is favored (e.g., Frazier, 1987; Gibson, 1998; Kimball, 1973). Thus, RC attachment has been used to investigate how the processing mechanism interacts with different grammars, in particular, how locality preferences are modulated by grammatical parameterizations. (See Table 1 for a partial list of proposals.) However, most studies thus far have dealt with European languages, and therefore their scope is often limited to postnominal RCs.

Results on prenominal RCs in Japanese have been contradictory. When shown ambiguous RCs that allow both interpretations (as in (2) from Kamide & Mitchell, 1997, Experiment 1), Japanese readers prefer the high noun (see also Hirose, 2001).

(2)   Dareka-ga   [$_{RC}$ barukonii-ni iru] joyuu-no   mesitsukai-o utta.
       somebody-nom   balcony-loc is   actress-gen servant-acc shot
       'Somebody shot the servant of the actress who is on the balcony.'

In contrast, when reading times were measured for unambiguous sentences (disambiguated through plausibility manipulations), low attachment sentences were read faster

i.	alternation between relative pronouns and complementizers in RCs (e.g., *who/that* was on the balcony; Cuetos & Mitchell, 1988)
ii.	the existence of an alternative construction (*colonel's daughter*) together with Gricean maxims (Frazier & Clifton, 1996; Thornton, Gil & Mac-Donald, 1998)
iii.	the subject is not allowed to appear after a direct object as in VOS (Gibson et al., 1996)
iv.	adverbs are not allowed to intervene between the verb and its direct object (Miyamoto, 1999)
v.	prosodic contours in the language disfavor the insertion of a pause between the head nouns and the RC (Fodor, 1998, 2002)

Table 1   Factors that may explain the low attachment preference in English.

than their high attachment versions at the low noun N_1, the genitive marker and the high noun N_2 in (3a), but that trend was reversed at sentence end (Kamide & Mitchell, 1997).

(3) a. RC | N_1 | gen | N_2 | ...   (Kamide & Mitchell, 1997, Experiment 2)

   b. RC | N_1-gen | N_2 | ...   (Kamide et al., 1998)

The initial advantage for local attachment in the reading time experiment may have been a segmentation artefact as the genitive marker was shown separated from N_1 (bars in (3) indicate the segmentations used in the self-paced reading presentations). When N_1 is read in (3a), there is no indication that another head noun is coming, thus the segmentation may have inadvertently boosted the preference for the low noun by making it the only candidate available initially. Another experiment partially supports this interpretation. When N_1 is shown together with the genitive marker as in (3b), there was no statistically reliable difference at that point, although the low attachment sentences were numerically faster (Kamide et al., 1998; but cf. Miyamoto et al., 1999, for a statistically reliable advantage for low attachment when locative postpositions are shown with N_1).

In order to address the segmentation controversy and further investigate the time course of RC attachment in Japanese, a series of experiments were conducted.

2.   Experiment 1

In this first experiment, we address the segmentation issue.

2.1.   Method

Twenty undergraduates at Kanda University of International Studies were paid for their participation. A non-cumulative moving-window self-paced reading setup (Just, Carpenter & Woolley, 1982) presented sentences one at a time on a single line. Each sentence was followed by a comprehension question presented on a new screen without feedback.

2.1.1. Materials

Twenty-four sets of sentence pairs (from Kamide & Mitchell, 1997, Experiment 2) were used in the experiment. The following is an example set.

(4) a. High attachment RC

	R1			R2	
Hoosekibako-no	sumi-ni	nokotteita	hannin-no	simon-o	...
jewelry-box-gen	corner-loc	remained	criminal-gen	fingerprint-acc	

'the fingerprint of the criminal (that) remained in the corner of the jewelry box'

b. Low attachment RC

	R1			R2	
Gojuudai	dansei-to	suiteisareru	hannin-no	simon-o	...
50s	male-as	supposed	criminal-gen	fingerprint-acc	

'the fingerprint of the criminal (who) is supposed to be a male in his 50s'

c. Matrix clause

	R3		R4
...	keisatsu-ga	nantoka	mitsukedasita.
	police-nom	somehow	found

'The police somehow found...'

The segmentation (indicated with vertical bars) shows the two head nouns together in region 2 (labelled R2), which makes both sites available simultaneously and avoids giving an artificial advantage to the low noun. Note that the low noun still has an advantage as it is going to be read first, but this is not an experimental artefact, rather it is a consequence of the word order in Japanese.

Two lists were created by distributing the test items according to a Latin square design and intermixing 40 filler items in pseudo-random order so that at least one filler intervened between consecutive test items. Each participant saw only one list.

2.1.2. Norming Study

To guarantee that the plausibility manipulation (that determines the RC attachment) was effective, 36 native speakers of Japanese who did not take part in the main study rated the

Edson T. Miyamoto, Michiko Nakamura and Shoichi Takahashi

naturalness of the RC attachment portions of the sentences from 1 (*natural*) to 5 (*strange*). For the set in (4), the following four conditions were created.

(5) a. High noun as part of the High RC (HH for short; plausible)
      Simon-wa   hoosekibako-no sumi-ni   nokotteita.
      fingerprint-top jewelry-box-gen corner-loc remained
      'The fingerprint remained in the corner of the jewelry box.'

    b. Low noun as part of the Low RC (LL; plausible)
      Hannin-wa   gojuudai dansei-to suiteisareru.
      criminal-top 50s   male-as   supposed
      'The criminal is supposed to be a male in his 50s.'

    c. High noun as part of the Low RC (HL; implausible)
      Simon-wa   gojuudai dansei-to suiteisareru.
      fingerprint-top 50s   male-as   supposed
      'The fingerprint is supposed to be a male in his 50s.'

    d. Low noun as part of the High RC (LH; implausible)
      Hannin-wa   hoosekibako-no sumi-ni   nokotteita.
      criminal-top jewelry-box-gen corner-loc remained
      'The criminal remained in the corner of the jewelry box.'

Analyses of the ratings for the four conditions (HH 1.49; LL 1.43; HL 3.96; LH 4.45) revealed that the plausible conditions (LL and HH) were more plausible than the implausible conditions ($Ps < 0.01$). The two plausible conditions did not differ ($Fs < 1$) as is desirable in this kind of experiment and it attests the care with which the original items (Kamide & Mitchell, 1997) were created.

However, the LH condition was rated more implausible than the HL condition ($Ps < 0.01$). Ideally, those two conditions should not differ but this is a difficult difference to control for when creating the items. These ratings are important because they may indicate how much the alternative interpretation competes with the intended interpretation during the online experiment (e.g., LH corresponds to: when reading the high RC, how natural it is for the RC to be attached to the low noun), and the different ratings for LH and HL will have to be taken into consideration when interpreting the reading time results.

2.2.   Results

Comprehension performance did not differ between the two conditions (Low 85.9%; High 86.7%; $Fs < 1$).

Reading time results were as follows. There was no difference in the first region (Fs < 1). In region 2 (the two head nouns), the high condition was read more slowly than the low condition ($F_1(1,19) = 28.7$, $P < 0.01$; $F_2(1,23) = 13.2$, $P < 0.01$). In region 3, the high condition was faster than the low condition in the participant analysis ($F_1(1,19) = 5.1$, $P < 0.05$; $F_2 < 1$). In region 4, the high condition was reliably faster in the participant analysis ($F_1(1,19) = 11.3$, $P < 0.01$; $F_2(1,22) = 3.5$, $P < 0.08$; one item was not included in the item analysis of this region because all its data points for the low condition had to be eliminated, e.g., because of mistakes to answer the comprehension question).

2.2.1. Correlation Analyses

In order to determine whether differences in plausibility accounted for the reading time patterns, a correlation analysis was conducted. For each region, the reading time differences (Low – High) for each item did not correlate with the rating differences in the norming study (with LL – HH or with HL – LH; all Ps > 0.13; all r^2s < 0.1). Therefore, despite the plausibility difference between HL and LH, the lack of correlation suggests that reading times were not affected by the plausibility of the competing interpretation.

Kamide et al. (1998) reported a reliable correlation between reading times and length of the RC. Thus, a similar analysis was conducted. A linear correlation between reading time differences for each item (Low – High) and length of the RC in number of characters yielded no reliable results for regions 1, 2 and 4 (Ps > 0.35). In region 3, there was a reliable correlation ($r^2 = 0.24$, $P < 0.05$), so that the longer the RC the greater the (Low – High) reading time difference. This is compatible with the claim that implicit prosodic contours (i.e., prosody computed for text read in silence) influence attachment decisions (Fodor, 1998, 2002; see Experiment 2 below).

2.3. Discussion

The faster reading times for the low attachment condition in region 2 confirm the initial preference that readers have for this type of attachment. Given the coarse segmentation used, it is unlikely that this was the result of segmentation artefacts, in particular, it cannot be due to the late availability of the high noun. The question then is why the initial preference for low attachment turns into a high attachment preference at sentence end (as attested by the reading times in the last region of the present experiment as well as in Kamide & Mitchell, 1997; Kamide et al., 1998; and in questionnaires reported by Hirose, 2001; Kamide & Mitchell, 1997). The following sections report the preliminary results of two experiments investigating two possible factors, namely, prosody and word order.

3. Experiment 2

In this experiment, prosody effects on RC attachment were investigated.

Literature on working memory reports that the continuous utterance of nonsense syllables prevents rehearsal in the phonological loop (*inner speech suppression*, ISS) and eliminates phonological effects in the recall of lists of words (e.g., effects of length and of confusability because of similarity; see Baddeley, 1990, for a summary and references). If implicit prosody is dependent on the phonological loop, it should be disrupted by ISS (see Slowiaczek & Clifton, 1980). By comparing attachment preferences while reading in silence and with simultaneous vocalization, prosodic effects can be isolated.

One possible prediction is that there is a locality preference in general (i.e., a preference for the closest candidate site; Frazier, 1987; Gibson, 1998; Kimball, 1973; inter alia), and that prosodic contours modulate locality based on the lengths of the modifier and the head. For the RCs investigated, length can favor the high noun for two reasons (Fodor, 1998, 2002). First, if the RC is long, a pause is more likely to be inserted between the RC and the head nouns, thus weakening the locality preference. Second, the high noun is always longer than the low noun as it includes the low noun as a modifier (e.g., for (1), the low noun is *the actress*, whereas the high noun is not just *servant*, but rather *the servant of the actress*). If readers have a preference to keep the length of the RC and the length of its head equal (*the same-size-sister constraint*, Fodor, 1998), then the longer the RC, the more likely for it to be attached to the high noun. The same-size sister constraint could be responsible for the correlation reported in Experiment 1 between RC length and reading time in region 3.

If ISS prevents implicit prosody from being computed, then pauses and length effects should be eliminated, and with locality being the only factor at play, the low noun should be favored throughout the sentence.

3.1.   Method

The test sentences and the setup were the same as the ones used in Experiment 1, except that there were two sessions. In one session, participants read 12 test items plus 42 filler sentences in silence, and, in the other session, they read a different set of 12 test items plus 42 fillers while repeating nonsense syllables (*ru* or *ne*) aloud. This created a 2×2 design (Silence/ISS ×High/Low). Order of the tasks was counterbalanced across participants, who were monitored throughout both sessions to ensure that they followed the instructions appropriately by reading in silence or repeating the nonsense syllables at a rapid constant pace (approximately three times per second).

Thirty-three native speakers of Japanese from the Nara Institute of Science and Technology (NAIST) were paid to participate in the study, none of which had participated in the first experiment or in the norming study. One participant's data were eliminated from further analysis because of low comprehension performance (less than 70%).

3.2. Results

There were no reliable effects in the comprehension performance of the four conditions (between 87.5% and 92.7%) except for a main effect of task with the ISS conditions reliably worse than the Silence conditions in the item analysis ($F_1(1,31) = 1.77$, p > 0.19; $F_2(1,23) = 5.93$, $P < 0.05$; see Slowiaczek & Clifton, 1980, for similar trends).

Reading time results were as follows. There were no reliable differences in region 1 (the RC; all $Ps > 0.17$).

In region 2 (the head nouns), there were main effects of task (ISS faster than Silence, $F_1(1,31) = 16.2$, $P < 0.01$; $F_2(1,23) = 21.6$, $P < 0.01$) and of attachment (High slower than Low; $F_1(1,31) = 17.2$, $P < 0.01$; $F_2(1,23) = 12.2$, $P < 0.01$). There was no interaction (ISS: High – Low, 227 ms; Silence: High – Low, 470 ms; $F_1(1,31) = 1.7$, $P < 0.2$; $F_2(1,23) = 2.1$, $P < 0.16$).

In region 3 (the first part of the matrix clause), the ISS conditions were slower than the Silence conditions in the item analysis ($F_1(1,31) = 3.0$, $P < 0.1$; $F_2(1,23) = 5.9$, $P < 0.05$). The High conditions were numerically faster than the Low conditions but the difference was not reliable ($Fs < 1$). There was no interaction ($Fs \leq 1$).

In region 4 (the matrix predicate), there was no effect of task ($Fs < 1$) nor interaction ($F_1 < 1$; $F_2(1,23) = 1.3$, $P < 0.27$). The High conditions were faster than the Low conditions ($F_1(1,31) = 13.1$, $P < 0.01$; $F_2(1,23) = 5.3$, $P < 0.05$).

3.2.1. Correlation Analyses

Linear regression analyses between RC length in number of characters and difference in reading times (Low – High) were conducted. For the Silence conditions, results were as follows. In region 1, RC length correlated marginally with reading time difference ($r^2 = 0.16$, $P < 0.06$). There were no reliable correlations in the remaining regions ($Ps > 0.3$). In the ISS conditions, there was no reliable correlation in any region ($Ps > 0.7$).

Numerically, the tendency for length effects were more apparent in the Silence conditions than in the ISS conditions, but we did not replicate the correlation in region 3 found in Experiment 1.

3.3. Discussion

There was no interaction between attachment (High/Low) and task (Silence/ISS), and the same pattern as in Experiment 1 was observed, namely, an initial bias towards Low attachment, and a High attachment advantage at the end. This suggests that ISS does not affect attachment and therefore prosody is unlikely to be the factor responsible for the preferences observed, in particular, it is unlikely to explain the high attachment preference at sentence-end.

Although there was no correlation between reading times and RC lengths in the ISS conditions, that was also the case for the ISS conditions. Therefore, there is no guarantee that the vocalization task achieved its intended purpose of eliminating implicit prosody. We are currently considering ways of addressing this point.

4.   Experiment 3

In this experiment, the effect of word order on RC attachment was investigated.

4.1.   Method

The experiment setup was the same as the one used in Experiment 1. Thirty-five native speakers of Japanese from NAIST were paid to participate. Three participants' data were eliminated because of low overall comprehension performance (72% or less).

4.1.1.   Materials

Apart from scrambled sentences (as in (4)), canonical versions were also included in a 2×2 design (Canonical/Scrambled × High/Low). The two sentences in (6) are an example of a Canonical pair (the scrambled versions can be obtained by moving regions 2 and 3 to the front of the sentence as in 2-3-1-4). The 24 sets of items of Experiment 1 were used with some of the matrix clauses modified to make their subjects implausible as part of the RCs.

(6) a. High attachment

      R1 | R2 |
      Satsujinka-wa | hoosekibako-no sumi-ni   nokotteita | ...
      homicide-dept-top   jewelry-box-gen corner-loc   remained

    b. Low attachment

      R1 | R2 |
      Satsujinka-wa | gojuudai dansei-to suiteisareru | ...
      homicide-dept-top   50s   male-as   supposed

    c. Remaining regions

                R3 | R4
      hannin-no   simon-o | nantoka   mitsukedasita.
      criminal-gen fingerprint-acc   somehow   found

      High condition: 'The homicide department somehow found the fingerprint of the criminal (that) remained in the corner of the jewelry box.'

      Low condition: 'The homicide department somehow found the fingerprint of the criminal (who) is supposed to be a male in his 50s.'

The test items were distributed into four lists according to a Latin Square design and were shown in pseudo-random order interspersed with 54 filler items.

4.1.2. Norming Study

In the canonical conditions, before the head nouns are read, the tendency is for the matrix subject to be interpreted as part of the RC leading to a garden path. At that point, plausibility is the only clue that this is incorrect. Thus, 28 native speakers of Japanese rated the plausibility of fragments like the following with the matrix subject and each RC.

(7) a. Matrix subject as part of the high attachment RC
     Satsujinka-wa   hoosekibako-no sumi-ni   nokotteita
     homicide-dept-top jewelry-box-gen corner-loc remained
     'The homicide department remained in the corner of the jewelry box.'

  b. Matrix subject as part of the low attachment RC
     Satsujinka-wa   gojuudai dansei-to suiteisareru
     homicide-dept-top 50s   male-as   supposed
     'The homicide department is supposed to be a male in his 50s'

The ratings for (7a) (4.42; scale from 1 = *natural* to 5 = *strange*) and for (7b) (4.48) did not differ ($F_1(1,27) = 1.34$, $P < 0.26$; $F_2 < 1$). Therefore, the likelihood of the matrix subject being interpreted as part of the RC is equally low for the two types of RCs.

4.2. Results

There was no reliable effect in the comprehension performance for the four conditions (between 87.5% and 91.7%; all Fs < 1).

There were no reading time differences for the matrix subject between the two Canonical conditions or between the two Scrambled conditions (all Fs < 1). There was no reliable difference at the RC region for the four conditions (all Fs < 1)

In the region containing the two head nouns, there was an interaction between word order (Canonical/Scrambled) and attachment (High/Low; Ps < 0.05). For the Scrambled conditions, Low was faster than High in the participant analysis ($F_1(1,31) = 4.77$, $P < 0.05$; $F_2(1,23) = 3.77$, $P < 0.07$), whereas for the Canonical conditions, High was numerically faster than Low (Fs < 1.2). There was also a main effect of word order as the Scrambled conditions were read more slowly than the Canonical conditions (Ps < 0.01); this is likely to be a position effect as fewer regions had been read in the Scrambled conditions at that point (readers tend to speed up as they read more words).

In the matrix predicate region, there was a main effect of attachment as the High conditions were faster than the Low conditions ($Ps < 0.01$). There was a main effect of word order as the Scrambled conditions were faster than the Canonical conditions (Fs < 0.01); this effect should be expected as the Canonical sentences involve a self-embedding configuration which is known to cause processing difficulties (Chomsky & Miller, 1963). There was no interaction (Fs < 1).

4.3. Discussion

The present experiment provides evidence that word order influences attachment decisions as attested by the interaction at the head nouns. One possible explanation is that in the scrambled conditions, the RC is initially interpreted as being a main clause and the mistake is only identified at the head nouns. In the canonical conditions, in contrast, the matrix subject is incompatible with the RCs, providing an early indicator for the higher clause. Thus, in the scrambled conditions, the higher predicate is not predicted until the head nouns are seeing, whereas in the canonical conditions the matrix subject may create the expectation for the matrix predicate earlier. It has been suggested that the matrix predicate is important in RC attachment decisions because the salience of the high noun is derived from the fact that this noun is the head of an argument of the matrix predicate (e.g., in (4), 'fingerprint' is the head of the direct object of 'found', whereas 'criminal' is not directly related to this verb; Frazier, 1990; Gibson et al., 1996). Thus, the late prediction of the matrix clause in the Scrambled sentences may weaken the salience of the high noun at first.

In the Canonical conditions, the High condition was numerically faster than the Low condition at the head nouns, but the difference was no statistically reliable. There are a number of possibilities that need to be considered for the reading time patterns in this region. First, the High is in fact faster than the Low condition at that point, but there was not enough statistical power. Second, although the matrix subject was equally implausible as part of both types of RCs (as attested by the norming study), it is conceivable that the NP was initially interpreted as part of the RCs, and that the ensuing reanalysis process necessary to expel the subject from the RC makes the reading times for the High and Low conditions indistinguishable. A third possibility is that this reanalysis process is in fact responsible for the interaction between attachment and word-order at the head nouns, and therefore the timing of the prediction of the matrix predicate per se is not critical. These three possibilities are being examined in ongoing work.

5.   Conclusion

Three self-paced reading experiments and two plausibility studies were reported in order to address various issues in the attachment of ambiguous relative clauses with two potential modifiees in Japanese. Using a coarse-grained segmentation, Experiment 1 confirmed the initial low attachment preference and its reversal at sentence-end (as in Kamide & Mitchell, 1997). The preliminary results of two experiments suggest future directions. In Experiment 2, no influence of prosodic contours on RC attachment was found. Experiment 3 detected an interaction between word order (Scrambled/Canonical) and attachment, which is compatible with the claim that awareness of an upcoming matrix predicate is critical in determining attachment preferences.

6.   Acknowledgements

The authors would like to thank Yuki Kamide and her collaborators for providing the items of their experiments. Experiment 1 was conducted at Kanda University of International Studies supported by this institution's Center for Language Sciences (CLS) and its Grant-in-Aid for COE Research (08CE1001) from the Japanese Ministry of Education, Science and Culture. The other experiments were conducted at the Laboratory of Natural Language Processing of NAIST. We would like thank professors Nobuko Hasegawa, Kazuko Inoue and Yuji Matsumoto for their support.

References

Baddeley, A. (1990). *Human memory — Theory and Practice*. Needham Heights, MA: Allyn and Bacon.

Brysbaert, M., & Mitchell, D. C. (1996). Modifier attachment in sentence parsing: Evidence from Dutch. Quarterly Journal of Experimental Psychology, *49*A, 3, 664-695.

Chomsky, N., & Miller, G. A. (1963). Introduction to the formal analysis of natural languages. In R. D. Luce, R. R. Bush, & E. Galanter (Eds.), *Handbook of Mathematical Psychology*, vol. 2 (pp. 269-321). New York: Wiley.

Cuetos, F., & Mitchell, D. C. (1988). Cross-linguistic differences in parsing: restrictions on the use of the Late Closure strategy in Spanish. *Cognition, 30*, 73-103.

Fodor, J. D. (1998). Learning to parse? *Journal of Psycholinguistic Research*, em 27, 285-319.

Fodor, J. D. (2002). Prosodic disambiguation in silent reading. *Proceedings of NELS 32*, M. Hirotani (ed.). Amherst, MA: GLSA, University of Massachusetts.

Frazier, L. (1987). Sentence processing: a tutorial review. In M. Coltheart (Ed.), *Attention and Performance XII* (pp. 559-586). Hillsdale, NJ: Lawrence Erlbaum.

Frazier, L. (1990). Parsing modifiers: special purpose routines in the human sentence processing mechanism? In D. A. Balota (Ed.), *Comprehension Processes in Reading* (pp. 301-330). Mahwah, NJ: Lawrence Erlbaum.

Frazier, L., & Clifton, C., Jr. (1996). *Construal*. Cambridge, MA: MIT Press.

Gibson, E. (1998). Linguistic complexity: locality of syntactic dependencies. *Cognition, 68*, 1-76.

Gibson, E., Pearlmutter, N., Canseco-Gonzalez, E., & Hickok, G. (1996). Recency preference in the human sentence processing mechanism. *Cognition*, *59*, 23-59.

Hirose, Y. (2001). L1 and L2 processing of RC attachment ambiguity. Talk presented at the Japanese Language Processing Workshop 2001. Nara Institute of Science and Technology, Ikoma, Japan. July 2001.

Just, M. A., Carpenter, P. A., & Woolley, J. D. (1982). Paradigms and processes in reading comprehension. *Journal of Experimental Psychology: General*, *3*, 228-238.

Kamide, Y., & Mitchell, D. (1997). Relative clause attachment: nondeterminism in Japanese parsing. *Journal of Psycholinguistic Research*, *26* , 247-254.

Kamide, Y., Mitchell, D. C., Fodor, J. D., & Inoue, A. (1998). Relative clause attachment ambiguity: further evidence from Japanese. Poster presented at the 11th Annual CUNY Conference of Human Sentence Processing. New Brunswick, NJ.

Kimball, J. (1973). Seven principles of surface structure parsing in natural language. *Cognition*, *2*, 15-47.

Miyamoto, E. T. (1999). Relative clause processing in Brazilian Portuguese and Japanese. Doctoral Dissertation. MIT.

Miyamoto, E. T., Gibson, E., Pearlmutter, N. J., Aikawa, T., & Miyagawa, S. (1999). A U-shaped relative clause attachment preference in Japanese. *Language and Cognitive Processes*, *14*, 663-686.

Slowiaczek, M. L., & Clifton, C., Jr. (1980). Subvocalization and reading for meaning. *Journal of Verbal Learning and Verbal Behavior*, *19*, 573-582.

Thornton, R., Gil, M., & MacDonald, M. C. (1998). Accounting for crosslinguistic variation: a constraint-based perspective. In D. Hilbert (Ed.), *A Crosslinguistic Perspective* (pp. 211-225), Syntax and Semantics, vol. 31. Academic Press.

Zagar, D., Pynte, J., & Rativeau, S. (1997). Evidence for early-closure attachment of first-pass reading times in French. *Quarterly Journal of Experimental Psychology*, *50A*, 421-438.

Edson T. Miyamoto   (miyamoto@alum.mit.edu)
University of Tsukuba
College of Japanese Language and Culture
Tsukuba, Ibaraki 305-8572 Japan

Michiko Nakamura   (michikon@is.aist-nara.ac.jp)
Nara Institute of Science and Technology
Graduate School of Information Science
8916-5 Takamaya, Ikoma, Nara 630-0192, Japan

Shoichi Takahashi   (s_t@mit.edu)
Massachusetts Institute of Technology
Department of Linguistics and Philosophy E39-230
77 Massachusetts Avenue Cambridge, MA 02139, USA

Two Constructions with *Most* and their Semantic Properties[*]

Kimiko Nakanishi and Maribel Romero

University of Pennsylvania

1.   Introduction

In this paper, we examine the semantic properties of two constructions involving *most* in English, namely, *most of the NPs* and *for the most part*, as exemplified in (1).

(1)   a.   Most of the linguists from the East Coast came to NELS.
       b.   For the most part, the linguists from the East Coast came to NELS.

In (1b), *for the most part* induces a so-called Quantificational Variability Effect (QVE) on the NP *the linguists from the East Coast*, yielding roughly the interpretation 'most of the linguists from the East Coast came to NELS'. We claim that the two constructions above differ in the domain where they apply, producing similar but not identical quantificational interpretations over the NP. In particular, we argue that *most of the NPs* applies to the nominal domain, while *for the most part* applies to the verbal domain. Our claim is based on two sets of novel semantic data. First, we show that the distribution of *most of the NPs* is parallel to that of *all the NPs* in terms of its selective compatibility with collective predicates. To account for this data, we extend Brisson's (1998, 2003) analysis of *all the NPs* to *most of the NPs,* concluding that *most* is an ∃-quantifier introducing a group of a certain proportion. Second, we show that, when *for the most part* gives rise to a QVE on a definite NP, the collective interpretation is not available. We develop a semantic analysis of *for the most part* as a verbal modifier that explains the lack of collective readings and that extends to interpretations other than QVE.

The structure of the paper is as follows: in section 2, we introduce some general background on events and distributivity that are relevant to the current paper. In section 3, we propose the analysis of *most of the NPs*, followed by the analysis of *for the most part* in section 4. Section 5 concludes the paper and discusses further issues.

---

[*] We would like to thank Dave Embick, Caroline Heycock, and Alexander Williams for valuable discussions, and our informants for their infinite patience. Thanks are also due to the audience at *NELS* 34. Of course, all errors are ours.

2.   General Background

Before we discuss the data on *most*, we introduce some background notions relevant to our analysis. First, a relation between a plural individual or event and its subparts is expressed by the ordering part-of relation ≤, as shown in (2) (Link 1983).

(2) $a \leq a{+}b{+}c$ (a is a part of the plural individual a+b+c)
          $e_1 \leq e_1{+}e_2{+}e_3$ (e_1 is a part of the plural event $e_1{+}e_2{+}e_3$)

Second, a distributive reading arises when a distributive operator D attaches to the verbal predicate, ^{D}P, as in (3). Furthermore, a VP predicate P can be pluralized, *P (Link 1983), yielding a reading that is vague between collective and distributive, as in (4).

(3)   IP   a. ^{D}P = $\lambda x \, \forall y \, [\, y \leq x \rightarrow P(y) \,]$

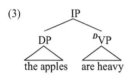

the apples   are heavy   b. $\forall y \, [\, y \leq$ the.apples $\rightarrow$ be.heavy(y) $]$

(4)   IP   a. $[\![$the.apples$]\!] = a{+}b{+}c$
                                          b. $[\![$be.heavy$]\!] = \{a, b, c, d, ...\}$
     DP   *VP $[\![$*be.heavy$]\!] = \{a,b,c,d,a{+}b, a{+}b{+}c, a{+}b{+}c{+}d, ...\}$
 the apples   are heavy   b'. $[\![$be.heavy$]\!] = \{a{+}b{+}c, d, ...\}$
                                              $[\![$*be.heavy$]\!] = \{a{+}b{+}c, d, a{+}b{+}c{+}d, ...\}$
                                          c. $[\![$IP$]\!]=1$ iff $a{+}b{+}c \in [\![$*VP$]\!]$

Third, we assume that thematic roles are introduced by neo-Davidsonian predicates (Higginbotham 1985, Parsons 1990, Landman 2000; Kratzer 1996 for the Agent head).

(5)   VP <v,t>[1] $\lambda e_v.$ lift(e) $\wedge$ Agent(e, the.boys) $\wedge$ Theme(e, the.piano)

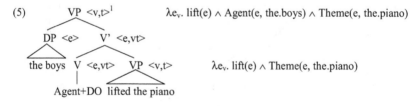

                                      $\lambda e_v.$ lift(e) $\wedge$ Theme(e, the.piano)

3.   The Analysis of *Most of the NPs*

3.1.   Data

Vendler (1957) proposed that verb phrases can be classified into four aspectual classes, that is, states, activities, accomplishments, and achievements. The examples in (6) show that predicates which allow both collective and distributive readings can be classified into

---

[1] We use type v for events.

the four classes and that definite plural NPs can have both a collective and distributive interpretations regardless of the aspectual classes.

(6)	a.	States:	The bottles are too heavy to carry.
			√collective, √distributive
	b.	Activities:	The boys lifted the piano.
			√collective, √distributive
	c.	Accomplishments:	The girls built a raft.
			√collective, √distributive
	d.	Achievements:	The girls found a cat.
			√collective, √distributive

However, definite NPs with *all* shows a different pattern: Taub (1989) found that these NPs allow a collective reading with activities and accomplishments, but not with states and achievements. Achievements can be coerced into accomplishments when predicates are understood to have some process. In such a case, a collective reading obtains.

(7)	a.	States:	All the bottles are too heavy to carry.
			*collective, √distributive
	b.	Activities:	All the boys lifted the piano.
			√collective, √distributive
	c.	Accomplishments:	All the girls built a raft.
			√collective, √distributive
	d.	Achievements:	All the girls found a cat.
			?collective, √distributive

As in (8), we found that *most of the NPs* shows the same distribution as Taub's pattern.

(8)	a.	States:	Most of the bottles are too heavy to carry.
			*collective, √distributive
	b.	Activities:	Most of the boys lifted the piano.
			√collective, √distributive
	c.	Accomplishments:	Most of the girls built a raft.
			√collective, √distributive
	d.	Achievements:	Most of the girls found a cat.
			?collective, √distributive

The question to be addressed is what is the source of the contrast between activities/accomplishments and states/achievements. We will turn in the next section to Brisson's (1998, 2003) analysis on definite NPs with *all* in (7).

3.2.   Brisson's (1998, 2003) Proposal on *All*

We have seen in (6) above that predicates applied to a definite plural NP allow for a collective and for a distributive interpretation. This fact is can be captured by saying that the distributive operator D can optionally apply to the verbal predicate: $[\![$ be.heavy$]\!]$ generates the collective reading, and $[\![^D$be.heavy$]\!]$ the distributive reading. Brisson (1998, 2003) claims that *all* signals the presence of a distributive operator D. Furthermore, Brisson assumes that activities and accomplishments, but not states and achievements, are syntactically decomposed into two VPs, as shown in (9): a lower VP whose head is a state and a higher VP whose head is the abstract verb DO (e.g. DOings of *build a raft* are hammering, sawing wood, etc.; a DOing of *sweep the floor* is moving a broom) (cf. McClure 1994, among others).

(9)   a.   Activities, Accomplishments   b.   States, Achievements

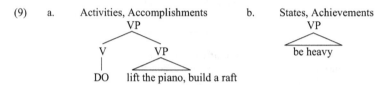

Given these structures, there are two possible insertion sites of the D operator in activities and accomplishments. If the operator is inserted at the higher VP, we obtain a distributive reading, roughly meaning that for each boy there is a different lifting the piano event e'. If the operator is attached to DO, we obtain a collective reading, roughly meaning that for each boy there is a different DOing event e' which is a part of the unique collective lifting e. For states and achievements, since they lack the head DO, the only possible attachment site of D is VP; hence, only the distributive reading is generated.[2]

(10)   a.   Activities, Accomplishments   b.   States, Achievements

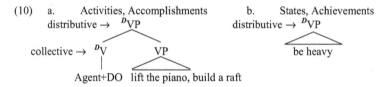

---

[2] In Brisson's (1998, 2003) analysis, *all* does not only signal the presence of the distributive operator D but it also imposes some constraints on D's cover variable *Cov*. A cover *Cov* of the set of individuals D_e is a subset of Pow(D_e) that exhausts D_e. *All* requires that *Cov* be a good fitting cover with respect to the relevant $[\![$NP$]\!]$, so that the $\forall$-quantification in reading (ii) of (i) does not leave aside any of the girls. By economy, Brisson also ensures that *all* is incompatible with a value of *Cov* for D that would accidentally generate a collective reading for (7a), e.g. a *Cov* where all the bottles (and only bottles) are in a set X member of *Cov*. Covers generating an intermediate reading for a bare definite, as paraphrased in (iii) for (6a), are allowed in Schwarzschild (1996) and are in principle predicted to occur under Brisson's account of *all the NPs*. However, intermediate readings for (7a) and (8a) are harder to obtain, and, if available, it is not clear whether the cover analysis would derive the correct truth conditions. We will leave this issue for future research and ignore intermediate readings in the present paper. (ii) can be thus simplified as in (iv).

(i)   All the girls jumped in the lake.

(ii) $\exists e \forall x$ [$x \le [\![$the.girls$]\!]$ $\wedge$ {z: Atom(z) $\wedge$ z$\le$x} $\in$ Cov $\rightarrow$ $\exists e'$ [e'$\le$e $\wedge$ jump(e') $\wedge$ $\exists e''$[e''$\le$e' $\wedge$ DO(e'') $\wedge$ Agent(e'', z)]]]

(iii)   Intermediate reading of (6a): 'Each group of bottles is too heavy to carry.'

(iv) $\exists e \forall x$ [$x \le [\![$the.girls$]\!]$ $\rightarrow$ $\exists e'$ [e'$\le$e $\wedge$ jump(e') $\wedge$ $\exists e''$[e''$\le$e' $\wedge$ DO(e'') $\wedge$ Agent(e'', z)]]]

3.3. The Extension of Brisson's Analysis to *Most of the NPs*

Brisson's analysis on *all the NPs* straightforwardly extends to *most of the NPs*, which shows the same pattern as *all the NPs*. We assume that *most of the NPs* introduces ∃-quantification over a group x whose cardinality is greater than a half of the NPs (i.e. 'a majority / major part of the NPs') (See Kroch 1974, cf. Kadmon 1987 for *at most three NPs*).[3] Furthermore, based on the parallelism between *all* and *most* with respect to Taub's generalization, we argue that *most* signals the presence of a distributive operator D in the same way as *all*. With the structures in (9), there are two possible insertion sites for the D operator with activities and accomplishments. The operator at the higher VP yields a distributive reading, where for each boy there is a different lifting the piano event e', as in (11a). In contrast, if the operator is at DO, we obtain a collective reading, where for each boy there is a different DOing event e" part of the unique collective lifting e, as in (11b).

(11)　a.　Distributive: $\exists e \exists x \,[\, x \le [\![\text{the.boys}]\!] \wedge \,|x\,|>1/2\,|\,[\![\text{the.boys}]\!]\,| \wedge \forall z \,[\, z{\le}x \rightarrow$
　　　　　$\exists e'[\, e'{\le}e \wedge \text{lift}(e', \text{the.piano}) \wedge \exists e"[\, e"{\le}e' \wedge \text{DO}(e") \wedge \text{Agent}(e", z)\,]\,]\,]\,]$
　　　b.　Collective: $\exists e \exists x \,[\, x \le [\![\text{the.boys}]\!] \wedge \,|x\,|>1/2\,|\,[\![\text{the.boys}]\!]\,| \wedge \text{lift}(e, \text{the.piano})$
　　　　　$\wedge \exists e' \,[\, e'{\le}e \wedge \forall z \,[\, z{\le}x \rightarrow \exists e"[\, e"{\le}e' \wedge \text{DO}(e") \wedge \text{Agent}(e", z)\,]\,]\,]\,]$

In sum, we argued that *most of the NPs* introduces ∃-quantification over a sum x of individual whose cardinality is greater than half of the cardinality of $[\![\text{the.NP}]\!]$, and that it signals the presence of the distributive operator D.

4.　The Analysis of *For the Most Part*

4.1.　Data

In this section, we shift our attention to the VP-spine modifier *for the most part*. Quantificational Variability Effects (QVE) with *for the most part* are illustrated in (12) and (13), where *for the most part* yields the effect of quantification over the individuals introduced by plural definite NPs (Berman 1991, cf. Lahiri 1991, 2002, Williams 2000).

(12)　(For the most part,) John (, for the most part,) likes his friends.
　　　≈ John likes most of his friends.
(13)　(For the most part,) the boys (, for the most part,) jumped in the lake.

Unlike *most of the NPs*, *for the most part* under QVE disallows a collective interpretation, even with activities and accomplishements:

---

[3] *Most* in *most NPs* is generally analyzed as a generalized quantifier in (i).
(i)　　$\lambda P_{<e,t>}\lambda Q_{<e,t>}.\,|\{x: P(x){\wedge}Q(x)\}| > 1/2\,|\{x: P(x)\}|$
Under this proportional analysis, we only obtain a distributive interpretation. We suspect that this prediction is empirically correct (e.g., the collective reading of *Most boys lifted the piano* seems quite hard, if possible at all). All the arguments in the present paper about adnominal *most* concern exclusively the construction *most of the NP*.

(14) a.   Activities: For the most part, the boys lifted the piano.
            *collective, √distributive
      b.   Accomplishments: For the most part, the girls built a raft.
            *collective, √distributive

These examples show that *for the most part* is semantically different from *most of the NPs*. While *most of the NPs* means 'a major part of [[NP]]', we cannot derive QVE from the claim that *for the most part* has a hidden argument semantically equal to [[NP]] (with the underlying syntactic structure *[for the most part ~~of NPs~~]* with ellipsis, or with the structure *[for the most part (of) C]*, where the value of the variable C is pragmatically determined). If QVE was simply the result of having [[NP]] as this hidden argument, it would mean 'for the major part of [[NP]]', incorrectly allowing collective readings in (14).

Note that *for the most part* allows readings other than QVE over an NP: (15)-(16). Crucially, in these readings, collective readings of that NP are available, as in (17)-(18).

(15) Quantification over times reading
      Q: What tasks did Jon perform last month?
      A: For the most part, he cooked.
            ≈ Most of the times he performed a task, the task consisted of cooking.

(16) Temporal span reading
      Q: What did Amy do yesterday?
      A: For the most part, she was building a sand castle.
            ≈ Most of yesterday was spent by Amy in building a sand castle.

(17) [In this dorm, the students in each room form a team to do household chores.]
      Q: What tasks did the students from Room A perform last month?
      A: For the most part, they cooked.

(18) Q: What did the boys do yesterday afternoon?
      A: For the most part, they were building a (large) sand castle.

The question is why *for the most part* behaves differently from *most of the NPs*, that is, why *for the most part* generates the effect of distributive quantification over [[NP]] (QVE reading) but not the effect of collective quantification over [[NP]].

4.2.   The Analysis of *For the Most Part*

The upshot of our analysis is that *for the most part* quantifies over the domain of events, unlike *most of the NPs* that applies to the nominal domain (cf. Nakanishi 2003, to appear).

4.2.1. Focus Sensitivity

For the most part adjoins to and modifies the VP spine (cf. Ginzburg 1995). Like other quantifiers over events adjoining to the VP spine, e.g. *only* in (19), *for the most part* is focus-sensitive, with different readings depending on the position of focus: (20)-(21).

(19)   a.   Sandy only feeds [Fido]$_F$ Nutrapup.

        b.   Sandy only feeds Fido [Nutrapup]$_F$.   (Beaver and Clark 2003:325)

(20)   a.   (Q: Who do the students admire?)

               A: For the most part, the students admire [Mary]$_F$. (But some admire Sue.)

        b.   (Q: What is the students' opinion about Mary?)

               A: For the most part, the students [admire]$_F$ Mary. (But some despise her.)

(21)   a.   For the most part, the conventioneers partied on [Friday]$_F$ night.

        b.   For the most part, the conventioneers [partied]$_F$ on Friday night.

These different readings result from different ways of dividing the content of the sentence between the Restrictor and Nuclear Scope of the adverbial quantification. In the case of *only*, Beaver and Clark (2003:349-50) propose the syntax-semantics mapping in (22), where the non-focused material is mapped both to the restrictor and to the nuclear scope and focused material is mapped exclusively to the nuclear scope (see also Bonomi and Casalegno 1993:16, Herburger 2000:18).

(22)   Truth conditions of 'NP only VP' in Beaver and Clark (2003):

        $\forall e\ [\ \mathbf{p}(e) \rightarrow \mathbf{q}(e)\ ]$, where

        RESTRICTOR $\mathbf{p}$ =   the meaning of 'NP VP' minus content related to any focused parts, and

        NUCLEAR SCOPE $\mathbf{q}$ =   the ordinary meaning of the sentence 'NP VP'.

Another possible syntax-semantics mapping is given in (23), where non-focused material is mapped only to the restrictor. Given the logical equivalence in (24), (22) and (23) yield the same truth-conditions for examples with *only*. Two readings are given in (25)-(26):

(23)   Modified truth conditions of 'NP only VP':

        $\forall e\ [\ \mathbf{p}(e) \rightarrow \mathbf{q}(e)\ ]$, where

        RESTRICTOR $\mathbf{p}$ =   the meaning of 'NP VP' minus content related to any focused parts, i.e., <u>the meaning of the non-focused material</u>, and

        NUCLEAR SCOPE $\mathbf{q}$ =   the meaning of 'NP VP' minus content related to any non-focused parts, i.e., <u>the meaning of the focused material</u>.

(24) $a \rightarrow a \wedge b$ iff $a \rightarrow b$

(25)   a.   Sandy only feeds [Fido]$_F$ Nutrapup.

        b. $\forall e\ [\ \text{feed}(e) \wedge \text{Agent}(e, \text{sandy}) \wedge \text{Theme}(e, \text{nutrapup}) \rightarrow \text{Goal}(e, \text{fido})\ ]$

(26)   a.   Sandy only feeds Fido [Nutrapup]$_F$.

        b. $\forall e\ [\ \text{feed}(e) \wedge \text{Agent}(e, \text{sandy}) \wedge \text{Goal}(e, \text{fido}) \rightarrow \text{Theme}(e, \text{nutrapup})\ ]$

We adopt the schema in (23) and extend it to *for the most part*.[4] A first try is (27). Then, we take our findings on *most of the NPs* from section 2 and we propose to apply them to *for the most part* as well: *most (part) of* introduces $\exists$-quantification over a sum x_e or e'_v whose cardinality is greater than half the cardinality of the relevant general individual ($[\![\, the\ boys\,]\!]$) or general event e described by the restrictor **p** – subformula $p(e) \wedge \exists e'$ [$e' \leq e \wedge |e'| \geq 1/2\ |e|$] in (28) – and it signals the presence of a distributive operator D – subformula $\forall e''[\ e'' \leq e' \rightarrow ...]$. The focused material mapped to the nuclear scope **q** falls under the scope of D. This gives us the syntax-semantics mapping in (28).

(27)   Truth conditions of 'For the most part NP VP':   (First try)
         MOST e [**p**(e)] [**q**(e)]
         Most events e for which **p**(e) holds are such that **q**(e) holds.
         RESTRICTOR **p**   =   the meaning of the non-focused material
         NUCLEAR SCOPE **q**   =   the meaning of the focused material.

(28)   Truth conditions of 'For the most part NP VP':   (Second try)
         $\exists e$ [$p(e) \wedge \exists e'$ [$e' \leq e \wedge |e'| \geq 1/2\ |e| \wedge \forall e''[\ e'' \leq e' \rightarrow q(e'')$]]]
         There is a general (possibly plural) event e for which **p**(e) holds and there is a (possibly plural) event e' that is a major part of e such that, for all subevents e'' of e', **q**(e'') holds.
         RESTRICTOR **p**   =   the meaning of the non-focused material
         NUCLEAR SCOPE **q**   =   the meaning of the focused material.

4.2.2. Deriving QVE over an NP

Several factors will further constrain the general truth-conditions in (28). First, the focus pattern of the sentence will determine what material is mapped to **p** and **q**. Second, the general event e must be somehow 'cut' into subevents e''_1, e''_2, e''_3, etc. so that there is a sum of them e' whose measure is more than half the measure of e, and so that, for each of the subevents of e that are part of the major event e', **q** holds. Different 'cuttings' of the general event e may yield different readings. Third and finally, for a given NP, it will be relevant whether or not that NP is interpreted distributively in a one-to-one mapping with respect to the verbal predicate. These parameters are summarized in (29):

(29)   Relevant factors
        (i)   What material is focused and non-focused in the sentence.
        (ii)   How the general event e is 'cut' into subevents e''_1, e''_2, e''_3, etc.
        (iii)   Whether the NP is interpreted distributively in a one-to-one mapping.

---

[4] For our analysis of *for the most part*, it is crucial that non-focused material is mapped *exclusively* to the restrictor **p**, as in (23) and contra (22) (see footnote 6). This means that we cannot derive the content of **p** and **q** directly from Rooth's (1992) alternative semantics of focus, which would assign (the great union of) the focus semantic value $[\![IP]\!]^f$ to **p** and the ordinary semantic value of the sentence $[\![IP]\!]^o$ to **q**, hence including non-focused material in **q** as well. Also, we leave for future research the question of whether the restrictor **p** of *for the most part* is entirely determined by focal structure (with its concomitant pragmatic restriction on relevant focus alternatives) or it includes other presuppositions, as discussed in Beaver and Clark (2003) for *only* and *always*.

We will show that the QVE-reading with respect to a given NP arises as a side effect of the following choices:

(30)   Choices for the QVE-reading:

> (i)   The semantic content and thematic predicate on the NP are within the restrictor **p**.
> (ii) The general event e is 'measured' by counting its atomic event units in $\llbracket V^0 \rrbracket$.
> (iii) The NP is interpreted distributively in a one-to-one mapping.

4.3.   Application to the Data

Let us now apply our analysis to some examples. The first example, in (31), involves an inherently distributive predicate *admire* and thus a plural general event e. The denotation of (31a) is given in (31b), which is paraphrased in (31c).

(31)   a.   For the most part, the students admire [Mary]$_F$.

   b. $\exists e$ [*admire(e) $\land$ Agent(e, the.students) $\land$ $\exists e'$ [$e' \leq e \land |e'| \geq 1/2|e| \land \forall e''$ [$e'' \leq e' \rightarrow$ Theme(e'', mary)]]]^5

   c.   There is a general (possibly plural) event e such that *admire(e) $\land$ Agent(e, the.students) and there is a (possibly plural) event e' that is a major part of e such that, for all subevents e'' of e', Theme(e'', mary).

The QVE reading results from the combination of the event quantification introduced by *for the most part* in (31b) and the factors discussed in (30). First, as in (32i), *the students*, i.e. Agent(e, the.students), is in the restrictor, since the NP is not focused. (This is already encoded in the truth conditions (31b-c).) Second, as in (32ii), the general event e such that *admire(e) $\land$ Agent(e, the.students) is semantically plural. This pluralized event e is measured by counting its atomic event units e''. Third, as stated in (32iii), since *admire* is inherently distributive, each atomic event is mapped to a student; let us assume that each student is mapped to exactly one (relevant) admiring event. This gives us the picture in (33): atomic events e'' part of the general event e are related to their agents in a one-to-one fashion, and thus quantification over the atomic events e'' yields the effect of quantification over the corresponding agents. This derives the QVE interpretation.^{6}

(32)   Relevant factors (cf.(29)):

   (i)   The meaning of *the students* is within the restrictor **p** (given the focus).

   (ii) The predicate *admire* is semantically plural: $\llbracket *admire \rrbracket = \{e''_1, e''_2, e''_3, e''_4, e''_5, e''_1+e''_2, e''_1+e''_2+e''_3, \dots \}$. The atomic units in the extension of *admire are taken as the units to measure the general event e.

---

^{5} To be precise, we obtain the following formula if we incorporate the decomposed DO in (9):
(i) $\exists e$ [*admire(e) $\land$ $\exists e''$[$e'' \leq e \land$ DO(e'') $\land$ Agent(e'', the.students)] $\land$ $\exists e'$ [$e' \leq e \land$ $|e'| \geq 1/2|e| \land$ $\forall e''$[$e'' \leq e' \rightarrow$ Theme(e'', mary)]]]
   ^{6} If we mapped non-focused material not just to the restritor **p** but also to the nuclear scope **q**, the truth condition of (31a) would be (i). (i) does not correspond to the QVE reading, since each e'' has the sum denoted by *the students* as its Agent. That is, (i) would be parallel to (39), which does not yield QVE.
(i) $\exists e$ [*admire(e) $\land$ Agent(e, the.students) $\land$ $\exists e'$ [$e' \leq e \land |e'| \geq 1/2|e| \land \forall e''$ [$e'' \leq e' \rightarrow$ *admire(e'') $\land$ Agent(e'', the.students) $\land$ Theme(e'', mary)]]]

(iii)   The NP necessarily has a distributive reading. Assume further that each
         student is the agent of exactly one admiring event.

(33)   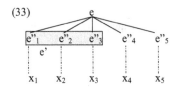   e: Agent(e, the.students) $\wedge$ *admire(e)

         e"$_1$, e"$_2$, e"$_3$: Theme(e"$_1$, mary);
                     Theme(e"$_2$, mary); Theme(e"$_3$, mary)

         x$_1$+x$_2$+x$_3$+x$_4$+x$_5$ = the.students

If we minimally modify (31a) as in (34a) so that the focus is on the verb instead of the
object, we obtain the truth condition in (34b). QVE results as before.

(34)   a.   For the most part, the students [admire]$_F$ Mary.
         b. $\exists$e [Agent(e, the.students) $\wedge$ Theme(e, mary) $\wedge$ $\exists$e' [e'$\leq$e $\wedge$ |e'|$\geq$1/2|e| $\wedge$
               $\forall$e"[e"$\leq$e' $\rightarrow$ *admire(e")]]]
         c.   There is a general (possibly plural) event e such that Agent(e, the.students)
               and Theme(e, mary) and there is a (possibly plural) event e' that is a major
               part of e such that, for all subevents e" of e', *admire(e").

         The second example involves a plural general event e and a predicate that allows
both distributive and collective readings, for example, *lift the piano* in (35).

(35)   For the most part, the students [lifted the piano]$_F$.
         $\exists$e [Agent(e, the.students) $\wedge$ $\exists$e' [e'$\leq$e $\wedge$ |e'|$\geq$1/2|e| $\wedge$ $\forall$e"[e"$\leq$e' $\rightarrow$ *lift(e") $\wedge$
         Theme(e", the.piano)]]]

Let us now examine the three factors given in (36). First, as in (36i), *the students*, being
non-focused, is in the restrictor. Second, as in (36ii), the general event e such that
Agent(e, the.students) is measured by counting its atomic events e". We can obtain either
a distributive or a collective reading depending on how to interpret the agent *the students*.
If we assume the one-to-one distributive reading described in (36iii), each student is the
agent of a different atomic event e", as in (37). This gives rise to the QVE reading:
quantifying over the atoms of the general event e"$_1$+e"$_2$+e"$_3$+e"$_4$+e"$_5$ produces the effect
of quantifying over the atoms of x$_1$+x$_2$+x$_3$+x$_4$+x$_5$. This reading is illustrated in (38).

(36)   Relevant factors (cf.(29)):
         (i)   The meaning of *the students* is within the restrictor **p** (given the focus).
         (ii)   The general event e is a plural event and it is measured by counting its
                atomic event e".
         (iii) Assume a distribute reading in which each student is paired with a single
                different atomic event of lifting the piano.
         (iii') Assume a collective reading in which each lifting of the piano is done
                collectively by the students.

(37)

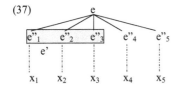

e: Agent(e, the.students)

e"₁, e"₂, e"₃:*lift(e"₁)∧Theme(e"₁, the.piano)
*lift(e"₂)∧Theme(e"₂, the.piano)
*lift(e"₃)∧Theme(e"₃, the.piano)
$x_1+x_2+x_3+x_4+x_5$ = the.students

(38)   [Each of the students must perform a difficult task. Each of them is given a choice between lifting the piano, taking a syntax exam and wrestling a grizzly bear.]
Q: What tasks did the students do?
A: For the most part, they lifted the piano (… but some took the syntax exam).

If we assume a collective reading in (36iii'), each atomic event e" has as its agent the sum of all the students x, as in (39). This does not evoke QVE on an NP, since quantifying over the atoms of e does not give rise to a parallel quantification over atoms of x. Instead, this yields the quantification over times reading in (17), repeated in (40), and in (41):[7]

(39)

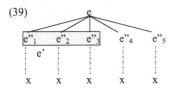

e: Agent(e, the.students)

e"₁, e"₂, e"₃:*lift(e"₁)∧Theme(e"₁, the.piano)
*lift(e"₂)∧Theme(e"₂, the.piano)
*lift(e"₃)∧Theme(e"₃, the.piano)
x = $x_1+x_2+x_3+x_4+x_5$ (the sum of students)

(40)   [In this dorm, the students in each room form a team to do household chores.]
Q: What tasks did the students from Room A perform last month?
A: For the most part, they cooked.

(41)   [In a TV contest, the student team has to accumulate points by performing one or more of the following tasks, possibly more than once: lifting the piano, taking a syntax exam, or wrestling a grizzly bear.]
Q: What tasks did the students perform?
A: For the most part, they lifted the piano.

The third example involves a singular general event e and a temporal span reading (again, not QVE). Consider (42), where we obtain the reading 'a major part of yesterday'. Such a temporal span reading often arises with a progressive, whose (simplified) lexical entry is given in (43). With this entry, the truth value of (42A) will be (44).

(42)   Q: What did the boys do yesterday afternoon?
A: For the most part, they were [building a raft]_F.

---

[7] QVE ceases to obtain as soon as there is no one-to-one mapping between the relevant events and relevant individuals. Hence, the quantification over times reading arises not only in the scenario (38), but also when some but not all atomic events have a collective agent, or when the same atomic individual is the agent of several events and the students as a group get "team credit" for each event.

(43)   Lexical entry for PROG(essive aspect) (Bennett and Partee 1972, Krifka 1992, but see also Dowty 1979, Parsons 1989, Landman 1992):

PROG = $\lambda P \lambda e'$ $\exists e$ [$P(e) \wedge e' \leq e$ $\wedge$ e' is not the final subevent of e]

(44)   a. $\exists e$ [Agent(e, the.boys) $\wedge$ At(e, yesterday) $\wedge$ $\exists e'$ [$e' \leq e$ $\wedge$ $|e'| \geq 1/2|e|$ $\wedge$ $\forall e''$[$e'' \leq e'$ $\rightarrow$ PROG([[build a raft]])(e'')]]]

        b. $\exists e$ [Agent(e, the.boys) $\wedge$ At(e, yesterday) $\wedge$ $\exists e'$ [$e' \leq e$ $\wedge$ $|e'| \geq 1/2|e|$ $\wedge$ $\forall e''$[$e'' \leq e'$ $\rightarrow$ $\exists e'''$[$e'' \leq e'''$ $\wedge$ e'' is not a final subevent of e''' $\wedge$ build(e''') $\wedge$ Theme(e''', a.raft)]]]]

First, as in (45i), *the boys*, being non-focused, is in the restrictor. Second, let us assume that *build* is semantically singular, that is, there is only one relevant – perhaps partial – building event e'. Still, PROG([[build a raft]]) yields a similar lattice of events as pluralization: e' is the sum of all the subevents of being in the process of building a raft.

(45)   Relevant factors (cf.(29)):
        (i)   The meaning of *the students* is within the restrictor **p** (given the focus).
        (ii)   Take *build* as semantically singular (there is only one – perhaps partial – building event e of a raft).
        (iii) Assume a collective reading: the boys are building the raft together.

(46)

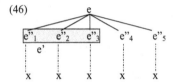

e: Agent(e, the.students)

e''$_1$, e''$_2$, e''$_3$: PROG([[build a raft]])(e''$_1$)
                            PROG([[build a raft]])(e''$_2$)
                            PROG([[build a raft]])(e''$_3$)
x = $x_1+x_2+x_3+x_4+x_5$ (the sum of students)

We have seen that *for the most part* in English gives rise to a variety of interpretations, including QVE over an NP, quantification over times, and a temporal span reading. A fourth reading that may fall under the present analysis is the path-quantification reading found in Japanese and Spanish. Besides the QVE interpretation in (47a), the Japanese example (47) has a reading (47b) where *for the most part* seems to quantify over (equally long) segments of a given path length l, meaning roughly 'John opened the door most of the way'. The same path reading obtains for Spanish in (48). Note that, under this reading, the NP *los chicos* 'the boys' can be interpreted collectively, i.e., the boys may have opened the door together.

(47)   John-ga   doa-o   isoide   hotondo   ake-ta
        John-NOM   door-ACC quickly   most   open-PAST
        a. NP-quantification reading: 'John opened most of the doors quickly'
        b. Path-quantification reading: 'John quickly opened the door most of the way'

(48)   Los chichos abrieron la   puerta   en su   totalidad.
        The boys   opened   the door   in its   totality

'The boys opened the door all the way.'   √collective, √distributive

We tentatively extend the current analysis to path-readings, generating the truth conditions in (49) and the schema in (50) for (47). To yield the correct interpretation, one would have to assume that, while e"$_1$, e"$_2$ and e"$_3$ are opening events, e"$_4$ and e"$_5$ are failing-to-open events.

(49)   ∃e [Agent(e, john) ∧ Theme(e, the.door) ∧ Path(e, l) ∧ ∃e' [e'≤e ∧ |e'|≥1/2|e| ∧ ∀e"[e"≤e' → open(e")]]]

(50)

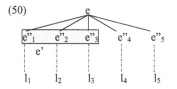

l$_1$ l$_2$ l$_3$ l$_4$ l$_5$

e: Agent(e, john) ∧ Theme(e, the.door) ∧
   Path(e, l)
e"$_1$, e"$_2$, e"$_3$: open(e"$_1$)∧Theme(e"$_1$,the.door)
                  open(e"$_2$)∧Theme(e"$_2$,the.door)
                  open(e"$_3$)∧Theme(e"$_3$,the.door)
l$_1$+l$_2$+l$_3$+l$_4$+l$_5$ = the complete path l

5.   Conclusions and Further Issues

In this paper, we argued that *most* in *most of the NPs* applies to the nominal domain and thus quantifies over individuals. It contributes an ∃-quantifier – introducing a sum x of a certain proportion – and a distributor operator *D* that makes the predicate ^{D}P distribute over the atoms of the sum x. Following Brisson's (1998, 2003) analysis on *all*, the predicate P$_{<e,<vt>>}$ that *D* adjoins to can be the VP or DO: ^{D}VP derives distributive readings and ^{D}DO derives collective readings for activities and accomplishments. In contrast, *most* in *for the most part* applies to the verbal domain and thus quantifies over events. It contributes an ∃-quantifier – introducing a sum e' of a certain proportion – together with a distributor over that sum e' of events. The question is how to cut e' into units and measure it. A plural event e' can be measured by counting its atomic units. When there is a one-to-one pairing between atomic events and individuals, quantification over event units will produce the effect of NP-quantification, i.e., QVE-reading. When each atomic event has the same collective agent, we obtain the quantification over times reading, with no QVE. A singular event e' with a progressive aspect can be measured by counting subparts of e' that belong to PROG([[VP]]). The result is a temporal span reading with no QVE. Finally, a singular event e with a path argument in Japanese and Spanish can be measured by counting subparts of the event e' as affecting each segment of the path, yielding the path reading.

   An interesting remaining question is how the type of quantification over events discussed in this paper differs from quantification over situations (von Fintel 1994, see also Endriss and Hinterwimmer 2003). When quantifying over events, we can quantify over the many (generic) events that make the sentence 'NP VP' true, as in (51a), or over parts of one episodic event that makes the sentence 'NP VP' true, as in (52a). In contrast, when quantifying over situations, only the first option seems possible, as the markedness of (52b) suggest.

(51) a.   For the most part, the students who sit over there are smart.
     b.   The students who sit over there are usually/always smart.

(52) a.   For the most part, the students sitting over there now are smart.
     b.   #The students sitting over there now are usually/always smart.

An open question is whether themes should have a separate neo-Davidsonian predicate Theme. The literature on focus-sensitive quantification over events assumes representations like (53a), whereas Kratzer (1996, to appear) argues that (core) themes should not be introduced by a separate predicate but should be represented as in (53b). For our analysis, we need to assume a separate Theme predicate for examples like (54), since the unfocused theme should appear exclusively in the restrictor **p** and not also in **q** with the focused verb (see footnote 6).

(53) Mary ate the pie.
     a. $\exists e\ [\ eat(e) \wedge Agent(e, mary) \wedge Theme(e, the.cake)\ ]$
     b. $\exists e\ [\ eat(e, the.cake) \wedge Agent(e, mary)\ ]$

(54) Q: What do you think about your classmates?
     A: For the most part, I [like]$_F$ them.
     $\exists e\ [\ Exp(e, I) \wedge Theme(e, my.classmates) \wedge \exists e'\ [\ e' \leq e \wedge |e'| \geq 1/2|e| \wedge \forall e''[\ e'' \leq e' \rightarrow {}^*like(e'')\ ]\ ]\ ]$

References

Beaver, David, and Brady Clark. 2003. *Always* and *only*: Why not all focus-sensitive operators are alike. *Natural Language Semantics* 11, 323-362.
Bennett, Michael, and Barbara Partee. 1972. *Toward the Logic of Tense and Aspect in English*. Santa Monica: System Development Corporation.
Berman, Stephen. 1991. *On the Semantics and Logical Form of Wh-Clauses*. Ph.D. dissertation, University of Massachusetts, Amherst.
Bonomi, Andrea, and Paolo Casalegno. 1993. *Only*: Association with focus in event semantics. *Natural Language Semantics* 2, 1-45.
Brisson, Christine. 1998. *Distributivity, Maximality, and Floating Quantifiers*. Ph.D. dissertation, Rutgers University.
Brisson, Christine. 2003. Plurals, *all*, and the nonuniformity of collective predication. *Linguistics and Philosophy* 26, 129-184.
Dowty, David. 1979. *Word Meaning and Montague Grammar: The Semantics of Verbs and Times in Generative Semantics and Montague's PTQ*. Dordrecht: Reidel.
Endriss, Cornelia, and Stefan Hinterwimmer. 2003. The role of tense and plurality in adverbial quantification. Manuscript. University of Potsdam.
von Fintel, Kai. 1994. *Restrictions on Quantifier Domains*. Ph.D. dissertation, University of Massachusetts, Amherst.
Ginzburg, Jonathan. 1995. Resolving questions, I&II. *Linguistics and Philosophy* 18, 459-527, 567-609.

Herburger, Elena. 2000. *What Counts: Focus and Quantification.* Cambridge, MA: MIT Press.

Higginbotham, James. 1985. On semantics. *Linguistic Inquiry* 16:4, 547-593.

Kadmon, Nirit. 1987. *On Unique and Non-Unique Reference and Asymmetric Quantification.* Ph.D. dissertation, University of Massachusetts, Amherst.

Kratzer, Angelika. 1996. Severing the external argument from its verb. J. Rooryck and L. Zaring eds., *Phrase Structure and the Lexicon*, 109-137. Dordrecht: Kluwer.

Kratzer, Angelika. to appear. *The Event Argument and the Semantics of Verbs.*

Krifka, Manfred. 1992. Thematic relations as links between nominal reference and temporal constitution. I. A. Sag and A. Szabolcsi eds., *Lexical Matters*, 29-53. Stanford: CSLI.

Kroch, Anthony. 1974. *The Semantics of Scope of English.* Ph.D. dissertation, MIT.

Lahiri, Utpal. 1991. *Embedded Interrogatives and Predicatives that Embed Them.* Ph.D. Dissertation, MIT.

Lahiri, Utpal. 2002. *Questions and Answers in Embedded Contexts.* Oxford: Oxford University Press.

Landman, Fred. 1992. The progressive. *Natural Language Semantics* 1, 1-32.

Landman, Fred. 2000. *Events and Plurality.* Dordrecht: Kluwer.

Link, Godehard. 1983. The logical analysis of plural and mass terms: A lattice theoretic approach. R. Bäuerle, C. Schwarze and A. von Stechow eds., M*eaning, Use and Interpretation of Language,* 302-323. Berlin: de Gruyer.

McClure, William. 1994. S*yntactic Projections of the Semantics o Aspect.* Ph.D. dissertation, Cornell University.

Nakanishi, Kimiko. 2003. The semantics of measure phrases. M. Kadowaki and S. Kawahara eds., T*he Proceedings of the 33rd Conference of the North East Linguistic Society (NELS 33),* 225-244.

Nakanishi, Kimiko. to appear. Semantic properties of Split Topicalization in German. C. Maienborn and A. Woellstein-Leisten eds., E*vents in Syntax, Semantics, and Discourse.* Tübingen: Niemeyer.

Parsons, Terence. 1989. The progressive in English: Events, states and processes. L*inguistics and Philosophy 12*, 213-241.

Parsons, Terence. 1990. E*vents in the Semantics of English.* Cambridge, MA: MIT Press.

Rooth, M. 1992. A theory of focus interpretation. *Natural Language Semantics* 1, 75-116.

Schwarzschild, Roger. 1996. *Pluralities.* Dordrecht: Kluwer.

Taub, Alison. 1989. Collective predicates, aktionsarten and al*l.* E. Bach, A. Kratzer and B. Partee eds., P*apers on Quantification.* University of Massachusetts at Amherst.

Vendler, Zeno. 1957. Verbs and times. Ph*ilosophical Review* 66, 143-160.

Williams, Alexander. 2000. Adverbial quantification over (interrogative) complements, T*he Proceedings of the 19th West Coast Conference on Formal Linguistics (WCCFL 19),* 574-587. Somerville, MA: Cascardilla Press.

Department of Linguistics
University of Pennsylvania
616 Williams Hall, Philadelphia, PA 19104

kimiko@ling.upenn.edu,   romero@ling.upenn.edu

On the Present Perfect Puzzle

Roumyana Pancheva and Arnim von Stechow

University of Southern California and University of Tübingen

1.   The Puzzle Illustrated

In English, the present perfect, unlike future, past, and non-finite perfects, cannot be modified by so-called 'positional' adverbials (Comrie 1976, McCoard 1978, a.o.). This phenomenon is known as the *present perfect puzzle* (Klein 1992).

(1)   a.   *Alicia has danced *on Monday / yesterday / at 10 o'clock.*
       b.   Alicia will have danced *on Monday / at 10 o'clock.*
       c.   Alicia had danced *on Monday / yesterday / at 10 o'clock.*
       d.   Alicia must have danced *on Monday / yesterday / at 10 o'clock.*

The prohibition against positional adverbials in the present perfect is not found in German (as seen in (2)), Dutch, Icelandic, or Italian. Notably, a present perfect morpho-syntax in these languages does not have the meaning of PAST[1], since it is compatible with present adverbials (Giorgi and Pianesi 1998, Musan 2001), a fact also illustrated in (2).

(2)   Hans ist {*gestern   um zehn / jetzt*}   weggegangen.   German
       Hans is   yesterday at 10   now   left   (Musan 2001)
       'Hans has left yesterday at 10 / now.'

The puzzle has proved rather difficult to solve (see Dowty 1979, Klein 1992, Giorgi and Pianesi 1998, Kiparsky 2002, Katz 2003, Portner 2003, a.o.). Lack of space prevents us from discussing the previous accounts in any detail. We can only note here that none are without problems, and hence we consider the puzzle still unresolved.

---

    * We are especially grateful to Philippe Schlenker for the extremely helpful discussions and ideas. Many thanks also to Rajesh Bhatt and to the audiences at NELS 34 at Stony Brook University, the University of Stuttgart, the University of Tübingen, the University of Texas, Austin, and UCLA.
    [1] We use capitalized regular font (e.g., Tense) for the syntactic category/node, small caps (e.g., PAST, PERFECT) for the semantic feature, and lowercase font (e.g., past, perfect) for the morpho-syntactic realization of the semantic feature (e.g. a –/d/-suffixed verb, an auxiliary + past participle).

2.   The Main Ingredients of the Proposal

A present perfect locates an eventuality (e.g., *Alicia's dance* in (1)) relative to a time interval that extends in the past. The intuition that we want to capture is that in English, though not in German, this interval necessarily includes the speech time, and hence cannot be modified by positional adverbials. This intuition is shared by many accounts of the perfect, most notably the Extended Now (XN) theory (McCoard 1978, Dowty 1979, a.o.). Our formalization of the intuition is novel in several respects.

Specifically, we propose that the inclusion/exclusion of the speech time is not solely due to the lexical meaning of PERFECT in its combination with PRESENT. The strictly compositional meaning of PRESENT PERFECT is compatible with intervals that precede the speech time. This meaning is, however, further restricted in English, because of competition with a semantic formative with a more specified meaning, namely PAST. The particular semantics of PRESENT is the reason PAST is a stronger scalar alternative to PRESENT PERFECT in English. PRESENT PERFECT is strengthened to non-PAST, requiring inclusion of the speech time. Failure of modification by positional adverbials then follows, as intervals including the speech time may not be modified by e.g. *yesterday*. PRESENT PERFECT is not strengthened in German, because of the different meaning of PRESENT in this language. Since inclusion of the speech time is not required, positional adverbials are predictably acceptable.

Below we present in more detail the three main components of our solution to the present perfect puzzle: (i) weak semantics for PERFECT, (ii) a cross-linguistic variation in the semantics of PRESENT, and (iii) a mechanism of grammatical competition and strengthening of meaning. But first we turn to the necessary background assumptions.

2.1.   Background Assumptions

We assume a tense-aspect architecture as in (3) and interpretations as in (4). Tenses relate an interval (commonly called *reference time*) with respect to the speech time (t_c).[2] Tenses are treated here as variables with presuppositions, after Partee (1973), Heim (1994), Schlenker (1999), von Stechow (2003)[3]. PERFECT relates an interval called here the *Perfect Time Span (PTS)*[4] and the reference time in a way, which will be made precise in the next subsection. The aspectual system is two-tiered (e.g., Smith 1991). Viewpoint aspects set up an interval – the interval at which an eventuality holds, called the *event time* – in relation to an evaluation interval. Composed with Tense, the Viewpoint aspects

---

[2] Embedded tenses are not directly interpreted relative to the speech time. We assume that tense features are deleted under semantic binding by verbs (see von Stechow 2003).

[3] Temporal variables may not be interpreted in the scope positions occupied by the tense features. Apposition to the variable, expressing the presupposition, is needed, as already reflected in (4a). Existential closure then applies (see Schlenker 1999, von Stechow 2003 for details of the formalization.)

[4] Perfect Time Span is a term introduced in Iatridou et al. (2001) for the concept of XN; it has the advantage of generalizing over intervals extending back in time from any reference time, not just a present one. The PTS in out proposal has weaker restrictions on its temporal location, than the PTS of Iatridou et al.

temporally situate the event time relative to the reference time. Composed with PERFECT, the Viewpoint aspects temporally situate the event time relative to the PTS. vPs denote predicates of eventualities.

(3)   [$_{TP}$ Tense [$_{PerfP}$ Perfect [$_{AspP}$ Viewpoint-Aspect [$_{vP}$ Aktionsart]]]]

(4)   a. $[\![$ PAST$_1$ $]\!]$ = $\lambda p_{(it)}.$ $\lambda t_{1(i)}$ [$t_1 < t_c$ & $p(t_1)$]
            $[\![$ PRESENT$_1$ $]\!]$ = $\lambda p_{(it)}.$ $\lambda t_{1(i)}$ [$t_1 = t_c$ & $p(t_1)$]   (to be further qualified)
        b. $[\![$ PERFECT $]\!]$ = $\lambda p_{(it)}.\lambda t_{(i)}.\exists t'_{(i)}$ [t' R t & $p(t')$]   (to be specified)
        c. $[\![$ IMPERFECTIVE$]\!]$ = $\lambda P_{(vt)}.\lambda t_{(i)}$.$\exists e_{(v)}$ [$t \subseteq \tau(e)$ & $P(e)$]
            $[\![$ PERFECTIVE $]\!]$ = $\lambda P_{(vt)}.\lambda t_{(i)}.\exists e_{(v)}$ [$\tau(e) \subset t$ & $P(e)$]
        d. $[\![vP]\!]$ = $\lambda e_{(v)}.P(e)$

We further assume that positional adverbials have different semantics from the time adverbials acceptable in a present perfect, such as e.g., *on (a) Monday,* certain instances of *on Monday/at 10 o'clock* (see (5)). As has been noted before, the prohibition is against specific temporal adverbials (cf. Heny 1982, Klein 1992, Giorgi and Pianesi 1998, a.o.). The meanings we assume are as in (6) (cf. Pratt and Francez 2001, von Stechow 2002, a.o.). Adverbials such as *on Monday, at 10 o'clock* conceal two structures and corresponding meanings: as in (6b) and (6c).

(5)   a. Alicia has danced *on a Monday.*
        b. Alicia has often/never danced *on (a) Monday/ at 10 o'clock.*

(6)   a. $[\![$ yesterday $]\!]$ = $\lambda p_{(it)}.\lambda t_{(i)}$ [$t \subseteq$ yesterday$_c$ & $p(t)$]
        b. $[\![$ on Monday $]\!]$ = $\lambda p_{(it)}.\lambda t_{(i)}$ [$t \subseteq$ Monday$_c$ & $p(t)$]
        c. $[\![$ on a Monday $]\!]$ = $\lambda p_{(it)}.\lambda t_{(i)}.\exists t'_{(i)}$ [Monday(t$'$) & t$'$ $\subseteq$ t & $p(t')$]

Consider now the question of where in the structure of a present perfect positional adverbials can be interpreted. Given the tense-aspect architecture and meanings we adopted, composing vP with time adverbials is not possible for type reasons. Three modification structures are in principle available: the adverbials can compose with TP, PerfP or AspP, as in (7). The LFs in (7a) yield semantically equivalent, and contradictory, statements. They involve reference time modification and a present reference time cannot be in yesterday$_c$ (a point made by pretty much every account).

(7)   a. i. *yesterday* [$_{TP}$ PRESENT$_1$ [$_{PerfP}$ PERFECT [$_{AspP}$ PERFECTIVE [$_{vP}$ Alicia dance]]]]
            ii. [$_{TP}$ PRESENT$_1$ *yesterday* [$_{PerfP}$ PERFECT [$_{AspP}$ PERFECTIVE [$_{vP}$ Alicia dance]]]]
            = $\exists t_1[t_1 = t_c$ & $t_1 \subseteq$ yesterday$_c$ & $\exists t_2[t_2$ R t_1 & $\exists e[\tau(e) \subset t_2$ & dance (A, e)]]]

        b. [$_{TP}$ PRESENT$_1$ [$_{PerfP}$ PERFECT *yesterday* [$_{AspP}$ PERFECTIVE [$_{vP}$ Alicia dance]]]]
            = $\exists t_1[t_1 = t_c$ & $\exists t_2$ [t_2 R t_1 & $t_2 \subseteq$ yesterday$_c$ & $\exists e[\tau(e) \subset t_2$ & dance (A, e)]]]

The only structure that can yield a contingent interpretation is (7b), where the adverbial modifies the PTS. Therefore, this has to be the source of the present perfect puzzle.

2.2.   Weak, Interval-Based Semantics for PERFECT

We propose that the semantic contribution of PERFECT, in both English and German, is to introduce an interval – the PTS – no part of which may be after the local evaluation time, as in (8).[5] Our proposal is in the spirit of the XN theory. But whereas the XN has to include the reference time as its final subinterval, the PTS has weaker restrictions: it may also precede and partially overlap with the reference time, or it may entirely precede it.[6]

(8) $[\![\text{PERFECT}]\!] = \lambda p_{(it)}.\lambda t_{(i)}.\exists t'_{(i)} \ [t' \leq t \ \& \ p(t')]$ $(t' \leq t$ iff there is no $t'' \subset t'$, s.t. $t'' > t)$

2.3.   Cross-Linguistic Variation in the Meaning of PRESENT

We adopt a suggestion by Klein (1992), Giorgi and Pianesi (1998), a.o., that the semantics of PRESENT$_i$ is different in English and German. Specifically, we propose that in English, PRESENT$_i$ introduces an interval coextensive with the speech time, whereas in German, it introduces an interval no part of which may precede the speech time.[7] The contrast between (10) and (11) illustrates the meaning difference: the English present is not compatible with future adverbials[8], whereas the German present is.

(9)   a. $[\![\text{PRESENT}_1]\!] = \lambda p_{(it)}. \ \lambda t_{1(i)} \ [t_1 = t_c \ \& \ p(t_1)]$ English

        b. $[\![\text{PRESENT}_1]\!] = \lambda p_{(it)}. \ \lambda t_{1(i)} \ [t_1 \geq t_c \ \& \ p(t_1)]$ German

             where $t' \geq t$ iff there is no $t'' \subset t'$, such that $t'' < t$

(10)   a.   # Fred is sick in 10 days.

         b.   # It {rains/is raining} next week.

---

[5] Musan (2001) proposes a similar meaning for the German PERFECT.

[6] There are no interesting consequences of the distinction between (i) the PTS partially intersecting with the speech time, or (ii) the PTS including the speech time as a final subinterval. The speech time is sometimes conceived of as a point, which would obliterate this distinction anyway.

[7] It has been argued that in German, the PRESENT$_i$ interval may extend prior to the speech time (Giorgi and Pianesi 1998, a.o.). The contrast between (i) and (ii) is often given as evidence. Our proposal does not depend on this specific aspect of the meaning of PRESENT$_i$. We note in passing that von Stechow (2002) gives an alternative explanation for the acceptability of (i), relating it to the meaning of *seit* (see also Musan 2003). When this factor is controlled for, German is like English (see (iii)-(iv)).

(i)   Maria   wartet   seit   gestern   auf Hans.   (Musan 2003)
       Maria   waits   since   yesterday   on Hans
       'Maria has been waiting on Hans since yesterday.'

(ii)   *Maria lives in LA since 2000.

(iii)   *Maria wohnt   in   LA   ab   dem   Jahr   2000.
        Maria   lives   in   LA   from   the   year   2000
        'Alexandra has lived in LA since 2000.'

(iv)   *Alexandra lives in LA from 2000 onwards / from 2000 till now.

Furthermore, if the PRESENT$_i$ interval could extend prior to the speech time, it should be possible for the calling event in (v) to be before the speech time. Yet this is not the case.

(v)   Ich rufe   Hubert heute   einmal   an
       I   call   Hubert today   once   up
       only: 'I will call Hubert today once.' not: 'I called Hubert today once.'

[8] Only planned events can receive future interpretation with the present in English.

(11)   a.   Fritz   ist   in 10 Tagen   krank.
           Fritz   is   in 10 days   sick
           'Fritz will be sick in 10 days.'

       b.   Nächste   Woche   ist das Wetter   schlecht.
           next   week   is the weather bad
           'Next week the weather will be bad.'

2.4.   Grammatical Competition between PRESENT PERFECT and PAST

Here are the outlines of a theory of feature distribution that is compatible with the idea of grammatical competition. Semantic features such as PRESENT$_i$, PAST$_i$, PERFECT, etc. are specified at syntactic terminal nodes, according to the architecture in (3). In the unmarked case, the feature PERFECT moves to Aux *have/be*. Feature-movement leaves no trace/copy behind. When the auxiliary is finite, it, together with the feature PERFECT, moves to T. PRESENT$_i$ and PERFECT thus meet at finite T (see (12)), and form the complex operator PRESENT$_i$ ° PERFECT, as in (13). If the auxiliary is non-finite, PRESENT$_i$ and PERFECT do not meet, as in (14). (In the trees below we ignore the issue of pronunciation, both with respect to the position of the subject, and concerning the morphology on the verb[9].)

(12)

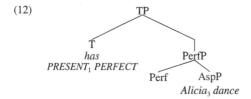

(13) $[\![$ PRESENT$_1$ ° PERFECT $]\!]$ = $\lambda p_{(it)}$. PRESENT$_1$ (PERFECT (p)) =
       = λp PRES$_1$ $\lambda t_1 \exists t_2$ [$t_2 \leq t_1$ & $p(t_2)$]

(14)

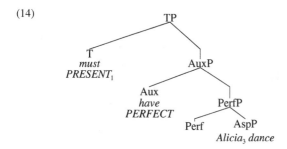

---

[9] The correspondence between the semantic temporal features and the verbal morphology can be stated in various ways. In von Stechow (2003), for instance, uninterpretable temporal features on verbs determine the morphology. These features are checked against the interpretable ones and deleted at LF.

A general principle dictates that meanings be expressed by the most specified form available. A familiar application of this principle is the realization of syntactic features by morphological forms. For instance, in a theory such as Distributed Morphology (Halle and Marantz 1993, a.o.), vocabulary items compete for insertion in syntactic terminal nodes, based on their feature specification. The vocabulary item that best matches the information in the syntactic node (i.e., the most specified one) wins the competition.

In an analogous way, semantic features realized at the same syntactic node compete with each other. The competition applies in the construction of an LF, both on the basis of an intended meaning (by a speaker), and on the basis of an utterance (by a hearer). Given an intended meaning, a speaker chooses the most specified semantic feature available in the language, to express at a syntactic node. Similarly, upon comprehending an utterance, a hearer chooses the most specified semantic feature available that corresponds to the morphology realized at a syntactic node. Among the temporal features, $PAST_i$, for instance, competes with $PRESENT_i$ as only one of them can occupy finite T. Since the two do not share aspects of their meaning, i.e., no interval can be described by both $PAST_i$ and $PRESENT_i$, the outcome of the competition is trivial. The interesting cases of competition are when one feature's meaning is less specified than that of another. The feature that has the more specified meaning wins in every case when it can be expressed as a value of the syntactic node. Therefore, when a feature with a less specified meaning is realized as a value of a syntactic node, it must be because its more highly specified competitor couldn't appropriately be used. As a result, the meaning of the less specified feature is restricted: those aspects of the meaning that are shared between the competing features are no longer available.

2.5.   Present Perfect in English and German

In both English and German, $PRESENT_i$ ° $PERFECT$ and $PAST_i$ compete for expression at the finite T node. The meaning of $PRESENT_i$ ° $PERFECT$, though, is different in the two languages, because the meaning of $PRESENT_i$ is. The results of the competition are thus different in the two languages.

In English, $PRESENT_i$ ° $PERFECT$ is less specified than $PAST_i$. $PAST_i$ denotes an interval that is strictly before the speech time, as in (15). The restrictions on $PRESENT_i$ ° $PERFECT$ are weaker: it sets up an interval that does not extend after the speech time, as in (16a). $PRESENT_i$ ° $PERFECT$ in English relates the PTS directly to the speech time, because $PRESENT_i$ makes the reference time coextensive with the speech time.

(15) $[\![PAST_1]\!] = \lambda p \, \exists t_1 \, [t_1 < t_c \ \& \ p(t_1)]$

(16) $[\![PRESENT_1 \ ° \ PERFECT]\!] = \lambda p \, PRES_1 \, \lambda t_1 \exists t_2 \, [t_2 \leq t_1 \ \& \ p(t_2)] =$
     a. $= \lambda p \, \exists t_1 \, [t_1 = t_c \ \& \ \exists t_2 \, [t_2 \leq t_1 \ \& \ p(t_2)]] = \lambda p \, \exists t_2 \, [t_2 \leq t_c \ \& \ p(t_2)]]$ English
     b. $= \lambda p \, \exists t_1 \, [t_1 \geq t_c \ \& \ \exists t_2 \, [t_2 \leq t_1 \ \& \ p(t_2)]]$ German

As a result, when PRESENT$_i$ ° PERFECT is the value of T, its meaning is restricted to the complement of PAST$_i$: i.e., the PTS has to overlap with the speech time, as in (17).

(17) $[\![$ PRESENT$_1$ ° PERFECT $]\!]$ = $\lambda p \, \exists t_1 \, [t_1 = t_c \, \& \, \exists t_2 \, [t_2 \cap t_1 \, \& \, p(t_2)]]$ (strengthened)
          where $t \cap t'$ iff $t \cap t'$ and there is no $t'' \subset t$, such that $t'' > t'$

Thus, we get essentially an XN meaning for the English present perfect, without positing in the lexical semantics of PERFECT that the PTS has to overlap with the reference time. Given the strengthened meaning of PRESENT$_1$ ° PERFECT, it follows that positional adverbials may not modify the PTS. (18) is clearly a contradiction.[10]

(18) $[_{TP}$ [PRESENT$_1$ PERFECT] $[_{PerfP}$ *yesterday* $[_{AspP}$ PERFECTIVE $[_{vP}$ Alicia dance]]]]
          = $\exists t_1 \, [t_1 = t_c \, \& \, \exists t_2 \, [t_2 \cap t_1 \, \& \, t_2 \subseteq$ yesterday$_c \, \& \, \exists e \, [\tau(e) \subset t_2 \, \& \,$ dance (Alicia, e)]]]

In English, PRESENT$_i$ ° PERFECT competes not only with PAST$_i$ but also with PRESENT$_i$. Note that the meaning of PRESENT$_i$ in English is a special case of the meaning of PRESENT$_i$ ° PERFECT (compare (9a) and (16a)). As a result of this competition, the meaning of PRESENT$_i$ ° PERFECT is strengthened such that the PTS may not coincide with the speech time. Rather some part of the PTS must precede the speech time.

Let us now turn to the analysis of the present perfect in German. In this language, PRESENT$_1$ ° PERFECT and PAST$_i$ are not scalarly ordered (see (16b) compared with (15). Therefore, when PRESENT$_1$ ° PERFECT is expressed as a value of finite T, its meaning is not restricted. As a result, the PTS may precede the speech time, and be modified by positional adverbials. (19) is not a contradiction.

(19) $[_{TP}$ [PRESENT$_1$ PERFECT] $[_{PerfP}$ *yesterday* $[_{AspP}$ PERFECTIVE $[_{vP}$ Alicia dance]]]]
          = $\exists t_1 \, [t_1 \geq t_c \, \& \, \exists t_2 \, [t_2 \leq t_1 \, \& \, t_2 \subseteq$ yesterday$_c \, \& \, \exists e \, [\tau(e) \subset t_2 \, \& \,$ dance (Alicia, e)]]]

Consider the following facts, which support the proposal that in the German present perfect the PTS need not intersect with the speech time. The so-called universal perfect requires the event time to include the PTS (cf. Iatridou et al. 2001). In the case of the English present perfect, this means that the event time includes the speech time, as the speech time and the reference time are coextensive. This is why, (20) may not be felicitously continued by *until recently*: *I live here* needs to be true at the speech time. In German, the facts are different, as (21) shows. The acceptability of *until recently* in (21) indicates that the event time precedes the speech time. But since the event time still includes the PTS, it follows that the PTS does not overlap with the speech time.

---

[10] In the case of *on Monday, at 10 o'clock*, the restriction obtains too, as these may not include the speech time. At 10 o'clock on Monday we may not say (i). Most likely, this is so because of competition with *today/now*. Similar facts obtain with proper names vs. 1st and 2nd personal pronouns in argument position. Speakers may not refer to themselves by name (see (ii)).
(i)   *We are writing *on Monday/at 10 o'clock.*
(ii)   *Roumi and Arnim are writing.*

(20)   I have always lived here (*... until recently).

(21)   Ich habe   hier   immer gewohnt   ... bis   vor kurzem
       I   have   here   always lived   until   recently
       'I have always lived here ... until recently.'

It is important to emphasize that the competition responsible for the strengthening of the meaning of a present perfect in English is strictly local, operating between two features that can potentially be realized at a single syntactic node. There is no global competition between proposition-expressing LFs. If there were such a global competition, the German present perfect too would have its meaning strengthened because of the existence of the past as a competitor. Consider the LF and interpretation in (22a). The location of the PTS with respect to the speech time is not directly specified. Yet it is still the case that the PTS is somehow situated relative to the speech time: it either precedes it, follows it, or intersects with it. When this inference is taken into consideration, it is clear that the interpretation in (22a) is less specified than that of the corresponding past sentence in (22b). If these LFs were allowed to compete, the interpretation in (22a) would be restricted in a way that makes the PTS overlap with or follow the speech time.

(22)   a. $[_{TP} [\text{PRESENT}_1 \text{ PERFECT}] [_{\text{PerfP}} [_{\text{AspP}} \text{PERFECTIVE} [_{vP} \text{Alicia dance}]]]]$
            $= \exists t_1 [t_1 \geq t_c \ \& \ \exists t_2 [t_2 \leq t_1 \ \& \ \exists e [\tau(e) \subset t_2 \ \& \ \text{dance (Alicia, e)}]]]$

       b. $[_{TP} [\text{PAST}_1 [_{\text{AspP}} \text{PERFECTIVE} [_{vP} \text{Alicia dance}]]]$
            $= \exists t_1 [t_1 < t_c \ \& \ \exists e [\tau(e) \subset t_2 \ \& \ \text{dance (Alicia, e)}]]$

The above discussion makes it clear that the strengthening of the meaning of the English present perfect is not the same phenomenon as the generation of scalar implicatures, as these are conceived of in traditional accounts such as Grice (1968), Horn (1972, 2001), a.o. According to the traditional view, scalar items such as e.g., numerals, are posited to have weak semantic content, i.e., *two* means "*two or more*". The strong reading "*exactly two*" in e.g. *John has two cats* comes about as a pragmatic effect. The addressee computes the meaning of this utterance as *John has two or more cats* and compares it with the stronger proposition *John has more than two cats*. On the assumption that speakers make the most informative contribution needed, the addressee concludes that the stronger assertion cannot be made, and thus, restricts the meaning of *John has two cats* to *John has exactly two cats*.

The traditional accounts of scalar implicatures compare propositional content, and this is not what we want in our competition account, if we are to have an explanation for the difference between the English and German present perfect. It does not follow, however, that the competition between PRESENT$_1$ ° PERFECT and PAST$_i$ and the strengthening of the meaning of PRESENT$_1$ ° PERFECT that it triggers, is a different phenomenon from the generation of scalar implicatures. Recent work in that domain by Kratzer (2003) (see also Chierchia, to appear) argues for a very local computation of the scalar implicatures to be followed by subsequent semantic composition. On that view, the lexical meaning of *two* is "*two or more*". Direct competition with e.g., *more than two,* restricts the meaning of *"two"* to *"exactly two"*.[11] Viewed from that perspective, the two competition phenomena are very similar.[12] It remains to be seen whether they are, in fact, essentially the same.

Before we move to the discussion of non-present perfects, consider the question of how a FUTURE semantic feature would figure in the tense system of German. The meaning of PRESENT$_i$ as defined in (9b), makes it a less specified tense feature than FUTURE$_i$. One might ask why PRESENT$_i$ and FUTURE$_i$ in German do not compete with the result that the meaning of the PRESENT$_i$ is restricted to non-future. The claim is that the competition with PRESENT$_i$ doesn't arise, because the FUTURE$_i$ is not productive in colloquial speech in German, i.e. the two are really not part of the same grammar. Grammatical competition across registers is not expected.

To summarize, the proposal makes the prediction that, keeping the meaning of PERFECT (and PAST) the same cross-linguistically, the semantics of PRESENT may by itself determine whether a language will prohibit positional adverbials in the present perfect.[13] It, of course, does not exclude the possibility that there may be cross-linguistic variation in the meaning of PERFECT itself.

3.   Positional Adverbials in Non-Present Perfects

The meanings of non-present perfects modified by positional adverbials follow directly from our proposal without any further provisions.

---

[11] See Fox (2003) for further discussion of various issues in the analysis of scalar implicatures.

[12] It may be further objected that scalar implicatures are cancelable, whereas the strengthening of the meaning of the English present perfect is not. As we will show, however, there is an environment where the meaning of a present perfect is not restricted. As discussed in section 4, PRESENT$_i$ and PERFECT sometimes remain on separate syntactic nodes; thus, the conditions for competition with PAST$_i$ are not met. In a similar way, the failure to generate scalar implicatures is conditioned by the grammatical environment. There appears to be no argument from cancelability then, that the strengthening of the meaning of a present perfect and the generation of scalar implicatures are unrelated phenomena.

[13] PRESENT$_i$ in Swedish, Norwegian, and Danish appears to be the same as in German.

(i)   a.   John   bliver   syg i   loebet   af   de   naeste   par   dage.   Danish
           John   becomes   sick   in-run   of   the   next   couple   days
           'John will become sick in the next few days.'
      b.   Det regner   paa deres   bryllupsdag.
           it   rains   on their   wedding-day
           'It will rain on their wedding day.'

Thus we would expect positional adverbials to be acceptable in the present perfect. However, Giorgi and Pianesi (1998) claim that in these languages the restriction with respect to positional adverbials obtains.

(ii)   *Johan har slutat   *klockan fyra.*   Swedish, (Giorgi and Pianesi 1998)
       Johan   has finished clock   four
       '*Johan has finished at four.'

The judgment in (ii) is challenged by some speakers (Bjorn Rothstein, p.c.). Similarly, we have found positional adverbials to be acceptable in Danish (Uffe Bergeton, p.c.)

(iii)   John   er   ankommet   *igaar /*   *klokken fem /*   *in   mandags*
        John   is   arrived   yesterday   clock   five   in   Monday's
        'John has arrived yesterday/at 5/on Monday.'

3.1   Past Perfect

The proposal predicts two readings for a past perfect modified by a positional adverbial. On one reading, the adverbial modifies the PTS, and on another it modifies the reference time. The lexical meaning of PERFECT is such that the PTS does not have to intersect with the reference time. Thus, when the PTS is modified by a positional adverbial, the reference time need not be included in the denotation of the adverbial (see (23) where clearly *last night$_c$*, which serves as the reference time for the subsequent past perfect, is not included in *Monday$_c$*). Here the proposal differs from the predictions of the XN account, which requires such inclusion, because of the lexical meaning of PERFECT.

(23)   a.   I saw Alicia last night. She had danced on Monday.
        b. $\exists t_1$ [$t_1 < t_c$ & $t_1 \subseteq$ last night$_c$ & $\exists t_2$ [$t_2 \leq t_1$ & $t_2 \subseteq$ Monday$_c$ & $\exists e$ [$\tau(e) \subset t_2$ & dance (Alicia, e)]]]

Importantly, the PTS is not required to overlap with the reference time through strengthening either. This is so, because there is no semantic tense with a more specified meaning of a PAST-under-PAST, i.e., a tense feature denoting an interval that precedes a past interval.

3.2   Non-Finite Perfects

The structure of non-finite perfects complements of modals is as in (14). The auxiliary is non-finite, so it doesn't move to T, therefore PRESENT$_i$ and PERFECT do not meet at the same node. One might ask why the feature PERFECT does not climb alone to T to form the alignment PRESENT$_i$ PERFECT *must*, which would make sense semantically. However, movement across a semantically non-empty head and across an intensional operator in particular seems not to be possible, a version of the head-movement constraint for feature movement.

Because PRESENT$_i$ and PERFECT are not together at the same node, competition with PAST$_i$ does not arise, and the meaning of the modal present perfect is not strengthened. Furthermore, competition may not arise between PAST$_i$ and PERFECT at the non-finite Aux node, as PAST$_i$ is a finite tense feature and needs to be expressed at T. Thus, despite the fact that (14) is semantically a *present* perfect, with a *present* reference time, its interpretation allows the lexical meaning of PERFECT to surface unrestricted. Since inclusion of the speech time in the PTS of a modal present perfect is not forced, the PTS may be modified by positional adverbials. (24), which roughly says that in every world that is compatible with what we believe in the actual world at the speech time, there is a time in *yesterday$_c$* that contains a dancing of Alicia, is not a contradiction.[14]

---

[14] Meanings have been suitably modified to include a world parameter.

(i)   [Alicia dance] = $\lambda e \lambda w.e$ is a dancing of Alicia in w   (vP: type v(st), v type of events)
(ii)   a   [PERFECTIVE] = $\lambda P_{v(st)}.\lambda t \lambda w \exists e$ [$\tau(e) \subset t$ & $P(e)(w)$]
          b.   [PERFECT] = $\lambda p_{i(st)}.\lambda t \lambda w \exists t'$ [$t' \leq t$ & $p(t')(w)$]
          c.   [PRESENT$_i$] = $\lambda p_{i(st)}.\lambda t \lambda w$ [$t = t_c$ & $p(t)(w)$]
(iii)   [ON yesterday] = $\lambda p_{i(st)}.\lambda t \lambda w$ [$t \subseteq$ yesterday^c & $p(t)(w)$]

(24) $[_{TP}$ [PRESENT$_1$ must$_H$] $[_{PerfP}$ PERFECT *yesterday* $[_{AspP}$ PERFECTIVE $[_{vP}$ A. dance]]]]
        $= \exists t_1 \lambda w[t_1 = t_c$ & $H(t_1)(w) \subseteq \lambda w' \exists t_2[t_2 \leq t_1$ & $t_2 \subseteq$ yesterday$_c$ & $\exists e$ $[\tau(e) \subset t_2$ & dance (Alice, w', e)]]]

Next, consider non-finite perfects in embedded clauses. No tense feature is expressed at the embedded non-finite T. In the absence of PRESENT$_i$ in the embedded clause, competition with PAST$_i$ does not arise. The lexical meaning of PERFECT allows modification of the PTS by positional adverbials.[15]

(25)   a.   Alicia claims to have danced yesterday.
        b.   PRESENT$_1$ A. claim λ_2 $[_{TP}$ $[_{PerfP}$ PERFECT *yesterday* [PERFECTIVE $[_{vP}$ t$_2$ dance]]]]

4.   Coordinated Perfects

We next consider an apparent violation of the generalization that positional adverbials are prohibited in the English present perfect. The exception to the generalization is reported in McCoard (1978) (where it is attributed to Diver 1963), but it has subsequently been forgotten in the literature. The example in (26) is not addressed by any account of the present perfect puzzle, as far as we are aware, and constitutes a problem for all.

(26)   How has he been occupying himself this week? Well, he's played golf on Tuesday, ridden horseback on Wednesday, and rested on Thursday.

The coordinated perfects in (26) are semantically and morphologically present. Yet, they allow modification by positional adverbials. Crucially, example (26) involves sharing of Tense. When Tense is repeated in each conjunct, the prohibition against positional adverbials resurfaces, as (27) (from Schein 2003) shows.

(27)   How has he been occupying himself this week? *He has played golf on Tuesday, has ridden horseback on Wednesday, and has rested on Thursday.

Sharing the subject but not the Tense is not what is causing the unacceptability of (27), nor is the initial question necessary for the contrast between (26) and (27) to obtain:[16]

(28)   a.   John has played golf on Tuesday and ridden horseback on Wednesday.
        b.   *John has played golf on Tuesday and has ridden horseback on Wednesday.
        c.   John has played golf and has ridden horseback.

Modals are evaluated with respect to a modal background *H*, which assigns to any world *w* and time *t* the sets of worlds accessible in *w* at *t*. Modals identify the local evaluation time with the time at which the complement of the modal is evaluated. *Must* is a universal quantifier over worlds.
(iv) $[\![$ must $]\!]= \lambda H_{i(s(s(st)))} \lambda p_{i(st)}. \lambda t \lambda w. H(t)(w) \subseteq p(t)$
    [15] For PRO, we assume with Chierchia 1987 that it is a semantically empty *de se* pronoun, which has to move at LF thereby creating a λ-abstract.
    [16] In fact, for some speakers, the presence of the question containing the adverbial *this week* obscures the contrast between (26) and (27), i.e., for them (27) is relatively acceptable. See the next section for discussion of the role of such adverbials.

The structure and interpretation of coordinated perfects are found in (29) and (30). There are two semantic features PERFECT, one in each conjunct. Since the auxiliary is shared, there is no feature movement of PERFECT to Aux. Across-the-board-style feature movement of PERFECT is syntactically possible, but would yield a single shared PERFECT, whose PTS will have to be simultaneously included in $Tuesday_c$ and $Wednesday_c$.

(29)

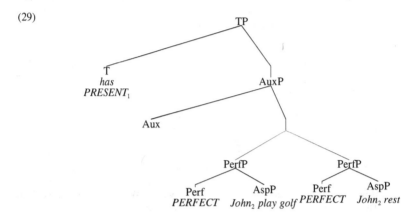

(30) $[_{TP}$ PRESENT$_1$ $[_{PerfP1}$ PERFECT *on Tue.* $[_{AspP}$ PERFECTIVE $[_{vP}$ he play golf]]] &
$[_{PerfP2}$ PERFECT *on Wed.* $[_{AspP}$ PERFECTIVE $[_{vP}$ he ride horseback]]]
$= \exists t\, [t = t_c$ & $\exists t_1\, [t_1 \leq t$ & $t_1 \subseteq Tuesday_c$ & $\exists e[\tau(e) \subset t_1$ & play-golf (he, e)]] &
$\exists t_2\, [t_2 \leq t$ & $t_2 \subseteq Wed._c$ & $\exists e[\tau(e) \subset t_2$ & ride-horseback (he, e)]]]]

PRESENT$_1$ and PERFECT are not at the same node, so no competition with PAST$_i$ arises. No competition arises at the Perf node either, as there is no non-finite PAST$_i$ in English. Because no competition with PAST$_i$ arises, the PTSs do not have to be interpreted as intersecting with the speech time, hence the acceptability of positional adverbials.

5. *So far...*

Another example of an apparent violation of the present perfect puzzle is found in McCoard (1978). Like the case of coordinated perfects, this example has not been analyzed by any of the previous accounts. It too is problematic for all previous proposals.

(31) Has he been playing much golf lately? Well, so far he has played on Tuesday.

The relevant factor is the presence of *so far* (*lately* in the question has a similar role) (see **(32)**). This adverbial obligatory requires perfect, not past, morphology (cf. McCoard 1978), as (33) shows. Other such adverbials are *since x, lately, for the past n years*. As Iatridou et al. (2001) argue, 'perfect-level' adverbials necessarily modify the PTS.

(32) Has he been playing much golf? *? Well, he has played on Tuesday.

(33) a. So far, John has visited the Getty and LACMA.
      b. *? So far, John visited the Getty and LACMA.

We give *so far* an analysis that is analogous to that of *since x*. Similarly to *since x*, *so far* has two readings – inclusive (as in (34)) and durative (as in (35)) (Mittwoch 1998, Iatridou et. al 2001, von Fintel and Iatridou 2002). The precise source of the two readings is not of direct concern here. Importantly for us, when these adverbials in their inclusive guise modify an interval (a PTS), they select a subset of the interval, where the underlying eventuality is located. The difference between *since x* and *so far* is that the former makes the left boundary of the interval precise.

(34) a. $[\![\text{since}^E]\!] = \lambda x. \lambda p. \lambda t. \exists t'\ [t' \subseteq t\ \&\ LB(\tau(x),t)\ \&\ p(t')]$
      b. $[\![\text{so far}^E]\!] = \lambda p. \lambda t. \exists t'\ [\ t' \subseteq t\ \&\ p(t')]$

(35) a. $[\![\text{since}^U]\!] = \lambda x. \lambda p. \lambda t. \forall t'\ [t' \subseteq t\ \&\ LB(\tau(x),t)\ \&\ p(t')]$
      b. $[\![\text{so far}^U]\!] = \lambda p. \lambda t. \forall t'\ [\ t' \subseteq t\ \&\ p(t')]$

A present perfect as in (31) has its meaning strengthened as the result of competition between PRESENT$_1$ ° PERFECT and PAST$_i$. Therefore, the PTS is interpreted as overlapping with the speech time. But because the PTS is modified by *so far*, a subinterval of the PTS is selected, and the event of him playing golf is situated within that subinterval. Now, the subinterval of the PTS need not intersect with the speech time, and therefore it could be modified by positional adverbials.

(36) [TP [PRESENT$_1$ PERFECT] [PerfP *so far* [*on Tue.* [PERFECTIVE [vP he play golf]]]]]
      $= \exists t_1\ [t_1 = t_c\ \&\ \exists t_2\ [t_2 \cap t_1\ \&\ \exists t'[t' \subseteq t_2\ \&\ t' \subseteq Tuesday_c\ \&\ \exists e\ [\tau(e) \subset t'\ \&\ \text{play-golf}\ (he, e)]]]]]$

PTS-modifying adverbials that have the effect of licensing positional adverbials in the present perfect need not be exclusively perfect-level, i.e., they need not require the perfect morphology. It is sufficient that they *may* modify the PTS and have the relevant semantics. Adverbials such as *this week, today* may modify the PTS, and they may be given an analysis analogous to *so far*. We suggest that this is the reason why there are some speakers who find (27) rather acceptable. These speakers posit an anaphoric PTS-modifying adverbial *this week* in their present perfect answer to the question containing *this week*, and this adverbial licenses positional adverbials in the same way *so far* does.

6. Conclusion

A simple account of the present perfect puzzle is offered. The proposal has three main parts: weak, interval-based semantics for PERFECT; cross-linguistic difference in the meaning of PRESENT, shown to be needed for phenomena independent of the perfect; and an independently needed mechanism of grammatical competition between features.

In both English and German, the feature PERFECT moves to the auxiliary (unless prevented by e.g., coordination). When the auxiliary moves to PRESENT$_i$-valued Tense, the complex feature PRESENT$_i$ ° PERFECT is formed. This feature competes with PAST$_i$. In English, PRESENT$_i$ ° PERFECT is less specified than PAST$_i$, because of the particular semantics of PRESENT$_i$, and as a result, its meaning is strengthened such that the PTS overlaps with the speech time. In German no such scalar relationship exists between the meanings of PRESENT$_i$ ° PERFECT and PAST$_i$. Hence, the PTS need not intersect with the speech time. As positional adverbials can only modify a PTS that does not intersect with the speech time, the cross-linguistic facts of the present perfect puzzle follow.

Ambiguities in the past perfect are captured by the proposal. The lack of a relative PAST (PAST-under-PAST) in the grammar of these languages is the reason no direct competition with PERFECT arises. Perfect complements of PRESENT$_i$-Tense modals are predicted to allow positional adverbials, despite being interpreted as present perfects. Similarly, coordinated perfect participles under PRESENT$_i$ Tense are also predicted to allow modification by positional adverbials, despite being morphologically and semantically present perfects. In both cases, PRESENT$_i$ and PERFECT do not meet at the same node, and no PRESENT$_i$ ° PERFECT is formed that can compete with PAST$_i$, and there is no non-finite relative PAST to compete with PERFECT directly. Perfects in non-finite clauses are also predicted to allow positional adverbials, as in the absence of PRESENT$_i$, the conditions for competition are not met. Finally, positional adverbials are acceptable with a present perfect, provided the PTS is modified by an inclusive perfect-level adverbial such as *so far, since x, lately*, etc., whose lexical semantics places the event time in a subset interval of the PTS. As the subset interval need not overlap with the speech time, it can be modified by positional adverbials.

The account makes strong predictions. The meaning of PRESENT$_i$ is sufficient to determine compatibility of the present perfect with positional adverbials in a given language (provided the meanings of PAST$_i$ and PERFECT are cross-linguistically the same). Furthermore, there is no need to posit ambiguity of the perfect morpho-syntax: every instance of *have...-ed* can be analyzed as containing a semantic PERFECT.

References

Chierchia, G. to appear. Scalar Implicatures, Polarity Phenomena, and the Syntax/Pragmatics Interface. In A. Belletti (ed.) *Structures and Beyond*. OUP.

Comrie, B. 1976. *Aspect*. Cambridge: Cambridge University Press.

Diver, W. 1963. The Chronological System of the English Verb. *Word* 19: 141-181.

Dowty, D. 1979. *Word Meaning and Montague Grammar*. Dordrecht: Reidel

von Fintel, K. and S. Iatridou. 2002. Since ~~Since~~. Ms. MIT.

Fox, D. 2003. The Interpretation of Scalar Items: Semantics or Pragmatics, or Both? Handout of a talk at UT Austin.

Giorgi, A. and F. Pianesi. 1998. *Tense and Aspect: From Semantics to Morphosyntax*. Oxford: Oxford University Press.

Grice, P. 1968. Logic and Conversation. In P. Grice. *Studies in the Way of Words*. HUP.

Halle, M. and A. Marantz. 1993. Distributed Morphology and the Pieces of Inflection. In *The View from Building 20*, ed. K. Hale and S. J. Keyser. MIT Press, 111-176.

Heny, F. 1982. Tense, Aspect and Time Adverbials. Part I. *Linguistics and Philosophy* 5: 109-54.

Heim, I. 1994. Comments on Abusch's Theory of Tense. Ms. MIT.

Horn, L. 1972. *On the Semantic Properties of Logical Operators in English.* Ph.D. thesis.

Horn, L. 2001. *A Natural History of Negation.* CSLI Publications.

Iatridou, S., E. Anagnastopoulou and R. Izvorski. 2001. Observations about the Form and Meaning of the Perfect, in *Ken Hale: A Life in Language.* Cambridge: MIT Press. 189-238.

Katz, G. 2003. A Modal Account of the Present Perfect Puzzle. SALT 13.

Kiparsky, P. 2002. Event Structure and the Perfect. In D. I. Beaver, L. D. C. Martnez, B. Z. Clark, and S. Kaufmann (eds.), *The Construction of Meaning.* CSLI Publications.

Klein, W. 1992. The Present Perfect Puzzle. *Language.* 68, 525-551.

Kratzer, A. 2003. Scalar Implicatures: Are there Any? Talk given at the Workshop on Polarity, Scalar Phenomena, and Implicatures, University of Milan-Bicocca

McCoard, R.W. 1978. *The English Perfect: Tense Choice and Pragmatic Inferences.* Amsterdam: North-Holland Press.

Mittwoch, A. 1988. Aspects of English Aspect: On the Interaction of Perfect, Progressive, and Durational Phrases. *Linguistics and Philosophy* 11: 203-254.

Musan, R. 2001. The Present Perfect in German: Outline of its Semantic Composition. *Natural Language and Linguistic Theory* 19, 355-401.

Musan, R. 2003. *Seit*-Adverbials in Perfect Construction. In A. Alexiadou, M. Rathert, and A. von Stechow (eds.) *Perfect Explorations.* Mouton de Gruyter. 253-276.

Partee, B. 1973. Some Structural Analogies between Tenses and Pronouns in English. *Journal of Philosophy* 70. 601-609.

Pratt, J. and N. Francez. 2001. Temporal Generalized Quantifiers. *Linguistics and Philosophy* 24: 187-222.

Portner, P. 2003. The Temporal Semantics and Modal Pragmatics of the Perfect, *Linguistics and Philosophy* 26, 459-510.

Schein, B. 2003. PredP *and* PredP. In *Conjunction Reduction Redux.* Ms. USC

Schlenker, P. 1999. Propositional Attitudes and Indexicality: A Cross-Categorial Approach, Ph.D Dissertation. MIT.

Smith, C. 1991. *The Parameter of Aspect.* Dordrecht: Kluwer.

von Stechow, A. 2002. German *Seit* 'Since' and the Ambiguity of the German Perfect. In *More than Words: A Festschrift for Dieter Wunderlich,* B. Stiebels and I. Kaufmann (eds.), 393-432. Berlin: Akademie Verlag.

von Stechow, A. 2003. Feature Deletion under Semantic Binding: Tense, Person, and Mood under Verbal Quantifiers". NELS 33.

Department of Linguistics
301 GFS
University of Southern California
Los Angeles, CA 90089

Seminar für Sprachwissenschaft
Universität Tübingen
Wilhelmstraße 19-23
72074 Tübingen, Germany

pancheva@usc.edu

Arnim.Stechow@uni-tuebingen.de

Nonlocal Reduplication

Jason Riggle

University of California, Los Angeles

1.   The edge-in generalization vs. the edge-in law

Marantz (1982) observed that reduplicative affixes generally copy the string of segments beginning with the segment at the edge to which the affix is attached and proceeding on into the word. Though he described this "edge-in association" as a tendency, many researchers have assumed, either tacitly or explicitly, that edge-in association is an inviolable principle governing reduplication (Yip 1988, McCarthy and Prince 1994, 1996, Kennedy 2004, Nelson 2003b, and others). This makes several typological predictions, including the prediction that reduplicative affixes should always occur adjacent to the material that they copy. In other words, reduplication should always be local.

In Optimality Theory (OT; Prince and Smolensky 1993), reduplication is usually analyzed using Base/Reduplicant-Correspondence constraints that govern the relationship between the reduplicative affix and the material that it copies (McCarthy and Prince 1995). In this setup, a portion of the output is designated as the base and base/reduplicant (B/R) correspondence demands that it be copied faithfully in the reduplicant. But how is the base delineated?

Kager (1999: 202), paraphrases McCarthy and Prince (1994) with "[t]he **'base'** is the output string of segments to which the reduplicant is attached, more specifically: for reduplicative *prefixes*, it is the *following* string of segments; for reduplicative *suffixes* the *preceding* string of segments." In (1) I give an example of reduplication with edge-in association. The reduplicant is underlined and bold and each segment in the reduplicant is connected by an arrow to the segment in the base with which it is in correspondence.

(1)   Edge-in association: **bad**-badupi

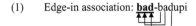

Many thanks to Pamela Munro for introducing me to Creek and for many insightful comments, to Kie Zuraw for excellent analytical advice and to the participants at NELS 34 at Stony Brook for useful comments and discussion, especially Shigeto Kawahara, Abigail Cohn , and Alan Yu.

Nonetheless, there are languages that evidence "nonlocal correspondence." I use this broad term for any case of correspondence between nonadjacent strings of segments. Nonlocal reduplication always shows nonlocal correspondence but the converse does not necessarily hold (e.g. correspondence-mediated agreement is the latter but not the former (Rose and Walker 2001, Zuraw 2003)). In (2) present a prototypical instance of nonlocal correspondence and in (3) I list twelve languages that show such patterns.

(2)   Nonlocal correspondence: mɪtqa**mɪt**

(3) | **Twelve languages with nonlocal correspondence** |
        | --- |
        | Chuukese (Goodenough and Sugita 1980) |
        | Creek (Martin and Mauldin 2000) |
        | Indonesian (Sneddon 1996) |
        | Itelmen (Bobaljik 2003) |
        | Koryak/Chukchee (Bogoras 1969, Kenstowicz 1979, Krause 1980) |
        | Madurese (Stevens 1968) |
        | Nancowry (Radhakrishnan 1981, Alderete et al. 1999, Nelson 2000) |
        | Tzeltal (Berlin 1963) |
        | Tillamook (Reichard 1959) |
        | Ulu Muar Malay (Hendon 1966) |
        | West Tarangan (Spaelti 1997) |
        | Yoruba (Awoyale 1989, Nelson 2003). |

Nelson (2003b) and Kennedy (2004) provide short descriptions and illustrations of many of the cases above. Much of the analysis of reduplication in the languages above has focused on the task of showing that what appears to be nonlocal reduplication is either "covertly" local or, in fact, not an instance of reduplication (especially McCarthy and Prince 1996, and Nelson 2003b).

Rather than examining each language in (3), I will consider here two representative cases. In §2 I present data showing nonlocal correspondence in Chukchee/Koryak and in Creek. In §3 I will argue that, while the former may be amenable to analysis as fake nonlocal reduplication, the latter must be analyzed as true nonlocal reduplication. In §4 I give an Optimality Theoretic analysis of nonlocal reduplication in Creek.

2.   Chukchee, Koryak, and Creek

Bogoras (1969) describes reduplication in absolutives in Koryak and Chukchee as in (4).

(4)   "The absolute form of the noun serves to express the subject of the intransitive verb and the object of the transitive verb. ... The reduplication consists in the repetition of the beginning of the word at the end, including the initial consonant, vowel, and the first consonant following the vowel." Bogoras (1969: 687-88)

In (5) I present data illustrating reduplication in the absolutive singular in Chukchee and Koryak. Though Chukchee is perhaps more well known, Koryak shows more striking reduplication in that an entire syllable may intervene between the two surface copies.

(5)

Chukchee			Koryak		
gloss	**stem**	**absolute**	**gloss**	**stem**	**absolute**
'land'	nute	nute**nut**	'oil'	mɪtqa	mɪtqa**mɪt**
'tears'	mêrê	mêrê**mêr**	'shellfish'	kilka	kilka**kil**
'voice'	quli	quli**gul**	'fire'	qanga	qanga**qan**
'meat'	tala	tala**tal**	'sleep'	yilqa	yilqa**yil**

Creek, a Muskogean language, has even more strikingly nonlocal correspondence. Booker (1980: 73) states that "Creek reduplicated stems are formed by copying the initial consonant and vowel of the root and placing them before the root final consonant." In (6) I illustrate this pattern with data from Haas (1977) and Martin and Mauldin (2000).

(6)

Creek		
gloss	**singular**	**plural**
a. 'precious'	a-cáːk-iː	a-caːcak-íː
b. 'sticking in'	cákh-iː	cakcah-íː
c. 'sticking in & on'	oh-cákh-iː	oh-cakcah-íː
d. 'sweet'	cámp-iː	camcap-íː
e. 'torn up, mashed'	citákk-iː	citakcik-íː
f. 'frozen, stiff	cóyh-iː	coycoh-íː
g. 'full' (of container)	fáck-iː	facfak-íː
h. 'split' (as of wood)	falápk-iː	falapfak-íː
i. 'crooked'	fayátk-iː	fayatfak-íː
j. 'white'	hátk-iː	hathak-íː
k. 'clean'	hasátk-iː	hasathak-íː
l. 'hot'	héyy-iː	heyhoy-íː
m. 'ugly, naughty'	holwak-íː	holwaːhok-íː
n. 'broken off'	kálk-iː	kalkak-íː
o. 'old'	lísk-iː	lislik-íː
p. 'nasty, dirty, filthy'	likácw-iː	likacliw-íː
q. 'soft'	lowáck-iː	lowaclok-íː
r. 'round'	polóːk-iː	poloːpok-íː
s. 'deep'	sófk-iː	sofsok-íː
t. 'hard, brittle'	takácw-iː	takactaw-íː
u. 'empty'	tánk-iː	tantak-íː
v. 'on tiptoe'	tikínk-iː	tikintik-íː
w. 'hard, firm'	wánh-iː	wanwah-íː

In (6) I have illustrated nonlocal correspondence in plural marking with adjectives. This pattern is robust and occurs with verbs as well. In (a) and (c) I show that the material targeted for reduplication is the initial portion of the stem, even when prefixes precede it.[1]

3.   Arguments and analysis

Is edge-in association an inviolable law or merely a tendency? In the face of apparent counterexamples like the ones in (5) and (6) there are two plausible answers to this question. If edge-in association is only a tendency then we must determine what factors promote this tendency and what factors can lead to exceptions. On the other hand, if edge-in association is indeed an inviolable principle then the apparent cases of nonlocal reduplication must be dealt with in one of two ways. Either they must be analyzed as instances of nonlocal correspondence that are not actually reduplication, or they must be analyzed as covertly local cases of true reduplication in which the edge-in law holds at an abstract level of representation.

3.1   Divide and dismiss

The claim that some putative cases of nonlocal reduplication are merely the result of non-reduplicative copying processes deals with some of the cases in (3) by classifying them as merely nonlocal copying. Nelson (2003b) makes this case for several languages including Chukchee. She points out that in Chukchee the nonlocal correspondence occurs with only a restricted subset of the stem shapes in the language. She argues that this restricted distribution would go unexplained if the pattern were true reduplication and claims that the pattern makes more sense when characterized as a tactic aimed at achieving some sort of prosodic target.

Coupled with the fact that the use of reduplication to mark absolutive forms is relatively anomalous cross-linguistically, it might be plausible to dismiss the Koryak and Chukchee data as instances of "copying to fill out a template" and not truly reduplication.

There is one catch though. Even if the mechanisms mediating correspondence in nonreduplicative and reduplicative copying are distinct, it must still be determined why the latter requires edge-in association and the former does not. Contrary to such an idea, Kawahara (this volume) proposes that echo epenthesis (another instance of nonlocal correspondence) is actually more stringently local than the copying that occurs in reduplication and that only reduplicative copying can skip intervening segments.

It is not tenable to dismiss the Creek data in (6) as a non-instance of reduplication. Not only is plural marking one of the most common uses for reduplication cross-linguistically, but the set of stems participating in the nonlocal correspondence pattern is representative of the general prosodic properties of stems in Creek.

---

[1] 'gray': sopakhátk-i:$_{sg.}$ sopakha**tha**k-í:$_{pl.}$ in Martin and Mauldin (2000) appears to be 'dregs': *sopak* compounded with 'white': *hátk-i:*. Note that in this case the initial CV of the second stem is copied.

3.2   Covert locality

Another strategy for explaining cases of apparently nonlocal reduplication is to claim that they arise when local reduplication is occluded by the action of independent phonological processes. This tack has also been taken in attempting to explain the Chukchee data.

McCarthy and Prince (1996) citing Kenstowicz (1979) note that Chukchee has an apocope rule that deletes stem-final vowels that would also occur word-finally. Under such an analysis, reduplication is opaquely local in the sense that the locality generalization is not surface true because reduplication occurs before apocope. Bobaljik (2003) argues for much the same analysis of this pattern in Itelmen. It is not immediately clear how this line of analysis would deal with the Koryak forms in which an entire CV intervenes between the copies, but it's possible that another rule could account for these cases.

In a rule-based framework, in which reduplicative copying can be preceded and followed by other operations like deletion, apparently nonlocal reduplication can be seen as a simple case of opacity. On the other hand, in a constraint-based framework that lacks the notion of precedence among phonological operations, it is hard to see what kind of empirical predictions covert locality makes and what role it plays in the theory.

Nonetheless, if it were indeed the case that every language showing instances of true nonlocal reduplication seemed to involve the action of an independent phonological process in that language, then the notion of covert locality would lead to a more restricted typology of reduplication and would lead to interesting research questions.

But reduplication in Creek does not appear to be covertly local. The claim that reduplication in Creek is covertly local by virtue of the action of an independent phonological process would have to appeal to something like a rule that deleted all but the initial CV of the reduplicant. At this level of abstraction it is hard to imagine a reduplicative pattern that couldn't be considered local. If the edge-in association law is only inviolate at arbitrarily high levels of abstraction then it doesn't seem to make any empirical predictions about the range of possible reduplicative patterns.

4.   Embracing nonlocality

In Correspondence Theory (McCarthy and Prince 1995), edge-in association is often assumed to delineate the "base" – the portion of the output that the reduplicant is obliged to copy. I argue here that nonlocal patterns of reduplication can be given a more straightforward analysis if we relax the definition of basehood in reduplication as in (7).

(7)   **The base generalized**
Everything in the output that isn't the reduplicant is the base.[2]

---

[2] This broad definition of the reduplicative base correctly predicts that epenthetic material and material from affixes will sometimes be copied in the reduplicant.

This general notion of the base makes it necessary to adopt proposals in Nelson (1998, 2003) and Riggle (2003) that the content of the reduplicant should be determined by the action of BASE/REDUPLICANT-MAX constraints that are indexed to salient elements like stems, edges, and stressed syllables. With the general notion of basehood and this natural extension of Beckman's (1998) positional faithfulness to the base/reduplicant dimension of correspondence, we capture straightforwardly the tendency for salient material to be copied in reduplication.

(8)   BASE/REDUPLICANT-MAX -C_1-ROOT: (**B/R-Mx-C_1^{RT}**)
        The initial consonant of the root must be copied in reduplication.

The placement of the reduplicant will then be determined by the (possibly conflicting) drives expressed by the ALIGNMENT family of constraints (McCarthy and Prince 1993) and a constraint demanding locality of the reduplicative affix and the material it copies. Consider in (9), Nelson's (2003) formalization of the locality constraint.

(9)   LOCALITY:
        The copied portion of the base and the corresponding reduplicant must be adjacent.

In (10) I give a more technically worded version of Nelson's constraint that doesn't refer to the base and makes it expressly clear that each segment intervening between the reduplicant and base incurs only one violation of LOCALITY.[3]

(10)   LOCALITY:
        No segment that isn't itself in the correspondence relation **Morph^1 $\mathcal{R}$ Morph^2** may intervene between two segments corresponding via $\mathcal{R}$ – One mark is assigned per segment y that lies between a pair $x, x' \in S$ where $x \mathcal{R} x'$, unless $\exists y' \in S$ and $y \mathcal{R} y'$.

The B/R-MAX-C_1^{RT} constraint must dominate LOCALITY or else the latter will select candidates that copy material other than the initial consonant. This is illustrated in (11).

(11)

'sweet' RED + camp + iː	B/R-Mx-C_1^{RT}	LOCALITY
a. ☞ cam.**ca**.piː		**
b. cam.**pi**.piː	*!	

        Another alternative would be to place the reduplicative affix next to the material it copies. An alignment constraint demanding that the reduplicant occur near the right edge of the word will prevent this. The alignment constraint in given in (12).

---

[3] This last point ensures that the number of constraint violations grows as a linear function of the length of the input and not a quadratic one, as is the case with Kitto and de Lacy's (1999) ADJACENCY and Kennedy's (2004) PROXIMITY. This also guarantees that the constraint can be represented with a regular expression and that it doesn't run afoul of the problems that McCarthy (2004) has observed with gradience.

(12) ALIGN-RED-RIGHT: (**RED-RT**)
The reduplicant must occur as close as possible to the right edge of the word.

Ranking RED-RT above LOCALITY will keep the reduplicant near the right edge.[4]

(13)	'sweet' RED + camp + i:	RED-RT	LOCALITY
a.	cam.**ca**.pi:	**	*
b.	ca.**cam**.pi:	***!	

Finally, as the reduplicant is not a suffix, some constraints must prevent RED-RT from being perfectly satisfied. One of these is a right alignment constraint on the -*i:* affix.

(14) ALIGN-*i:*-RIGHT: (**i:-RT**)
The -*i:* affix must occur as close as possible to the right edge of the word.

Ranking *i:*-RT above RED-RT will make the reduplicant occur as close as possible to the right edge but before -*i:* suffix. This is illustrated in (15).

(15)	'sweet' RED + camp + i:	i:-RT	RED-RT
a. ☞	cam.**ca**.pi:		**
b.	cam.pi:**c**	*!	

A couple of standard markedness constraints will explain why the reduplicant is always infixed before the final consonant of the stem. First consider *COMPLEX in (16).

(16) *COMPLEX: (***CPLX***)
Consonant clusters are not permitted.   (Prince and Smolensky 1993)

The reduplicant will interrupt the stem, cleaving off its last consonant, if *COMPLEX is ranked above RED-RT and CONTIGUITY, which penalizes cases in which the stem is interrupted by the reduplicant (McCarthy and Prince 1995). This is illustrated in (17).

(17)	'sweet' RED + camp + i:	*CPLX	RED-R	CONTIGUITY
a. ☞	cam.**ca**.pi:		**	*
b.	camp.**c**i:	*!	*	
c.	camp.**ca**.**m**i:	*!	*	

---

[4] Alternatively the reduplicant might be aligned to the syllable bearing main stress.

The constraint NoCODA must also dominate the alignment constraint on the reduplicant.

(18)   NoCODA:
        Codas are not permitted.   (Prince and Smolensky 1993)

The action of the constraint NoCODA will ensure that the reduplicant is infixed at the right edge of the stem even when the stem does not end in a consonant cluster.

(19)	'round' RED+ poloːk + iː	NoCODA	RED-R
a. ☞ po.loː.**po**.kíː		**
b. po.loːk.**pí**ː	*!	*
c. po.loːk.**po**.îː	*!	*

There are no stems in my database of verbs and adjectives in Creek drawn from Martin and Mauldin (2000) that end in vowels. If there were vowel-final stems, this analysis predicts that the reduplicant would be placed between the stem and suffix in such cases.

To ensure that the reduplicative affix does not copy more than an a single syllable, Zoll's (1993) *STRUCTURE-SYLLABLE can be ranked in the emergence of the unmarked ranking (McCarthy and Prince 1995); below INPUT/BASE-MAX but above BASE/REDUPLICANT-MAX. *STRUCTURE-SYLLABLE is presented in (20).

(20)   *STRUCTURE-SYLLABLE: (*STRUC-σ)
        Each syllable in the output incurs one penalty.

Ranking *STRUC-σ below the INPUT/BASE-MAX constraint but above B/R-MAX will keep the reduplicant small but leave base forms unaffected. This is shown in (21).[5]

(21)	'round' RED + poloːk + iː	B/R-Mx-C$_1^{RT}$	I/B-MAX	*STRUC-σ	B/R-MAX
a. ☞ po.loː.**po**.kiː			****	loki
b. po.loː.**po.loː**.kiː			*****!	ki
c. po.**po**.kiː		**!	****	ki
d. poloːkiː	*!		****	poloki

Candidate (21d) might alternatively be ruled out by a REALIZE-MORPHEME constraint which forbids the plural form from being homophonous with the singular (see. Kurisu

---

[5] Plug in your favorite size restrictor for (20), e.g. ALLSYLLABLELEFT (Spaelti 1997), Hendricks' (2001) COMPRESSION model, or DEP-OO (Gouskova 2004), to name a few. There are interesting issues lurking here but they are orthogonal to the central concern of accounting for nonlocal reduplication.

2001). I include (21d) to show that B/R-Mx-C$_1^{RT}$ isn't vacuously satisfied by failure to reduplicate, so if it dominates *STRUC-σ then the size of the Creek reduplicant is derived.

To keep *STRUC-σ from predicting single-consonant reduplicants it must be dominated by the constraint against consonant clusters. This is illustrated in (22).

(22)

'empty' RED+ tank-iː	*COMPLEX	*STRUC-σ
a. ☞ tan.**ta**.kiː		***
b. tan**t**.kiː	*!	**

NOCODA must also dominate *STRUC-σ to prevent single-consonant reduplicants.

(23)

'round' RED+ poloːk -iː	NOCODA	*STRUC-σ
a. ☞ po.loː.**po**.kiː		***
b. po.loː**p**.kiː	*!	***

To keep NOCODA from repairing codas by selecting candidates that copy a vowel rather than the initial consonant, it must be dominated by B/R-Mx-C$_1^{RT}$. This is shown in (24).

(24)

'sweet' RED + camp + iː	B/R-Mx-C$_1^{RT}$	NOCODA
a. ☞ cam.**ca**.píː		*
b. ca.m**a**.piː	*!	

Finally, because both consonant clusters and codas are tolerated in Creek at large, NOCODA and *COMPLEX must both be dominated by I/B-MAX. With this last piece of information I present in (25) the master-ranking for nonlocal reduplication in Creek.

(25) **Ranking diagram for Creek reduplication**

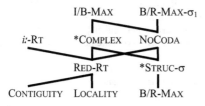

5.   Typology

In (26) I illustrate the four distinct patterns of reduplication and affixation that arise from the twenty four possible rankings of the constraints LOCALITY , RED-R, RED-L, and B/R-MAX-$\sigma_1{}^{RT}$. With each pattern I list one language in which the pattern is attested.

(26)

Pattern1:	a copy of the initial syllable is prefixed. This occurs if: RED-L >> RED-R E.g. Ilokano (McCarthy and Prince 1996)
Pattern2:	a copy of the final syllable is suffixed. This occurs if: RED-R >> RED-L and LOCALITY, RED-R >> BR-MAX-$\sigma_1{}^{RT}$ E.g. Manam (McCarthy and Prince 1996)
Pattern3:	a copy of the initial syllable is suffixed. This occurs if: RED-R >> RED-L and RED-R, BR-MAX-$\sigma_1{}^{RT}$ >>LOCALITY. E.g. Creek
Pattern 4:	a copy of the initial syllable is infixed at the left edge. This occurs if: RED-R >> RED-L and BR-MAX-$\sigma_1{}^{RT}$, LOCALITY >> RED-R. E.g. Pima (Riggle 2003).

6.   Conclusions

There are feasible alternatives for some of the details of this analysis of reduplication in Creek. For instance, there are many ways to restrict the size of the reduplicant that would work equally well here. Also, the reduplicant's position could be derived through alignment to the stressed syllable instead of the right edge. If this were the case NOCODA would no longer need to dominate RED-R but would still need to dominate CONTIGUITY to cause the infixation into the root.

Regardless of the specifics of these details, Creek clearly shows nonlocal reduplication and shows that some constraint other than LOCALITY will be needed to derive the position of the reduplicant (e.g. RED-RT). Most importantly, the copying pattern in Creek does not seem to be amenable to any but the least restrictive (empirically vacuous) notion of covert locality.

Nonlocal reduplication is a marked alternative that can arise only when LOCALITY is dominated by B/R-MAX and an alignment constraint that are at odds. The tendency for edge-in association is expressed in all other cases where either LOCALITY is dominant or the alignment constraints on the reduplicant and B/R-Max are not at odds.

I have presented a simplified notion of the base and shown that LOCALITY, B/R-MAX, ALIGNMENT, and ordinary markedness constraints and can derive Creek's nonlocal reduplication. Moreover, all the patterns that arise from these constraints' interactions are typologically attested. Thus it seems that we obtain a simpler theory of (nonlocal) reduplication by allowing the edge-in tendency to arise through constraint interaction.

References

Alderete, John, Jill Beckman, Laura Benua, Amalia Gnanadesikan, John McCarthy and Suzanne Urbanczyk. 1999. Reduplication and with Fixed Segmentism. *Linguistic Inquiry* 30:327-364.

Awoyale, James Oladuntoye Yiwoya . 1989. Reduplication and the Status of Ideophones in Yoruba. *The Journal of West African Languages*, Calgary, AB, Canada. May, 19:1, 13-34.

Beckman, Jill. 1998. Positional Faithfulness. Doctoral dissertation, University of Massachusetts, Amherst.

Berlin, Brent. 1963. Some semantic features of reduplication in Tzeltal. *International Journal of American Linguistics*, 29, 211-218.

Bobaljik, Jonathan David. 2003. Itelmen Reduplication: Edge-In Association and Lexical Stratification. Ms. McGill University.

Bogoras, Waldemar. 1969. 'Chukchee', in F. Boas, (ed.), *Handbook of American Indian Languages, Bureau of American Ethnology Bulletin 40, Part 2*, Government Printing Office, Washington, DC, pp. 631-903.

Booker, Karen. M. 1979. *Comparative Muskogean: Aspects of Proto-Muskogean Verb Morphology.* Doctoral Dissertation. U. Kansas.

Goodenough, Ward H., and Hiroshi Sugita. 1980. Trukese-English dictionary.

Gouskova, Maria. 2004. Minimizing RED without Economy: an OO-Faith Approach. Handout from LSA annual meeting. Boston, MA.

Haas, Mary R. 1977. Nasals and Nasalizatiton in Creek. Proceedings of the Third Annual Meeting of the Berkeley Linguistics Society, 194-203,. Berkeley: Berkeley Linguistics Society, University of California, Berkeley.

Hendon, Rufus. 1966. *The Phonology and Morphology of Ulu Muar Malay.* Yale University Publications in Anthropology number 70.

Hendricks, Sean. 2001. Bare consonant reduplication without prosodic templates: expressive reduplication in Semai. *Journal of East Asian Linguistics* 10, 287–306. Kluwer.

Kager, René. 1999. Optimality Theory. Cambridge.

Kawahara, Shigeto. this volume. Echo Epenthesis and Reduplication.

Kennedy, Robert. 2004. "A Formal Replacement For Reduplicative Anchoring." Ms. University of Arizona.

Kenstowicz, Michael. 1979. Chukchee vowel harmony and epenthesis. In P. Clyne, W. Hanks & C. Hofbauer (eds.), CLS 15: The Elements: Parasession on Linguistic Units and Level (pp. 402– 412). Chicago: Chicago Linguistic Society.

Kitto, Catherine and de Lacy, Paul. 1999. Correspondence and epenthetic quality. *Proceedings of Austronesian Formal Linguistics Association* 4, 181-200.

Kurisu, Kazutaka. 2001. The Phonology of Morpheme Realization, Doctoral dissertation, University of California, Santa Cruz.

Krause, Scott. 1980. Topics in Chukchee phonology and morphology. Doctoral dissertation, University of Illinois, Urbana-Champaign, Illinois.

Marantz, Alec. 1982. Re Reduplication. *Linguistic Inquiry* 13:3, 435-482.

Martin, Jack B. 1994. Implications of plural reduplication, infixation, and subtraction for Muskogean subgrouping. *Anthropological Linguistics* 36:27-55.

Martin, Jack B., and Margaret McKane Mauldin. 2000. *A Dictionary of Creek/Muskogee, with notes on the Florida and Oklahoma Seminole dialects of Creek.* Lincoln/London: University of Nebraska Press.

McCarthy, John, and Alan Prince. 1994. Two lectures on prosodic morphology. Handouts of lectures at OTS/HIL workshop on Prosodic Morphology, Utrecht University.

McCarthy, John and Alan Prince. 1996. Prosodic Morphology 1986. Technical Report 32, Rutgers University Center for Cognitive Science.

McCarthy, John. & Alan Prince. 1995. 'Faithfulness and Reduplicative Identity.' In *University of Massachusetts Occasional Papers in Linguistics [UMOP] 18: Papers in Optimality Theory,* J. Beckman, L. Walsh Dickey & S. Urbanczyk, eds. GLSA UMass, Amherst. 249-384.

McCarthy, John. 2004. OT constraints are categorical. *Phonology* 20, 75-138.

Nelson, Nicole. 1998. "Right Anchor, Aweigh." Ms., Rutgers University.

Nelson, Nicole. 2000. Stressed rhyme faithfulness: a case study of Nancowry. In *WCCFL 19*, ed. Billery and Lillehaugen. Sommerville, MA: Cascadilla Press. 329-342.

Nelson, Nicole. 2003a. *Asymmetric Anchoring.* Doctoral Dissertation. Rutgers University.

Nelson, Nicole. 2003b. Wrong side reduplication is epiphenomenal: evidence from Yourba. To appear in: *Studies in Reduplication* [tentative title], ed. Bernhard Hurch. Mouton de Gruyter.

Radhakrishnan, R. 1981. *The Nancowry Word: Phonology, Affixal Morphology and Roots of a Nicobarese Language.* Carbondale, Illinois, and Edmonton, Alberta: Linguistic Research.

Reichard, Gladys A. 1959. A comparison of five Salish languages: V. *International Journal of American Linguistics* 59, 239-253.

Riggle, Jason. 2003. Infixation in Pima Reduplication and Its Theoretical Consequences. Handout from LSA annual meeting. Atlanta, GA.

Rose, Sharon and Rachel Walker. 2001. A typology of consonant agreement as correspondence. Ms. University of California, San Diego and University of Southern California.

Sneddon, James Neil. 1996. *Indonesian Reference Grammar.* Allen & Unwin.

Steriade, Donca. 1988. Reduplication and syllable transfer in Sanskrit and elsewhere. *Phonology*, 5, 73-155.

Spaelti, Peter. 1997. *Dimensions of Variation in Multi-Pattern Reduplication.* Doctoral Dissertation, University of California-Santa Cruz.

Stevens, Alan. 1968. *Madurese Phonology and Morphology.* American Oriental Series vol. 52, American Oriental Society, New Haven CT.

Yip, Moira (1988) Template morphology and the direction of association. *Natural Language & Linguistic Theory*, 6, 551–577.

Zuraw, Kie. 2003. Aggressive reduplication. *Phonology* 19, 395-439.

Department of Linguistics
University of California, Los Angeles
3125 Campbell Hall Box 951543
Los Angeles, CA 90095-1543

riggle@ucla.edu

The Influence of Binding Theory on the On-line Reference Resolution of Pronouns

Jeffrey T. Runner, Rachel S. Sussman and Michael K. Tanenhaus

University of Rochester

1.   Introduction

1.1.   Binding Theory and Sentence Processing

This paper addresses the following main question: How do the structural constraints of Binding Theory interact with on-line sentence processing? There have been two types of answers to this question hypothesized in the literature: (1) the Initial Filter hypothesis, which claims that Binding Theory constrains the sentence processing system from the earliest moments of reference resolution (Nicol & Swinney, 1989; Sturt, 2003); and (2) the Multiple Constraints hypothesis, which claims that Binding Theory constraints are among a larger set of constraints applying simultaneously during sentence processing (Badecker & Straub, 2002).

We present the results of a study using eye-movements to investigate the role of Binding Theory during sentence processing. Our results show that from the very earliest moments participants consider both Binding Theory-compatible and Binding Theory-incompatible referents, which is inconsistent with the initial filter hypothesis, but consistent with the multiple constraints hypothesis.

1.2   Background

In Runner, Sussman & Tanenhaus (2003) we examined the role of Binding Theory on pronouns and reflexives in "picture" noun phrases (NPs) containing possessors (e.g., 'Harry's picture of him/himself'). Our participants were seated in front of display containing three male dolls (Joe, Ken, Harry); behind each doll was a column of digitized photos of all three dolls (Figure 1).

Keir Moulton and Matthew Wolf (eds.): Proceedings of NELS 34,
Stony Brook University: 497 – 504. GLSA, Amherst.

Figure 1

Participants listened to pre-recorded instructions (see (1)) containing two "lead-in" phrases asking them to pick up one doll and look at another. The lead-ins were followed by an "action" sentence instructing the participant to touch one of the photos with the doll she has just picked up. The lead-in phrases varied in order:

(1) { Pick up Joe. Look at Ken. } Have Joe touch Harry's picture of him/himself
      { Look at Ken. Pick up Joe. }

The study yielded two types of results: target choices and eye movement data. For target choice (which doll's picture the participant had the actor doll (here Joe) touch), Binding Theory (BT) correctly predicted the targets of pronoun trials, with fewer than 10% of trials violating BT; however, Binding Theory did significantly worse predicting the target choice for reflexives, with almost 30% of trials violating BT (Figure 2).

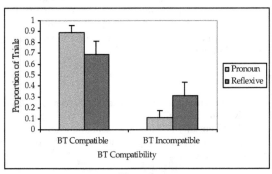

Figure 2

The second type of result we reported was the proportion of looks to the relevant pictures over time. Focusing on the reflexive trials in which participants followed BT (i.e., where they chose the picture of the possessor as target choice), Figure 3 graphs the proportion of looks over time to the picture of the doll mentioned in the lead-in phrase, the picture of the subject doll, and the picture of the possessor. What this graph illustrates is that the picture of the BT-incompatible subject doll is being considered from the earliest moments of sentence processing, even on trials in which the participants actually chose the BT-compatible interpretation. If these reflexives are constrained by Binding Theory, this is strong evidence that BT is *not* acting as an initial filter.

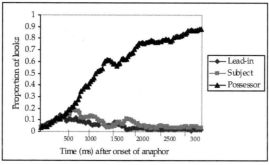

Figure 3

However, it may not be justified to reject the initial filter hypothesis based on these results. As argued by Runner, Sussman & Tanenhaus (2002) and Runner (2003), these reflexives may actually be logophors, a type of coreferential anaphor that is not constrained by Binding Theory. If this is the case, then Figure 3 does not illustrate the interaction of BT and sentence processing.

The Runner et al. (2003) study, though, did provide a candidate for testing the initial filter hypothesis. It showed that pronouns do seem to be constrained by Binding Theory. Recall the basic results presented in Figure 2, which showed that BT did a good job at predicting the target choices for pronouns. If pronouns are constrained by BT, then an analysis of the early looks on the pronoun trials should illustrate the role of BT in sentence processing.

Figures 4 and 5 show the proportion of looks over time on the pronoun trials. Figure 4 contains the trials in which the subject doll was mentioned first (the "pick up" lead-in preceded the "look at" lead-in); Figure 5 shows the trials in which the subject doll was mentioned second. What we see by examining these graphs is that there are early looks to the relevant pictures of the BT-compatible subject and lead-in dolls, but there also seem to be early looks to the picture of the BT-incompatible possessor doll.

Figure 4

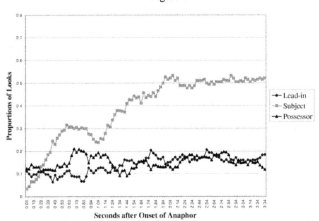

Figure 5

Unfortunately, because of the design of the experiment, the relevant comparison is missing. As (1) shows, every instruction began with two lead-in phrases. This provided two BT-compatible potential referents, and only one BT-incompatible one. What may have happened, then, is that the looks to the two BT-compatible referents may have been divided, providing the impression that the looks to the BT-incompatible possessor were higher than they actually were. The comparison that is needed is one in which there is only one BT-compatible potential referent and one BT-incompatible potential referent. If the looks to these two potential referents do not differ early on, then this will show that the Binding Theory is not acting as an early filter on sentence processing.

2.   Current Study

2.1.   Experiment

The main question we were interested in was the following: How does the Binding Theory constraint on pronouns apply during on-line sentence processing? In particular, we wanted to do this in a way that would provide the appropriate comparisons (see above). Our secondary goal was to replicate the basic results of Runner, Sussman & Tanenhaus (2003) using instructions recorded by "naïve" speakers.

Participants were again seated in front of the display in Figure 1. They heard instructions like the following:

(2)   Pick up Joe. Have Joe touch Ken's picture of him/himself.

These instructions contained only a single lead-in phrase, which asked the participant to pick up the doll that would be the subject of the action sentence. Thus, there is one BT-compatible potential antecedent mentioned (the subject) and one BT-incompatible potential antecedent (the possessor).

The instructions were recorded by three naïve speakers, who were told they were recording instructions for an experiment. They pronounced the instructions after having the Binding Theory-compatible action modeled by one of the researchers. These instructions were then used in the current experiment with 24 additional listeners. The intent here was to see what effect pronunciations intended to elicit a BT-compatible action would have on the actual actions of listeners.

2.2.   Results

First, our results successfully replicated the basic target choice results of Runner et al. (2003): Binding Theory did a good job of predicting the pronoun choices (less than 5% BT violation) but a worse job of predicting the reflexive choices (over 20% BT violation). This result is particularly interesting given that the instructions were recorded by naïve speakers and were intended to elicit BT-compatible actions only.

To evaluate our main question of whether Binding Theory is acting as an early filter on the reference resolution of pronouns we isolated the earliest looks, the first 1000 ms after the onset of the pronoun. As Figure 6 shows, looks to the picture of the BT-compatible subject (Ken's picture of Joe in the example) and to the picture of the BT-incompatible possessor (Ken's picture of Ken) increase together from the earliest moments of processing. It is only later on that looks to the picture of the possessor start to decrease. This seems inconsistent with the main claim of the early filter hypothesis. It is consistent with the claim of the multiple constraints hypothesis, since the effects of

Binding Theory do gradually appear, resulting in a pattern of looks very similar to the final target choices.

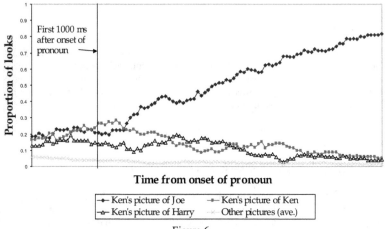

Figure 6

To help clarify the details of the time course graph we also analyzed the total proportion of looks to the objects in the display during that first 1000 ms. Figure 7 shows these results.

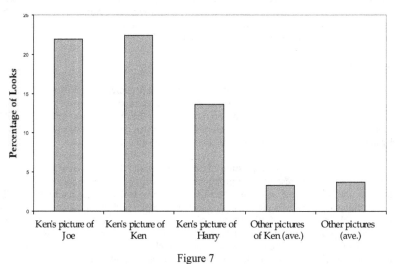

Figure 7

Looks to the picture of the BT-compatible subject (Ken's picture of Joe) and looks to the picture of the BT-incompatible possessor (Ken's picture of Ken) do not differ (unless otherwise stated, all differences mentioned are at the standard p-level of <.05). That means that during the earliest moments of processing, looks to these two pictures are equally likely. This is very strong evidence against the initial filter hypothesis, which would predict looks to the BT-compatible referent (the subject) to be increased in comparison with looks to BT-incompatible referents during this time period.

To rule out the possibility that the increased looks to the possessor were simply due to the fact that participants had to scan the relevant column of pictures before finding the correct photo, we compared the proportion of looks to the possessor to those of the third unmentioned doll in the same column (Ken's picture of Harry); the proportion of looks to the possessor were significantly greater than those to that third picture (Figure 7), suggesting again that participants were considering the possessor as a potential referent contra Binding Theory.

Finally, to rule out the possibility that participants were primed to look at pictures of the possessor simply because it had been mentioned, we compared looks to the other pictures of the possessor with looks to the other pictures (including those of the subject); these proportions were not different either (Figure 7), again suggesting that the prior mention of the possessor cannot alone account for the increased looks.

3.   Conclusions

The results of the current experiment are inconsistent with the initial filter hypothesis. From the earliest moments of pronoun reference resolution, pictures of both the BT-compatible subject and BT-incompatible possessor were equally considered. The early looks cannot be attributed to scanning the scene or to prior mention of the possessor. What we find instead is that the effects of Binding Theory are gradual, only clearly appearing well after the first 1000 ms of processing, a result consistent with the multiple constraints hypothesis.

References

Badecker, William and Kathleen Straub. 2002. The Processing Role of Structural Constraints on the Interpretation of Pronouns and Anaphors. *Journal of Experimental Psychology: Learning, Memory, and Cognition* 28: 748-769.

Nicol, Janet and David Swinney. 1989. The Role of Structure in Coreference Assignment During Sentence Comprehension. *Journal of Psycholinguistic Research* 18: 5-19.

Runner, J.T. 2003. Insights into Binding and Ellipsis from Head-mounted Eye-tracking Experiments. In *Chicago Linguistic Society 39 Proceedings*.

Runner, Jeffrey T., Rachel S. Sussman and Michael K. Tanenhaus. 2002. Logophors in Picture Noun Phrases. In *WCCFL 21 Proceedings*, ed. L. Mikkelsen and C. Potts. Somerville, MA: Cascadilla Press.

Runner, Jeffrey T., Rachel S. Sussman and Michael K. Tanenhaus. 2003. Assignment of
    Reference to Reflexives and Pronouns in Picture Noun Phrases: Evidence from
    Eye Movements. *Cognition* 89: B1-B13.
Sturt, Patrick 2003. The Time-Course of the Application of Binding Constraints in
    Reference Resolution. *Journal of Memory and Language* 48: 542-562.

Department of Linguistics
Box 270096
University of Rochester
Rochester, NY 14627

runner@ling.rochester.edu

A Silent Noun in Partitives[*]

Uli Sauerland and Kazuko Yatsushiro

University of Connecticut

1 Introduction

Determiner quantifiers have been an area of intense investigation in generative linguistics. One central insight has been that quantificational determiners are often the main functors of the clause they occur in (Ajdukiewicz 1935). Within generalized quantifier theory (Montague 1974[1970] and others), quantifiers are analyzed as functors of type $\langle\langle e, t\rangle, \langle\langle e, t\rangle, t\rangle\rangle$ (see Heim and Kratzer's 1998 textbook for the type notation). As an example, we give the lexical entry of *every* in (1).

(1) $[[\text{every}]](R)(S) = 1$ iff. $\forall x : R(x) = 1 \Rightarrow S(x) = 1$

In the analysis of (2), NP and VP are the two arguments of *every*.

(2)   Every boy is singing.

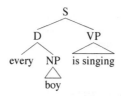

[*]We are grateful to Helen Stickney, Shoichi Takahashi, Satoshi Tomioka, and Akira Watanabe for helpful comments. Uli Sauerland received financial support from the DFG as an Emmy-Noether-Fellow (Grant SA 925/1-1) at the time of writing this paper.

Keir Moulton and Matthew Wolf (eds.): Proceedings of NELS 34,
Stony Brook University: 505 – 516. GLSA, Amherst.

Uli Sauerland and Kazuko Yatsushiro

Ajdukiewicz's insight is preserved in Matthewson's (2001) recent modification of generalized quantifier theory: In her analysis, quantifiers are of type $\langle e, \langle\langle e, t\rangle, t\rangle\rangle$ (see also Sauerland 2003), as is illustrated for *every* in (3). Therefore the complement of *every* is analyzed as a definite with the interpretation of *the boys*, but nevertheless *every* is main functor of the clause.

(3) $[[\text{every}]](X)(S) = 1$ iff. $\forall x : x \sqsubseteq X \wedge \text{atom}(x) \Rightarrow S(x) = 1$

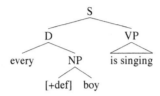

Japanese quantificational expressions present a puzzle for the view that quantificational determiners are the main functors of the clause they occur in.[1] In the examples in (4), the quantifiers *subete* (*every*) and *san-satu* (*three* followed by the classifier for books) seem to be marked with genitive case.

(4)   a.   subete-no hon
             every-GEN book
             'every books'
       b.   san-satu-no hon
             three-CL-GEN book
             'three books'

Compare the examples in (4) with the possessive genitive in (5):

(5)   Lina-no hon
       Lina-GEN book

       'Lina's book'

Morphologically and syntactically (4) and (5) look alike. However, the genitive *Lina-no* in (5) is analyzed as either a modifier of the noun *hon* or as an argument of it (Jensen and Vikner 1994 and others, see also footnote 5). The quantifiers in (4), on the other hand, as we just saw are semantically analyzed as taking the noun as its argument. It seems that the genitive quantifiers in (4) represent a genuine mismatch between syntax and semantics.[2]

---

[1]We are not considering the Japanese quantificational particles *mo* ('every') and *ka* ('a') here (see Yatsushiro 2001).

[2]Note, however, that a similar situation obtains between VP and the argument DPs: a non-quantificational subject is the argument of VP, while a quantificational subject takes VP as its argument.

Japanese quantifiers can also combine with nouns in the three other syntactic constructions shown in (6). (As shown, the entire DP bears accusative case. For a different case-marking, replace any occurrence of *o* with the appropriate case-marker.) [3]

(6) a. hon-o   san-satu / hon-o   subete / hon-o   hotondo
         book-ACC three-CL / book-ACC every / book-ACC most
     b. hon san-satu-o   / hon subete-o   / hon hotondo-o
         book three-CL-ACC / book every-ACC / book most-ACC
     c. san-satu hon-o   / subete hon-o   / hotondo hon-o
         three-CL book-ACC / every book-ACC / most   book-ACC

While previous analyses (Kawashima 1994, Watanabe 2003) try to relate (4) transformationally to one of the constructions in (6), we propose to analyse (4) as a kind of partitive. One argument for our analysis comes from (7). (7) can only be true if John read a number of books which is greater than half of the total number of books. If however *hotondo-no* is replaced with any of three other constructions with *hotondo* in (6), the resulting sentence is also true in a scenario where there is one relevant book, and John read most of that book.

(7) John-wa hotondo-no hon-o   yomi-oeta
     John-TOP most-GEN   book-ACC read-finished

     'John finished reading most of the books.' / *'John read most parts of the book(s).'

If (7) is transformationally related to one of (6), the absence of an interpretation available in (6) is unexpected, and we presently know of no proposal to account for it. As we argue in section 3 below, our analysis directly account for this restriction of (7).

The idea of our analysis is related to an analysis of the regular partitive which we adopt with some modifications from Jackendoff (1977). The proposal is that regular partitives always involve two NPs one of which is phonologically deleted, which in the following is indicated by strike out.

(8) a. most ~~parts~~ of the book / most ~~books~~ of the books
     b. hon-no   ~~hon~~ hotondo
         book-GEN ~~book~~ book

We propose that phonological deletion in (8) is subject to the same principles as deletion of XPs in general. Semantically, the deleted noun provides a way of dividing up the plurality

---

[3]The DPs *hon subete-o* in (6b) and *subete hon-o* in (6c) seem to have an interesting distributional restriction, at least in the judgements of one native speaker. They cannot occur as the objects of the simple verb *yonda* ('read') contrasting with (7), while the floated *hon-o subete* ((6a)) and also *subete-no hon-o* with the genitive quantifier can occur. This seems to support our analysis of the genitive quantifier as having a different structure from (6b) and (6c). It also might support Nakanishi's (2003) analysis of the floated construction which does not derive it from (6b) or (6c). More work, however, is call for on this interesting distributional restriction of *subete*.

the argument of *of* denotes into countable units. Hence, interpreting the singular variant in (8a) involves comparing the sizes of parts of a book, while interpreting the plural variant in (8a) involves comparing numbers of books.

Our main claim is that (7) is derived by deletion from a similar structure with two NPs. (9) shows the analysis of the object DP of (7) we propose. Note that (9) could be called a 'reverse partitive' because not the lower noun, but the higher noun is deleted.

(9)   hotondo [~~hon~~-no   hon-o]
        most   book-GEN book-ACC

We show in section 3 that our analysis explains the facts in (7) and has other advantages. But, first consider the English partitive.

2   The Structure of Partitives

The prior investigations of partitives that we are presently aware of are those of Selkirk (1977), Jackendoff (1977), Ladusaw (1982), Keenan and Stavi (1986), Barker (1998), and Matthewson (2001). Unfortunately not much is agreed upon even within this limited selection from the literature. Consider the different proposals for the DP *three of the books*: Keenan and Stavi assume that *three of the* forms a constituent, while the other authors assume that *of the books* does. Matthewson assumes that *of* has no semantic content, while Ladusaw and Barker argue that semantic content of *of* accounts for the partitive and anti-uniqueness constraints of partitives they discuss.

The proposal we adopt is that partitives always involve two NPs (Jackendoff 1977), and the *of* denotes the part relation (Ladusaw 1982). We consider these two assumptions in turn, starting with the two NPs. In example (10), both of the NPs in the partitive are pronounced. In other partitives, we argue that one or both of these two NPs is phonologically deleted. We assume (10) has the structure in (11).[4]

(10)   three books of all the books Gina has

(11)

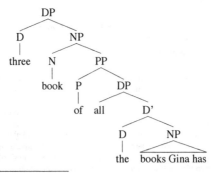

---

[4]We assume Brisson's (2003) analysis of *all* here, but this will not be crucial for the following.

One or both of the nouns in the partitive construction can undergo PF-deletion. In (12a), the higher NP is deleted, in (12b), it is the lower noun, and in (12c) both are deleted.

(12)   a.   three ~~books~~ of all the books Gina has.
        b.   three books of those ~~books~~
        c.   three ~~books~~ of those ~~books~~

We assume that NP-deletion in partitives is subject to the same conditions that NP-deletion in general is subject to. One of Jackendoff's (1977) arguments for the deletion analysis is based on a restriction on which determiners license NP-deletion. The determiners in (13b) don't license NP-deletion in English.

(13)   a.   Sue read all these books, but John didn't read all/most/three/those/none ~~books~~
        b.   *Sue read all these books, but John didn't read the/every/no ~~books~~

As (14b) shows, the same determiners cannot occur in the higher position of a partitive if the noun is deleted.

(14)   a.   John read all/most/three/those/none ~~books~~ of the books.
        b.   *John read the/every/no ~~books~~ of the books.

Because of the partitive constraint, only definite NPs are possible in the lower position of a partitive. (15) shows that deletion of the lower noun is possible with the demonstrative determiner and with a genitive, but not with the definite *the*. This is predicted by our claim that (15) involve NP-deletion.[5]

(15)   a.   John read most books of these/those/Bill's ~~books~~
        b.   *John read most books of the ~~books~~

The construction *most books of Bill's* that we consider as part of (15a) is sometimes referred to as the *Double Genitive*. Barker (1998) defends this assumption in detail. One point he makes is both double genitives and partitives where the higher noun is deleted are subject to an anti-uniqueness condition. This is shown by (16) and (17) ((17) from Barker 1998).

(16)   a.   *John read the one of Bill's books.
        b.   *John read the book of Bill's.

(17)   a.   *I met the one of John's friends.
        b.   *I met the friend of John's.

---

[5]It is interesting to note that the licensing of NP-deletion in (15a) with the genitive *Bill's* below requires an analysis of the genitive as a modifier, because the two occurrences of *books* must have the same interpretation.

Barker points out that the parallel between the constructions extends further: Both constructions are acceptable again when a restrictive modifier is attached to the higher NP as in (18).

(18)   a.   I met the one of John's friends that you pointed out last night.
        b.   I met the friend of John's that you pointed out last night

Barker (1998) proposes the lexical entry in (19) for partitive *of* which predicts the facts in (16) through (18).

(19) $[[\text{of}]](x)(y) = 1$, if and only if y is a proper part of x.

Following Link (1983), we assume that humans can form conceptualizations that involve atomic, indivisible entities. Furthermore, they can form pluralities of these entities which are characterized by the atomic parts they have. Hence, this conceptualization amounts to an atomic semi-lattice in mathematics. If for example a, b, and c are atoms corresponding to individual humans, $a \oplus b$, $a \oplus c$, $b \oplus c$, and $a \oplus b \oplus c$ are the entities corresponding to pluralities of humans. $a \oplus b$ is the plurality that has a and b as its only atomic parts. X is a proper part of Y holds if and only if all atomic parts of X are also atomic parts of Y and furthermore X is distinct from Y. For example, $a \oplus b$ is not a proper part of $a \oplus b$, but only of $a \oplus b \oplus c$.

As Barker shows in detail, the facts in (16) through (17) follows directly from the semantics in (19). In particular the definite descriptions in (16) and (17) lead to a presupposition failure because any countable entity has either no proper parts (atoms) or at least two proper parts (pluralities).[6]

While this was the case in the examples above, our analysis does not require that the two nouns in a partitive construction be identical. If another antecedent for NP-deletion is salient, it can license PF-deletion of a noun in the partitive construction as in (20).

(20)   a.   John had to sort five stacks of books and two stacks of papers. He already managed three ~~stacks~~ of the books.
        b.   Annoyingly some of the papers have missing pages. Two ~~pages~~ of the one I'm reading are gone.

Furthermore, we assume that the higher noun in a partitive construction can also be a mass noun as it is overtly in (21).

---

[6]Possibly, Barker's proper part of should be derived from pragmatic principles, rather than built into the semantics. For example, (i) seems to require only that at least one of the relevant people have more than one sister, while Barker's proposal predicts that all of them should be required to have more than one. This is frequently found with requirements derived from pragmatics (Sauerland 2003).

(i)   Everybody should invite one of his sisters.

A pragmatic derivation of the proper-parthood requirement could possibly start from the observation that if it is not fulfilled use of just the lower DP instead of the partitive is appropriate.

(21)   Some money of the stolen amount reappeared.

Consider now (22) where the lower DP is a singular definite. Because the set of determiners that can occur with a singular definite is a subset of those that can occur in NP-deletion (see (13)), we assume that here, too, there is a silent NP. Specifically, we assume that it is a silent mass noun with a very bland meaning like *stuff* or *content*. We assume that deletion of this noun does not require an antecedent.

(22)   a.   Most/None ~~content~~ of the book is interesting.
        b.   *No of the book is interesting.

Even with plurals the silent higher mass noun seems to be possible. This assumption predicts that singular agreement is possible in (23a) (Selkirk 1977).

(23)   a.   Most ~~content~~ of these papers is boring.
        b.   Most ~~papers~~ of these papers are boring.

Since masses can be a part of individuals, we adopt Link's (1983) μ-operator which maps an individual to the stuff that makes up that individual. (24) shows a lexical entry for *of* that allows for masses.

(24) $[[of]](x)(y) = 1$, if and only if y is a proper part of x or y is a part of $\mu(x)$

3   Japanese

In this section, we address the Japanese construction where quantifiers seem to bear genitive case. (25) (repeated from (4)) shows examples of this with the quantifiers *three, all,* and *most*. As we mentioned in the introduction, the quantificational expression seems to be an argument of the noun. But, this would be puzzling from the perspective of general theories of nominal quantification (Montague 1974[1970], Matthewson 2001, among others), because these assume that quantificational determiners are the main functors of the clause they occur in.

(25)   san-satu-no   hon / subete-no hon / hotondo-no hon
        three-CL-GEN book / all-GEN   book / most-GEN   book

        'three of the books / all of the books / most of the books'

We will argue that the quantifiers in (25) neither are arguments of the noun, nor bear genitive case. Our proposal is that (25) is a partitive construction similar to the English example in (26) (repeated from (12b)), where we argued above that a lower occurrence of *books* is deleted.

(26)   three books of those ~~book~~

The base-generated structure of Japanese partitive constructions that we assume is shown in (27). Note that this is essentially the structure of the English partitives we adopted in (11), except for word-order, and for the need to accommodate classifiers into the structure. Following Watanabe (2003), we assume that the classifier *satsu* is head, and the numeral *san* occupies the specifier position of this head.[7] We make this assumption for concreteness and our proposal could probably restated on the basis of different assumptions about classifiers.

(27)

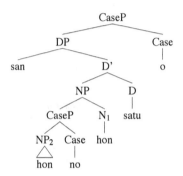

We propose that (25) is derived from the structure (27) in three steps: First, the NP moves to adjoin to CaseP, deriving (28a) (this movement may also target a Specifier of CaseP). Secondly, the DP remnant also moves to adjoin to CaseP, targetting a position higher than the earlier movement as shown in (28b) (again, movement to a Specifier is an option we cannot rule out). Finally, the noun lower occurrence of the noun *hon* is deleted to derive (28c).

(28) a.   [[hon-no hon]$_{NP}$ [san t$_{NP}$ satsu]$_{DP}$-o]$_{CaseP}$
      b.   [[san t$_{NP}$ satsu]$_{DP}$ [hon-no hon]$_{NP}$ t$_{DP}$-o]$_{CaseP}$
      c.   [san t$_{NP}$ satsu]$_{DP}$ [~~hon~~-no hon]$_{NP}$ t$_{DP}$-o]$_{CaseP}$

For the following, we use the terms *whole-NP-movement* for the first step, *Q-inversion* for the second step, and *part-NP deletion* for the third step of this derivation. We address each of these assumptions in more detail to show that they are all independently justified.

Consider first the *whole-NP-movement*. As Watanabe (2003) already shows, this operation must be assumed to be obligatory on his analysis of numerals and classifiers, because the NP cannot occur between the numeral and the classifier as (29a) shows.

---

[7]Watanabe proposes that the classifier is a #-head, rather than a determiner. We actually agree with his conclusion, but for the sake of simplicity, we kept the D-label.

(29) a. *san hon satu-o
          three book CL-ACC
      b. hon san-satu-o
          book three-CL-ACC

Now, consider *Q-inversion*. This operation is also present in Watanabe's proposal as well. Namely, he proposes that (30a) is derived from (29b) by means of remnant movement of the phrase *san-satu* as shown in (30b).

(30) a. san-satu hon-o
          three-CL book-ACC
      b. [[san t_{NP} satu]$_{DP}$ [hon]$_{NP}$ t_{DP} o]$_{CaseP}$

Hence, the operation underlying Q-inversion is also independently required. However, in (30a) the application of Q-inversion is optional, as (29b) is fully grammatical as well. This is not the case for the the genetive quantifier construction in (25) as (31) illustrates.

(31) *no hon san satu o
       GEN book three CL ACC

Why is Q-inversion obligatory in (31)? We propose that *no* requires the presence of a noun to its left that is contained in the same CaseP. Such an assumption may be independtly needed to account for the difference between English *one* and Japanese *no* illustrated in (32)(to be read as occurring in a conversation about bears):

(32) a. I have seen one / a black one.
      b. *no-(o)   mita
           one-(ACC) saw
      c. kuroi no-o   mita
          black one-ACC mita

In English, *one* can occur bare as the object of *see* in (32a). Japanese *no*, which, as (32c) shows, can be used in a similar fashion as *one*, cannot occur on its own as in (32b): *no* requires a phonologically overt noun or adjective to its right it can attach to. If the genetive case marker *no* is subject to the restriction that the NP-pronoun *no* is subject to in (32b), it follows that Q-inversion in (31) is obligatory.

   Finally, consider the third stop of (28): part-NP deletion. NP-deletion is independently known to be possible in Japanese (Saito and Murasugi 1990). However, NP-deletion in partitives has not been discussed in Japanese before, as far as we know. Consider the regular Japanese partitive in (33). We assume that (33) has essentially the same structure as the regular English partitive in (12a) above.

(33) (Gina-ga motteiru) hon-no   san-satu-o
      (Gina-NOM has)   book-GEN three-CL-ACC

      ' three of the books (that Gina has).'

We propose that (33) like (12a) is derived by deletion of the higher noun in the partitive structure. (27) shows the underlying structure of (33). (33) is derived by the application of whole-NP-movement and deletion of the higher occurrence of *hon*.

In difference to English, it is impossible in the Japanese partitive construction to pronounce both the higher and the lower NP of structure (27). Recall that we analyzed the English example (10) as a partitive structure in which two occurrences of the same NP are pronounced. All our attempts to translate (10) literally into Japanese yielded an ungrammatical sentence:

(34) *Gina-ga   motteiru (subete-no) hon-no   hon   san-satsu-o
       Gina-NOM has   (all-GEN)   book-GEN three-CL-Macc

Hence, we assume that the application of NP-deletion is obligatory in partitive structures in Japanese, though we do not know why the application of NP-deletion is forced. NP-deletion of the higher occurrence of the noun *hon* in (34) derives (35).

(35)   Gina-ga motteiru (subete-no) hon-no ~~hon~~ san-satsu-o

And as we argued in (28) above, deletion of the lower NP generally derives the quantifier genetive construction. (In (35), though, deletion of the lower occurrence of *hon* is blocked by the presence of a relative clause.)

Now consider the interpretation of the Japanese partitive structure. We assume that the *no* has the same interpretation as the English *of*, and therefore our account of English partitives following Barker (1998) carries over straighforwardly to the Japanese construction. Recall that we assume that the two NPs in the partitive structure are not required to be identical. The deleted noun can also have a bland interpretation that is paraphrasable as *stuff*. This predicts the fact that the interpretation of the genetive quantifier construction differs from that of the partitive with respect to the partitivity requirement: While the normal partitive (36a) is unacceptable in a situation where only three books are relevant, (36b) is acceptable in the same scenario.

(36)   a.   Taroo-wa hon-no   san-satu-o yomi-oeta
            Taro-TOP book-ACC san-CL-ACC read-finished
            'Taro has finished reading three of the books.'
       b.   Taroo-wa san-satu-no hon-o   yomi-oeta
            Taro-TOP san-CL-GEN book-ACC read-finished
            'Taro has finished reading three books.'

The unacceptability of (36a) follows directly from Barker's proper-parthood requirement, which amounts to a presupposition of (36a) that there be more than three books around. That (36b) lacks this presupposition is also predicted by our analysis: If the deleted lower noun in (36b) is not *book*, but something less specific like *stuff*, the proper-parthood requirement then amounts to just a presupposition that there be some other thing other than the three books. But, this presupposition is essentially vacuous.

Further support for our analysis comes from the interpretation of *hotondo* in these constructions. As is the case with the numeral quantifier, there are two possible constructions with *hotondo*, as shown in (37). In (37a), the higher noun is deleted, and in (37b), the lower noun is deleted. For the ease of exposition, let us call the construction of type (37b), *reverse partitive*.

(37) a. John-wa hon-no   *hotondo*-o yomi-oeta.
          John-TOP book-GEN most-ACC read-finished
          'John has finished reading most of the book(s).'
      b. John-wa *hotondo*-no   hon-o   yomi-oeta
          John-TOP three-CL-GEN book-ACC read-finished
          'John has finished reading most of the books.'

These two sentences differ in interpretation. (37a) allows the two readings in (38). The difference comes from what is divided: in (38a), what is divided is a single book (higher noun = *hon* 'a single book', lower noun = 'pages'), while in (38b), it is a set of books (higher noun = *hon* 'books', silent lower noun = 'books'). When the higher noun is interpreted as a single book, and the lower noun is understood to be 'pages', the interpretation where *hotondo* quantifies over parts of a book arises.

(38) a. John has finished reading most pages of the book.
      b. John has finished readings most books of the books.

In (37b), one the other hand, one of the readings that is available for the normal partitive construction in (37a) is missing. The only available reading for (37b) is that John has read three books of all the books relevant in the discourse ((38b)). But, a reading in which quantification of *hotondo* is over parts of a single book as in (38a)is not allowed.

This is predicted by our theory. According to our analysis, the lower noun is deleted to derive the reverse partitive construction. The reading in which quantification is over parts of a book is possible only when the higher noun is covert, being interpreted as *pages*. This is not possible in (37b), however, since the higher noun is pronounced, and therefore, can be only interpreted as *books*.

It is useful to point out that non-partitive DPs with *hotondo* allow the same range of readings that the partitive (37a) does. Specifically, both (39a) and (39b) allow an interpretation paraphrasable as *most of the book*.

(39) a. John-wa hon hotondo-o yomi-oeta
          John-TOP book most-ACC read-finished
      b. John-wa hotondo hon-o   yomi-oeta
          John-TOP most   book-Macc read-finished

The difference in interpretation between (37b) and (39) therefore corroborates our claim that (37b) is not transformationally related to the non-partitives in (39). In this assumption, our analysis differs from that of Watanabe (2003) who does transformationally relate (37b) with (39). In this way, (37b) argues for our analysis.

References

Ajdukiewicz, K. 1935. Die syntaktische Konnexität. *Studia Philosophica* 1:1–27.
Barker, C. 1998. Partitives, double-genitives, and anti-uniqueness. *Natural Language & Linguistic Theory* 16:679–717.
Brisson, C. 2003. Plurals, *all*, and the nonuniformity of collective predication. *Linguistics and Philosophy* 26:129–184.
Heim, I. and A. Kratzer. 1998. *Semantics in Generative Grammar*. Oxford: Blackwell.
Jackendoff, R. 1977. *X̄-bar Syntax: A Study of Phrase Structure*. Cambridge: MIT Press.
Jensen, P. and C. Vikner. 1994. Lexical knowledge and the semantic analysis of Danish genitive constructions. In *Topics in Knowledge-Based NLP-systems*, ed. S. Hansen and H. Wegener, 37–55. Copenhagen, Denmark: Samfundslitteratur.
Kawashima, R. 1994. The structure of noun phrases and the interpretation of quantificational NPs in Japanese. Doctoral Dissertation, Cornell University.
Keenan, E. and Y. Stavi. 1986. A semantic characterization of natural language determiners. *Linguistics and Philosophy* 9:253–326.
Ladusaw, B. 1982. Semantic constraints on the English partitive construction. In *Proceedings of WCCFL 1*, ed. D. Flickinger, *et al.*, 231–242. Stanford, Calif.
Link, G. 1983. The logical analysis of plurals and mass terms. In *Meaning, Use, and the Interpretation of Language*, ed. R. Bäuerle *et al.*, 302–323. Berlin: de Gruyter.
Matthewson, L. 2001. Quantification and the nature of crosslinguistic variation. *Natural Language Semantics* 9:145–189.
Montague, R. 1974[1970]. The proper treatment of quantification in ordinary English. In *Selected Papers*, 247–270. New Haven: Yale University Press.
Nakanishi, K. 2003. The semantics of measure phrases. In *Proceedings of NELS 33*, ed. M. Kadowaki and S. Kawahara, 225–244. Amherst: GLSA, Univ. of Mass.
Saito, Mamoru, and Keiko Murasugi. 1990. N′-deletion in Japanese. In *UConn Working Papers in Linguistics 3*. Storrs: University of Connecticut.
Sauerland, U. 2003. A new semantics for number. In *The Proceedings of SALT 13*. Cornell University, Ithaca, N.Y.: CLC-Publications. (in print)
Selkirk, L. 1977. Some remarks on noun phrase structure. In *Studies in Formal Syntax*, ed. P. Culicover, T. Wasow, and A. Akmajian, 285–316. New York: Academic Press.
Watanabe, A. 2003. Functional projection of nominals in Japanese: Syntax of classifiers. Ms., University of Tokyo. (presented at AFLA2, MIT, Cambridge, Mass.)
Yatsushiro, K. 2001. The distribution of *mo* and *ka* and its implications. In *Proceedings of the Third Formal Approaches to Japanese Linguistics*, 181–198. Cambridge, Mass.: MIT Working Papers in Linguistics.

Department of Linguistics, U-1145
University of Connecticut
Storrs CT 06269
U.S.A.

uli@alum.mit.edu, kazuko@mac.com

Presupposition & Root Transforms in Adjunct Clauses[*]

Miyuki Sawada and Richard K. Larson

Ming Chuan University and Stony Brook University

Hopper & Thompson (1973; hereafter H&T) observe an interesting correlation between the syntax and pragmatics of adverbial clauses. As shown in (1a), adverbial *when-*, *before-* and *after-* clauses resist root transformations like Left Dislocation; correspondingly their content is presupposed (1b). By contrast, *because*-clauses like those in (1b) allow Left Dislocation (2a), and their content is asserted, not presupposed:

(1)   a.   *Mildred bought a Mercedes
            [**when/before/after** her son, he purchased stock in Xerox].
      b.   Mildred bought a Mercedes
            [**when/before/after** her son purchased stock in Xerox].
            Presupposes: Mildred's son purchased stock in Xerox.

(2)   a.   Mildred drives a Mercedes [**because** her son, he owns stock in Xerox].
      b.   Mildred drives a Mercedes [**because** her son owns stock in Xerox].
            Asserts: Mildred's son purchased stock in Xerox.

The robustness of H&T's correlation between root transform availability and presupposition is underscored by example (3). Here presupposition is forced on the *because*-clause by association with negation; notice now that Left Dislocation is blocked.

(3)   *Sam is going out for dinner [**not because** his wife, she can't cook],
       but **because** he wants to discuss Q-magic with Stella. (= H&T 's (245))
       Presupposes: Sam's wife can't cook

Hopper & Thompson's observations raise some simple, but intriguing questions:

   • Why should a semantic/pragmatic phenomenon like presupposition be correlated
     with the possibility of certain syntactic operations—specifically, root

---

[*] The authors are grateful to audiences at the 2003 LSA Annual Meetings (Atlanta, GA), and at NELS 34 (Stony Brook, NY)   for helpful feedback. We particularly thank G. Cinque and O. Ciucivara for discussion of the Italian and Romanian data in section 3.3.

transformations?
• How is this correlation achieved?

In this paper, we suggest an answer based on work by Michael Johnston (1994), who argues for an important semantic difference between *because*-adjuncts versus *when-*/*before-*/*after*-adjuncts. We propose that Johnston's semantic difference explains the presupposed/asserted contrast, and correlates with a syntactic difference, which explains the differential availability of root transforms.

1.   The Breadth of the Phenomenon

Hopper & Thompson's correlation is exhibited across a wide variety of root transforms in English, including not only with Left Dislocation, but also other root transformations such as VP Preposing, Negative Constituent Preposing, Directional Adverb Preposing, Participle Preposing, PP Substitution, Subject Replacement, Direct Quote Preposing, Complement Preposing, Adverb Dislocation, Right Dislocation Tag Question Formation, and Topicalization.   As shown in (4a-g), temporal adverbial clauses resist all of these operations:

(4)   a.   *Helen and Jack had dinner [**before into the kitchen trooped the children**]
            (Directional Adverb Preposing)
      b.   *The villagers all burst into song [**when in came the bride and groom**].
            (Directional Adverb Preposing)
      c.   *We were all much happier [**when upstairs lived the Browns**].
            (PP Substitution)
      d.   *The guests laughed out loud [**after Mary stopped singing, strangely**]
            (Adverb Dislocation)
      e.   *The customer stomped out [**after the clerk, I guess, insulted her**]
            (Complement Preposing)
      f.   *Max left the room [**after "I won," Alice exclaimed**]
            (Direct Quote Preposing)
      g.   *Max was quiet [**before Alice was sleeping, wasn't she?**]
            (Tag Question Formation)

But when these operations occur in *because*-clauses, as in (5a-g), the results are considerably better:

(5)   a.   Helen and Jack stopped eating
            [**because into the kitchen trooped the children**]
      b.   The villagers burst into song [**because in came the bride and groom**].
      c.   We were all much happier [**because upstairs lived the Browns**].
      d.   The guests laughed out loud [**because Mary stopped singing, strangely**]
      e.   The customer stomped out [**because the clerk, I guess, insulted her**]
      f.   ?Max left the room [**because "I won," Alice exclaimed**]
      g.   Max was quiet [**because Alice was sleeping, wasn't she?**]

1.1. Swedish (Andersson 1975)

Hopper & Thompson's correlations also extend beyond English. As discussed by Andersson (1975), Swedish *because*-clauses permit root transforms when their content is asserted (6):

(6)   a.   USA har startat ett nytt krig   [**därför   att   Nixon, han är ju inte klok**].
            U.S has started   a new war   because   that   Nixon   he is EMPH not
sane
            'The US has started a new war because Nixon is insane.'
            (Left Dislocation)
      b.   Vi foljer inte med   [**därför   att ÖIS   gillar vi   inte**].
            We follow not with   because that ÖIS (= a sports team) like   we   not
            'We aren't coming along because we don't like ÖIS.'
            (Topicalization)
      c.   Vi blev   överraskade [**därför   att   ut i köket   sprang plötsligt Olle**].
            We were surprised   because that out into kitchen-the sprang suddenly Olle'
            'We were surprised because Olle suddenly ran into the kitchen.'
            (Directional Adverb Preposing)

But, as in English, Swedish *when*-clauses block root transforms when their content is presupposed (7):

(7)   a.   *Vi   kom till Stockholm [**när   Henry, han var på väg till Kairo**].
            We came to Stockholm   when Henry,   he was on way to Cairo
            'We came to Stockholm when Henry was on the way to Cairo.'
            (Left Dislocation)
      b.   *Vi   åkte genast   hem   [**när   Peter vi   hade   talat   med**].
             We   went immediately home   when   Peter we   had   spoken to
            'We went immediately home when we had spoken to Peter.'
            (Topicalization)
      c.   Vi satt och talade [**när ut i   köket   sprang plötsligt   Olle**].
            We sat and talked when out into kitchen-the sprang   suddenly Olle'
            'We sat and talked when Olle suddenly ran into the kitchen.'
            (Directional Adverb Preposing)

1.2. Japanese (Minami 1974, 1993, Noda 1986, Takubo 1987, Takayama 1987, Koizumi 1993)

Japanese also exhibits the Hopper & Thompson correlation. Japanese root transformations are restricted to a construction involving Topicalization (NP-*wa*) + a modal element. This construction may occur in non-presupposed *kara*-clauses (*because*-clauses), as shown in (8a-d):

(8) a. **kondo-no typhoon-wa ookii-rashii-kara**,
        this-gen   typhoon-top big-seem-because,
        dansui-ya   teiden-ni   sonaeta   hou-ga   ii.
        cutting water-and cutting electricity-for prepare(PST) way-nom good
        'Because the coming typhoon seems to be very strong, (we) had better prepare
         for the water and electricity being cut off.'
     b. **mukou-no   hodou-wa   kawaite-iru-youda-kara**, mukou-ni   wataro-u.
        over there-gen sidewalk-top dry-is-seem-because,   over there-to cross-will
        'Because the sidewalk on the other side seems drier,(I) will cross the road.'
     c. **sake-wa karadani yoku-nai-darou-kara**,   oolong-cha-o   nomo-u.
        sake-top health   good-Neg-May-because,   oolong-tea-acc drink-will
        'Because sake may not be good for (our) health, I will have oolong tea.'

(9) a. **ame-ga   futta-kara**,   Taroo-wa soccer-o   shi-nakatta-no-de-wa nai,
        rain-nom fell-because, Taro-top soccer-acc didn't-Comp-be Top Neg,
        totemo samukatta-kara-da.
        very   cold(PST)-because-be(NPST)
        'Taro didn't not play soccer because it was raining, but because it was very
         cold.'
     b. ***ame-wa futta-darou-kara**,   Taroo-wa soccer-o
        rain-top fall(PST)-may-because Taro-to soccer-acc
        shi-nakatta-no-de-wa nai,   totemo samukatta-kara-da.
        didn't-Comp-be Top Neg,   very cold(PST)-because-be(NPST)
        'Taro didn't not play soccer because it may have rained, but because it was
         very cold.'

But Japanese *toki*- (*when*-), *mae*- (*before*-) or *ato*-clauses (*after*-clauses), which are presupposed, block topicalization (NP-*wa*) + modal (10):

(10) a. ***Taro-wa raishuu   kuru-darou-toki**, soba-o   motte kite   morau
        Taro-top next week come-may-when,   noodles-o   bring come BENE
        'When Taro may come next week, (I) will ask him to bring soba noodles.'
     b. ***Taro-wa ki-ta-darou-ato**,   minna-no naka-ga   warukunat-ta
        Taro-top come(PST)-may-after, everyone-gen relation-nom bad-become-PST
        'After Taro came, everyone was in a bad mood.'

   c. ***Taro-wa kuru-darou-mae**, minna-no   naka-ga   warukunat-ta.
        Taro-top come-may-**before**, everyone-gen relation-nom bad-become-PST
        'Before Taro came, everyone was in a bad mood.'

2.   Our Analysis

We propose an account of the Hopper & Thompson correlation based on the semantics for adverbial clauses offered by Johnston (1994), who draws an important distinction between temporal clauses headed by *when, before* and *after*, and causal clauses headed by *because.* [1]

2.1. Temporal Clauses as Q-Restrictions

According to Johnston, temporal connectives combine with an <u>open</u> event sentence, to create a time-interval description.   The basic idea is shown in (11) for the temporal clause *when Marcia was at the cafe. Marcia was at the cafe* denotes an open event description - an event of Marcia being at the cafe (11b). *When* is analyzed as taking an open event description and yielding an interval description, namely, the interval that is the temporal "run-time" of the maximal event that it combines with (11c).   In this case, *when Marcia was at the cafe* denotes the interval i that is the temporal runtime of the maximal event of Marcia being at the cafe (11d).

(11) a.   when Marcia was at the cafe
      b. *Marcia was at the cafe* $\Rightarrow$ **at'**(Marcia, the, cafe, e)
      c. *when* $\Rightarrow$ $\lambda\phi\lambda i[\exists e[MAX(\phi)(e) \,\&\, i = f(e)]$
      d. *when Marcia was at the cafe* $\Rightarrow$
                                   $\lambda i [\exists e[MAX(\mathbf{at'}(Marcia, the, cafe, e))(e) \,\&\, i = f(e)]$

In this approach, combination with an open event description is crucial. As we see, *when* needs to apply the temporal runtime function (f) to the <u>maximal</u> e in its complement, hence the latter cannot be closed off by binding. In combing with its complement *when* itself supplies the existential e-binding. We will follow Johnston in adopting the notation on the handout, where the result in (11d) is abbreviated as shown. This notation captures the event-binding nature of *when* via the subscripted e variable.

$\lambda i [\exists e[MAX(\mathbf{at'}(Marcia, the, cafe, e))(e) \,\&\, i = f(e)]$ $\Leftrightarrow$ **when'**$_e$(**at'**(Marcia, the, cafe, **e**))

    Following a number of authors, Johnston assumes that temporal clauses always restrict a (covert or overt) adverb of quantification (AoQ). (12) gives Johnston's analysis

---

[1] An appeal to Johnston's semantics for *because*-clauses may not be essential to our account. Davidson (1967) analyzes *cause* as a binary relation between event individuals (cause(e1,e2)) rather than propositions, An analysis of (restrictive) *because*-clauses as existential quantifiers over events, involving Davidson's cause-relation is given in Larson (2004). The latter would appear to have the same desired result: that because combines with (existentially) closed event descriptions.

of episodic *when*-clauses, where the latter are taken to restrict an implicit existential adverb. (13) gives his analysis of a case where the adverb is overt.

(12) a. Marcia wrote a letter when she was at the cafe.   Episodic *When*
     b. ∃**when'**$_{e1}$(**at'**(Marcia, the cafe, **e1**))) [**write'**(Marcia, the cafe, **e2**)]

(13) a. Marcia **always** writes a letter when she is at the cafe.   *When* + Overt AoQ
     b. ∀**when'**$_{e1}$(**at'**(Marcia, the cafe, **e1**))) [**write'**(Marcia, the cafe, **e2**)]

Under the usual view that quantifier-restrictions are presupposed or background entailed to be non-empty, this will yield the presuppositional character of temporal clauses that Hopper & Thompson note.   That is, it will be presupposed that there IS a run-time interval i, and hence that there IS a maximal event e that i is the runtime of.

In brief, then, for Johnston temporal connectives combine with an open event sentence, creating an interval description that restricts a quantificational adverb. This explains why temporal clauses presuppose the existence of the complement event.

2.2. "Because" –Clauses as Event Relations

Causal clauses have a very different analysis. For Johnston *because* takes a <u>closed</u> event sentence as its complement, and expresses a binary relation between <u>closed</u> event sentences.   The truth-conditions for *because* are given in (14) and the analysis of a basic case, *Marty sold his bike because the gears broke*, is given in (15).

(14) **Truth-conditions**: If X and Y are propositions, then
     because'(X,Y) is true iff X is true as a result of Y being true.

(15) a. Marty sold his bike because the gears broke.
     b. **because'**($\exists e_1$[**sold'**(Marty, his bike, e_1)], $\exists e_2$[**break'**(Marty, his bike, e_2)])

Notice that, under the truth conditions given, the existential quantifier over events is <u>not</u> provided by *because*.

Furthermore, since *because* and its complement do not yield a description of events or intervals, it cannot function as a restriction on an adverb of quantification.   As Johnston discusses, there is no reading of (16a) equivalent to (16b) where all relevant events caused by John's wrecking the car are ones in which Jane fixes it.

(16) a. Jane **always** fixes the car because John wrecks it.
     b. #∀**because'**($\exists e_1$[**wreck'**(John, the car, e_1)]) [**fix'**(Jane, the car, e_2)]

     # 'All (relevant) events caused by John's wrecking the car are ones of Jane's fixing it.'

Since the *because*-clause does not (and cannot) restrict an adverb of quantification, its content is <u>not</u> presupposed.

In summary, then, causal connectives combine with a closed event sentence, and create a functor that selects another closed event sentence. They do not create restrictions on adverbs of quantification, and this explains why they do not presuppose the existence of the complement event, but merely assert it.

2.3. A Structural Conjecture

Looked at from a certain perspective, Johnston's semantics implies that *because* thus applies to a "larger" semantic domain than temporal connectives. Temporals combine with <u>open</u> eventuality descriptions. *Because* combines with a closed eventuality description; that is, an open eventuality description <u>plus</u> a quantifier:

> *when Marcia was at the cafe*
> **when'**   + **at'**(Marcia, the cafe, **e**)
>
> *because Marcia was at the cafe*
> **because'** + ∃**e** + **at'**(Marcia, the cafe, **e**)

It is attractive to suppose that this semantic difference is reflected in a syntactic difference: that along with having a larger semantic domain than *when*, *before*, and *after*, *because* also has a larger <u>syntactic</u> domain. Suppose temporals combine with some projection YP (17a). Then we may propose that *because* combines with some larger projection XP, which includes YP, and whose head contributes the existential quantifier ∃ over events (17b).

(17) a. **when/before/after** $[_{YP} \ldots]$
      b. **because** $[_{XP}$ $[_{X'} \exists e$ $[_{YP} \ldots]]]$
      c. **because** $[_{XP}$ her son $[_{X'} \exists e$ $[_{YP}$ he owns stock in Xerox]]]

Notice that this extra layer of structure will bring with it an extra specifier position (Spec of XP). We propose that it is just this area that is accessed by root transformations, along the lines in (17c).

3.   Some Cross-linguistic Data

We will not attempt to supply the details of (17) here, or identify the specific categories X and Y, but rather will close by noting, very briefly, the existence of some apparent cross-linguistic evidence that *because*-complements are in fact syntactically "larger" than *when/before/after*-complements, as expected under our proposal. We do not present these data as definitive, but only suggestive. Plainly a good deal of further work would be required on each construction to show that the distinctions observed are due to the structural one we are proposing.

3.1. Haitian Creole Verb-Doubling (Lefebvre & Ritter 1993)

Lefebvre and Ritter (1993) note that Haitian Creole can form temporal and causal adjunct clauses by "doubling" the main clause predicate in initial position. This process is illustrated in (18a-c):

(18) a. **[Bwè**   li   bwè   remèd   la   ],   l   ap   geri
        drink   he   drink   medicine   DM   he   FUT   recover
        'As soon as he takes the medicine, he will get better'
    b. **[Vini**   Jan   te   vini   an],   manman li   kontan
        come   John   PST   come DM   mother   his   happy
        'Since John has come, his mother is happy'
    c. **[Rive**   Jan   rive   (a)   ],   Mari   pati
        arrive   John   arrive   DM   Mary   leave
        'As soon as/since John arrived, Mary left'

Lefebvre and Ritter argue that in temporal adjuncts, the doubled V resides in T; whereas in causal adjuncts, the doubled V is positioned higher, in C; see (19a,b). Among other things, this explains why clausal adjuncts can contain tenses, modals and negation, but temporal adjuncts cannot; compare (20a) and (20b).

(19) a.   [$_{TP}$ V   ... V ...]   doubled *when*-clauses in HC
    b. [$_{CP}$ V ... [$_{TP}$ ... V ...]]   doubled *because*-clauses in HC

(20) a. **Achte**   Jan   pa   te   achte   flè   yo,   Mari   fache.
        buy   John   NEG   PST   buy   flower Det, Mary   angry
        'Because John didn't buy the flowers, Mary is angry.'
    b. ***Di**   m   pa   di   l   sa,   li   ale.
        tell   I   NEG   tell him   that,   he   go
        'As soon as/When I didn't tell him that, he left.'

So the size-difference in temporal vs. causal adjuncts is reflected in a difference in V scope.

3.2. Sakha Agreement (N. Vinokurova p.c.)

Agreement patterns in Sakha (N. Vinokurova) also appear to furnish evidence for a size difference. In Sakha root sentences, subject and verb agree, and *pro* is possible; see (21). *Because*-clauses show normal subject agreement (21a), but temporal clauses do not (21b):

(20) a. Marty/pro amerika-qa   baar-**a**
        Marty/he   Amerikca-DAT   exist-**3**
        'Marty/he was in America'

(21) a. Marty belesipie-ti-n atylaa-bat-a [**toqo dieri   pro   amerika-qa   baar-a**].

Marty bike-3-ACC sell-NEGPST-3 because   he   America-DAT   exist-**3**
'Marty didn't sell his bike, because he was in America.'
b.   Marty belesipie-ti-n atylaa-bat-a   [amerika-qa   pro baar-(***a**)   kemiger].
Marty bike-3-ACC sell-NEGPST-3 America-DAT he   exist-(***3**)   time-dat-3
'Marty didn't sell his bike, when he was in America.'

Assuming that subject agreement resides in a projection AgrsP above TP (Chomsky 1993), this suggests *because*-type adjuncts include AgrsP, but *when*-type adjuncts do not, a result consistent with Lefebvre and Ritter.

3.3. Romance Clitic Left Dislocation (CLLD)

Romance clitic left dislocation (CLLD) is known to be possible front of virtually any subordinate clause type (see Cinque 1990:58 for Italian; Zubizarreta 1998:187 for Spanish).   Interestingly, however, whereas only <u>single</u> CLLD is available with temporal adverbial clauses, <u>multiple</u> CLLD is possible with causal clauses.   The Italian facts in (22) and (23) from G. Cinque (p.c.) illustrate the contrast:[2]

(22) **Da quando**   di vestiti   a me   Gianni non **(??me)**   **ne**   compra più,
When/since of clothes   to me   G.   not   to me of them   buys   no longer
sono costretto   ad andare in giro   mal vestito
I am   forced   to   go   around   ill-dressed
'Since the time that Gianni stopped buying clothes for me, I have been forced to go around ill-dressed'

(23) **Poiché   di** vestiti   a me   Gianni non **me**   **ne**   compra   più,
Because of clothes   to me   G.   not   to me of them   buys   no longer
sono   costretto   ad   andare   in giro   mal vestito
I am   forced   to   go   around ill-dressed
'Because Gianni stopped buying clothes for me, I have been forced to go around ill-dressed'

On the hypothesis that multiple CLLD is made possible by the existence of an additional position at the left-periphery of the clause, providing additional space for a dislocated element (Haegeman 2003), this contrast is consistent with the basic analysis proposed here.

---

[2] The contrast observed here appears to be distinct from one observed by Haegeman (2002, 2003), who argues for a structural difference between what she calls "central adverbial clauses" (conditional *if*-clauses, temporal *when*-clauses, purposive *so that*-clauses, among others), and "peripheral adverbial clauses," which (in her terms) "anchor to the speaker' like root clauses, and accept RTs (evidential *if*-clauses, contrastive *when*-clauses, resultative *so that*-clauses, etc.). According to Haegeman, Romance allows a single clitic left dislocation (CLLD) in 'central adverbial clauses', whereas multiple CLLDs are possible in 'peripheral adverbial clauses'.   We will not attempt to relate Haegeman's claims with the data presented here.

A potentially similar phenomenon is pointed out to us by Oana Ciucivara (p.c.) for Romanian. In Romanian CLLD constructions two word orders are possible: the IO may precede the DO, or vice versa. For Ciucivara, the IO-DO order is more natural, and in this case,   the presence of both clitics is possible, and indeed obligatory, in both temporal and *because*-clauses (24):

(24) a. IO>DO
         De cand   bunicului   nepoatele-i   nu   i   **le-**
         of when   grandpa-dat granddaughters.the-his not to him   them (fem, pl)
         am   mai   trimis, se simte din ce in ce mai   singur
         have.1st anymore sent   SE-refl feels   more and more alone.
         'Ever since I no longer sent grandpa his grandaughters, he has been feeling
         more and more alone.'
     b. **Fiindca** bunicului nepoatele-i   nu **i**   **le** am   mai   trimis,
         Because grandpa-dat granddaughters-his not to him them have.1sg anymore
         sent
         se simte din ce in ce mai singur.
         se-refl feels more and more alone.
         'Because I no longer sent grandpa his grandaughters, he has been feeling more
         and more alone.'

However, Ciucivara reports that when the DO precedes the IO, there appears to be a contrast: specifically multiple clitics remain acceptable in the *because*- clause (25b), whereas the indirect object clitic in the temporal clause is marginal (although not completely unacceptable) (25a).

(25) DO>IO
     a. ?**De cand**   nepoatele-i, bunicului nu **i** **le**-am mai trimis, el se simte din ce in ce
         mai singur
     b. **Fiindca** nepoatele-i, bunicului nu **i le**-am mai trimis, el se simte din ce in ce mai
         singur

One potential interpretation of this fact is that DO>IO represents a derived order in which the direct object has been moved to the at the left-peripheral position that we have been discussing, a position available in *because*-clauses, but unavailable (or only marginally so) in temporal clauses.

4. Conclusions

In this paper, we have that proposed that Hopper & Thompson's striking correlation between presupposition and the availability of root transformations in adjunct clauses is essentially an artifact of semantics, and its projection into syntax. Specifically, using the semantics for adverbials proposed by Johnston (1994) we have explored the following claims:

- Temporal connectives combine with open event sentences, yielding interval descriptions.
- These restrict (covert or overt) adverbial quantifiers and are presupposed.
- Causal connectives combine with closed event sentences, do not restrict adverbial quantifiers, and are not presupposed

Closed event sentences are semantically and syntactically "larger" than open ones, and the larger syntactic domain of causal adjuncts makes room for root transforms. We briefly reviewed some independent syntactic evidence that such a "size difference" does indeed exist.

References

Andersson, L. 1975. Form and Function of Subordinate Clauses. Doctoral Dissertation. Göteborg University. Göteborg.

Cinque, G. 1990. *Types of A'-Dependencies*. Cambridge: MIT Press.

Davidson, D. 1967. Causal Relations. *Journal of Philosophy* 64: 691-703.

Diesing, M. 1992. *Indefinites*. Cambridge: MIT Press.

Haegeman, L. 2002. "Anchoring to Speaker. Adverbial Clauses and the Structure of CP." In S. Mauck and J. Mittelstaedt (eds) *Georgetown University Working Papers in Theoretical Linguistics*, Volume 2, Fall 2002, 117-180.

Haegeman, L. 2003. The Syntax of Adverbial Clauses and its Consequences for Topicalisation . (unpublished ms.)

Heinämäki, O. 1978. *Semantics of English Temporal Connectives*. Univ. of Indiana: IULC.

Herburger, E. 2000. *What Counts*. Cambridge: MIT Press.

Hooper, J. B. and Thompson, S.A. 1973. On the Applicability of Root Transformations. *Linguistic Inquiry* 4: 465-497.

Johnston, M. 1994. *The Syntax and Semantics of Adverbial Adjuncts*. Doctoral Dissertation. UCSC.

Keenan, E. 1971. Two Kinds of Presupposition in Natural Language, In C. Filmore and D,T. Langendoen (eds.) *Studies in Linguistic Semantics*. New York: Holt Rinehart and Winston.

Koizumi, M .1993. Modal Phrase and Adjuncts. *Japanese/Korean Linguistics* 2: 409-428.

Larson, R. (2004) Sentence-Final Adverbs and Scope. In K. Moulton and M. Wolf (eds.) *Proceedings of NELS 34* (this volume).

Lefebvre, C. and Ritter, E. 1993. Two Types of Predicated Doubling Adverbs in Haitian Creole, In Byrne, F and Winford, D (eds.) *Focus and Grammatical Relations in*

Creole Languages. (pp.65-91) Amsterdam/Philadelphia: John Benjamins.

Minami, F. 1974. *Gendai Nihongo no Kozo [Structure of Modern Japanese]*. Tokyo: Taishukan Shoten.

Minami, F. 1993. *Gendai Nihongo Bunpoo no Rinkaku [The Frame of Modern Japanese Grammar]*. Tokyo: Taishukan Shoten

Noda, H. 1986. Hukubun ni okeru "wa" to "ga" no Kakarikata. [The Function of "wa" and "ga" in Multiple Sentences] *Nihongogaku* 5-2: 31-43.

Takayama, Y. 1987. Juzokusetu ni okeru mood keishiki no jittai ni tsui te [The Appearance of Modals in Adjunct Clauses]. *Nihongogaku* 6-12: 85-97.

Takubo, Y. 1987. Toogo Koozoo to Bunmyaku Joho [Syntactic Structure and Contextual Information]. *Nihongogaku* 6-5: 37-48.

Zubizaretta, M-L. 1998. *Prosody, Focus and Word Order*. Cambridge: MIT Press.

Department of Applied Japanese
Ming Chuan University
5 Tehming Rd. Tatung Village, Taoyuan
333 Taiwan ROC

msawada88@hotmail.com

Department of Linguistics
Stony Brook University
Stony Brook, NY 11794-4376

richard.larson@stonybrook.edu

Preverbal Negative Polarity Items in Cantonese[1]

Scott Shank

University of British Columbia

1.   Introduction

Cantonese has a set of negative polarity items (NPIs) which are derived from wh-words. As polarity items, they must occur within the scope of an appropriate licensor (1a-2a). When not in the scope of negation, these wh-words are construed as wh-questions (1b-2b).

(1)   a.   Ngóh   móuh   gin   bīngo.
             I   neg.pfv   see   who[2]
             'I didn't see anyone.'

       b.   Léih   gin-jó   bīngo   a?
             you   see-pfv   who   prt
             'Who did you see?'

(2)   a.   Ngóh   móuh   sihk   mātyéh.
             I   neg.pfv   eat   what
             'I didn't eat anything.'

       b.   Léih   sihk-jó   mātyéh a?
             you   eat-pfv   what   prt
             'What did you eat?'

In this paper I focus on preverbal NPIs associated with *dōu* "even" (3-4). These forms are emphatic, and are naturally translated into English with a stressed *ANY* or *NO*.

---

[1] Thanks to my consultants Susan Hung, Rebecca Lee and Florence Woo. Thanks also to Henry Davis, Lisa Matthewson, Chung-hye Han, Florence Woo, Anastasia Giannakidou and participants at NELS 34 for helpful discussion. All errors are my own.

[2] Abbreviations used are as follows: cl= classifier, dat = dative, fam = familiar, neg = negative, pfv = perfective, prt = particle, rhet = rhetorical, v-prt = verbal particle.

Keir Moulton and Matthew Wolf (eds.): Proceedings of NELS 34,
Stony Brook University: 529 – 540. GLSA, Amherst.

(3)   a.   Ngóh bīngo dōu   móuh   gin.
             I   who   even   neg.pfv   see
             'I didn't see ANYBODY at all.'

       b.   Bīngo dōu   móuh   gin   ngóh.
             who   even   neg.pfv   see   me
             'NOBODY saw me.'

(4)   Ngóh mātyéh   dōu   móuh   sihk.
       I   what   even   neg.pfv   eat
       'I didn't eat ANYTHING at all.'

These preverbal NPIs are somewhat puzzling. Although they are translated as negative polarity indefinites, on the surface they are not within the scope of negation. As NPIs, these indefinites are predicted not to be licensed if not c-commanded by their licensor. Negation cannot normally scope over subject NPs, in keeping with Huang's (1982) observation that scopal relations in Chinese are reflected at surface structure. Sentences with more than one operator are normally unambiguous. For instance, in (5) a universal quantifier in subject position may only have wide scope over negation..

(5)   Go-go dōu   mh   jūngyi sihk   gāt.
       cl-cl all   neg   like   eat   tangerine
       (i) $\forall\neg$:   'Everyone doesn't like to eat tangerines.'
       (ii) $\neg\forall$: * 'Not everyone likes to eat tangerines.'

My solution to the problem of the preverbal NPIs in (3-4) is to link their behaviour to that of preverbal indefinites containing yāt "one". In negative sentences containing dōu "even", yāt indefinites only allow a reading in which the NP is interpreted below the scope of negation. I argue that dōu forces lowering of the indefinite at LF to satisfy its presuppositions. I also show how extending this analysis to the preverbal NPIs in (3-4) is empirically superior to an alternative proposal which extends the work of Cheng (1995) and treats dōu as a universal "all" in these sentences.

2.   Analysis

2.1.   Preverbal yāt indefinites

I begin the discussion with the particle dōu, whose presuppositions are key to my analysis. The particle dōu functions as an additive focus particle meaning "even". The focused item with which dōu associates normally occurs to the left of the particle.

(6)   Ngóh a-John   dōu   gin-jó.
       I   fam-John   even   see-pfv
       'I even saw John.'

Even does not affect the truth conditions, but rather brings certain presuppositions to the sentence. It has an existential presupposition that there is another true alternative proposition besides the one denoted by the sentence in which it occurs. The particle furthermore has a scalar presupposition that the asserted proposition is the least likely of all the alternative propositions under consideration (Karttunen and Peters 1979).

When *dōu* is associated with a preverbal *yāt* "one" indefinite in a negative sentence, the indefinite must be interpreted below negation. The following examples with subject *yāt* indefinites provide a striking minimal pair. In (7), where there is no *dōu* associated with the subject, the numeral must be interpreted with wide scope over negation. The example in (8) is exactly the opposite. In this case, the indefinite is focused and associated with *dōu*, and only the reading in which the indefinite takes scope under negation is possible.[3]

(7) Yāt   go   yàhn móuh   sihk.
     one   cl   person neg.pfv   eat
     (i) $\exists\neg$: 'One person did not eat.'
     (ii) $\neg\exists$: * 'Not one person ate.'

(8) Yāt$_F$ go   yàhn dōu   móuh   sihk.
     one   cl   person even neg.pfv   eat
     (i) $\exists\neg$: * 'Even one person didn't eat.'
     (ii) $\neg\exists$: 'Not even one person ate.'

The pattern is that when a low-scalar indefinite is focused and associated with *dōu* "even", the indefinite must be interpreted with narrower scope than negation. In order to account for this, I will pursue the hypothesis that the indefinite has lowered back to its base position at LF to a position within the scope of negation. I will argue that the lowering in these examples is forced on semantic grounds. Outside the scope of negation, the presuppositions of *dōu* "even" cannot be satisfied.

2.2. Semantic Analysis

I begin by discussing (8i) and show how interpreting the *yāt* indefinite in its surface position leads to *dōu* carrying impossible presuppositions. The argument derives from Lahiri (1998), who observed that low-scalar indefinites associated with *even* only have coherent presuppositions in downward entailing environments.

The sentence in (8i) has the LF in (9).

(9) Yāt go yàhn dōu móuh sihk.
     LF: [dōu [[yāt$_F$ go yàhn][móuh sihk]]].

---

[3] The acceptability of preverbal numeral phrases in non-negative sentences in Chinese is a matter of some debate. See Li (1998) for an overview of the issue. The Cantonese speakers I have consulted accept (7).

Adopting Rooth's (1985, 1992) alternative semantics of focus, this sentence has the ordinary semantic value given in (10) and is interpreted against the background of salient focal alternatives given in (11).

(10) $|\lambda x[\text{person}(x)] \cap \lambda x[\neg\text{eat}(x)]| \geq 1$
        = There is one person who did not eat.

(11)   C = $\{^\wedge[|\lambda x[\text{person}(x)] \cap \lambda x[\neg\text{eat}(x)]| \geq 1], {}^\wedge[|\lambda x[\text{person}(x)] \cap \lambda x[\neg\text{eat}(x)]| \geq 2],$
        $^\wedge[|\lambda x[\text{person}(x)] \cap \lambda x[\neg\text{eat}(x)]| \geq 3]\}$
        = {There is one person who didn't eat, There are two people who didn't eat,
        There are three people who didn't eat}

Dōu has no effect on the truth conditions, but it carries both an existential and a scalar presupposition. These presuppositions are given in (12a) and (12b) respectively.

(12)   a. $\exists q[q \in C \wedge q \neq {}^\wedge[|\lambda x[\text{person}(x)] \cap \lambda x[\neg\text{eat}(x)]| \geq 1] \wedge q(w) = 1]$
              = There is another true proposition in the salient set of alternatives besides
              "There is one person who didn't eat".

        b. $\forall q[[q \in C \wedge q \neq {}^\wedge[|\lambda x[\text{person}(x)] \cap \lambda x[\neg\text{eat}(x)]| \geq 1] \wedge \neg\text{eat}(x)]$
                                $\rightarrow {}^\wedge[|\lambda x[\text{person}(x)] \cap \lambda x[\neg\text{eat}(x)]| \geq 1] <_{\text{likely}} q]$
              = All salient unasserted alternative propositions are more likely than the
              proposition "There is one person who didn't eat".

The presupposition given in (12b) cannot be satisfied and this is why the *yāt* indefinite does not in fact have the option of not lowering. According to this scalar presupposition, the asserted proposition is less likely than its focal alternatives.

    Since the alternatives contain higher numerals, each alternative entails the asserted proposition but is not entailed by it. For example, the alternative "There are two people who didn't eat" entails the asserted proposition "There is one person who didn't eat". This is a problem because entailment relations are the inverse of the likelihood relation. If p entails q then q is weaker and more likely than p. Since the asserted proposition with *yāt* must be true for any of the alternatives to be true, but not vice versa, then the asserted proposition is the most likely of the alternatives. Therefore, the scalar presupposition of *dōu* in (12b) that the asserted proposition is the least likely cannot be satisfied.

    This problem does not arise if the indefinite lowers, because then the entire proposition is within the scope of negation. To see why this is so, let's now assume that in (8) the indefinite subject lowers at LF to its base position. This LF is given in (13).

(13)   Yāt go yàhn dōu móuh sihk.
        LF: [dōu [móuh [[yāt_F go yàhn] sihk]]].

This sentence has the semantic value in (14) and the salient alternatives in (15).

(14) $\neg[| \lambda x[person(x)] \cap \lambda x[eat(x)]| \geq 1]$
      = There is not one person who ate.

(15) $C = \{^\wedge \neg[| \lambda x[person(x)] \cap \lambda x[eat(x)]| \geq 1], ^\wedge \neg[| \lambda x[person(x)] \cap \lambda x[eat(x)]| \geq 2],$
        $^\wedge \neg[| \lambda x[person(x)] \cap \lambda x[eat(x)]| \geq 3]\}$
       = {There is not one person who ate, There are not two people who ate,
        There are not three people who ate.}

The existential and scalar presuppositions of *dōu* in this sentence are given in (16).

(16)   a. $\exists q[q \in C \wedge q \neq ^\wedge \neg[| \lambda x[person(x)] \cap \lambda x[eat(x)] | \geq 1] \wedge q(w) = 1]$
            = There is another true proposition in the salient set of alternatives besides
            "There is not one person who ate".

     b. $\forall q[[q \in C \wedge q \neq ^\wedge \neg[| \lambda x[person(x)] \cap \lambda x[eat(x)] | \geq 1]$
            $\rightarrow ^\wedge \neg[| \lambda x[person(x)] \cap \lambda x[eat(x)] | \geq 1] <_{likely} q]$
            = All salient unasserted alternative propositions are more likely than the
            proposition "There is not one person who ate".

This is a fair rendering of what (8) means. The problem with the scalar presupposition of *dōu* does not arise here.

Because negation takes scope over the entire proposition, the entailment relations among the alternatives are reversed (Fauconnier 1978). For example, the asserted proposition "There isn't one person who ate" entails "There aren't two people who ate". Since the asserted proposition entails its alternatives, it is less likely than them. This matches the scalar presupposition of *dōu* in (16b).

I conclude that LF lowering of preverbal *yāt* indefinites is licensed in order to satisfy the presuppositions of *dōu*. Before extending the analysis to the preverbal wh-indefinites in (3-4), I will briefly comment on example (7). In this sentence there is no focus on the numeral *yāt* and no *dōu*, and only a reading where the indefinite gets wide scope is possible. This sentence has an LF which closely resembles the surface structure.

(17)   a.   LF: [[yāt go yàhn]$_i$ [móuh [t$_i$ sihk]]].
     b. $| \lambda x[person(x)] \cap \lambda x[\neg eat(x)]| \geq 1$

Since there are no focal alternatives and no presuppositions of *dōu* "even" which must be satisfied, a wide scope reading of the indefinite is completely acceptable.

This leaves the puzzle of why reconstruction is not possible in this sentence. That is, why is (18) an impossible LF and interpretation of (7)?

(18)   a.   *   LF: [[móuh [[yāt go yàhn]$_i$ sihk]]].
       b.   *   ¬[| λx[person(x)] ∩ λx[eat(x)] | ≥ 1]

This is an interesting question, and at this point I do not have a very firm answer. However, I will speculate a little and draw a parallel with some similar data in English. Since negation cannot normally scope over an indefinite subject in English, I will discuss an example with the indefinite in object position. The sentence in (19) has the two scopal readings in (i) and (ii).

(19)   I didn't talk to one student.
       (i)   ∃¬:   There is one student that I did not talk to.
       (ii)   ¬∃:   There is not one student that I talked to.

The two readings are brought out by the following dialogues.

(20)   Q: Have you talked to the students yet?
       A: ∃¬ Mostly. I haven't talked to one student. Bill is out of town until Monday.

(21)   Q: Have you talked to the students yet?
       A: ¬∃ I'm sorry. I haven't talked to one student. It's been a hectic week.

These examples differ in that focal stress is used on the numeral *one* in (21) in order to get the narrow reading of the indefinite below negation. In this case, the sentence essentially means the same thing as (22) with *even*.

(22)   I haven't even talked to one$_F$ student.

If this observation holds for other languages as well, then the question of why the *yāt* indefinite in Cantonese cannot take low scope unless *dōu* is used arguably has its roots in this independent crosslinguistic pattern.

2.3.   Preverbal emphatic NPIs

The data in the preceding section demonstrated that preverbal *yāt* indefinites associated with *dōu* had to be interpreted below negation. Now I return to the problem of preverbal emphatic NPIs. In this section I extend the observations from the previous section and show the NPI analysis is possible. This follows if these wh-phrases are regarded as focused low-scalar NPIs which denote very general properties and which are entailed by their more specific alternatives, as in Lahiri's (1998) analysis of Hindi NPIs.

Lahiri is concerned with the distribution of NPIs which incorporate the particle *bhii* "even". He provides a semantic account of these items, and finds that their distribution is dictated by the environments in which the presuppositions of *bhii* can be satisfied. These NPIs are of interest here, because like the preverbal wh-words in Cantonese, these forms in Hindi are generally considered emphatic (Haspelmath 1997).

Lahiri observes that the indefinites that the focus particle *bhii* associates with all denote very general properties. The focal alternatives of these indefinites are thus necessarily more specific in some way and will be subsets of the indefinite. For example, the alternatives of *anybody*, which can be treated as the property *person*, might be other human-denoting properties such as *woman* and *child*. As subsets, these alternatives stand in the same entailment relation to the indefinite as higher numerals do to the low numeral *one*. Consequently, the indefinites which denote very general properties can be regarded as being at the bottom of a scale of alternative properties.[4]

Once we acknowledge that preverbal wh-phrases are low-scalar, then they can receive an analysis completely parallel to the analysis of *yāt* "one" indefinites from the previous section. The example which I will use throughout the discussion is given in (23).

(23)   Bīngo   dōu   móuh   gin   ngóh.
       who   even   neg.pfv   see   me
       'NOBODY saw me.'

Following Lahiri, I assume that the wh-word *bīngo* denotes a very general property such as *person*. As in the earlier discussion of *yāt* indefinites, I will first show how interpreting the indefinite outside the scope of negation results in unsatisfactory presuppositions. In this case, example (23) has the LF and semantic value in (24).

(24)   LF: [dōu[[bīngo$_F$] [móuh [sihk]]]].
       [λx[person(x)] $\cap$ λx[$\neg$eat(x)] $\neq$ $\varnothing$]
       =There is a person who did not eat.

We can assume that the contextually supplied alternatives are other person-denoting properties, such as *woman* and *child*. These are given in (25).

(25)   C = {$^\wedge$[λx[person(x)] $\cap$ λx[$\neg$eat(x)] $\neq$ $\varnothing$], $^\wedge$[λx[woman(x)] $\cap$ λx[$\neg$eat(x)] $\neq$ $\varnothing$],
           $^\wedge$[λx[child(x)] $\cap$ λx[$\neg$eat(x)] $\neq$ $\varnothing$]}
       = {There is a person who didn't eat, There is a woman who didn't eat,
           There is a child who didn't eat}

The existential and scalar presuppositions of *dōu* in this sentence are as in (26).

(26)   a. $\exists$q[q$\in$C $\wedge$ q $\neq$ [λx[person(x)] $\cap$ λx[$\neg$eat(x)] $\neq$ $\varnothing$] $\wedge$ q(w) = 1]
             = There is another true proposition in the salient set of alternatives besides
             "There is a person who didn't eat".

---

[4] Unlike in the case of numerals, the scale may be partially ordered. As long as the indefinite is ranked below all other alternatives, it does not matter how the other alternatives are ranked.

b. $\forall q[[q \in C \wedge q \neq [\lambda x[\text{person}(x)] \cap \lambda x[\neg\text{eat}(x)] \neq \varnothing]$
$\rightarrow [\lambda x[\text{person}(x)] \cap \lambda x[\neg\text{eat}(x)] \neq \varnothing] <_{\text{likely}} q]$
= All salient unasserted alternative propositions are more likely than the proposition "There is a person who didn't eat".

The scalar presupposition in (26b) cannot be met. Each of the alternatives entails the asserted proposition, but is not entailed by it. For instance, "There is a woman who didn't eat" entails "There is a person who didn't eat" but not vice versa. Therefore, the asserted proposition is in fact more likely than any of the alternative propositions. This conflicts with the scalar presupposition of *dōu* in this sentence, and so this sentence has an unsatisfiable presupposition.

Just as with the *yāt* indefinite, the problem with *dōu*'s scalar presupposition does not arise if the indefinite lowers. In this case, (23) has the LF and semantic value given in (27) and is interpreted against the salient alternatives in (28).

(27)   LF: [[dōu[móuh [[bīngo$_F$] sihk]]]]
$\neg[\lambda x[\text{person}(x)] \cap \lambda x[\text{eat}(x)] \neq \varnothing]$
= There is no person who ate.

(28) $C = \{^\wedge \neg[\lambda x[\text{person}(x)] \cap \lambda x[\text{eat}(x)] \neq \varnothing], ^\wedge\neg[\lambda x[\text{woman}(x)] \cap \lambda x[\text{eat}(x)] \neq \varnothing],$
$^\wedge\neg[\lambda x[\text{child}(x)] \cap \lambda x[\text{eat}(x)] \neq \varnothing]$
= {There is no person who ate, There is no woman who ate,
There is no child who ate.}

Because of *dōu*, the sentence has the existential and scalar presuppositions in (29).

(29)   a. $\exists q[q \in C \wedge q \neq \neg[\lambda x[\text{person}(x)] \cap \lambda x[\text{eat}(x)] \neq \varnothing] \wedge q(w) = 1]$
= There is another true proposition in the salient set of alternatives besides "There is no person who ate".

        b. $\forall q[[q \in C \wedge q \neq \neg[\lambda x[\text{person}(x)] \cap \lambda x[\text{eat}(x)] \neq \varnothing]$
$\rightarrow \neg[\lambda x[\text{person}(x)] \cap \lambda x[\text{eat}(x)] \neq \varnothing] <_{\text{likely}} q]$
= All salient unasserted alternative propositions are more likely than the proposition "There is no person who ate".

This adequately captures what (23) means. The indefinite has lowered and the scalar presupposition in (29b) is satisfiable because the asserted proposition is within the scope of negation. The result is that all of the alternative propositions are also negated, and the entailment relations among them are reversed. For example, the asserted proposition "There is no person who ate" entails the alternative "There is no woman who ate" but not vice versa. Therefore, the asserted proposition entails each of the alternative propositions and is hence the least likely of them. This is exactly the presupposition in (29b).

I conclude from this discussion that the presuppositions of *dōu* cannot be satisfied unless the wh-word has lowered to a position below negation. This lowering mechanism is independently required to account for indefinites containing the numeral *yāt* "one".

3. An alternative analysis

In this section I sketch a completely different analysis of preverbal wh-phrases in negative sentences that does not draw upon the parallel of preverbal *yāt* indefinites at all. Rather than trying to motivate LF lowering which is otherwise atypical of the language, the proposal that I will now consider simply abandons the intuition that the preverbal wh-words in (3-4) are indefinites that need to be licensed by negation. This alternative is to treat the wh-word as the restrictor of a universal quantifier which has wide scope.

As is well known by work on Mandarin, *dōu* can often be regarded as a quantifier meaning "all" that quantifies over a preverbal NP to its left (Lee 1986, Cheng 1995). When the NP is a wh-word, the result is something like a universal pronoun meaning "everybody", "everything", etc., depending on the wh-word used. An example from Cantonese is given in (30).

(30) Ngóh mātyéh   dōu   yiu   jihgéi máaih.
      I   what   all   need   self   buy
      'I have to buy everything myself.'   Matthews & Yip 1994: 262

Treating *dōu* as a genuine universal quantifier purchases us an easy solution to the scope problem. If the universal takes scope over negation, it will give rise to the illusion of a negative existential reading due to the law of quantifier negation, whereby $\forall x[\neg\varphi(x)]$ is truth conditionally equivalent to $\neg\exists x[\varphi(x)]$. Under this analysis, (31) does not contain a preverbal NPI but a preverbal universal quantifier.

(31) Ngóh mātyéh   dōu   móuh   sihk.
      I   what   dōu   neg.pfv eat
      'I didn't eat ANYthing at all.' (*literally* 'Everything is such that I didn't eat it.')

Adopting this treatment allows us to avoid the unconventional lowering outlined above because it abandons the idea that the examples in (3-4) are negative polarity indefinites. Rather, these are ordinary universals which take wide scope.

Although elegant, I nonetheless believe this analysis is wrong. In the next section, I compare the empirical consequences of the "even" analysis with this universal "all" analysis of *dōu*, and show that the "even" analysis generates better predictions.[5]

---

[5] Apart from the arguments I present below that the "even" analysis better deals with the preverbal wh-words in negative sentences in (3-4), there is reason to doubt that the universal *dōu* analysis is even appropriate for examples like (30) in non-negative sentences. Such sentences are often more adequately translated by free choice rather than as a universal in English, as in (i) below.

(i)   A-Wāi   mātyéh dōu   sihk.
      fam-Wai   what   dou   eat
      'Wai will eat anything'

3.1. Comparing the two analyses

This section discusses why the NPI analysis, which treats *dōu* as "even", is superior.

The most obvious benefit of the emphatic NPI analysis is that it accounts for why the data in (3-4) are emphatic. As reported, these preverbal indefinites are most naturally translated with a stressed *ANY* or *NO*.

(32) Ngóh bīngo dōu   móuh   gin.
      I   who   dōu   neg.pfv   see
      'I didn't see ANYBODY at all.'

The use of focus and the scalar semantics of *dōu* "even" in the NPI treatment account for why the preverbal wh-phrases are emphatic. This is absolutely missed by the universal analysis, which makes no use of focus.

A second piece of evidence supporting the emphatic NPI analysis has to do with the restricted use of these preverbal wh-words in yes-no questions. A well known property of NPIs which incorporate the semantics of "even" is that they are unacceptable in unbiased questions (Heim 1984). The following example containing the NPI *(even) a finger* is very biased towards a negative answer to the point that it sounds rhetorical.

(33) Did you even lift a finger to help?

In Cantonese, unbiased questions are formed with the A-not-A construction (Law 2001). In the case of a preverbal universal quantifier, the A-not-A complex takes the form of *haih-mhaih* "be-neg.be" which precedes the quantifier.

(34) Haih-mhaih   go-go dōu   séung yāusīk a?
      be-neg.be   cl-cl all   want   break prt
      Does everyone want a break?   Matthews & Yip 1994: 263

A preverbal wh-phrase cannot have a negative polarity reading with such an A-not-A question. Using *haih-mhaih* before the wh-word gives rise to a somewhat pragmatically odd reading in which the wh-word is actually construed as a free choice item (see footnote 5). The example in (35) is best glossed in English with "just anything", which suggests this is an example of free choice rather than an NPI.

(35) ? Léih   haih-mhaih   mātyéh   dōu   góng?
        you   be-neg.be   what   even   say
        'Do you say just anything?'

Crosslinguistically, free choice items often incorporate an additive particle meaning "even" as well (König 1991). Therefore, one could argue that even in these sentences this *dōu* means "even".

Using the A-not-A complex to the left of the preverbal wh-phrase does not help. The example in (36) does not even have a free choice reading.

(36)   * Léih mātyéh   dōu   yáuh-móuh   góng?
         you   what   even   pfv-neg.pfv   say
       'You didn't say anything?'

In order to use a preverbal wh-word with a reading that could be understood as negative polarity, the rhetorical question maker *mē* must be used, as in (37).

(37)   Léih   mātyéh   dōu   móuh   góng   mē?
        you   what   even   neg.pfv   say   rhet
       'Didn't you say ANYTHING at all?'

These data show that preverbal wh-phrases can only be licensed in biased questions, just like NPIs incorporating *even* in English. This suggests the wh-word in (37) is a NPI and not a universal quantifier, since universals can be used in unbiased questions (34).

Finally, the universal *dōu* analysis predicts that the quantifier should be presuppositional. As a strong quantifier, the preverbal *wh...dōu* universal is predicted to presuppose that members of the set denoted by the restriction exist (de Jong and Verkuyl 1985). However, preverbal wh-phrases in negative sentences do not presuppose that members of the set denoted by the wh-word actually exist (38).

(38)   Gāmyaht   bīngo   dōu   móuh   wán   dóu   léih.
        today   who   even   neg.pfv   contact   v-prt   you
       'Nobody found you today.'   (≠ 'None of them found you today.')

Speakers report that this sentence conveys an expectation that somebody would call, but that there are no specific people in mind who are expected to call. This contrasts with a genuine universal quantification, such as the reduplicated classifier in (39).

(39)   Gāmyaht   go-go   dōu   móuh   wán   dóu   léih.
        today   cl-cl   all   neg.pfv   contact   v-prt   you
       'Everybody didn't find you today.'   (= 'None of them found you today')

This sentence conveys that there is an expectation that members from some known group would call today. Thus, this sentence presupposes that members of set denoted by the restriction actually exist. The evidence here clearly favours an NPI analysis of these preverbal wh-phrases.

4.   Conclusion

In this paper I have argued that preverbal wh-phrases in negative sentences should be treated as negative polarity items that lower at LF to satisfy the presuppositions of the additive particle *dōu* "even". This mechanism is independently needed in the language in order to account for the interpretation of preverbal *yāt* "one" indefinites in negative sentences when associated with *dōu*. The parallel behaviour of the two types of preverbal indefinites follows if preverbal NPIs are regarded as low-scalar focused items, as in the approach of Lahiri (1998).

References

Cheng, Lisa Lai-Shen. 1995. On Dou-Quantification. *Journal of East Asian Linguistics* 4 197-234.

De Jong, Franciska and Henk Verkuyl. 1985. Generalized Quantifiers: The Properness of their Strength. In J. van Benthem and A. ter Meulen (eds.), *Generalized Quantifiers in Natural Language*, 21-44. Dordrecht: Foris.

Fauconnier, Gilles. 1978. Implication Reversal in a Natural Language. In F. Guenthner and S.J. Schmidt (eds.), *Formal Semantics and Pragmatics for Natural Languages*, 289-301. Dordrecht: D. Reidel.

Haspelmath, Martin. 1997. *Indefinite Pronouns*. Oxford: Clarendon Press.

Heim, Irene. 1984. A note on negative polarity and downward entailingness. *NELS 14*, 98-107. GLSA: UMass, Amherst.

Huang, C.T. James. 1982. *Logical Relations in Chinese and the Theory of Grammar*. Ph.D. dissertation, MIT.

Karttunen, Lauri and Stanley Peters. 1979. Conventional Implicature. In Ch. Oh and D. Dinneen (eds.), *Syntax and Semantics 11: Presupposition*, 1-56. Academic Press.

König, Ekkehard. 1991. *The Meaning of Focus Particles: A Comparative Perspective*. London: Routledge.

Lahiri, Utpal. 1998. Focus and Negative Polarity in Hindi. *Natural Language Semantics* 6, 57-125.

Law, Ann. 2001. A-not-A questions in Cantonese. *UCLWPL* 3, 295-317.

Lee, Thomas H. 1986. *Studies in Quantification in Chinese*. Ph.D. dissertation, UCLA.

Li, Yen-hui Audrey. 1998. Argument Determiner Phrases and Number Phrases. *Linguistic Inquiry* 29, 693-702.

Matthews, Stephen and Virginia Yip. 1994. *Cantonese: A Comprehensive Grammar*. New York: Routledge.

Rooth, Mats. 1985. *Association with focus*. Ph.D. dissertation, University of Massachusetts, Amherst.

Rooth, Mats. 1992. A theory of focus interpretation. *Natural Language Semantics* 1, 75-116.

Department of Linguistics
University of British Columbia
E-270, 1866 Main Mall
Vancouver, BC. V6T 1Z1

sjshank@interchange.ubc.ca

Two Types of Multiple Accusative Constructions in Korean[*]
-Inalienable Possession Type and Set Relation Type-

Chang-Yong Sim

University of Delaware, Newark

1. Introduction

In Korean, more than one NP can surface with the accusative case marker *-lul*.[1] Sentence (1a) is an instance of the inalienable possession (IAP) type of Multiple Accusative Construction (MAC), since the body-part *son* 'hand' is not alienable from the possessor, *Sunhee*. Sentence (1b) shows a construction similar to (1a), in which the relationship between the two *lul*-marked NPs is a superset-subset relation; the set denoted by the second NP, *Marlboro*, is a proper subset of the set denoted by the first NP, *tambae* 'cigarette' (hence, the set relation (SR) type of MAC).

(1)   a.   Chelswu-ka   **Sunhee-lul**   **son-ul**   cap-ass-ta.   (IAP)
            Chelswu-nom   Sunhee-acc   hand-acc   grab-past-decl
            'Chelswu grabbed Sunhee by the hand.'

      b.   Chelswu-ka   **tambae-lul**   **malboro-lul**   piu-ess-ta.   (SR)
            Chelswu-nom   cigarette-acc   Marlboro-acc smoke-past-decl
            'As for fruits, Chelswu smoked Marlboro.'

The relations between the two NPs in (1a) and (1b) are similar in that the second NP denotes a smaller portion of the first NP. That is, a part-whole relation is observed between the two accusative case marked NPs, since *the hand* is a physical part of *Sunhee* and *Marlboro* is a subset of *cigarettes*.

In addition, the two ACC-marked NPs do not form a single constituent in these two constructions. For instance, a postpositional phrase, such as *in the car*, or an adverb like *always,* may occur between the two ACC-marked NPs, as illustrated below:

---

[*] I would like to thank Satoshi Tomioka and Benjamin Bruening for their valuable comments and suggestions. The previous version of this paper was presented at the U.D Linguistics and Cognitive Science Graduate Student Conference (2003 Spring).

[1] The markers *-un* and *-nun, -i* and *-ka, -ul* and *-lul* alternate depending on their phonological environments: *-un, -i* and *-ul* are used after a consonant and *-nun, -ka,* and *-lul* are used after a vowel.

© 2003 Chang-Yong Sim
Keir Moulton and Matthew Wolf (eds.): Proceedings of NELS 34,
Stony Brook University: 541 – 553. GLSA, Amherst.

(2)   a. Chelswu-ka   Sunhee-lul   **cha-ese**   pal-ul   palp-ass-ta.   (IAP)
          Chelswu-nom   Sunhee-acc   car-at   foot-acc   step.on-past-decl
          'Chelswu stepped on Sunhee's foot in the car.'

      b. Chelswu-ka   kwail-ul   **hangsang**   sakwa-lul   mek-ess-ta.   (SR)
          Chelswu-nom   fruit-acc   always   apple-acc   eat-past-decl
          'As for fruits, Chelswu always eats apples.'

Despite these similarities, they also exhibit different syntactic behaviors. Therefore, I argue that they are structurally different. Section 2 demonstrates their different syntactic behaviors. Section 3 illustrates the structure of the IAP type of MAC and accounts for the inalienable possession relation between the possessor and the possessee. Section 4 shows the structure of the SR type of MAC is different from the IAP type of MAC. Section 5 accounts for the *–lul* marking system as well as passives. Finally, Section 6 summarizes the paper.

2.   **Differences**

Under passivization, the IAP type of MAC allows for the possessed NP to bear either a nominative (*-ka*) or an accusative case marker (*-lul*), as in (3a), while in the SR type of MAC, both NPs must be nominative case marked, as in (3b).

(3)   a. Sunhee-ka   **son-i/-ul**   cap-**hi**-ess-ta.   (IAP)
          Sunhee-nom   hand-nom/-acc   grab-Pass-Past-decl
          'Sunhee's hand was grabbed.'

      b. Koki-ka   **piraemi-ka /*-lul**   cap-**hi**-ess-ta.   (SR)
          fish-nom   small.fish-nom/-acc   grab-pass-past-decl
          'As for fish, small ones were caught.'

Another distinction between the two constructions is found in relativization: The IAP type of MAC allows either one of the two NPs to be the head noun of a relative clause, as exemplified in (4), but neither of the NPs can be relativized in the SR type of MAC, indicating that the SR type of MAC cannot occur in relative clause, as shown in (5):

(4)   a. [Chelswu-ka   t$_i$ ppam-ul   ttali-n]   Sunhee$_i$ (IAP)
          Chelswu-nom   cheek-acc   hit-Rel   Sunhee
          'Sunhee whose cheek Chelswu hit'

      b. [Chelswu-ka   Sunhee-lul   t$_i$ ttali-n]   ppam$_i$ (IAP)
          Chelswu-nom   Sunhee-acc   hit-Rel   cheek
          'The cheek where Chelswu hit Sunhee'

(5)   a. *[Chelswu-ka   t$_i$ piraemi-lul   cap-un]   mulkoki$_i$ (SR)
          Chelswu-nom   small.fish-acc catch-Rel   fish
          'lit. the fish that Chelswu caught a small fish'

  b. *[Chelswu-ka   mulkoki-lul   t$_i$ cap-un]   piraemi$_i$ (SR)
      Chelswu-nom fish-acc   catch-Rel small.fish
      'lit. the small fish that Chelswu caught a fish'

These syntactic differences indicate that the two types of MAC have different syntactic structures.

3   The Inalienable Possession Type of MAC

An analysis of the IAP type of MAC must account for the inalienable possession relation between the possessor and the possessee which do not form a constituent (e.g., 2a).

3.1   Against the Possessor Raising Analysis

There has been an attempt to explain the inalienable possession relation between the two NPs by positing that the possessor and the possessee form a constituent at some level, and the possessor moves away from the base-generated position to some other position, (Cho 2000, Kitahara 1993, O'grady 1998, among others). Based on the observation that there are two patterns, the ACC-ACC pattern in (1a), and the GEN-ACC pattern in (6), proponents of this analysis tried to derive (1a) from (6).

(6)   Chelswu-ka   **Sunhee-euy son-ul**   cap-ass-ta.
        Chelswu-nom Sunhee-gen hand-acc grab-past-decl
        'Chelswu grabbed Sunhee's hand.'

The possessor raising analysis crucially relies on the assumption that the sentences in (1a) and (6) have the same meaning. This assumption, however, turns out to be incorrect: In a situation in which the hands are physically detached from Sunhee, and the doctor, Chelswu, grabbed her hands for a surgical operation, the GEN-ACC pattern in (6) CAN describe such a situation, but the ACC-ACC pattern in (1a) CANNOT. That is, the ACC-ACC pattern requires body-parts to be physically attached to the possessor (i.e., inalienably possessed). The possessor raising analysis, however, predicts incorrectly that both sentences (1a) and (6) can describe the situation. The semantic difference between the two patterns demonstrates that it is unlikely that they are derivationally related. One might assume an additional constraint such that the possessed NP must be physically attached to the raised (i.e., the ACC-marked) possessor in order to maintain the derivational relation. It is evident that this additional constraint should not apply to the GEN-marked counterpart, since the sentence in (6) does not require the hand to be physically attached to the possessor. Thus, this additional semantic constraint like the inalienable possession relation has to apply to the derived structure only, which is not conceivable.

     Idiomatic expressions provide further evidence against the derivational relation between (1a) and (6); Expressions such as *son-ul po-ta* 'to see the hand; to deal with', *son-ul ppes-ta* 'to stretch the hand; to extend the area of business', etc. have idiomatic meanings with the ACC-ACC pattern, as in (7a). In contrast, the GEN-ACC pattern in (7b), does not have the idiomatic reading:

(7) a. Chelswu-ka   Sunhee-lul   son-ul   po-ass-ta.
         Chelswu-nom   Sunhee-acc   hand-acc   see-past-decl
         literal   'Chelswu saw Sunhee's hand.'
         idiomatic   'Chelswu dealt with (punished) Sunhee.'

     b. Chelswu-ka   Sunhee-euy   son-ul   po-ass-ta.
         Chelswu-nom   Sunhee-gen   hand-acc   see-past-decl
         literal   'Chelswu saw Sunhee's hand.'
         *idiomatic 'Chelswu dealt with (punished) Sunhee.'

Under the possessor-raising analysis, we have to assume that possessor raising triggers an idiomatic reading, which is dubious, as pointed out by Yoon (2001). This fact, in addition to the semantic difference between (1a) and (6), rejects the derivational relation between the ACC-ACC pattern and the GEN-ACC pattern.

3.2   An Alternative Analysis: A Layered Event Structure

Since the ACC-ACC pattern is not derivationally related to the GEN-ACC pattern, an immediately following question is how the inalienable possession relation is accounted for. I propose that the IAP type of MAC has a recursive VP structure, and that the inalienable possession relation between the two NPs is derived from the material part-whole relation between two events denoted by each verb and its argument.

Choe (1986) observes that the accusative possessor NPs must bear the same relation to the verb as the accusative possessed NPs. Following his observation, Cho (2000) proposes the Entailment condition.

(8)   A Conditioning Factor in Possessor Agreement (Cho 2000:14)
        V(Possessor-Possessee) → V(Possessor)

For example, since (9a) satisfies (8), it is grammatical, whereas (9b) is ungrammatical, since it violates (8). That is, kicking John's leg entails kicking John in (9a), whereas kicking John's car does not entail kicking John in (9b).

(9) a. Mary-ka   John-ul   tali-lul   cha-ass-ta.
         Mary-nom   John-acc   leg-acc   kick-past-decl
         'Mary kicked John's leg.'

     b. *Mary-ka   John-ul   cha-lul   cha-ass-ta.
         Mary-nom   John-acc   car-acc   kick-past-decl
         'Mary kicked John's car.'

I argue that the Entailment Condition is derived from the syntactic structure and that the IAP type of MAC has a recursive VP structure with two identical verbs, as shown in (10).

(10)

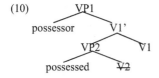

The structure in (10) shows that the possessor NP is an argument of the higher V (V1) and the possessed NP is an argument of the lower V (V2). The lower verb is deleted at PF under identity. Since the possessor NP is an argument of V1 and the possessed NP is an argument of V2, it is natural that the possessor NP has the same relation to the verb as the possessed NP does to the verb.[2] Thus, the Entailment Condition is derived from the syntactic containment relation between VP1 and VP2. The fact that both NPs can be relativized naturally follows, since both NPs are arguments.

Semantically, the events denoted by the two VPs are layered in that the event of VP2 (i.e., the lower verb and the possessee) is part of the event of VP1 (i.e., the higher verb and the possessor). This part-of relation, however, is not sufficient, since the kicking the car event may be part of the kicking John event in a situation where John was in the car, and Mary kicked the car in her effort to kick John.

This situation is blocked if the two events have the material part-whole relation. There are two kinds of part-of relations between events: The ⊆ or individual relation and the ◄, or material part-whole relation (Brisson 1998). Sentences like *John and Mary ate dinner* assert the existence of plural events, which have subevents: Mary eating dinner, and John eating dinner. The ⊆ relation captures the part-of relation between the event of John and Mary eating dinner and the subevents of John eating dinner and Mary eating dinner. The ◄ relation, in contrast, represents material part-whole relations such that some subevents of an event are not themselves the individual event. That is, the event of John picking up his fork, or Mary cutting her steak are subevents of an eating dinner event, but they are not themselves the eating dinner event. Now, consider the following examples:

(11) a. John-i   kep-ul   cap-ass-ta.
       John-nom   cup-acc   grab-past-decl
       'John grabbed the cup.'

     b. John-i   kep-ul   soncapi-lul   cap-ass-ta.
        John-nom   cup-acc   handle-acc   grab-past-decl
        'John grabbed the handle of the cup.'

---

[2] In fact, there are cases where this relation does not hold straightforwardly, when the possessor is interpreted as Source or Goal. *Buffy* in (ia) is interpreted as Source, and *robot* in (ib) is interpreted as Goal. Furthermore, these sentences do not satisfy the Entailment Condition. For more details of the Source and Goal possessors, see Tomioka and Sim (2004).

(i) a.   Vampire-ka   **Buffy-lul**   **phi-ul**   ppal-ass-ta.
         vampire-nom   Buffy-acc   blood-acc   suck-past-decl
         'The vampire sucked the blood from Buffy.'

    b.   Annie-ka   **robot-lul**   **phal-ul**   tal-ass-ta.
         Annie-nom   robot-acc   arm-acc   attach-past-decl
         'Annie attached the arm to the robot.'

In the material domain, the handle of the cup is in the material part-whole relation to the cup. Therefore, events of grabbing the material part of the cup such as grabbing the handle of the cup constitute a set of subevents of the grabbing the cup event, but they are not themselves the grabbing the cup event. In (11b), the material part of the cup, *soncapi* 'handle' is instantiated with an accusative case marker. Since the overtly expressed grabbing the handle event is material part of the grabbing the cup event, the part-of relation between the two events in the IAP type of MAC is the material part-whole relation. The recursive VP structure in (10), therefore, represents a layered event structure in (12).

(12)   A Layered Event Structure
        The event denoted by the possessed NP and the verb is **material part of** the event
        denoted by the possessor NP and the verb.

The layered event structure accounts for the inalienable possession relation between the two NPs without relying on the GEN-ACC pattern. The inalienable possession relation is derived from the material part-whole relation between the two events.[3] For instance, in (9a) the event of kicking the leg is material part of the event of kicking John. Therefore, the leg belongs to John. The event of kicking the car in (9b), however, is not the material part of the kicking John event, and the car is not the material part of John. Furthermore, a set of eventualities 'exemplifies the proposition' (Kratzer 2002). In these eventualities, no irrelevant entities are included. Thus, the irrelevant entity, the car, cannot exist in the kicking John event. Therefore, (9b) is ungrammatical.

Another welcome result is that this layered event structure automatically captures the Affectedness Condition (Yoon 1989) which requires the possessor NP to be 'affected' by the action denoted by the possessed NP and the verb. Since the kicking the leg event is a material part of the kicking John event, it is natural that the possessor John is affected by the action denoted by the event of kicking the leg.

3.3   Interpretation

To compute the denotation of (1a), I assume that the two identical verbs have the identical semantic type, viz., $<e,<s,t>>$. In addition, to combine the type $<s,t>$ and the type

---

[3] The distinction between eventive and non-eventive predicates is important in this paper. Verbs like *alta* 'know' do not take an event argument. However, non-eventive predicates allow multiple accusative case marked NPs.

(i)   Chelswu-ka   **pemin-ul**   **elkul-ul**   a-n-ta.
       Chelswu-nom   criminal-acc   face-acc   know-present-decl
       'Chelswu knows the criminal's face.'

The sentence in (i) seems to be a counter-example to the layered event structure since the inalienable relation holds between *pemin* 'criminal' and *elkul* 'face'. Non-eventive predicates, however, do not allow the normal passive morphemes such as *–hi*, but allow only the periphrastic passives (*-ci* passives), as shown in (ii).

(ii)   pemin-i   elkul-i   **ali-e-ci-ess-ta**   / ***ali-hi-ess-ta**.
       criminal-nom   face-nom   know-E-become-past-decl / know-pass-past-decl
       'The criminal's face was/became known.'

This fact indicates that the semantic properties of predicates affect their syntactic properties despite the fact that the two NPs have the inalienable possession relation. See Tomioka and Sim (2004) for more details.

$<e,<s,t>>$, we need two composition principles, Event Identification (Kratzer 1996)[4] and Event Composition (Brisson 1998), as shown in (13).

(13)

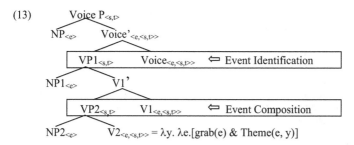

VP2 and V1 are combined by Event Composition in (14) and VP1 and the Voice head are combined by Event identification in (15). Both composition principles take the functions f and g as input and yield a function h as output. Input functions g and output functions h are of type $<e,<s,t>>$. Input functions f are of type $<s,t>$. If s is the type of events, *e* the type of individuals, and t the type of truth-values, then entities of type $<s,t>$ are functions from events to truth-values, and entities of type $<e,<s,t>>$ are functions that map individuals to functions from events to truth-values. The crucial difference between them is that Event Composition represents the material part-of or ◄ relation between the two events of input functions, while Event Identification does not necessarily represent the part-of relation.

(14)   Event Composition (Brisson 1998, 156)
$$\begin{array}{cccc} f & g & \rightarrow & h \\ <s,t> & <e,<s,t>> & & <e,<s,t>> \\ \lambda e.\, f(e) & \lambda x.\, \lambda e.\, g(x)(e) & & \lambda x.\, \lambda e.[g(x)(e) \,\&\, \exists\, e'[e' \!\blacktriangleleft e \,\&\, f(e')]] \end{array}$$

(15)   Event Identification (Kratzer 1996, 122)
$$\begin{array}{cccc} f & g & \rightarrow & h \\ <e,<s,t>> & <s,t> & & <e,<s,t>> \\ & & & \lambda x_e.\, \lambda e_s.\, [f(x, e) \,\&\, g(e)] \end{array}$$

The application of Event Composition to VP2 (f) and V1 (g) is illustrated below:

(16)   f: $\lambda e.$ [grab (e) & Theme (e, the hand)]
         g: $\lambda y.\ \lambda e.$ [grab (e) & Theme (e, y)]
    →   h: $\lambda y.\ \lambda e.$[grab(e) & Theme (e, y) & $\exists$ e' [e'◄e & grab (e') & Theme (e', the hand)]]

A rule called 'existential closure' takes the predicate of event in f and changes it to a proposition by binding the variable over events *e* with an existential quantifier. Consequently, the event argument in the denotation of VP2 is existentially closed.

---

[4] I thank Kimiko Nakanishi for her suggestion to use Event Identification.

The result of the application of Event Identification which combines the denotation of VP1 and the denotation of the Voice head is shown in (17).

(17)   λe. [Agent (e, Chelswu) & [grab(e) & Theme (e, Sunhee) & ∃ e' [e'◄e & grab (e')
        & Theme (e', the hand)]]]

4.   The Set Relation MAC

One might attempt to apply the layered event structure to the set relation type of MAC since *smoking Marlboro* entails *smoking cigarette*, in (1b). There are, however, predicates with which the entailment relation does not hold. For instance *hating Marlboro* does not entail *hating cigarettes*, in (18).

(18)   Chelswu-ka   tambae-lul   malboro-lul   **silhe-ha-ass-ta**.
        Chelswu-nom   cigarette-acc   Marlboro-acc   hate-do-past-decl
        'As for cigarettes, Chelswu hated Marlboro.'

        Furthermore, the superset NP is always interpreted outside of the scope of negation, regardless of the form of negation:

(19) a. Short Form Negation
        Chelswu-ka   **tambae-lul   malboro-lul   an**   piu-ess-ta.
        Chelswu-nom   cigarette-acc   Marlboro-acc   Neg   smoke-past-decl
        'As for cigarettes, Chelswu did not smoke Marlboro.'
              cigarette > Neg   *Neg > cigarette

    b. Long Form Negation
        Chelswu-ka   **tambae-lul   malboro-lul** piu-ci   **ani**   ha-ess-ta.
        Chelswu-nom   cigarette-acc   Marlboro-acc   smoke-CI Neg   do-past-decl
        'As for cigarettes, Chelswu did not smoke Marlboro.'
              cigarette > Neg   *Neg > cigarette

        In addition, as noted in Section 2, the set relation type of MAC cannot occur in relative clauses. To account for these patterns of the SR type of MAC, I propose a structure with a sentence-internal topic position in which the superset NP occurs, as shown in (20) (cf. mini topics in Kuroda 1992, type-token in Yoon 2001):

(20)

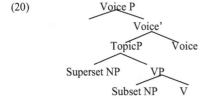

The superset NP is a sentence-internal topic, and it moves to the sentence external topic position at LF.⁵ Therefore, it does not fall in the scope of negation, in (19). Sentence-internal topics also account for the observation that the SR type of MAC cannot occur in relative clauses. As shown in (21), topics cannot occur inside relative clauses (Yang 1990, Han 1998, among others).

(21)   *[TP John-i [NP [CP [TP Mary-nun coaha-nun]]   salam-ul] man-ass-ta.]
          John-nom   Mary-top like-Rel   person-acc meet-past-decl
          'John met a person who Mary likes.'

In (21), the subject of the relative clause is topic-marked. Since the relative clauses form a complex NP island, and the topic moves to the sentence external position at LF (Han 1998), topics are not compatible with these constructions. Therefore, the superset NP, being a topic, cannot appear in the relative clauses.

5.   *-lul* Marking and Passives

The *–lul* marked superset NP is a sentence-internal topic, while the *–lul* marked subset NP and the possessor and the possessed NPs are arguments. The fact that both of the superset and the subset NPs cannot be *–lul* marked under passivization indicates that a head that checks the accusative case feature of the argument licenses the *–lul* marker on the sentence-internal topic. Thus, the *–lul* marker on the topic has an identical form to that of the case marker on the arguments, and both the topic and the argument move to the subject position under passivization. Furthermore, the fact that the possessed NP shows the NOM-ACC alternation under passivization indicates that the accusative case checking head of the possessed NP is independent from the accusative case checking head of the possessor NP. That is, the *–lul* marking mechanism allows multiple occurrence of the case checking head and each argument requires an accusative case checking head of its own. Thus, arguments are different from non-arguments (i.e., the superset NP) with respect to *–lul* marking in that arguments require the case checking head of their own, but non-arguments do not.

5.1   The NOM-ACC Case Alternation in Passives

The possessed NP in the IAP type of MAC shows the NOM-ACC alternation in passives. In (3a), the agent is suppressed, but the possessed NP, *son* 'hand', may still bear the accusative case marker. Languages like Ukrainian (Sobin 1985) also show a similar fact that the agent is suppressed but the object is still assigned accusative case under passivization. If a head that introduces an agent and a head that checks the accusative case of the object are the same (Kratzer 1996, and Chomsky 1995), the sentence with the accusative case marker in (3a) should be predicted to be ungrammatical, which is not true. This indicates that a head that introduces an agent must be distinguished from a head that checks the accusative case of the object (Baker and Stewart 2002). Therefore, I assume that

---

⁵ The structure in (20) does not observe endocentricity. However, I will leave this problem open for the time being.

the agent is introduced by Voice, whereas the accusative case feature is checked by a distinct accusative case checking head v.[6] The fact that the possessor NP cannot be ACC-marked in (3a) indicates that there is more than one case checking head, one for the possessor NP and one for the possessed NP, and that the case checking head for the possessor NP must be absent under passivization. Thus, assuming that each argument NP requires a case checking head, (22) illustrates the structure of the active sentence with multiple accusative NPs (the order of head-complement is reversed for the sake of simplicity).

(22)   [$_{VoiceP}$ NP$_{agent}$ [$_{Voice'}$ Voice [$_{vP1}$ $v1$ [$_{VP1}$ NP1 [$_{V1'}$ V1 [$_{vP2}$ $v2$ [$_{VP2}$ NP2 V2]]]]]]]

In (22), the case checking head, v, occurs twice, and $v1$ checks the accusative case feature of the possessor NP and $v2$ checks the accusative case feature of the possessed NP.

The separation of the agent introducing head from the accusative case checking head provides a natural account for the NOM-ACC alternation of the possessed NP in passives. Consider the following possible structures:

(23) a.   [$_{VoiceP}$ [$_{Voice'}$ Voice$_{passive}$ [$_{VP1}$ NP1 [$_{V1'}$ V1 [$_{VP2}$ NP2 V2]]]]]

      b.   [$_{VoiceP}$ [$_{Voice'}$ Voice$_{passive}$ [$_{VP1}$ NP1 [$_{V1'}$ V1 [$_{vP2}$ $v2$ [$_{VP2}$ **NP2** V2]]]]]]

      c.   *[$_{VoiceP}$ [$_{Voice'}$ Voice$_{passive}$ [$_{vP1}$ $v1$ [$_{VP1}$ **NP1** [$_{V1'}$ V1 [$_{VP2}$ NP2 V2]]]]]]

In (23a), both NPs move to the subject position and are nominative case marked, since no accusative case checking heads are present (the NOM-NOM pattern). When one accusative case checking head is present, two structures are possible as in (23b) and (23c). In (23b), the case feature of the possessor is not checked because of the absence of the case checking head, while the case feature of the possessed NP is checked by the case checking head $v2$. Consequently, the possessor NP moves to the subject position (the NOM-ACC pattern). In contrast, in (23c), the case feature of the possessor NP is checked, but not that of the possessed NP. Thus, the possessed NP moves to the subject position crossing the possessor NP. This derivation, however, crashes because there is an NP closer to T than the possessed NP, and thus violates the Minimal Link Condition (Chomsky 1995). The well-formed structures in (23a) and (23b), therefore, account for the NOM-ACC alternation of the possessed NP in passivization.

5.2   *-lul* marked Topic

Since the *–lul* marked superset NP is not an argument, but a topic, and both the superset and the subset NPs are *–ka* marked under passivization in (3b), it is plausible to assume that there is only one accusative checking head in the SR type of MAC and that the *–ka* and *–lul* markers on the superset NPs are topic markers. Yoon (to appear) argues that a *-ka* marked

---

[6] I assume that the case checking head is semantically vacuous.

NP, *pihayngki* 'airplane' in (25) is a generic topic. This generic topic can be *-lul* marked when the sentence is embedded in an ECM context as shown in (24).

(24)   Na-nun **pihayngki-ka/-lul**   747-i   khu-ta-ko   sayngkak-ha-n-ta
        I-top   airplane-nom/-acc   747-nom big-decl-comp believe-do-pres-decl
        'I think that as for airplanes, the 747 is big.'

(25)   **Pihayngki-ka/*-lul** 747-i khu-ta.

Schütze (1996, 2001) also proposes an analysis with two distinct focus/topic domains and argues that the *-lul* marker in (24) is a topic marker, based on the NOM-ACC (i.e., *-ka/-lul*) alternation in (24) and the fact that *pihangki* cannot be *-lul* marked in (25).

(26)   Distribution of discourse particles (Schutze 2001, 219)
        If a constituent XP can be marked as topic or focus by a case particle, that particle
        will correspond to the case assignable by XP's focus- or topic-licensing head.

That is, the *-ka* and *-lul* markers on the superset NPs are topic markers, which are different from the case-markers, though they are licensed by the case assigning heads (T and *v*). Thus, the superset NP is licensed by the accusative case checking head, *v* is *-lul* marked, as illustrated below:

(27)

In (27), the accusative case checking head *v* is present, and it checks the case feature of the subset NP and licenses the topic marker *-lul* to the superset NP. In passives, the accusative case checking head *v* is not present, and the subset NP, which is an argument, moves to the subject position. The superset NP also moves to the outer specifier position of TP, since it cannot be licensed and be *-lul* marked by the head *v*. Since the nominative case checking head, T, checks the case feature of the subset NP and licenses the superset NP, both NPs in the SR type of MAC are *-ka* marked under passivization.

6.   Conclusion

The two superficially similar constructions, the IAP type of MAC and the SR type of MAC, have distinctive structures: The IAP type of MAC has the recursive VP structure reflecting the layered event structure, while the SR type of MAC has a sentence-internal topic position. The recursive VP structure accounts for the syntactic behavior such as relativization. By separating the agent-introducing head from the case checking head, the NOM-ACC case alternation of the possessed NP under passivization is also accounted for. The inalienable possession relation between the two NPs is derived from the material part-whole relation between the two events denoted by the possessor NP and the verb and the possessed NP and the verb. The superset NP is a sentence-internal topic, and is *-lul* marked by the case checking head *v*. It moves at LF to the scope position. Thus, the superset NP does not fall in the scope of negation and it cannot occur in relative clauses.

References

Brisson, Christine. 1998. *Distributivity, Maximality, and Floating Quantifiers*. Rutgers University Ph.D. thesis.

Cho, Seng-Eun. 2000. *Three Forms of Case Agreement in Korean*, SUNY-Stony Brook Ph.D. thesis.

Choe, H.-S. 1986. Syntactic Adjunction, A-chains and Multiple Identical Case Construction. In *Proceedings of NELS* 17. GLSA, University of Massachusetts, Amherst.

Chomsky, Noam. 1995. *The Minimalist Program*. Cambridge, Mass.: MIT Press.

Chomsky, Noam. 1998. Minimalist Inquiries: the Framework. *MIT Occasional Papers in Linguistics* Number 15, Cambridge, Mass.: MIT Press.

Han, Chung-Hye. 1998. Asymmetry in the Interpretation of –*(n)un* in Korean. *Japanese/Korean Linguistics* 7, 1-15.

Kitahara, Hisatsugu. 1993. Inalienable possession constructions in Korean: Scrambling, the proper binding condition, and case-percolation. *Japanese/Korean Linguistics* Vol.2: 394-408.

Kratzer, Angelika. 1996. Severing the External Argument from its Verb. In J. Rooryck & L. Zaring (eds.) *Phrase Structure and the Lexicon*. Dordrecht.: Kluwer Academic Publishers.

Kuroda, S.-Y. 1992. Judgment Forms and Sentence Forms. In *Japanese Syntax and Semantics*, 13-77. Dordrecht.: Kluwer Academic Publishers.

O'Grady, William. 1998. Korean Case: A Computational Approach. Keynote paper at the 11th ICKL Meeting, Honolulu, HI.

Schütze, Carson T. 1996. Korean case stacking isn't: Unifying noncase uses of case particles. In *Proceedings of NELS* 26, 351-365. GLSA, University of Massachusetts, Amherst.

Schütze, Carson T. 2001. On Korean "case stacking": the varied functions of the particles *ka* and *lul*. *The Linguistic Review* 18, 193-232.

Tomioka, Satoshi and Chang-Yong Sim. 2004. Event Structure of Inalienable Possession in Korean. A paper presented at the 28th Penn Linguistics Colloquium. University of Pennsylvania, Philadelphia.

Sobin, Nicholas. 1985. Case assignment in Ukrainian morphological passive constructions. *Linguistic inquiry* 16(4), 649-662.

Yang, Hyun Kwon. 1990. *Categories and Barriers in Korean*. University of Texas at Austin. Ph.D. thesis.

Yoon, J H-S. 1989. The Grammar of Inalienable Possession Constructions in Korean, Mandarin, and French. In *Harvard Studies in Korean Linguistics III*, 357-368.

Yoon, J H-S. 2001. Multiple (Identical) Case Constructions. Lecture notes. LSA Summer Institute at UC Santa Barbara.

Yoon, J H-S. To appear. Non-nominative (Major) Subjects and Case Stacking in Korean. In P. Bhaskararao & K. V. Subbarao (eds.), *Non-nominative Subjects*, Berlin: Mouton de Gruyter.

Department of Linguistics
University of Delaware

46 East Delaware Avenue
Newark, DE 19716-2551

simyong@udel.edu

Event Decomposition and the Syntax and Semantics of *–kan* in Standard Indonesian

Minjeong Son and Peter Cole[1]

University of Delaware, Newark

1.   Introduction

A widely held position in the literature on verbal meaning is that the lexical semantic representation of verbs involves complex event structure (e.g., Dowty 1979) and that components of event structure are directly reflected in the syntax (e.g., Hale & Keyser 1993). A growing number of recent works on predicate decomposition in the syntax (Travis 2000; van Hout 2000, among others) have further shown that there is a tight correlation between the (morpho)-syntax and the semantics of event structure. For instance, the morphological transparency of the component expressing the causing event in causative constructions has often been noted with respect to such languages as Malagasy, Japanese and Korean (e.g., Harley 1995; Travis 2000; Son 2003).

Adopting such a general approach, we argue that in Indonesian there is a close correspondence between the morpho-syntax and an aspectual component expressing a result state: we argue that the verbal suffix–*kan* is an overt realization of the result head that projects a result-state-denoting constituent, i.e., a Result Phrase (RP), analogous to RP proposed by Ramchand (2003).

On first examination, the suffix *–kan* in Indonesian gives the appearance of having multiple functions since it occurs in a variety of constructions, among them, causatives and benefactive applicatives.[2] The main goal of this paper is two fold: First, we offer a unified semantic and syntactic account of *–kan* that explains its uses in these seemingly unrelated constructions. Secondly, by analyzing *-kan* as an overt instantiation of the result head, we provide a new empirical argument for the view that there is a direct mapping between semantic decomposition of predicates and the (morpho-)syntax.

---

[1] An earlier version of this paper was presented at the Workshops on Complex Predicates at the Linguistic Society of Korea International Summer Conference 2002 held in Kyunghee University, Seoul, Korea. We thank the audience for their comments and questions. We have benefited greatly from the insightful comments and suggestions of Satoshi Tomioka and Benjamin Bruening. Thanks also go to Yassir Tjung for the data reported on in this paper. It should be noted that the system of applicatives described here is different from that found in colloquial varieties of the language like Jakarta Indonesian.

[2] The suffix *–kan* is also found in Goal-PP constructions and with inherently ditransitive verbs like 'give'. Readers who are interested in how our analysis of *–kan* extends to these constructions are referred to Son & Cole (2004) forthcoming.

Keir Moulton and Matthew Wolf (eds.): Proceedings of NELS 34,
Stony Brook University: 555 – 569. GLSA, Amherst.

Minjeong Son and Peter Cole

2.   Distribution of *-kan*

Let us first consider examples where the suffixation of *–kan* derives causative sentences. This is shown in (1-2).

(1) a. Cangkirnya pecah
        cup-3   break
        'The cup broke'

    b. Janet memecah-**kan**   cangkirnya
        Janet meN-break-KAN cup-3
        'Janet broke her cup.'

(2) a. Banyak orang tewas
        Many   people dead
        'Many people died.'

    b. Kecelakaan itu menewas-**kan** banyak orang
        accident that meN-dead-KAN many people
        'The accident killed many people.'

The causative verbs in the (b) sentences are formed by attaching the suffix *–kan* to inchoative verb stems like *pecah* 'break' and *tewas* 'dead'. The use of *–kan* as a causative morpheme is quite productive with various grammatical categories such as unaccusative verb stems (shown in (1-2)), stative predicates (i.e., adjectives) and psychological predicates. Some examples are provided in (3).[3]

(3)   Type of Base Predicates with Causative *–kan* (Sneddon 1996)

   a.   Adjectives

Non-Causatives		Causatives	
bersih	'clean'	*membersihkan*	'clean x'
lebar	'wide'	*melebarkan*	'widen x'
kering	'dry'	*mengeringkan*	'dry x'
bebas	'free'	*membebaskan*	'set x free'

   b.   Unaccusative verbs

Non-Causatives		Causatives	
jatuh	'fall'	*menjatuhkan*	'drop x'
kembail	'return'	*mengembalikan*	'return x'
naik	'go up'	*menaikkan*	'raise x'

   c.   Psychological predicates

Non-Causatives		Causatives	
bosan	'bored'	*membosankan*	'bore x'
puas	'satisfied'	*memuaskan*	'satisfy x'
kejut	'startled'	*mengejutkan*	'startle x'
senang	'pleased/happy'	*menyenangkan*	'please x'

While (1-3) illustrate the use of *–kan* as a morpheme deriving causatives, the following examples show the use of *–kan* as a seeming applicative suffix associated with a benefactive interpretation. When *–kan* is attached to transitive verb bases, the

---

[3] Arka (1992) and Kaswanti Purwo (1995) provide many examples of *–kan* causatives, the base forms of which range from nouns to prepositions. In this paper, our discussion of causatives will focus only on causative verbs, the base forms of which are unaccusative.

beneficiary, which is expressed as an optional adjunct phrase in the (a) sentences, occurs as a bare NP adjacent to the derived verb (henceforth, NP+NP frame).

(4) a. Tika memanggang roti   itu (**untuk** Eric).
Tika meN-bake   bread the   for   Eric
'Tika baked the bread for Eric'

b. Tika memanggang-**kan** Eric roti   itu
Tika meN-bake-KAN   Eric bread the
'Tika baked Eric the bread.'

(5) a. Eric membuat   rumah-rumahan (**untuk** anak-nya).
Eric meN-make RED-house   for   child-3
'Eric made a toy house for his child.'

b. Eric membuat-**kan**   anak-nya rumah-rumahan
Eric meN-make-KAN   child-3   RED-house-AN
'Eric made his child a toy house.'

When the benefactive argument occurs as a bare NP in the (b) sentences, it behaves like the primary object of the derived verb. This is shown by the fact that it is the benefactive NP that can be passivized, not the theme argument, as shown in (6).[4]

(6) a. Eric dipanggang-**kan** roti   itu (oleh Tika)
Eric DI-bake-KAN   bread the   (by Tika)
'Eric was baked the bread (by Tika).'

b. *Roti itu dipanggang-**kan** Eric (oleh Tika)
bread that DI-bake-KAN   Eric (oleh Tika)
'The bread was baked for Eric (by Tika).'

On the basis of examples like (4-6), -*kan* might appear to be an applicative suffix with a distribution similar to that of prototypical applicatives in such language groups as Bantu (Baker 1988; Marantz 1993, *inter alia*). However, the consideration of a broader range of examples suggests that Indonesian benefactives with –*kan* differ from typical applicatives with respect to the effect of the affix on the argument structure. In prototypical applicatives the nominal corresponding to the object of a preposition in the base sentence must appear as the primary object in the applicative construction. In Indonesian, however, the applied NP may also occur in a prepositional phrase (hereafter, NP+PP frame). This is despite the presence of –*kan* on the verb, as shown in (7).

---

[4] By 'primary (or direct) object' we mean the internal NP object, the NP that receives structural case from the functional head, Voice, and that can be passivized.

(7) a. Tika memanggang-**kan** roti   itu ***untuk Eric***.
        Tika meN-bake-KAN   bread the for   Eric
        'Tika baked the bread for Eric.'

   b. Eric membuat-**kan**   rumah-rumahan itu ***untuk   anak-nya***.
       Eric meN-make-KAN RED-house-AN the for   child-3
       'Eric made the toy house for his child.'

Furthermore, on the assumption that it is the primary object that is made subject by
passivization, the theme, not the beneficiary, is the primary object in (7), as shown in (8).

(8) a. Roti   itu dipanggang-**kan** untuk Eric.
        bread the DI-bake-KAN   for   Eric
        'That bread was baked for Eric (by him).'

   b. Rumah-rumahan itu dibuat-**kan**   untuk   anak-nya.
       RED-house-an   the DI-make-KAN   for   child-3
       'The toy-house was made for his child (by him).

    While the examples in (7) appear to have the same structure as those sentences
with a *for*-beneficiary without –*kan* (e.g., 4a-5a), they differ from each other in two
respects. First, when –*kan* is absent, as in (4a-5a), the PP is an optional adjunct phrase. In
contrast, when –*kan* is present, the PP is an obligatory oblique complement (i.e., a
subcategorized constituent). This is shown by the fact that when the PP in (8) is omitted,
the sentence is interpreted as having a null benefactive interpretation, as illustrated in (9).

(9) a. Roti   itu dipanggang-**kan**
        bread the DI-bake-KAN
        'The bread was baked *for someone* (by him).'

   b. Rumah-rumahan itu   dibuat-**kan**
       RED-house-an   the DI-make-KAN
       'The toy-house was made *for someone* (by him).

When –*kan* is absent, this interpretation is not available in the passive if the *untuk* phrase
is omitted, as shown in (10).

(10) a. Roti   itu   dipanggang
         bread the DI-bake
         'That bread was baked (by him).'

    b. Rumah-rumahan itu   dibuat
        RED-house-an   the DI-make
        'The toy-house was made (by him).

Secondly, the NP+PP frame with *–kan* is synonymous with the NP+NP frame shown in the (b) sentences of (4-5). When *–kan* is present on the verb, the benefactive argument is interpreted as a prospective possessor of the theme argument in both the NP+NP and the NP+PP frame. For instance, sentence (4b), repeated as (11a), carries the strong implication that Eric is the possessor of the bread that Tika baked, and only this interpretation is possible. The corresponding NP+PP frame, given in (11b), also has the interpretation in which Eric is expected to possess the bread as a result of Tika's baking event.

(11) a. Tika memanggang-**kan** Eric roti itu.
  Tika meN-bake-KAN Eric bread the
  'Tika baked Eric the bread.'

  b. Tika memanggang-**kan** roti itu **untuk** **Eric**.
  Tika meN-bake-KAN bread the for Eric
  'Tika baked the bread for Eric.'

An implication of possession is not necessary in the corresponding transitive sentence without *–kan* in (4a), repeated as (12); the sentence is vague with respect to two readings, a possessive reading, as shown in (12a), and a purely benefactive reading, as shown in (12b).

(12) Tika memanggang roti itu **untuk** **Eric**.
  Tika meN-bake bread the for Eric
  a. 'Tika baked the bread to give it to Eric.'
  b. 'Tika baked the bread in place of Eric (since Eric was busy).'

The semantic contrast between sentences with *–kan* and those without *–kan* is parallel to the semantic contrast between double object and oblique complement constructions in English given in (13).

Harley (2002)
(13) a. Sally knitted John a sweater.   (Only possession reading)
  'John has the sweater as a result of Sally's kitting.'

  b. Sally knitted a sweater for John.   (Ambiguous)
  i) John may be intended to be a possessor.
  ii) Sally knitted the sweater in place of John.

It is often noted (e.g., Gropen, Pinker et al. 1989; Pesetsky 1995; Harley 2002) that the double object construction in English shown in (13a) is interpreted with a strong implication that there is a possession relation between the goal and the theme, hence the possessor account (e.g., Pesetsky 1995; Beck and Johnson 2002; Harley 2002). In contrast, the oblique complement construction in (13b) is vague with respect to whether the beneficiary is the possessor. In both the possessive reading in (13b-i) and the purely benefactive reading in (13b-ii), the sentence is true.

The 'possessor' account proposed for the English double object construction applies to two variants of the *–kan* benefactives as well, given that there is an animacy restriction on the applied argument, which has been a basis for justifying the possessor account for English. This is evidenced by the examples from (14) through (17).

(14) a. *Saya men-(p)anggang-***kan** ***perayaan*** ***ulangtahun*** ***Eric*** biskuit itu
        1SG meN-bake-KAN   celebration birthday   Eric   biscuit the
        'I baked a biscuit for Eric's birthday.'

    b. *Dia   mem-buat-***kan***   ***perayaan*** ***Halloween*** rumah-rumahan itu
       3SG   meN-build-KAN celebration Halloween RED-house-AN the
       'He built a toy house for Halloween.'

(15) a. Saya men-(p)anggang-***kan*** biscuit itu untuk perayaan   ulangtahun Eric
        1SG meN-bake-KAN   biscuit the   for   celebration birthday   Eric
        'I baked ***someone*** the biscuit for Eric's birthday.'

    b. Dia   mem-buat-***kan***   rumah-rumahan itu untuk perayaan   Halloween
       3SG   meN-build-KAN RED-house-AN the for   celebration Halloween
       'He built ***someone*** the toy house for Halloween.'

(16)[5] Saya menyulam baju hangat ini untuk bayi kita.
        1SG   meN-knit   shirt   warm   this   for   baby 1PL
       'I knitted this sweater for our baby. (The baby need not exist in a real world.)

(17) a. Saya menyulam-***kan*** bayi kita   baju hangat ini.
        1SG meN-knit-KAN   baby 1PL   shirt warm   this
        'I knitted our baby this sweater.'

    b. Saya menyulam-***kan***   baju hangat ini untuk bayi   kita
       1SG meN-knit-KAN shirt warm   this   for   baby 1PL
       'I knitted this sweater for our baby.' (The baby must exist in a real world to be a prospective possessor of the theme.)

As shown in (14), the inanimate object cannot appear as an applied argument in the NP+NP frame of *–kan* benefactives. The animacy restriction on the benefactive argument also applies to the NP+PP frame, as shown in (15); although it may appear that the NP+PP frame with *–kan* allows a wider range of benefactive arguments including inanimate referents in (15), the sentences are interpreted as having a null 'animate' beneficiary interpretation. In (17), both frames of the *–kan* benefactive have the strong implication that the baby exist. If the baby must bear a possessor role in (17) by virtue of occurring in the *–kan* construction, it must be alive, and hence has been born already. In (16), in contrast, the baby may or may not exist when *–kan* is absent on the verb; the (female) speaker may not have a baby at present, but be planning to have one.

---

[5] The examples with 'knit' are inspired by the corresponding English examples provided by Harley (2002).

Based on the facts described so far, the problems that should be addressed are the following: First, what is the correct characterization of -*kan* that gives rise to the observed occurrence of the suffix in the two seemingly unrelated constructions?: 2) In the benefactive construction, unlike prototypical applicatives in many languages, -*kan* has the effect of allowing either an NP or a PP benefactive argument to function as internal arguments and allows two different argument structures, the NP+NP and the NP+PP structure. How do we account for the compatibility of both structures with –*kan* and for the fact that –*kan* has the effect of allowing both types of arguments to be internal arguments?

In order to correctly characterize the function of –*kan* based on the causative and benefactive constructions, we provide an event-based approach which argues for a tight correlation between the semantics of events and the syntax. We argue that –*kan* has a single function as the head of a Result Phrase and that the presence of –*kan* in the aforementioned constructions is not coincidental but is attributed to the internal event structure of these constructions. The issues noted above are intended to receive a natural explanation in our event-based account, no matter what specific implementation is proposed for each construction. Our proposal is outlined in the following section and is explicitly executed with respect to each –*kan* construction in the subsequent sub-sections.

3.   Proposal: An Event-Based Approach

In order to explain the occurrence of –*kan* in seemingly unrelated constructions that we have seen above, we would like to offer a unified semantic and syntactic account. Instead of treating –*kan* as a transitivizer which has a position somewhere above VP (e.g., as proposed by Postman 2002), we claim that –*kan* is an overt realization of the head of the Result Phrase which is embedded in the lower domain of the VP. We further argue that despite their superficial differences the aforementioned constructions share certain aspectual properties. To implement this idea, we adopt the view that predicates are decomposable into sub-components of event structure and that these event structures are directly reflected in the phrase structure along the lines proposed by Hale and Keyser (1993), among others. Under this view, we argue that causative and benefactive constructions associated with –*kan* contain the same aspectual component of a causing event and a result state which corresponds to a separate verbal projection in the phrase structure. The verbal head responsible for projecting a result-state-encoding constituent, i.e., Result, is explicitly expressed by the suffix –*kan* in Indonesian.

3.1   Representation of Causatives

Let us consider first how the idea of treating –*kan* as an overt instansiation of the Result head can be implemented for causative constructions. Example (1) is repeated as (20).

(20) a. Cangkirnya pecah   b.   Janet memecah-**kan**   cangkirnya
        cup-3   break   Janet meN-break-KAN cup-3
        'The cup broke'   'Janet broke her cup.'

Various streams of research on predicate decomposition (e.g., Dowty 1979; Levin and Rapoport 1988) have converged on the idea that the meaning of causative verbs with complex event structure like 'break' can be represented along the lines of (21), which can be paraphrased as 'x causes y to change into a state of being broken.'

(21)   [x CAUSE [y BECOME [$_{AP}$ broken]]

Following this view of lexical decomposition and the idea that (21) is directly represented in the syntax (Hale & Keyser 1993), we propose that –*kan* is an overt realization of the verbal head that roughly corresponds to BECOME in (21). In our analysis, we call this verbal head Result (R), and argue that it projects a Result Phrase (RP) in the sense of Ramchand (2003).[6] We further propose that, unlike the BECOME predicate in (21) whose semantics is associated only with eventive interpretation (see Hale and Keyser 1993), the semantics of R head gives rise to causative interpretation by introducing a causing event to the semantics of non-causative counterparts; Result is interpreted as building a relation between two events, a result state and a causing event. Therefore, the R head receives the semantic denotation shown in (22).

---

[6] On the basis of the cross-linguistic pattern in which causation is often marked by overt morphology in causative constructions (e.g., Harley 1995; Pylkkänen 2000), one might argue that the suffix –*kan* in (20b) should be represented as an overt realization of CAUSE (as is normally assumed for causative constructions for which the forms are derived by an overt causative morpheme like –*kan*). However, we reject this idea for the following reason: Unlike causative morphemes in other languages (see Travis 2000, for example), –*kan* is not always associated with the introduction of an external argument (e.g., a causer) into non-causative sentences. On the assumption that the prefix *meN*- is an external-argument-introducing head, Voice, in the sense of Kratzer (1996), -*kan* may appear to be responsible for introducing an external causer, since the presence of *meN*- in apparent causatives is dependent on –*kan* suffixation; *meN*- can attach to the verb base (in causatives, e.g., 20b) only when –*kan* is present. However, it should be noted that -*kan* is not always associated with an external argument; -*kan* does not always license the presence of Voice. For instance, in benefactive instances of -*kan*, the external argument is already present in the base sentence, regardless of whether –*kan* is present (e.g., 4a). Or, in some instances, -*kan* may be present on the verb independent of a Voice morpheme, as in the Passive 2 construction (see Sneddon 1996, *inter alia*). Furthermore, in the benefactive, -*kan* adds an internal argument to the derived verb, rather than an external argument. Therefore, if we take seriously the idea of lexical decomposition along the lines of (21), the only component to which we can relate -*kan* is the BECOME head, i.e., Result for our purpose. Result, in our analysis, bears similarities to Cause in other people's semantics (e.g., Pylkkänen 2000), in the sense that both derive causative interpretation by building a relation between two events, a causing and a caused event. However, we choose 'Result' over 'Cause' because the caused eventuality is always a state for the –*kan* constructions under investigation. Once the proposed semantics of R is adopted, the postulation of an abstract CAUSE predicate in the semantic-syntactic representation of causatives is not, since R entails the relevant semantic function provided by CAUSE.

(22)   Semantics of R^0 (*-kan*) [7,8]

- Causatives: $\lambda f.{<}e,{<}s,t{>>} \lambda x. \lambda g.{<}s,t{>} \lambda e. \exists e'$ [Result (e',e) & f(e',x) & **g(e)**]
- Benefactives: $\lambda f {<}e{<}s,t{>>} \lambda x. \lambda g {<}e{<}s,t{>} \lambda e. \exists e'$ [Result (e',e) & f(e',x) & g (e,x)]

'Result' is defined as 'for all eventualities *e, e'*, Result (e', e)=1 iff *e'* is a result state of *e*. Under the current analysis of *-kan*, the causative sentence in (20b) can have the lexical-semantic representation as (23), and this can be paraphrased roughly as 'the event in which Janet is doing something brings about a result state in which the cup is broken.'

(23) [$_{VoiceP}$ Janet VOICE [$_{VP}$ V-do (something) [$_{RP}$ **RESULT** [$_{AP}$ the cup broken]]]]

Based on the lexical semantic representation in (23) the causative sentence receives a fully-specified semantic and syntactic representation as (24). [9]

(24)

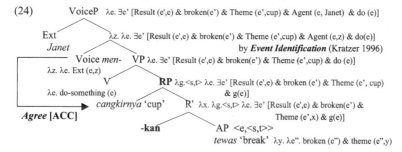

In (24), the result state, 'the cup is broken', is expressed inside the RP whose head is overtly realized as *–kan*. Based on the proposed semantics of R, the R head takes the function *f* as its first argument, which corresponds to the result state expressed by the AP in (24). The R further takes the function *g* denoted by the verb as a solution for deriving the correct semantic composition. [10] The compositional interpretation of (24) then proceeds as indicated in the proposed structure. The interpretation based on the semantic composition in (24) can be expressed as 'a set of eventualities *e* such that Janet is the

---

[7] The semantic types involved here are *e* for individuals, *t* for propositions, *s* for eventualities

[8] Notice that the type of *-kan* can vary depending on the type of the functional argument *g*. The semantic type of function *g* is either $<s,t>$ or $<e<s,t>>$ depending on the base predicate which *–kan* combines with. If the base verb is intransitive, *g* is of type $<s,t>$ as in the case of causatives. If the base verb is transitive, *g* is of type $<e <s,t>>$ as in the case of benefactives. Given that *–kan* has a different type depending on whether it is causative or benefactive, the semantic function of *–kan* may appear to be only semi-uniform. However, the core meaning of *–kan* is unified in the sense that it is interpreted as establishing a relation between two eventualities in both causative and benefactive constructions.

[9] We omit tense-related complexities in the logical form of sentences.

[10] This approach in which *-kan* takes a VP as its argument is inspired by the interpretation of a low applicative head proposed by Pylkkänen (2002).

agent of doing something in *e* and there is *e'* such that the cup is broken in *e'*, and *e'* is the result of *e*.

Another key assumption adopted here is that that all arguments receive case in their base position, as also hypothesized for case assignment in Tagalog by Rackowski (2002). Case is assigned either by the licensing head (i.e., inherent case) or through a structural case mechanism via Agree, in the sense of Chomsky (1998, 1999) (i.e., accusative and nominative). Chomsky (1998, 1999) argues that feature checking, the mechanism of syntactic licensing (i.e., case assignment) takes place via an abstract operation called Agree, as stated in (25).

(25) **Agree**: establishes a relation (agreement, Case checking) between an LI (lexical
        item) α and a feature F in some restricted search space (its domain).

In Chomsky's terms, the Voice head *meN-* probes for the feature [+accusative case] in its c-command domain. When it finds this feature it establishes an Agree relation with the NP bearing the feature, i.e., *cangkirnya* 'the cup' in (24). The direct object is thus assigned accusative case by the agreeing head Voice. T assigns nominative case to the subject via Agree; T is also a Probe looking for a [+ nominative case] goal. T^0 is in an Agree relation with the subject NP, which is in T's c-commanding domain and which is closer to T than is the object NP. The subject raises to [Spec, TP] to satisfy the EPP feature of T^0. (The projection of TP is implied in all sentential representations, although it is omitted throughout the paper.)

3.2 Representation of Benefactives

The idea that *–kan* is deeply embedded in the VP structure as the head of RP can be extended fairly straightforwardly to benefactives.

There has been a growing body of literature (e.g., Beck and Johnson 2002; Harley 2002) that argues that benefactive double-object verbs like 'make' are parallel in lexical meaning and underlying structure to explicit causatives. In particular, Harley (2002) has claimed that the double-object verb 'make' (e.g., *John made his son a robot*) is lexically decomposable into two heads; an external argument-selecting CAUSE predicate and a prepositional element P_{HAVE} which encodes a result state. If we adopt the idea of treating (benefactive) double object verbs as parallel to explicit causatives in Indonesian, the structural configuration and semantics proposed for causatives can extend naturally to the *–kan* benefactives. For example, the lexical semantics of the benefactive sentences in (4), repeated as (26), can be roughly represented along the lines of (27).

(26) a. Eric   membuat-**kan**   anak-nya rumah-rumahan itu
       Eric   meN-make-KAN   child-3   RED-house-AN the
       'Eric made his child a toy house.'

   b. Eric   membuat-**kan**   rumah-rumahan itu **untuk** anak-nya
       Eric   meN-make-KAN RED-house-AN the   for   child-3
       'Eric made a toy house for his child.'

(27)   [*VoiceP* Eric VOICE [*VP* making (toyhouse) [*RP* **RESULT** the child has the toyhouse.]]]

In the earlier section, we observed that the two variants of the –*kan* benefactive involve a necessary possession relation. Therefore, we assume that the logical representation of benefactive 'make' in (27) implies that the verb stem plus -*kan* denotes causation of change of possession as part of its lexical meaning, as represented in (27). (27) can be paraphrased as 'the event of Eric's making the toyhouse brings about a result state in which the child is the possessor of the toyhouse.' The result state denoting the possession relation between two individuals then is expressed inside the Result Phrase.

Given that the two variants of the –*kan* benefactive show different syntactic patterns in terms of passivization, as observed in Section 2, we take a base-generation approach to the two different structures compatible with –*kan* (cf. Beck and Johnson 2002; Harley 2002; Ramchand 2003). We assume that the benefactive argument can be realized either in [Spec, RP] as a subject of the result state, as shown in (28a), or as a complement of PP selected by the R head, as shown in (28b).

(28)   a.   NP+NP Frame   b.   NP+PP Frame

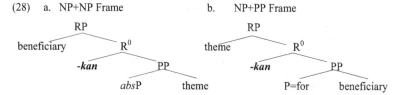

In the previous section, it was shown that in the NP+NP frame -*kan* adds a benefacitve NP to the argument structure of the derived verb. In the NP+PP frame, -*kan* makes the benefactive PP a subcategorized constituent. In the former, we assume that the benefactive NP is introduced by –*kan* in [Spec, RP] in a form similar to the introduction of an applied argument in low applicatives in Pylkkänen (2002). In the latter, we assume that the benefactive PP is selected by –*kan* as its complement. This explains the status of the benefactive PP (or *for*-benefactive) as integral to the argument structure of the derived verb when –*kan* is present.[11] Thus, under the proposed structures in (28), a close relation between –*kan* and the benefactive argument in both frames is ensured; -*kan* is the locus of projection of the benefactive argument regardless of whether it is realized as an NP or a PP. A fully specified semantic and syntactic representation of (28b) is given in (29).

---

[11] The *for*-benefactive in the corresponding transitive sentence without –*kan* is external to VP, and presumably is adjoined to some higher functional projection as a modifier (cf. Beck & Johnson 2002).

(29)

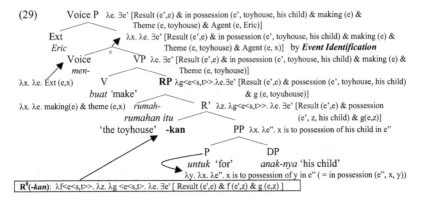

Voice P   λe. ∃e' [Result (e',e) & in possession (e', toyhouse, his child) & making (e) &
                  Theme (e, toyhouse) & Agent (e, Eric)]

Ext   λx. λe. ∃e' [Result (e',e) & in possession (e', toyhouse, his child) & making (e) &
Eric   Theme (e, toyhouse) & Agent (e, x)]   by *Event Identification*

    Voice   VP λe. ∃e' [Result (e',e) & in possession (e', toyhouse, his child) & making (e) &
    men-   Theme (e, toyhouse)]
λx. λe. Ext (e,x)   V   RP λg<e<s,t>>.λe.∃e' [Result (e',e) & possession (e', toyhouse, his child)
                  buat 'make'   & g (e, toyuhouse)]
λx. λe. making(e) & theme (e,x)   rumah-   R' λz. λg<e<s,t>>. λe. ∃e' [Result (e',e) & possession
                             rumahan itu   (e', z, his child) & g(e,z)]
                          'the toyhouse' -kan   PP λx. λe". x is to possession of his child in e"

                                              P   DP
                                         untuk 'for'   anak-nya 'his child'
                                         λy. λx. λe". x is to possession of y in e" (= in possession (e", x, y))

R⁰(-kan): λf<e<s,t>>. λz. λg <e<s,t>>. λe. ∃e' [Result (e',e) & f (e',z) & g (e,z)]

In the benefactive, the result state is expressed by PP, which involves a necessary possession relation between the goal and the theme. This denotation is reflected in the semantics of P, as shown above.

We assume that the semantic representation of the NP+NP frame is identical with that of (29), except for the reversed order of the theme and the benefactive argument that is first interpreted. As shown in (28a), we further postulate an empty category P for the NP+NP frame which corresponds to an overt 'with' (cf. Pesetsky 1995). We assume that the phonologically empty category P is not semantically vacuous but has the same semantic denotation as that of the overtly realized P in (29).[12] The structure in (28a), however, makes it hard to derive our intended semantics. We, therefore, propose that the null P head is incorporated into R, as depicted in (30), in order to derive the correct semantic interpretation.

(30)   Syntactic and Semantic Incorporation of P to R⁰ [13, 14]

a.

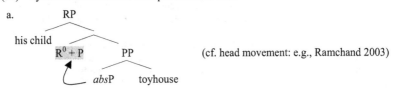

            RP
    his child
          R⁰ + P   PP   (cf. head movement: e.g., Ramchand 2003)

              absP   toyhouse

b. **R⁰ + P** : λx. λz. λg <e<s,t>. λe. ∃e' [Result (e', e) & possession (e', x, z) & g (e, x)]]

---

[12] Positing an empty category P in the NP+NP frame is conceptually plausible, since it allows the core part of the logical form of *–kan* to be uniform in apparent causatives and benefactives; *-kan* takes a function of type <e<s,t>> denoting a result state as its first argument.

[13] The incorporation of P into R applies only when P is phonologically null.

[14] We assume that this incorporation process does not leave a trace, unlike standard head movement.

Applied to RP, (30) then yields our intended semantics for the NP+NP frame as follows:

(31) a. ⟦R'⟧ = λz. λg <e<s,t>. λe. ∃e' [Result (e',e) & possession (e',x, toyhouse) & g (e, **toyhouse**)]]

   b. ⟦RP⟧ = λg <e<s,t>. λe. ∃e' [Result (e',e) & possession (e', child, toyhouse) & g (e, **toyhouse**)]]

   c. ⟦VP⟧ = λe. ∃e' [Result (e',e) & possession (e', child, toyhouse) & making (e) & theme (e, toyhouse)]

   d. ⟦Voice'⟧ = λx. λe. ∃e' [Result (e',e) & in possession (e', child, toyhouse) & making (e) & Theme (e, toyhouse) & Agent (e,x)] (by ***Event Identification***)

   e. ⟦Voice P⟧ = λe. ∃e' [Result (e',e) & in possession (e', child, toyhouse) & making (e) & Theme (e, toyhouse) & Agent (e,x)]

The interpretation based on the semantic computation given in (31e) where incorporation has applied can be expressed as: 'a set of eventualities *e* such that *e* is making the toyhouse and Eric is the agent of *e* and there is an *e'* such that his child is in possession of the toyhouse in *e'* and *e' is* the result state of *e*.'

5.   Conclusion

In this paper, we provided a unified syntactic and semantic account of *–kan* that accounts for its presence in two seemingly unrelated constructions, causatives and benefactives. We proposed that the verbal suffix *–kan* has a single function as the head of RP which is deeply embedded in the expanded VP structure in the sense of Hale & Keyser (1993). We further showed that the two constructions associated with *–kan* share certain aspectual properties and that they have similar lexical-semantic representations which contain a result state. We argued, therefore, that the presence of *–kan* in these constructions is not coincidental, but comes from the internal event structure that these constructions share.

     The postulation of an abstract CAUSE head in verbal meaning has been argued to be (morpho)-syntactically substantial since in many languages the component that expresses the meaning of a causing event is overtly realized (e.g., a causative morpheme associated with an external causer). However, in many languages the result state is not expressed by special morphology, but is incorporated in the meaning of specific verbs in apparent causatives and double object constructions. In Indonesian, however, we argued that it is the result head that is overtly realized in the morpho-syntax of such constructions, rather than the CAUSE head. Furthermore, we proposed that it is the RESULT head that gives rise to the causative interpretation, in perfect analogy to the CAUSE head proposed in other people's semantics. For this reason, we did not need to postulate a separate verbal head CAUSE in the semantic and syntactic representation of *–kan* constructions.

     By analyzing *–kan* as an overt instansiation of the Result head, the current analysis not only leads to a unified account of *–kan* but also provides new empirical support for the existence of a result-state-denoting constituent in the syntax of double-object verbs (e.g., Beck and Johnson 2002; Harley 2002).

References

Arka, Wayan. 1992. The -kan Causative in Indonesian. MPhil Thesis, University of Sydney, Sydney.

Baker, M. (1988a). Theta Theory and the Syntax of Applicatives in Chicheŵa, *Natural Language and Linguistic Theory* 6:353-389.

Beck, S. and Johnson, K. 2002. Double Object Again. Ms. U. Conn. Storrs. and U Mass. Amherst.

Chomsky, Noam. 1998. Minimalist Inquiries. *MIT Occasional Papers in Linguistics*, NO.15. MITWPL, Cambridge, MA.

Chomsky, Noam.1999. Derivation by Phase. *Number 18 in MIT Occasional Papers in Linguistics*, Cambridge, Mass: MIT WPL

Dowty, D. R. 1979. Word Meaning and Montague Grammar. Dordrecht, Reidel.

Gropen, J., S. Pinker, et al. 1989. The Learnability and Acquisition of the Dative Alternation in English. Language 65 (2), pp. 203-257.

Hale, Ken & Jay Keyser. 1993. On Argument Structure and The Lexical Expression of Syntactic Relations. In Ken Hale and Jay Keyster (eds.) *The View from Building 20: A Festschrift for Sylvain Bromberger.* pp. 53-108. MIT.

Harley, Heidi. 1995. Subjects, Events, and Licensing, Ph.D. Thesis, MIT.

Harley, Heidi. 2002. Possession and The Double Object Construction. To appear in the second volume of the Yearbook of Linguistic Variation, edited by Pierre Pica and Johan Rooryck.

Kaswanti Purwo, Bambang. 1995. The Two Prototypes of Ditransitive Verbs: The Indonesian Evidence. Werner Abraham, T. Givon and Sandra A. Thompson (eds). *Discourse Grammar and Typology*, John Benjamins Publishing Company

Kratzer, Angelika. 1996. Severing the External Argument from Its Verb. In Johan Rooryck & Laurie Zaring, (eds). *Phrase Structure and lexicon*, 109-137. Dordrecht: Kluwer.

Levin, Beth and Tova Rappaport Hovav. 1988. Lexical Subordination. Proceedings of the Chicago Linguistics Society.

Marantz, Alec. (1993). Implications of Asymmetries in Double Object Constructions. In Sam A. Mchombo, ed., *Theoretical Aspects of Bantu Grammar 1.* CSLI Publications, Stanford, CA, 113-151.

Pesetsky, David. 1995. *Zero Syntax*. MIT Press, Cambridge.

Postman, W. A. 2002. Thematic Role Assignment in Indonesian: A Case Study of Agrammatic Aphasia. Doctoral Dissertation, Cornell University, Ithaca, NY.

Pylkkänen, Liina. 2000. Representing Causatives. *SALTX Proceedings.* Jackson, B. and T. Matthews (eds.). CLC Publications. Cornell University, Ithaca, NY

Pylkkänen, Liina. 2002. Applicatives and Depictive Secondary Predication.. *Ling-Lunch.* Department of Linguistics and Philosophy, MIT. Cambridge, MA.

Rackowski, Andrea. 2002. Voice and Configurational Case in Tagalog. (to appear). *The proceedings of AFLA* 9. Cornell University, Ithaca, NY.

Ramchand, Gillian. 2003. First phase syntax. Unpublished Ms. Oxford University.

Sneddon, James N. 1996. Indonesian: a Comprehensive Grammar. London and New York: Routledge.

Son, M.J. 2004. A Unified Syntactic Account of Morphological Causatives. to appear in the Proceedings of the 13th Japanese/Korean Linguistics Conference. Stanford:CSLI.

Son, M.J. & Cole, Peter. 2004. An Event-Based Approach to *–kan* constructions in Standard Indonesian. Ms. University of Delaware.

Travis, L. 2000. Event Structure in Syntax. In C. Tenny & J. Pustejovsky (eds.), *Events as* grammatical *objects* (pp. 145-185). Stanford: CSLI.

Van Hout, A. 2000. Event Semantics in the Lexicon-Syntax Interface. In C. Tenny & J. Pustejovsky (eds.), *Events as grammatical objects* (pp. 239-282). Stanford: CSLI.

Department of Linguistics
University of Delaware
Newark, DE 19716

karmamin@udel.edu
pcole@udel.edu

Pseudogapping and Cyclic Linearization[*]

Shoichi Takahashi

Massachusetts Institute of Technology

1.   Introduction

The main empirical concern of this paper is an ellipsis construction called Pseudogapping, given in (1).[1]

(1)   John will select me, and Bill will ~~select~~ you.   (Lasnik 1999:141)

One might speculate that only a verb *select* is elided in (1). However, as (2) demonstrates, a constituent larger than a verb is elided in Pseudogapping.

(2)   I didn't expect your mother to like the picture; but I did ~~expect~~ you ~~to like the picture~~.
                                                                              (Jayaseelan 1990:67)

Jayaseelan (1990) argues that a remnant (e.g., *you* in (1) and (2)) undergoes Heavy NP Shift (HNPS) and VP (the matrix VP in (2)) is elided together with a trace of the remnant. Since Jayaseelan's work, there is a general consensus that Pseudogapping is another incarnation of VP-ellipsis (Lasnik 1999, among others). However, the controversial issue is what type of movement is involved in Pseudogapping. Pointing out some empirical difficulties that Jayaseelan faces, Lasnik (1999) proposes that a remnant moves out of an ellipsis site by Object Shift. The main goal of this paper is to understand the nature of movement involved in Pseudogapping.

        Parts of this paper have been presented in the Ling-Lunch at MIT (September 2003), in the 18th Comparative Germanic Syntax Workshop at University of Durham (September 2003), in NELS 34 at Stony Brook University (November 2003) and in a colloquium talk at Kanda University of International Studies (January 2004). I would like to thank the audience in these talks for their comments. I am very grateful to Danny Fox, Jon Nissenbaum and David Pesetsky for invaluable discussion and their suggestions. I would also like to thank Klaus Abels, Pranav Anand, Marcel den Dikken, Norvin Richards and Akira Watanabe for their helpful comments. Thanks are also due to the speakers for their judgments. All remaining errors and inadequacies are my own.
    [1] The strikeout material is intended to be elided.

Keir Moulton and Matthew Wolf (eds.): Proceedings of NELS 34,
Stony Brook University: 571 – 585. GLSA, Amherst.

The predictions that Jayaseelan and Lasnik make are clear. For Jayaseelan, we expect that whether some element can be a remnant should be dependent on its possibility of undergoing HNPS. An analogous prediction can be made for Lasnik. In section 2, I examine these predictions primarily on the basis of Pseudogapping in the double object construction. It is shown that both of them are not fully borne out. It is also revealed that if some fact is problematic for the HNPS approach, it can be explained by the Object Shift approach, and vice versa. In section 3, I, therefore, argue that the union of the two approaches is the right way to analyze Pseudogapping. The remainder of the paper considers two potential counterarguments for the Object Shift approach. In section 4, I discuss that facts from contraction in Pseudogapping, which Fox and Pesetsky (2003) present as an argument against the Object Shift approach, are in fact compatible with it. There is another issue which arises in approaches which assume Object Shift in Pseudogapping. That is, there is no clear indication that Object Shift takes place in environments other than Pseudogapping in English. In section 5, I provide a suggestive solution within Fox and Pesetsky's framework of cyclic linearization.

2.   Comparing the Approaches

2.1.   The HNPS Approach

In this section, I examine Jayaseelan's (1990) approach, which assumes that a remnant in Pseudogapping escapes an ellipsis site by HNPS. This is shown in (3).

(3)   ... and Bill will [$_{VP}$ select t_i] you$_i$
                          |___↑ HNPS

As mentioned above, the prediction made by the HNPS approach is that only items that can undergo HNPS can be remnants in Pseudogapping.

There are two cases in which this prediction is not borne. The first one has been pointed out by Lasnik (1999). As illustrated in (4), there is an asymmetry in the possibility of undergoing HNPS between an indirect object and a direct object.

(4)   a.   *John gave a lot of money the fund for the preservation of VOS languages.
        b.   John gave Bill yesterday more money than he had ever seen.
                                                                    (Lasnik 1999:143)

The HNPS approach correctly explains the fact that Pseudogapping with a direct object remnant in (5) is grammatical since the remnant is an element that can undergo HNPS.[2]

(5)   Although John wouldn't give Bill the book, he would give Bill the paper.

However, an indirect object can also be a remnant in Pseudogapping, as shown in (6).

---

[2] Lasnik (1999) claims that a direct object cannot be a remnant. See Baltin (2003) and Bowers (1998) for the observation that it can be a remnant under certain circumstances.

(6)   Although John wouldn't give Bill the book, he would ~~give~~ Susan ~~the book~~.

Since an indirect object cannot undergo HNPS, there is no constituent that can be deleted in (6). Thus, the HNPS approach has a difficulty in deriving (6), as Lasnik points out.

Second, more than one item cannot undergo HNPS in a clause, as shown in (7).

(7)   a.   *John gave t_1 t_2 yesterday [the tall man]$_1$ [the book written by the professor at MIT]$_2$.
       b.   *Sue gave t_1 t_2 on Friday [the book about HNPS]$_1$ [to the student who works on Parasitic Gaps]$_2$.

The HNPS approach predicts that Pseudogapping with multiple remnants would be ungrammatical. However, Baltin (2003) and Bowers (1998) observe that two objects in the dative construction can remain as remnants, as shown in (8a). For unknown reasons, the presence of two remnants in the double object construction makes Pseudogapping degraded, as shown in (9a). Bowers suggests that grammaticality of Pseudogapping improves in the comparative context and I adopt this strategy in (8b) and (9b).[3]

(8)   a.   Although John would give a book to Mary, he wouldn't ~~give~~ a paper to Susan.
       b.   John would give a book to Mary more often than he would ~~give~~ a paper to Susan.

(9)   a.   ??Although John would give Bill a book, he wouldn't ~~give~~ Susan a paper.
       b.   ?John would give Bill a book more often than he would ~~give~~ Susan a paper.

Since there are at least some cases of legitimate Pseudogapping with multiple remnants, we here have an argument against the HNPS approach.

The discussion above leads us to conclude that some movement other than HNPS should also be involved in Pseudogapping (I put aside the possibility that a completely different movement operation plays a role here). However, it is important to notice that HNPS can straightforwardly treat Pseudogapping with a direct object remnant in (5). This case is problematic for the Object Shift approach, as we will discuss in the next section.

2.2.   The Object Shift Approach

As briefly mentioned in the introduction, Lasnik's (1999) Object Shift approach, illustrated in (10), faces a serious problem. It needs to explain why there is no clear case of Object Shift in contexts other than Pseudogapping in English:

(10)   … and Bill will [you$_1$ ~~[$_{VP}$ select t_1]~~]
                            |_____| Object Shift

---

[3] There are speakers' variations on acceptability in Pseudogapping in general. The variation also exists here. In (8), some speakers find the same contrast as (9).

It is clear that the HNPS approach does not face this problem because there are observable cases of HNPS in English. In addition to this issue, there are two types of challenges to the Object Shift approach.

The first type is analogous to the problem for HPNS. There is a case in which an element that cannot undergo Object Shift can be a remnant:

(11)   a.   Although John wouldn't give Bill the book, he would ~~give~~ Susan ~~the book~~.
        b.   Although John wouldn't give Bill the book, he would ~~give Bill~~ the paper.

Maintaining the idea that an ellipsis operation only applies to constituents, the Object Shift approach would analyze (11a) and (11b) as (12a) and (12b), respectively.[4]

(12)   a.   he would [Susan₁ ~~[give tᵢ the book]~~]
        b.   he would [the paper₁ ~~[give Bill tᵢ]~~]

Since we do not find any clear case of Object Shift in English, we observe the one in Scandinavian languages to understand whether the operations in (12a) and (12b) might be allowed in English. As we will observe shortly, an indirect object can undergo Object Shift in these languages. Thus, I assume that Object Shift in (12a) is allowed in English. However, I suggest that Object Shift in (12b) is prohibited in English. Let us first observe the facts in Swedish in which either an indirect or a direct object can undergo Object Shift across the other object, as shown in (13). This is also the case in Norwegian:

(13)   a.   Han   visade   henne   inte   den.   (Swedish)
              he   showed   her   not   it
              'He did not show it to her'
        b.   Han   gav   den   inte   henne.
              he   gave   it   not   her
              'He did not give it to her.'
                                          (Anagnostopoulou 2002:5; see also Hellan and Platzack 1999)

However, a direct object cannot cross over an indirect object by Object Shift in Icelandic, as shown in (14b). This is also true in Danish:

(14)   a.   Ég   skilaði   manninum   ekki   bókinni.   (Icelandic)
              I   returned   the-man-DAT   not   the-book-DAT
        b.   *Ég   skilaði   bókinni   ekki   manninum.
              I   returned   the-book-DAT   not   the-man-DAT
              'I did not return the book to the man.'
                                          (Anagnostopoulou 2002:7; see also Hellan and Platzack 1999)

---

[4] Lasnik adopts the split VP hypothesis (Koizumi 1995). In this hypothesis, there is no stage in which a direct object is structurally higher than an indirect object. Thus, there is no way to derive (11b) in this approach. My argument here is that even if we would dispense with the hypothesis and take the potential derivation in (12b) into account, (11b) is still a challenge to the Object Shift approach.

Interestingly, Anagnostopoulou (2002) observes that this difference between the two classes of the languages is correlated with whether a direct object can be passivized across an indirect object in these languages. First, either one of the two objects can be passivized in Swedish, as shown in (15).

(15)   a.   Johan forärades   en   medalj.   (Swedish)
              John   was-presented a   medal
              'John was presented a medal.'
       b.   Medaljen   forärades   Johan.
              the-medal   was-presented John
              'The medal was presented to John.'   (Anagnostopoulou 2002:9)

In contrast, Icelandic and Danish do not allow a direct object to move across an indirect object by passivization, as illustrated in (16).

(16)   a.   Jóni   var   skilað   bókunum.   (Icelandic)
              John-DAT   was   returned   the-book-DAT
              'John was given back the book.'
       b.   *Bókunum   var   skilað   Jóni.
              the-book-DAT   was   returned   John-DAT
              'The book was returned to John.'   (Anagnostopoulou 2002:8)

The generalization that we reach on the basis of the facts above is that a direct object can undergo Object Shift across an indirect object in languages where the former can be passivized across the latter. As shown in (17), passivization of a direct object across an indirect object is not allowed in most dialects of English.

(17)   a.   *A book was given Mary.
       b.   Mary was given a book.

Consequently, I suggest that a direct object cannot move across an indirect object by Object Shift in English. This suggests that the derivation in (12b) is not a possible analysis of Pseudogapping in (11b).

The second type of challenge to the Object Shift approach is as follows. There is some evidence from Scandinavian languages which suggests that Object Shift is A-movement (e.g., the lack of parasitic gap licensing in (21)). Thus, the Object Shift approach predicts that the movement of a remnant patterns with A-movement. However, this prediction is not borne out. To set the stage, recall the following contrast between complements and adjuncts in reconstruction:

(18)   a.   *[Whose claim that John$_i$ is nice]$_1$ did he$_i$ believe t$_1$?
       b.   [Which story that John$_i$ wrote]$_1$ did he$_i$ like t$_1$?   (Lebeaux 1988:146)

The contrast above shows that there is an asymmetry in the possibility of reconstruction between an argumental sentential complement and an adjunct relative clause in A'-

movement. The former must undergo reconstruction and hence, (18a) is ruled out by Principle C. In contrast, a sentential complement does not show an obligatory reconstruction effect in A-movement. Therefore, (19) is grammatical, unlike (18a).

(19)   [The claim that John$_i$ was asleep]$_1$ seems to him$_i$ [t$_1$ to be correct].

                                                                        (Chomsky 1993:37)

Given the discussion above, the Object Shift approach predicts that the movement of a remnant should not exhibit an obligatory reconstruction effect of an argumental sentential complement. Sauerland (1998), however, observes that this prediction is not borne out:

(20)   a.   *While some granted/told him$_i$ everything, others did grant/tell him$_i$ only
                the story that John$_i$ had met aliens.
        b.   While some granted/told him$_i$ everything, others did grant/tell him$_i$ only
                the story that John$_i$ had evidence for.
                                                        (adapted from Sauerland 1998:144)

The fact that (20a) is ungrammatical indicates that an argumental sentential complement obligatorily undergoes reconstruction in the movement involved in Pseudogapping, unlike in A-movement. We here have a reason to suggest that the movement involved should not be A-movement, at least in all cases.

The next evidence against the Object Shift approach comes from the parasitic gap licensing. It is observed that Object Shift cannot license a parasitic gap in Scandinavian languages and this seems to suggest that it patterns with A-movement:

(21)   *Þú   setur   [Þetta blað]$_1$ ekki t$_1$ á   borðið   (Icelandic)
        you   put   this   paper not   on   the table
        [án Þess að   lesa   e$_1$].
        without   reading
        'You didn't put this book on the table without reading.'   (Jónsson 1996:72)

Contrary to what the Object Shift approach would predict, the movement of a remnant in Pseudogapping can license a parasitic gap, as (22) shows.

(22)   Although John didn't file a recent article about HNPS, he did [without reading e$_1$]
        [a recent article about Object Shift]$_1$.

In this section, we have observed some challenges to the Object Shift approach. However, it is crucial to notice that it can account for Pseudogapping with an indirect object remnant in (11a), which is problematic for the HNPS approach.

2.3.   Interim Conclusion

Among other facts, I have shown that the following Pseudogapping contrast is a challenge to both the HNPS approach and the Object Shift approach:

(23)   a.   Although John wouldn't give Bill the book, he would ~~give Bill~~ the paper.

       b.   Although John wouldn't give Bill the book, he would ~~give~~ Susan ~~the book~~.

As mentioned above, (23a) is dealt with by the HNPS approach, which cannot treat (23b). Conversely, the Object Shift approach can explain (23b), but not (23a). Thus, we are led to conclude that both approaches are insufficient.

3.   Proposals

3.1.   The Eclectic Approach

Based on the discussion above, I argue that the right approach to Pseudogapping is the union of the HNPS approach and the Object Shift approach.[5] This eclectic approach not only explains the facts, but has the following conceptual naturalness. Both HNPS and Object Shift are shown to be operations observed in natural language. Thus, there is no a priori reason to assume that a VP constituent derived by either one of operations cannot be elided at a later stage of the derivation (see Lasnik 1999 for relevant discussion).[6]

We are now in a position to explain how the eclectic approach deals with the facts above. Let me first explain the pair of Pseudogapping in (23). Their derivations are given in (24) and (25), respectively.[7]

(24)   ... he$_1$ would [$_{vP}$ ~~[$_{vP}$ t$_1$ give Bill t$_2$]~~ the paper$_2$]

                           |_____↑ HNPS

(25)   ... he$_1$ would [$_{XP}$ Susan$_2$ ~~[$_{vP}$ t$_1$ give t$_2$ the book]~~]

                ↑_____| Object Shift

It is clear that this approach faces no difficulty in explaining these examples. We have already seen that each is successfully dealt with by one of the two approaches. In each case, if we choose the wrong type of movement operation, the resulting derivation is ruled out for independent reasons. Although the derivations of (23a) and (23b) are unambiguous, the eclectic approach predicts that derivations would be ambiguous if we could apply both HNPS and Object Shift to some remnant. I suggest that one of such cases is (26a) in which a remnant is a direct object in the dative construction.

(26)   a.   Although John wouldn't give the book to Bill, he would ~~give~~ the paper ~~to Bill~~.

       b.   ... he$_1$ would [$_{vP}$ ~~[$_{vP}$ t$_1$ give t$_2$ to Bill]~~ the paper$_2$]

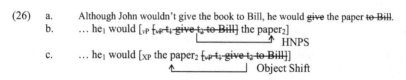

       c.   ... he$_1$ would [$_{XP}$ the paper$_2$ ~~[$_{vP}$ t$_1$ give t$_2$ to Bill]~~]

                ↑_____| Object Shift

---

[5] Bowers (1998) also proposes that both rightward and leftward movements are necessary for deriving all instances of Pseudogapping on the basis of the independent facts.

[6] Baltin (2003) and Johnson (2001) argue that the movement involved in Pseudogapping is the one analogous to scrambling in Dutch. A detailed examination of this proposal awaits another occasion.

[7] I assume that Object Shift targets some position above vP, which is represented as XP in the text.

The grammaticality of (27) shows that the HNPS option should be available.

(27)   We gave t_1 to John on Friday [a brand-new toy]$_1$.   (Pesetsky 1995:249)

It is more involved to show that the Object Shift option should also be available. In this respect, the following fact is suggestive. As shown in (28), Object Shift is applicable to a direct object in so-called inversion construction in Icelandic, which is analyzed as the dative construction.

(28)   Ég   gaf   ambáttina$_1$ ekki   [t_1 konunginum].   (Icelandic)
        I   gave   the maidservant-ACC   not   the king-DAT
        'I didn't give the maidservant to the king.'
                        (Collins and Thráinsson 1996:415; see also Holmberg and Platzack 1995)

Consequently, I suggest that both (26b) and (26c) are the legitimate derivations of (26a). In addition to (26a), there are also two derivations for Pseudogapping with a direct object remnant of a transitive verb in (29a) because both HNPS and Object Shift are clearly applicable to the direct object.[8]

(29)   a.   John will select me, and Bill will ~~select~~ you.
        b.   ... Bill$_1$ will [$_{vP}$ ~~$_{VP}$ t_1 select t_2~~ you$_2$]
                                  └────↑ HNPS
        c.   ... Bill$_1$ will [$_{XP}$ you$_2$ ~~$_{VP}$ t_1 select t_2~~]
                                  ↑_____| Object Shift

        In contrast to this, a unique derivation is assigned to (30a), which involves a dative prepositional phrase as a remnant.

(30)   a.   Although John wouldn't give the book to Bill, he would ~~give the book~~ to Susan.
        b.   ... he$_1$ would [$_{vP}$ ~~$_{VP}$ t_1 give the book t_2~~ to Susan$_2$]
                                  └──────↑ HNPS
        c.   *... he$_1$ would [$_{XP}$ to Susan$_2$ ~~$_{VP}$ t_1 give the book t_2~~]
                                  ↑_____| Object Shift

Since HNPS in (31) is grammatical, we can conclude that the derivation in (30b) is available.

(31)   Sue gave the book t_1 on Friday [to John]$_1$.   (Pesetsky 1995:261)

However, the derivation in (30c) is not allowed because a prepositional phrase cannot undergo Object Shift in Icelandic, as shown in (32).

---

[8] Lasnik (1999:fn 14) leaves open the possibility that Pseudogapping with a direct object of a transitive verb can be produced by HNPS. However, this is not a possibility in other cases.

(32) a.   Jón   talaði   ekki   [PP   við   Maríu].   (Icelandic)
            Jon   spoke   not   to   Mary
      b.   *Jón   talaði   [PP   við   Maríu]₁   ekki t₁.
            Jon   spoke   to   Mary   not
            'John didn't speak to Mary.'   (Thráinsson 2001:151)

Let me finally examine Pseudogapping with multiple remnants. The case in the double object construction is repeated here as (33a). As shown in (34), multiple applications of Object Shift are legitimate in Scandinavian languages. Thus, the derivation in (33b) is available to the eclectic approach.

(33) a.   ?John would give Bill a book more often than he would ~~give~~ Susan a paper.
      b.   ... than OP₁ he₂ would [XP Susan₃ [XP a paper₄ ~~[vP t₂ give t₃ t₄ t₁ often]~~]]

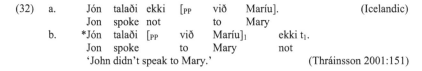

Object Shift

(34) Jag   gav   honom den   inte.   (Swedish)
      I   gave   him   it   not
      'I didn't give it to him.'   (Anagnostopoulou 2002:7)

An alternative derivation is also available to (33a). The direct object and the indirect object undergo Object Shift and HNPS, respectively, as shown in (35).

(35) ... than OP₁ he₂ would [XP Susan₃ [vP ~~[vP t₂ give t₃ t₄ t₁ often]~~ a paper₄]]
      Object Shift ↑_____| |_____↑ HNPS

Pseudogapping with multiple remnants in the dative construction is given in (36a). Since a prepositional phrase cannot undergo Object Shift and HNPS cannot apply multiple times, (36a) should be analyzed as (36b) in the eclectic approach.

(36) a.   Although he wouldn't give the book to Bill, he would ~~give~~ the paper to Susan.
      b.   ... he₁ would [XP the paper₂ [vP ~~[vP t₁ give t₂ t₃]~~ to Susan₃]]
            Object Shift ↑_____| |_____↑ HNPS

In conclusion, I have shown that the eclectic approach straightforwardly captures the possibility of being a remnant. The next section reveals that this approach can also account for the A'-movement properties exhibited by the movement of a remnant.

3.2.   Explaining the A'-movement Properties

The fact that the movement of a remnant shows A'-movement properties is not problematic for the eclectic approach because it is equipped with not only Object Shift, but HNPS, which is considered as A'-movement.

First, we have observed that the argumental sentential complement of the remnant must undergo reconstruction, but not the adjunct relative clause, as illustrated in (37).

(37)   a.   *While some granted/told him₁ everything, others did ~~grant/tell him₁~~ only
                the story that John₁ had met aliens.
        b.   While some granted/told him₁ everything, others did ~~grant/tell him₁~~ only
                the story that John₁ had evidence for.

                                                    (adapted from Sauerland 1998:144)

This contrast, which is generally observed in A'-movement, straightforwardly follows
from the proposed approach. Notice that the remnants in (37) are the direct objects in the
double object construction. As discussed above, they must undergo HNPS in order to
escape an ellipsis site since Object Shift is not an option for it. Thus, the eclectic
approach assigns the representation in (38) to (37a).

(38)   ... others₁ did [$_{vP}$ ~~[$_{vP}$ t₁ grant him₁ t₂]~~ [only the story that John₁ had met aliens]₂]
                            └_____↑ HNPS

Since HNPS is generally regarded as A'-movement, the contrast observed is expected.[9]

        Second, it has been shown that a parasitic gap is licensed by the movement of a
remnant, as shown in (39).

(39)   Although John didn't file a recent article about HNPS, he did [without reading e₁]
        [a recent article about Object Shift]₁.

It is clear from the word order in (39) that the remnant moves out of an ellipsis site by
HNPS. The fact in (39) is explained by the current approach because HNPS can license a
parasitic gap, as observed in Larson (1988), Nissenbaum (2000), among others (see also
Postal 1994 for relevant discussion):

(40)   John filed [without reading e₁] [a recent article about global warming]₁.

                                                    (Nissenbaum 2000:32)

In contrast to (39), Baltin (2003) observes that a parasitic gap cannot be licensed by the
movement in Pseudogapping. The relevant example is given in (41).

(41)   *Although John didn't kiss Mary, he did Sally₁ without looking at e₁.

                                                    (adapted from Baltin 2003:241)

The crucial difference between (39) and (41) is the position of the remnant relative to the
adjunct phrase. Since it precedes a gap in (41), I suggest that the movement involved is
Object Shift, which cannot license a parasitic gap (see (21) for relevant observation).
What the eclectic approach predicts based on the discussion above is that a parasitic gap

---

[9] The eclectic approach makes the following prediction. In cases where an indirect object in the
double object construction is a remnant, it should show an anti-reconstruction effect with respect to
Principle C, as we have observed in A-movement in (19). This is because Object Shift is the only option
for it. Unfortunately, I have not found a configuration in which this prediction can be examined. But, see
the discussion on the parasitic gap licensing, which is based on the same logic.

is licensed by the movement of a direct object, but not an indirect object in the double object construction. This is because HNPS is applicable to the former, but not to the latter. As shown in (42) and (43), this prediction is borne out.

(42)   Although John didn't give the boy a short paper, he did [without reading e₁] [a long paper]₁.

(43)   a.   *Although John didn't give the tall boy a book, he did [without meeting e₁] [the short boy]₁.
        b.   *Although John didn't give the tall boy a book, he did [the short boy]₁ [without meeting e₁].

Pseudogapping in (43a) is ruled out independently of the parasitic gap because it just cannot undergo HNPS and cannot follow the adjunct phrase. On the other hand, the existence of the parasitic gap makes (43b) ungrammatical since the movement of the remnant is Object Shift in this case and the parasitic gap is not licensed.

This section has shown that the facts that are challenges to the Object Shift approach can be accounted for by the eclectic approach because it has HNPS as an option. In the next section, I take up an apparent argument against the Object Shift appraoch raised by Fox and Pesetsky (2003).

4.   Contraction in Pseudogapping

This section deals with an apparent counterevidence to the analysis that Object Shift can be involved in Pseudogapping. The issue that is raised by Fox and Pesetsky (2003) is the following. It is well known that contracted forms are disallowed immediately before an ellipsis site (Bresnan 1973, King 1970, among others). This point is illustrated in (44b).[10]

(44)   a.   John is leaving and Mary is, too.
        b.   *John is leaving and Mary's, too.
        c.   John is leaving but Mary's not.   (Lobeck 1995:156)

As shown in (44c), if there is a phonologically overt item like negation between the tensed auxiliary and the elided constituent, a contracted form of the tensed auxiliary is allowed. This paradigm raises a question under the assumption that Object Shift can be a movement operation in Pseudogapping. I have argued that if an indirect object in the double object construction is a remnant, it must move out of vP by Object Shift, as shown in (45).

(45)   a.   Although he wouldn't give Bill the book, he would Susan.
        b.   [TP he₁ would [XP Susan₂ [vP t₁ give t₂ the book]]]

---

[10] Although contracted forms are also prohibited immediately before an extraction site (see King 1970 for relevant discussion), I concentrate on facts in ellipsis here.

Given this structure, we predict that a contracted form of the tensed auxiliary would be possible in Pseudogapping with an indirect object remnant because there is a phonologically overt material between an auxiliary and an elided site, namely, the indirect object. However, this prediction is not borne out, as shown in (46a).

(46)   a.   *Although I didn't give Mary a book, I'll Sue.
        b.   Although I didn't give Mary a book, I will Sue.

In the following, I suggest that the facts should be viewed differently. A motivation for this suggestion is that contraction can sometime take place immediately before an ellipsis site. As King (1970) observes, negation can be contracted in this environment, as shown in (47).

(47)   John is leaving, but Mary isn't.

What is the difference between (44b) and (47)? If the facts were captured based on the relative position between a contracted element and an ellipsis site, like the way we described above, it would be difficult to distinguish one from the other. My suggestion is that there should be a structural condition which states that VP-ellipsis is licensed by a non-contracted licensing head.[11] This captures the contrast between (44a) and (44b) because there is a non-contracted licensing head (i.e., the tensed auxiliary) in the former, but not in the latter. At the same time, this accounts for (47). Since the tensed auxiliary is a non-contracted licensing head, negation can be contracted even though it is immediately before the ellipsis site. I suggest that contraction of the tensed auxiliary is possible in (44c) because negation as well as the tensed auxiliary is a licensing head and the former is not contracted.

As discussed in Potsdam (1997), this idea is supported by VP-ellipsis in subjunctive complements. To set the stage, let us first observe the fact that no element under T node can appear overtly in subjunctive complements:

(48)   *Jack asks that we do not/don't cut down his beanstalk just yet.
                                                    (Potsdam 1997:536)

Under the assumption that VP-ellipsis requires an overt licensing head, we expect that VP-ellipsis is not allowed in subjunctive complement and this is what we observe in (49a). Interestingly, VP-ellipsis becomes possible if there is negation, as shown in (49b).

(49)   a.   *We think that Mary should present her case to the committee and we ask
              that Bill too.
        b.   We think that Mary should present her case but we will ask that Bill not.
                                                    (Potsdam 1997:538)

---

[11] This licensing condition is the first approximation. It is very likely that there are some other constraints on licensing VP-ellipsis, which are not relevant for the present discussion (see Lobeck 1995 for detailed discussion on the licensing condition on VP-ellipsis).

The fact that (49b) is legitimate VP-ellipsis indicates that negation is a licensing head.

Given this characterization of the facts, the impossibility of contraction in (46a) is not problematic for the Object Shift approach. Even though the indirect object intervenes between the auxiliary and the ellipsis site, it is not a licensing head and hence, the auxiliary is prevented from being contracted. Thus, (46a) is compatible with the proposed approach.

5. Cyclic Linearization

The eclectic approach inherits one of the problems of the Object Shift approach. While (50) is illegitimate, it is the structure in which vP is elided in Pseudogapping. In the proposed approach, the question is why (50) becomes legitimate if vP is elided.

(50)   *John$_1$ [$_{XP}$ Mary$_2$ [$_{vP}$ t$_1$ gave t$_2$ the book]]

Adopting Fox and Pesetsky's (2003) insights, I discuss that this issue should be examined in the context of linearization and can be solved by their cyclic linearization theory, which explains several relevant facts in a unified way.

The fact that (50) is not allowed is strongly reminiscent of Holmberg's (1986, 1999) generalization. Holmberg observes that Object Shift in Scandinavian languages is dependent on verb movement, as illustrated by the contrast in (51).[12]

(51)   a.   Jag   kysste   henne$_1$ inte   [$_{VP}$ t$_v$ t$_1$].   (Swedish)
              I   kissed   her   not

        b.   *Jag   har   henne$_1$ inte   [$_{VP}$ kysst   t$_1$].
              I   have   her   not   kissed   (Holmberg 1999:1)

We can characterize a situation common to (50) and (51b) in the following way. A verb precedes an object at one stage of the derivation (i.e., at the underlying structure), but the latter precedes the former at another stage of the derivation (i.e., at the surface structure).

Based on this characterization, Fox and Pesetsky propose that relative orders among lexical elements are determined by Spell-out in a cyclic fashion. Furthermore, once relative orders are established, they must be preserved throughout a derivation (see also Müller 2001, Sells 2001 and Williams 2003 for similar ideas). On the assumption that the first Spell-out domain contains a verb and an object, they argue that (51a) is legitimate because the relative order between the two established by the first Spell-out (i.e., the former precedes the latter) is preserved throughout the derivation as a consequence of verb movement and Object Shift. However, this is not the case in (50) and (51b), due to the lack of verb movement and hence, Object Shift is illegitimate in

---

[12] Holmberg (1999) emphasizes that this fact is an incarnation of a more general generalization.

these cases.[13] As suggested in Fox and Pesetsky, their framework provides an answer to the issue raised above. The relative order between the verb and the object established by the first Spell-out has loses its effect in Pseudogapping because vP is elided and the verb is not linearized. This is the reason why an otherwise illegitimate Object Shift in (50) is saved by ellipsis.[14]

6.   Conclusion

The main claim of this paper has been that both HNPS and Object Shift are necessary to derive all instances of Pseudogapping. I have argued that this eclectic approach not only explains the facts, but is conceptually most natural. In order to understand the nature of Object Shift in English, which I have argued is involved in Pseudogapping, we have observed the one in Scandinavian languages in which Object Shift is clearly observable. It has been revealed that two potential counterarguments against the Object Shift approach can be explained away.   First, I have argued that, given a different characterization of the contraction facts in Pseudogapping, they are compatible with the Object Shift approach. I have also suggested that Fox and Pesetsky's cyclic linearization framework accounts for the issue that Object Shift is confined to Pseudogapping in English, together with Holmberg's generalization.

References

Anagnostopoulou, E. 2002. Movement across Phonologically Visible Categories. Handout of the talk at Ling-Lunch at MIT.

Baltin, M. 2003. The Interaction of Ellipsis and Binding: Implications for the Sequencing of Principle A. *Natural Language and Linguistic Theory* 21:215-246.

Bowers, J. 1998. On Pseudo-gapping. Ms., Cornell University.

Bresnan, J. 1973. Syntax of the Comparative Clause Construction in English. *Linguistic Inquiry* 4:275-343.

Chomsky, N. 1993. A Minimalist Program for Linguistic Theory. In *The View from Building 20: Essays in Linguistics in Honor of Sylvain Bromberger*, ed. by K. Hale and S. J. Keyser, 1-52. Cambridge, Mass: MIT Press.

Collins, C., and H. Thráinsson. 1996. VP-internal Structure and Object Shift in Icelandic. *Linguistic Inquiry* 27:391-444.

Fox, D., and D. Pesetsky. 2003. Cyclic Linearization and the Typology of Movement. Lecture Notes, MIT.
[downloadable from http://web.mit.edu/linguistics/www/fox/July_19_handout.pdf]

Hellan, L., and C. Platzack. 1999. Pronouns in Scandinavian Languages: An Overview. In *Clitics in the Languages of Europe*, ed. by H. van Riemsdijk, 123-142. Mouton de Gruyter.

Holmberg, A. 1986. Word Order and Syntactic Features in the Scandinavian Languages and English. Doctoral dissertation, University of Stockholm.

---

[13] It is certainly true that an object sometimes ends up with preceding a verb, just like (50) and (51b) (e.g., *wh*-movement of an object). See Fox and Pesetsky (2003) for the analysis of such cases.
[14] Holmberg (1999:fn. 13) suggests a prediction which is similar to this idea.

Holmberg, A. 1999. Remarks on Holmberg's Generalization. *Studia Linguistica* 53:1-39.

Holmberg, A., and C. Platzack. 1995. *The Role of Inflection in Scandinavian Syntax.* Oxford University Press.

Jayaseelan, K. A. 1990. Incomplete VP Deletion and Gapping. *Linguistic Analysis* 20:64-81.

Johnson, K. 2001.What VP Ellipsis Can Do, and What It Can't, But Not Why. In *The Handbook of Contemporary Syntactic Theory*, ed. by M. Baltin and C. Collins, 439-479. Blackwell Publishers.

Jónsson, J. 1996. Clausal Architecture and Case in Icelandic. Doctoral dissertation, University of Massachusetts, Amherst.

King, H. 1970. On Blocking the Rules for Contraction in English. *Linguistic Inquiry* 1:134-136.

Koizumi M. 1995. Phrase Structure in Minimalist Syntax. Doctoral dissertation, MIT, Cambridge, Mass.

Larson, R. 1988. Light Predicate Raising. *MIT Centre for Cognitive Science: Lexicon Working Papers vol. 27.* Cambridge, Mass.: MITWPL.

Lasnik, H. 1999. Pseudogapping Puzzles. In *Fragments: Studies in Ellipsis and Gapping*, ed. by S. Lappin and E. Benmamoun, 141-174. Oxford University Press.

Lebeaux, D. 1988. Language Acquisition and the Form of Grammar. Doctoral dissertation, University of Massachusetts, Amherst.

Lobeck, A. 1995. *Ellipsis: Functional Heads, Licensing, and Interpretation.* Oxford University Press.

Müller, G. 2001. Order Preservation, Parallel Movement, and the Emergence of the Unmarked. In *Optimality-Theoretic Syntax*, ed. by G. Legendre, J. Grimshaw and S. Vikner, 279-313. Cambridge, Mass.: MIT Press.

Nissenbaum, J. 2000. Investigation of Covert Phrase Movement. Doctoral dissertation, MIT, Cambridge, Mass.

Pesetsky, D. 1995. *Zero Syntax.* Cambridge, Mass.: MIT Press.

Postal, P. 1994. Parasitic and Pseudoparasitic Gaps. *Linguistic Inquiry* 25:63-117.

Potsdam, E.1997. NegP and Subjunctive Complements in English. *Linguistic Inquiry* 28:533-541.

Sauerland, U. 1998. The Meaning of Chains. Doctoral dissertation, MIT, Cambridge, Mass.

Sells, P. 2001. *Structure, Alignment and Optimality in Swedish.* CSLI Publications.

Thráinsson, H. 2001. Object Shift and Scrambling. In *The Handbook of Contemporary Syntactic Theory*, ed. by M. Baltin and C. Collins, 148-202. Blackwell Publishers.

Williams, E. 2003. *Representation Theory.* Cambridge, Mass.: MIT Press.

Department of Linguistics and Philosophy, E39-230
Massachusetts Institute of Technology
77 Massachusetts Avenue
Cambridge, MA 02139

s_t@mit.edu

Prosody as a Diagonalization of Syntax. Evidence from Complex Predicates[†]

Michael Wagner

Massachussetts Institute of Technology

1. The Transformational Cycle vs. XP-Alignment

Chomsky and Halle (1968) derive prosody and phonological domains by an algorithm that recursively operates on sister constituents in a surface tree structure: the transformational cycle. Prosodic phonology, on the other hand, phrases an output string into a universal prosodic hierarchy based on conventions that map certain types of syntactic constituents into certain types of prosodic constituents, e.g via XP-Edge Marking (Chen, 1987; Selkirk, 1986) or XP-Alignment (Selkirk, 1995; Truckenbrodt, 1995, 1999).

An asymmetry in the assignment of prosody is established that connects syntactic relation, linear order, and prosodic structure. The data serves to illustrate why XP-edge marking does not provide a viable model of the syntax–phonology interface, and is used to argue in favor of a syntax–phonology mapping closer to the transformational cycle, along the lines of recent proposals in Cinque (1993) and Arregi (2002).

2. Prosodic Asymmetry

This section presents evidence for the following generalization about prosodic asymmetry:

(1) Prosodic Asymmetry

- When a projecting element A *precedes* its complement B, a sequence of two prosodic domains that are on a par is derived: Á Ɓ. The last domain provides the 'nuclear stress'.

- When a projecting element A *follows* an element from the complement domain B , A is subordinated: Ɓ A (unless A is focused or B is old information)

In the following, I present evidence in favor of (1) from different dialects of West-Germanic (Dutch, English, German), involving predicates with infinitival and nominal complements.

[†]Thanks to the audience at NELS, and David Adger, Karlos Arregi, Asaf Bachrach, Corrien Blom, Edward Flemming, Jon Gajewski, Morris Halle, Paul Kiparsky, Alec Marantz, Ad Neeleman, David Pesetsky, Henk van Riemsdijk, Lisa Selkirk, Donca Steriade, Hubert Truckenbrodt, Susi Wurmbrand, Jan Wouter Zwart for comments and suggestions. This work was partly conducted at Stanford University in Spring 2003.

Keir Moulton and Matthew Wolf (eds.): Proceedings of NELS 34,
Stony Brook University: 587 – 601. GLSA, Amherst.

2.1. Predicates and Infinitival Complements

West Germanic languages differ in their prosody. However, once linear order is taken into account, the apparent prosodic differences actually reduce to syntactic differences. This section looks closely at sequences of predicates.[1] Consider first the case of Dutch:

(2)   Dutch Predicate Cluster: Final Stress

...[dát hij] [wílde   ] [hélpen] [vérven].
    that he   wanted.to   help.to   paint

The predicates are ordered according to their embedding. The actual output for (2) contains less accents than given here: The accent on 'helpen' is dropped, as indicated in (3a). This seems to be due to rhythmic restructuring, which gets rid of clashes. One indication that this is the correct characterization of the data is example (3b). If a preposition separates the last two predicates, they are separated enough to both maintain their accents.

(3)   a. ...[dát hij] [wílde helpen] [vérven]
      b. ...[dát hij] [wilde hélpen] [met vérven]

(3a,b) suggest that nuclear stress in the Dutch predicate clusters is final, pre-final predicates may also bear an accent. Predicate 2 in (3a) is in an accented position as indicated in (2), but gets rhythmically deaccented. The sentence in (2) can also be pronounced with only one accent on the last predicate. The rhythmic nature of accent-placement in the pre-nuclear domain is further evidenced by (4a vs. b) and (4c vs. d) respectively.

(4)   Hij zéi   dat hij...
      he said that he....

      a. ...wilde   vérven.   b. ...wílde   helpen vérven.
          wanted.to paint   wanted.to help.to paint

      c. ...wílde   kunnen   helpen vérven.
          wanted.to be.able.to help.to paint

      d. ... wílde mogen kúnnen helpen vérven.
          ... wílde mogen kunnen helpen vérven.

      e. Hij wílde mogen kunnen helpen vérven.

          'He wants to be allowed to be able to help to paint.'

---

[1]In presenting the cluster data I am tacitly assuming that they form constituents. These may have been derived via head movement—if we allow for head-movement in the first place. I will not explore the possibilities in detail. The numbers in the examples indicate the path of selection between the predicates, starting from the highest predicate '1', to the one selected by it '2' and so forth. The tree-representation encodes projecting constituents by uninterrupted lines. Predicates that receive an accent are indicated by a bold-faced branch. All sentences presented involve sentence wide focus.

One way to make sense of this pattern is to say that the mapping to prosody places accents on *each* predicate, which are then rhythmically organized resulting in the omission of certain accents. This would explain non-local effects such as in (4e), where the first predicate counts for rhythm although it has risen to second position. The syntactic and phonological conditions on rhythmic restructuring are beyond the scope of this paper.[2] Consider now the German counterparts of the Dutch predicate clusters:

(5) German Predicate Cluster: Initial Stress

...dass er málen helfen wollte.
...that he paint help want.

Main stress in German falls on the first predicate. No accents are possible under neutral focus in the post-nuclear domain although secondary stresses are present. This is true independent of the number of predicates that follow.

(6) [Er ságte dass er] [málen helfen kònnen dürfen   wòllte].
     he said that he   paint help   can   be.allowed wanted

The two languages also differ in the linear order of predicates, apart from the linear location of main word stress: while the predicates in Dutch are ordered according to embedding, the order in German is the exact inverse. The two differences, initial vs. final stress, embedding vs. inverse order, conspire to the following communality: Both languages keep main stress on the *most deeply embedded predicate according to the path of selection.*

The following paradigm shows three of the possible orders of a particular predicate sequence in German. When predicates are ordered according to embedding as in (a), this order is often taken to involve 'extraposition'. Haider (1997) convincingly argues that 'extraposed' material is actually within VP and in-situ, resulting in a right branching structure for (7). Different orders are possible, however, in so-called 'restructuring' environments (e.g. in b,c). There are many syntactic differences between 'extraposition' and 'restructuring' constructions that I will not address in this paper—restructuring derives what appear to be monoclausal constructions that, e.g. , facilitate scrambling between clauses, and allow pronouns that are arguments in the lower clause to be affixed on the matrix verb in second position, etc. (cf. Wurmbrand, 2003). Restructuring, however, does not always result in a different word order between the predicates (Haider, 1994).

It could very well be that these syntactic differences play a crucial role. For example, one could argue that subordinated predicates are not really XPs, but heads, which is part of the restructuring process. A syntax–phonology theory that makes reference to XP-status could then exploit this difference to predict the asymmetries. A first problem with

---

[2]Some speakers are not able place the middle accent in (4d). As will become apparent in the discussion later, the reverse solution with assigning nuclear stress to the most embedded predicate and subsequent insertion of accents in the pre-nuclear domain is not tenable.

this approach is that it makes no prediction about the directionality of the asymmetry. More serious problems will be pointed out in the last section. The important point here is that the prosodic asymmetries already follow from the generalization in (1), *without* reference to these differences.

(7)   '...weil   er   ihr...
       '...because he...

   a. [versprách] [zu versúchen] [zu schwéigen].   *í≺2̌≺3̌*
   b. [versprách] [zu schwéigen zu versuchen].   *í≺3̌≺2̌*
   c. [zu schwéigen zu versuchen versprach.]   *3̌≺2̌≺1*

   be silent try promise
   '...promised her to try to be silent.'

The example (7a) is similar to predicate clusters in Dutch (4), in that main stress is right-most and secondary accents precede the main one. The fact that the median predicate does not necessarily lose its accent rhythmically as in the Dutch example (2) (although it may in fast speech), maybe due to the fact that there is unstressed phonological material—the preposition—intervening, preventing a clash. Remember the similar pattern in the Dutch example in (3), where also a preposition separated two predicates. The prosody in Dutch extraposition constructions is generally equal to that of the German cases. Note also that the facts are equivalent in the relevant constructions in English:[3]

(8)   He wánted to be áble to hélp to succéed.

That Dutch and German indeed do not differ in their prosodic systems is also evidenced by those word orders in predicate clusters that are attested in both languages (Wurmbrand, 2003, for discussion of possible word orders):[4]

(9)   Dutch and German

---

[3]The asymmetry equally holds in other syntactic domains. consider complex nominals. Again, the following constructions obviously differ in their semantics and syntax in various ways, and the compound could be argued to include less functional structure, similar to restructured predicates—the correlation is certainly not accidental. The crucial observation here is that the prosody follows the expected pattern:

(1)   a. [A téacher] [of sláyers] [of vámpires]
       b. A vámpireslayerteacher.

It is certainly possible that the fact that (b) is a called a compound and (a) is not is a factor, or that the fact that the phrases in (a) are full DPs and can be modified plays a role. However, the prosodic asymmetries are also already captured by (1)—so there may be *no need* for phonology to refer to these differences. More discussion of this point follows in the last section.

[4]Here, the DP argument preceding the cluster is made 'given' (old information), in order to prevent subordination of the cluster (see next section)

a. ...dat Ján Maríe*given* kan₁ gezíen₃ hebben₂.
  that Jan Mary   could seen   have

b. ...wéil sie ihn hat₁ málen₃ wollen₂.
  because she him has paint   wanted

In this example, the second predicate 'hebben' is preceded by its complement 'gezien', which effects its subordination. The modal is unstressed, which is unsurprising since it in a position that loses stress via the rhythmic principles that disallow clashes. The next example again illustrates that it is in fact sufficient if a subconstituent from the complement domain precedes.

(10)   Dutch and German

a. ...dat Ján Maríe*given* gezíen₃ kan₁ hebben₂.
  'that Jan could have seen Mary.'

b. ...wéil er es káufen₃ wird₁ können₂.
  because he it buy will can

The distribution of accents so far follows the generalization in (1) plus rhythmic deaccenting. A theory placing accents stricty by XP–alignment would have to posit arbitrary XP–boundaries inside clusters in cases of non-peripheral accents. Consider the following cases of particle climbing:

(11)   Climbing up the Cluster (cf. Evers, 2001, and ref. therein)
       Het labyrinth waar we hem niet over...

a. zul̄len hoeven laten nā́ denken.   1≺2≺3≺5≺4

b. zul̄len hoeven nā́ laten denken.   1≺2≺5≺3≺4

c. nā́ zullen hoeven laten denken.   subordination 5≺1≺2≺3≺4
  about will need let think
  'The labyrinth about which we won't let him reflect.'

The correlation between prosody and syntax in predicate clusters and extraposition constructions was already observed in Bech (1955/57). While the generalization that nuclear stress falls on the most deeply embedded constituent is already predicted based on the approach based on major and minor projection lines in Cinque (1993, 269ff), the asymmetry observed here is not: predicates are subordinated exactly when their complement or a subconstituent from their complement precedes. This generalization appropriately covers the distribution of accents in the constructions discussed here—without reference to $\bar{X}$-status (XP vs. non-XP).

592   Michael Wagner

2.2. Predicates and Nominal Complements

Predicates preceding their complement can receive an accent in English (a). This is also true for DP-complements (b).

(12) a. She wánted to hélp to succéed.

  b. She wánted to hélp to páint the hóuse.

The case of an infinitival complement preceding its selector is unattested in English, but consider DP-complements:

(13) What did she want to change before moving in?
  She wánted to have the wálls painted.

Integration with *subjects* is in generally possible in English, both with unaccusative (a) and unergative (b) verbs[5]. Subordination is also observed when there is more than one predicate (c):

(14) a. [Gasolíne evaporated].

  b. [the déan/a télemarketer called]

  c. [The déan was expected to come.]

Subordination of predicates following arguments can also be observed in Dutch and German when multiple predicates follow an argument.[6]

(15) a. ...dat hij [een múur$_6$ wilde$_1$ mogen$_2$ kùnnen$_3$ helpen$_4$ vèrven$_5$.]
      that he a   wall   want allow can   help   paint
      'he says that he wants to be allowed to be able to help to paint a wall.'

  b. ...wéil er [einen Míxer$_3$ versprach$_1$ zu kaufen$_2$.]
      because he a blender promised to buy

---

[5]It has been reported, however, that unaccusatives tend to phrase with the subjects whereas unergatives don't (Selkirk, 1995; Hoskins, 1996)

[6]At this point, we can look at evidence that the asymmetry outlined in (1) also applies to accentual domains that are pre-nuclear. Consider the case of a complement of a predicate that is not the lowest predicate in a sequence:

(1) a. Sie hat María versprochen zu schwéigen.
      she has mary promised   to be.silent

  b. Sie hat María versprochen zu versúchen/versuchen zu schwéigen.
      she has mary promised   to try/try   to be   silent.

The argument *Maria* is selected by *versprochen* 'promise', which then takes a second argument *zu bleiben* 'to stay'. This example illustrates that indeed only those predicates subordinate that are preceded by an element from its complement domain—not all predicates in a cluster blindly subordinate to a preceding DP argument. The nuclear stress falls on the rightmost accentual phrase, provided by the predicate 'bleiben'. This example illustrates that the distribution of secondary accentual phrases obeys the same principles and shows the same asymmetry. It is not simply guided by rhythmic principles. This is not a rhythmic effect, as is illustrated by (b). While predicates that do get an accent may optionally omit if adjacent to an accent (b, try), 'promise' obligatorily subordinates (a,b) since an argument locally precedes.

Not that the secondary prominence in post-nuclear position has an least severely reduced pitch range. The predicates are distinctly subordinated, nuclear stress is on the object.[7]

As is well known, the subject phrases separately from the verb when it is 'given' in the context. The following context is set up to facilitate wide focus in the embedded clause — but with a backgrounded subject.

(16)   What did you say the dean did?
       I just said that [The déan] [arríved].

Consider the following example:

(17)   Why did they close the factory?
       a.   [The fáctory] [went báckrupt]
       b.   [Gasolíne evaporated].
       c.   [A wórker] [eváporated].

'The factory' is given in (17a) and thus the verb receives main stress. A DP containing new information (as in 17b) shows the normal pattern. 'A worker' in (17c) can be treated as a member of a set inferred from the background (the factory). As in (a), the verb receives an independent accent.[8] Similar asymmetries exist with unergative verbs. In (18b), the subject is again an indefinite that is interpreted as a member of set made salient by the discourse (i.e. a partitive relating to a set in the background).

(18)   Why did they interrupt the play?
       a.   [A chíld was crying].
       b.   [An aćtor] [was crýing].

These prosodic contrasts may point to a structural difference. Consider the case of 'scrambled' vs. 'unscrambled' word order in German. Given or partitive DPs in German undergo scrambling. This may involve adjunction of the scrambled constituent. The prosodic difference follows from this syntactic restructuring. I refer the reader to the discussion of scrambling and focus in Dutch in Neeleman and Reinhart (1998, 343). I will not explore issues relating to focus further at this point.[9]

---

[7]The post-nuclear rhythmic pattern is actually almost the *same* as in German (6) — despite the different order. A detailed investigation of the rhythmic patterns remains to be undertaken.

[8]Also, the unlikelihood of the predicate may play a role. See also discussion of the thetic/categorical distinction in Krifka (1984).

[9]The stage-level, individual-level distinction has also been argued to be relevant Schmerling (1976); Diesing (1992). Individual-level predicates resist subordination, and this may in fact indicate a structural asymmetry as proposed in Kratzer (1989).

(1)   a.   [Your éyes a red].
      b.   [Your éyes] [are blúe].

Again, we may speculate about a higher structural position of subjects relative to the predicates in the case of individual level predicates, which may ultimately explain the prosodic difference.

(19)   a. Er will   das Búch verkáufen.
            he wants the book sell

        b. Er will   das Búch wahrscheinlich verkáufen.
            he wants the book (probably)   sell

The asymmetry relevant here is that in a neutral context, *two* accentual phrases are derived
when the predicate *precedes* the complement—while *one* accentual domain is derived in
cases the predicate *follows* the complement. Relevant data were already noted in Newman
(1946); Bresnan (1971), though only looking at nuclear stress.

(20)   a. He had pláns to leave. (selectee ≺ selector)

        b. He had pláns to léave. (selector ≺ selectee)

The discussion so far contradicts the common assumption that in English the verb phrases
together with a *following* argument, usually the direct object, thus contrasting with Dutch
and German in the directionality of phrasing. One piece of evidence adduced in favor of
this is the application of the rhythm rule, claimed to apply within phonological phrases.

(21)   Evidence for Phrasing Kenesei and Vogel (1995)

        a. ...in English: Rhythm Rule:
            [They mánaged] [to óutclass] [Délaware's cantéen].

        b. ...in German: No Accent on Verb
            [Sie haben Délaware's Kantíne übertroffen].

The application of Rhythm rule presupposes assignment of Accent—however, in Dutch
and German, the verb does not receive an accent due to subordination. The phrasing of a
predicate together with the object in English must be a higher level prosodic domain. It
will leave two adjacent accentual phrases (verb and object) within a single higher prosodic
domain—and thus result in later rhythmic restructuring if there is a clash. Note, finally,
that both Dutch and German show a similar prosody to English when the verb precedes a
direct object:

(22)   Sie tánzte Tángo
        she danced tango

Considering the evidence discussed, it seems that the three languages have a very similar if
not identical mapping from syntax to prosody, and all show the asymmetry outlined in (1).

3. Deriving the Asymmetry

How does the syntax–phonology mapping work? The claim proposed here is that prosody
can be derived using exactly one type of syntactic information: the information of which

of two sister constituents projects,[10], by a recursive mechanism following the transformational cycle in SPE, similar to the proposals in Jacobs (1991, 1992); Cinque (1993); Arregi (2002). Relative prominence will be represented by metrical grids (Liberman, 1975; Libermann and Prince, 1977). The prosodic foot structure imposed on the grid marks prosodic phrasing. I assume a version of the bracketed grid as outlined in Halle and Idsardi (1995). Higher grid marks are introduced by grid mark projection:

(23) Projection: Project all top-line grid-marks of a constituent to a new top grid-line, and foot them.

Projection as proposed here leaves relative prominence within the projected material intact, contrary to projection in the literature on the metrical grid, where only the head of a foot projects. This is a necessary modification of the theory, since the claim is that subordination is only negotiated via syntax.

(24) Examples of Projection

The conventions about what to project when computing the relative prominence between sisters constitutes the phonology-syntax interface. 'Equalize' is a different version of the stress equalization principle proposed in Halle and Vergnaud (1987)[11].

(25) Projection convention for $< \alpha, \beta >$, where α projects:

  a. Equalize if α precedes β: Project α and Project β.

  b. Subordinate if β precedes α : Project β.

The two types of cases that have to be distinguished are the following:

(26) Two Cases

  a. Head Intial Structure   b. Head Final Structure

---

[10]Following (Wagner, 2002), where evidence from phrases, compounds and derivatives is presented. Johnson (2002) posits an asymmetric operation MERGE (essentially, the formation of an ordered pair), argues that focus projection and island conditions can be derived from properties of recursive Merge. This proposal contrasts with Chomsky (2001), who assumes a symmetric operation of set-merge. I assume that the relation between sisters is asymmetrical at least at the interface to phonology.

[11]The reason why I adopt a different version relate to the pre-nuclear rhythmic pattern. The approaches to stress in SPE, Libermann and Prince (1977), and Halle and Vergnaud (1987) are modeled based on the assumption that in the pre-nuclear domain, prominence is declining. In terms of relative prominence: 2 3 4 5 1, whereas the present proposal derives a sequence of equal stresses that are rhythmically organized. The output of the algorithm here is similar to the output of Libermann and Prince (1977) *after stress leveling has applied*. The last or nuclear accent is special in that it is not subject to rhythm, and is followed by a boundary.

To illustrate how this works, consider first a right-branching structure.

(27) versprach zu versuchen zu schweigen
      promised to try   to be.silent

      'promised to try to be silent'

    a. First Step: Create γ
```
      ( ×
   ×  ( × ×
   z u schweig e n
```
    b. Second Step: Create β
```
      (×
   × ×(×  ×
   z u vers u ch e n
```

    c. Third Step: < α, β >
```
      (×            ( ×
      (×            ( ×
   × ×(×  ×   ×  ( × ×
   z u vers u ch e nz u schweig e n
```
    d. Fourth Step: Create γ
```
      ( ×
   ×  (  ×
   versprach
```

    e. Fifth Step: < γ < α, β >>
```
      ( ×        ×            ×
      ( ×        (×           ×
      ( ×        (×       ( ×
   × (  ×  × ×(×   ×   × ( × ×
   versprachzuvers u ch e nz u schweig e n
```

The representation derived has a crucial property: Three accents, i.e. top-level grid marks, are derived, which are essentially on a par. They count as the heads of three accentual domains. There are several lines in the grids that would seem superfluous. Why would the simpler version not suffice?

(28) versprach zu versuchen zu schweigen
      'promised to try   to be silent'
```
      ( ×        (×          ( ×
   × (  ×  × ×(×   ×   × ( × ×
   versprachzuvers u ch e nz u schweig e n
```

When two complex right-branching structures are put together, e.g. in coordination, the need for further structure becomes apparent. Otherwise, the expectation would be a sequence of accents on a par.

(29) Two complex Right-Branching Structures

    'promised to try to be silent and asked to allow to whisper'

```
(  ×        ×              ×        ×    ×        ×
(  ×        ×              ×      ( ×    ×        ×
(  ×       ( ×             ×      ( ×    ×        ×
(  ×       ( ×        (  ×        ( ×  ( ×        ×
×  (  ×  × × ×( ×    ×    ×  (   ×  ( ×  (× × ×(×   ×   ×  (×   ×
versprachzuvers u ch e nz u schw ei genundbatzuerl aub e n z ufl ü stern
```

The additional grouping in (29) is necessary, since the pitch level is reset at the break between the two predicate sequences. Within each predicate sequence downstep between the three accents can be observed. The relative pitch level of the six accents in the structure can be approximated by looking at the left brackets: the highest left bracket in the column represents the relative pitch level. The grouping arises through the brackets that delimit feet at the relevant grid line. Consider now two different linearizations:

(30) *1 ≺ 3 ≺ 2*

versprach zu schweigen zu versuchen
promised to be silent   to try

'promised to try to be.silent'
```
        (  ×      ( ×
        (  ×      ( ×              (×
        ×  (   ×  (×  (   × ×  × ×(×   ×
        versprachz u schw ei g e nz u vers u ch e n
```

The next example illustrates the case of a completely inverted structure.

(31) *3 ≺ 2 ≺ 1*

zu schweigen zu versuchen versprach
to be silent   to try   promised

'to promise to try to be silent
```
        (  ×
        (  ×            (×         ( ×
        (×  (   × ×   × ×(×   × ×( ×
        z u schw ei g e nz u vers u ch e n v ersprach
```

The recursive projection mechanism outlined here derives the corrrect prominence relations between constituents. The foot structure imposed on the grid marks models intuitions about prosodic domains, serves to mark domains for down-stepping and reset, and captures mismatches in constituency between syntax and prosody.

The linear order effect was stipulated here: ultimately, the very mechanism that fixes linear order should be linked to the prosodic differences. One way to conceive of how this works is to view subordination as a syntactic PF-operation of postponement, that is of linearizing a projecting element to the right of the non-projector. Exploring this possibility would go beyond the scope of this paper.

The syntax–phonology interface proposed here transforms the asymmetric relations of syntactic trees into a prosodic representation. It provides a 'diagonalized' representation, in that, similar to the diagonalized representation of a matrix in algebra, it encodes all the relevant information, just in transposed form, facilitating further computation in phonology (rhythm), and making the relevant syntactic information available for parsing.[12]

4. Against XP-Aligment

So far, evidence was presented to argue that the information of projection is sufficient to derive the correct prosody. The theory of XP-alignment presupposes an $\bar{X}$-theory, and predicts a correlation between phrasing and XP-status. In this section I present evidence that there is no such correlation and that the prosodic hierarchy is 'diagonal' (in the sense of 'lying or passing astray', OED) to the assumed $\bar{X}$-hierarchy. First, modifiers often subordinate despite of their XP-status (the prosody of modification is discussed in Wagner (2004)):

(32)   a. Oh no, I léft the ínbox open *yesterday/again*.

     b. María hat getánzt, *den ganzen Abend*.
       Mary has danced, the entire evening

Second, particles (e.g. Toivonen, 2001, argues they are non-projecting X^0) are treated just like XP-objects for NSR, whether or not the verb raises to second position:

(33)   a. She próbably went óut.

     b. Sie gíng wahrscheinlich áus.

     c. Sie íst wahrscheinlich áusgegangen.

Maybe: Particles are stranded inside VP, XP-alignement kicks in although it only contains X^0, thus the edge of VP receives nuclear stress. But: Dutch 'creepers' (11) show the effect of nuclear stress assignment even within the cluster, presumably deep inside of the VP— there is a loss of generalization if one wants to link the accent in (33) to the particle being at the edge of VP, while all prosodic facts follow from the projection approach.

      Third, multiple accents domains *within words* are unexplained under XP-edge marking. Right-branching words show multiple accents (just like right-branching structures involving XPs). Compare:

(34)   Right-branching constituent in NSR position: multiple accents.

     a. He was hóping for her to see Dón in Bóston.

     b. She hóped for it to be nón-prepáckaged.

The prefixes in (34b) can receive an accent. Of course not all prefixes can—but those that form a foot can bear an accent. The accent on 'pre' is deleted for rhythmic reasons[13]

---

[12]Whether or not phonological and syntactic derivations apply cyclically as was suggested in Bierwisch (1968), Bresnan (1971), and Adger (2003) is not apparent from the data discussed here, and requires further research. An obvious alternative to the flattened prosodic representation chosen here would be so say that prosodic structure itself allows recursive constituency, as most recently assumed in Truckenbrodt (1999). This issue will have to remain undiscussed at this point.

[13]Note that the observations on rhythm observed in this paper mirror those observed in Halle and Kenstowicz (1991). This points to a parallel in the way main word stress relates to structure and higher level stress and should be discussed elsewhere.

Derivational Affixes that form a foot are not always allowed to bear an accent—precisely those that are *suffixes* are subordinated[14], as expected based on (1):

(35) fríendshipworthy

Fourth, consider compounds. Again some readjustment according to rhythm takes place. Still, right-branching compounds show multiple accents:

(36) a. She was trýing to pass the láw degree éntry requirements.

  b. She prómised to try to lóok for the Éast Boston Mónthly.

To summarize, there are ample mismatches between XP-boundaries and the distribution of accents. There are XP's that do not line up with accentual domain boundaries, and at the same time there are accentual domain boundaries in the absence of XP-boundaries, namely within predicate clusters, as outlined in the first part of the paper, and also within words and compounds. The unifying factor in all the cases of accentual domain–whether or not they coincide with what one may want to call the edge of an XP–is that they involve right-branching configurations, that is configurations in which the projecting and selecting element is on the left. This follows from the suggested principle of subordination that only uses linear order and the asymmetry of projection.

XP-edge marking/alignment runs into various empirical problems, once a wider array of facts than just accented XPs are considered. It also rests on an unspecified $\bar{X}$-theory. How many different $\bar{X}$-categories for alignment are needed to cover all accent domains, within and above the word level? Are they independently motivated? No extra assumptions are necessary under the projection approach: the pattern above and below the 'word' does not differ (cf. Wagner, 2002, for more examples from derivational morphology and compounding).

5. Conclusion

This paper presented a pattern of prosodic asymmetry, and proposed to compute prosody by recursively looking at the syntactic asymmetries of projection and of linear order, without reference to syntactic categories such as 'XP'-status. Apparent prosodic differences between the three languages reduce to independently motivated syntactic differences.

References

Adger, David. 2003. Phonology and phasal syntax. Paper presented at GLOW.

Arregi, Karlos. 2002. Focus on Basque movement. Doctoral Dissertation, MIT, Cambridge, Ma.

---

[14]This of course does not hold true for so called level-one affixes, which are only not just not subordinated, but they in fact receive main word stress or at least shift them to a closer syllable. I will not discuss their structure here.

Bech, Gunnar. 1955/57. *Studien über das deutsche Verbum Infinitum*. Tübingen: Niemeyer.

Bierwisch, Manfred. 1968. Two cricitcal problems in accent rules. *Linguistics* 4:173–178.

Bresnan, Joan. 1971. On sentence stress and syntactic transformations. In *Contributions to generative phonology*, ed. Michael K. Brame, 73–107. University of Texas Press.

Chen, M. Y. 1987. The sytax of Xiamen tone sandhi. *Phonology Yearbook* 4:109–49.

Chomsky, Noam. 2001. Derivation by phase. In *Ken Hale. a life in language.*, ed. Michael Kenstowicz, 1–52. MIT Press.

Chomsky, Noam, and Morris Halle. 1968. *The sound pattern of English*. New York: Harper & Row.

Cinque, Guglielmo. 1993. A null-theory of phrase and compound stress. *Linguistic Inquiry* 24:239–298.

Diesing, Molly. 1992. *Indefinites*. Cambridge, Ma.: MIT Press.

Evers, Arnold. 2001. Verb clusters and cluster creepers. Utrecht.

Goldsmith, John A., ed. 1995. *The handbook of phonological theory*. London: Blackwell.

Haider, Hubert. 1994. Fakultativ kohärente infinitivkonstruktionen im Deutschen. In *Zur satzwertigkeit von Infinitiven und Small Clauses*, ed. Anita Steube and Gerhild Zybatow. Tübingen: Niemeyer.

Haider, Hubert. 1997. Extraposition. In *Rightward movement*, ed. H. van Riemsdijk D. Beerman, D. LeBlanc, 115–151. John Benjamins.

Halle, Morris, and William Idsardi. 1995. General properties of stress and metrical structure. In Goldsmith (1995), 403–443.

Halle, Morris, and Michael Kenstowicz. 1991. The free element condition and cyclic versus noncyclic stress. *Linguistic Inquiry* 22:457–501.

Halle, Morris, and Jean-Roger Vergnaud. 1987. *An essary on stress*. Cambridge: MIT Press.

Hoskins, Steve. 1996. A phonetic study of focus in instransitive verb sentences. In *Proceedings of the ICSLP 96*.

Jacobs, Joachim. 1991. Focus ambiguities. *Journal of Semantics* 8:1–36.

Jacobs, Joachim. 1992. Neutral stress and the position of heads. In *Informationsstrukur und Grammatik*, ed. Joachim Jacobs, Linguistische Berichte Sonderheft 4, 220–244. Opladen: Westdeutscher Verlag.

Johnson, Kyle. 2002. Towards an etiology of adjunct islands. Umass Amherst.

Kenesei, István, and Irene Vogel. 1995. Focus and phonological structure. University of Szeged, University of Delaware.

Kratzer, Angelika. 1989. Stage-level and individual-level predicates .

Krifka, Manfred. 1984. Fokus, Topik, syntaktische Struktur und semantische Interpretation. Universität Tübingen.

Liberman, M. 1975. The intonational system of English. Doctoral Dissertation, MIT.

Libermann, M., and A. Prince. 1977. On stress and linguistic rhythm. *Linguistic Inquiry* 8:249–336.

Neeleman, Ad, and Tania Reinhart. 1998. Scrambling and the pf interface. In *The projection of arguments*, ed. Miriam Butt and Wilhelm Geuder, 309–353. CSLI.

Newman, S.S. 1946. On the stress system of English. *Word* 2:171–187.

Schmerling, S. F. 1976. *Aspects of English sentence stress*. Austin: University of Texas.

Selkirk, Elizabeth O. 1986. On derived domains in sentence phonology. *Phonology Yearbook* 3:371–405.

Selkirk, Elizabeth O. 1995. Sentence prosody: Intonation, stress, and phrasing. In Goldsmith (1995), 550–569.

Toivonen, Ida. 2001. The phrase structure of non-projecting words. Doctoral Dissertation, Stanford University.

Truckenbrodt, Hubert. 1995. Phonological phrases: Their relation to syntax, focus, and prominence. Doctoral Dissertation, MIT, Cambridge, Mass.

Truckenbrodt, Hubert. 1999. On the relation between syntactic phrases and phonological phrases. *Linguistic Inquiry* 30:219–255.

Wagner, Michael. 2002. Configurational stress in derivatives, compounds, and phrases. Paper presented at the Workshop on Pertinacity, University of Konstanz.

Wagner, Michael. 2004. Asymmetries in prosodic domain formation. To appear in Proceedings of Workshop on Phases, MIT, January 2003.

Wurmbrand, Susi. 2003. Verb-clusters in West-Germanic: The emipirical domain. In *The verb-cluster Sprachbund: Verb clusters in germanic and hungarian*, ed. Katalin É. Kiss and Henk van Riemsdijk. Amsterdam: John Benhamins.

MIT Department of Linguistics and Philosophy
77 Massachusetts Avenue, 32-D962A
Cambridge, MA 02139-4307

chael@mit.edu

Demonstratives, Definiteness and Determined Reference[1]

Lynsey Wolter

University of California, Santa Cruz

1. Introduction

This paper is concerned with three puzzles about English demonstrative descriptions. Addressing these puzzles leads to a new analysis of the English demonstrative determiner *that* and to new considerations about the relation of demonstrative descriptions to other definite noun phrases.

First, even if we limit our attention to demonstrative descriptions (noun phrases with a demonstrative determiner and descriptive content) and to the demonstrative determiner *that*, we find several varieties of demonstrative descriptions. One well-known variety is the *deictic* use, illustrated in (1) below. Deictic demonstratives refer to something in the context of utterance, they are optionally accompanied by an extralinguistic demonstration, and they are the focus of foundational work on demonstratives by Kaplan (1989).

(1)   [Pointing at John] That man is tall.

A second variety of demonstrative description is the *anaphoric* use, illustrated in (2) below. This use is not considered in detail in Kaplan 1989, but it has since been described in other research, notably King 2001 and Roberts 2002.

(2)   A dog$_i$ lives next door. That dog$_i$ likes to howl at fire trucks.

The third variety of demonstrative description that will be considered in this paper is a construction that has previously received little attention in the literature. I'll call it the *explicit demonstrative* construction; it is illustrated below and is characterized by an obligatory postnominal modifier.

---

[1]I am grateful for insightful comments from Donka Farkas, Michela Ippolito, Jim McCloskey, James Isaacs, Line Mikkelsen, and audiences as the UCSC Semantics Reading Group and NELS 2003. Remaining mistakes are mine. The research for this paper was supported by a National Science Foundation Graduate Research Fellowship.

Keir Moulton and Matthew Wolf (eds.): Proceedings of NELS 34,
Stony Brook University: 603 – 617. GLSA, Amherst.

(3)   That hero who kills the dragon will inherit half the kingdom.

I will argue that these varieties of demonstrative descriptions can and should be given a unified treatment, and that the consideration of explicit demonstratives leads to new insights into the interpretation and semantic type of the demonstrative determiner *that*.

The second puzzle is concerned with the scopal properties of demonstrative descriptions. Kaplan 1989 argues that demonstratives are scopally inert, based on examples like (4) and (5) below. Example (4) is false, while example (5) is true for most speakers.

(4)   [Pointing at John throughout] If John and Mary switched places, that person would be a woman.

(5)   [Pointing at John throughout] If John and Mary switched places, the person I'm pointing at would be a woman. (Kaplan 1989; Roberts 2002)

Even though the phrase *that person* can be paraphrased as *the person the speaker is pointing at*, the two phrases don't mean the same thing. The definite description can take narrow scope in this sentence, and the demonstrative appears to be scopally inert, taking widest scope only. This led Kaplan to argue that demonstratives have direct reference: that is, the content of the demonstrative does not play a direct role in the main assertion.

Subsequent research has shown that in some circumstances, demonstrative descriptions *can* take scope under various operators. Representative examples are shown below.

(6)   Every dog in the neighborhood has an owner who thinks that dog is a sweetie. (Roberts 2002)

(7)   Scott is going to pick a number. That number could be odd. (King 2001)

I will argue that different varieties of demonstrative descriptions have different scopal possibilities, and that the scopal possibilities of each variety follow from its interpretation.

In addition to accounting for fine distinctions among demonstratives, an account of demonstrative descriptions should address the similarities and differences between demonstrative descriptions as a whole and other definite noun phrases. The distinction between definite descriptions and demonstrative descriptions is of particular interest, given that both have substantive descriptive content. I will argue that the adoption of the determined reference approach to definiteness (Farkas 2002) leads to new insights into the place of demonstrative descriptions among other definite noun phrases.

Section 2 of the paper considers types of demonstrative and definite descriptions in more detail. The observations in section 2 lead to a preliminary analysis of the demonstrative determiner *that*, presented in section 3. The final section implements the analysis in the determined reference approach to definiteness in order to show the place of demonstrative descriptions among other noun phrases.

2. Types of Demonstrative and Definite Descriptions

2.1 Deictic Descriptions

Demonstrative and definite descriptions can be used to refer to something in the context of utterance. For example, (8-a)–(8-b) below are felicitous if the context contains a cat:

(8)   a.   The cat is purring.
        b.   That cat is purring.

The conditions on the deictic use of these expressions are not identical. Example (8-b) is felicitous in a context containing more than one cat. Example (8-a) is not felicitous in a neutral context containing more than one cat, and the standard wisdom (following Russell 1905) is that a definite description requires a unique referent in the context. On the other hand, (8-a) is acceptable if additional information from the context allows the identification of a unique referent: for example, if one cat is more salient than the others or belongs to the speaker. (The relevant pragmatic factors have been described by Löbner 1985, Hawkins 1991 and von Heusinger 1997a,b.)

In a context containing a single most prominent cat, the subject of (8-b) may refer to that most prominent cat, and no demonstration is required. However, provided that the demonstrative in (8-b) is accompanied by an appropriate demonstration, that is, an extralinguistic act that allows the interpreter to identify a unique referent, it can equally well refer to a cat that was not previously "salient" in any sense. Demonstrative descriptions thus refer uniquely, but their referent is not determined by descriptive content alone or even by the descriptive content supplemented by pre-existing pragmatic factors.

Deictic descriptions, whether definite or demonstrative, have widest scope only. In (9) below, if the definite and demonstrative descriptions are taken to be anaphoric to *every dog in my neighborhood*, then they have narrow scope under the universal quantifier. If the descriptions are taken to be deictic, then they have wide scope. In (10) below, the demonstrative description is accompanied by a demonstration to force a deictic interpretation.

(9)   Every dog in my neighborhood has an owner who thinks the/that dog is a sweetie.

(10)   Every dog in my neighborhood has an owner who thinks that dog [pointing at Fido] is a sweetie.

Since definite descriptions are not accompanied by demonstrations, a deictic use of a definite description is harder to force, but the deictic reading is possible for the definite description in (9) if there is a salient dog in the context, such as the speaker's dog. On the deictic reading, the definite description has wide scope.

The conventional wisdom that definite and demonstrative descriptions always take wide scope with respect to negation has been challenged by King (2001), who argues that deictic demonstratives can take narrow scope under negation. This position is based on examples like (11) below, which he argues can be used to correct a mistaken belief.

(11)   [pointing at a jewel] That diamond isn't real. (p. 107)

Example (11) is said to be possible in a situation in which the speaker is trying to correct the addressee's false belief that a piece of cubic zirconium is a diamond. Notice, however, that the examples in (12) below can also be used to correct the same mistaken belief:

(12)   a.   That diamond is cubic zirconium.
        b.   That diamond isn't a diamond.

It seems that in (11)–(12), the speaker "plays along" with the false belief that the demonstratum is a diamond in order to identify the referent, then goes on to contest that false belief. Something special is happening – but it doesn't require the demonstrative to be in the scope of negation. The other examples that King provides have an equally ironic feel. I will assume that the conventional wisdom is correct in this case: deictic definite and demonstrative descriptions cannot take narrow scope under negation.

Though the conventional wisdom following Kaplan 1989 is that deictic demonstrative descriptions are scopally inert, this has been challenged in two cases besides the examples with negation: King (2001) argues that deictic demonstratives can take narrow scope under attitude verbs, and Roberts (2002) argues that deictic demonstratives can take scope under (epistemic) modals. Let's take a look at each of these claims in turn.

King (2001) argues that deictic demonstratives can occur in the scope of attitude verbs. Here is a representative example. Suppose that Sherry, who works for Chanticleer toy company, believes that Alan has been elected CEO of Chanticleer. Sherry also believes that Alan dislikes her, and she's unhappy about having Alan as her boss. Under these circumstances, one can point at Alan and say:

(13)   Sherry believes that that man who was just elected CEO of Chanticleer hates her.[2]

However (*pace* King), this sentence can only be used if the speaker believes that Alan has been elected CEO. If Sherry's belief is false, and the speaker knows that Alan has not been elected CEO, (13) is infelicitous. The demonstrative cannot have narrow scope here.

Example (14) below, which Roberts (2002) attributes to Heim, is argued to be a case of a deictic demonstrative in the scope of a modal. This example is uttered in a room containing two panels that are either mirrors or windows, but the speaker isn't sure which. Each panel displays an identical chair. It is not clear whether we are viewing two chairs behind separate panes of glass or multiple reflections of one chair, and we can say:

(14)   That (chair) [pointing to the left panel] could well be that (chair) [pointing to the right panel].

If (14) is not to be trivially true or trivially false, the demonstratives must have narrow scope under the modal. However, it's important to recognize that (14) is interpreted with epistemic modality, and epistemic modals can take wide scope with respect to anything, even proper names. Names in standard examples of modalized identity statements,

---

[2]This example, and many of King's other examples of demonstratives with narrow scope, is acceptable if it is interpreted as an explicit demonstrative. My claims in this section are about the *deictic* reading of examples that King takes to be deictic. One way to force a deictic reading is to consider the examples when they are accompanied by an extralinguistic demonstration.

such as *Hesperus might be Phosphorus*, take narrow scope under epistemic modals just like the demonstratives in (14). Sentences like (14) do not allow us to conclude anything about the interaction of deictic demonstratives with other types of modals.

In fact, deictic demonstratives do not take narrow scope under metaphysical modals. Suppose that Mary has just pulled a scarf at random out of a drawer. Mary pulled out a red scarf, but she could just as well have taken a blue one. This situation can be described as in (15) below, where the definite description takes narrow scope under a metaphysical modal. Example (16) can only mean that a particular red scarf could have been a different color; the referent of *that scarf* does not vary across worlds.

(15)   Mary actually pulled out a red scarf, but the scarf could have been blue.

(16)   Mary actually pulled out a red scarf, but that scarf [pointing] could have been blue.

The conclusion that deictic demonstrative and definite descriptions have wide scope is not a surprising one. Scope-taking operators induce variation, and the hallmark of a noun phrase with narrow scope is that its referent varies along with some parameter. If the referent of a noun phrase is fixed as an entity in the context, then we certainly do not expect to find the referent of that noun phrase varying.

2.2   Anaphoric Descriptions

Demonstrative and definite descriptions can be used as anaphors, as shown below.

(17)   A woman$_i$ entered from stage left. The/that woman$_i$ was carrying flowers.

Here, again, definite descriptions and demonstrative descriptions are subject to slightly different conditions. Roberts (2002) observes that, when there are two equally likely potential antecedents, an anaphoric definite description is unacceptable, while a demonstrative description (or a pronoun) refers to the most recently mentioned potential antecedent.

(18)   A woman$_i$ entered from stage left. Another woman$_j$ entered from stage right.

    a.   #The woman/That woman$_j$/She$_j$ was carrying a basket of flowers.

As we saw with the deictic use, in a bland context an anaphoric definite description is acceptable just when there is exactly one potential antecedent. And as before, if we enrich the context enough to make one potential antecedent more salient than the others, we can use an anaphoric definite description even when there appears to be more than one potential antecedent. Below, the last occurrence of *the cat* refers to the cat in New Zealand, who has been made more salient by the preceding text than the cat in the context of utterance.

(19)   [A cat is running around the room.]
    The cat is in the carton. The cat will never meet our other cat, because our other cat lives in New Zealand. Our New Zealand cat lives with the Cresswells. And there he'll stay, because Miriam would be sad if the cat went away. (Lewis 1979)

Abbott (2002) makes similar observations about definite and demonstrative paraphrases of donkey pronouns, such as (20) below. Donkey pronouns and their paraphrases are anaphoric definites whose antecedents happen to be interpreted as bound variables.

(20)   Every farmer who owns a donkey feeds the/that donkey.

Definite descriptions are not perfect paraphrases of donkey pronouns. When there is more than one potential referent for a definite in a relevant situation, definite descriptions are less acceptable than donkey pronouns, as shown by these well-known examples, the latter of which Abbott attributes to Elbourne:

(21)   a.   Everybody who bought a sageplant here bought 8 others along with it.
        b.   ?Everybody who bought a sageplant here bought 8 others along with the sage-
              plant. (Heim 1982)

(22)   a.   Whenever a bishop meets another bishop, he blesses him.
        b.   ?Whenever a bishop meets another bishop, the bishop blesses the bishop.

Abbott observes that a demonstrative description can paraphrase the pronoun in the sage-plant example, although not in the bishop example:

(23)   Everybody who bought a sageplant here bought 8 others along with that sageplant.

(24)   ?Whenever a bishop meets another bishop, that bishop blesses that bishop.

Intuitively speaking, the unique referent of a definite description is identified based on its descriptive content, and the descriptive content in these examples is not enough to identify a unique referent. The referent of a demonstrative description is identified by an extra factor, namely contextual salience. In the sageplant example, one sageplant is already salient, namely the one that was used to verify the truth of the relative clause. In the bishop example, neither bishop is more salient than the other. What this suggests, then, is that salience plays a central role in identifying the referent of a demonstrative description. Earlier, we saw that a notion of salience might be one of the pragmatic factors used to license a definite description. These examples show that salience plays a more central role for demonstrative descriptions than for definite descriptions.

As we saw with the deictic use, anaphoric demonstrative and definite descriptions refer uniquely, but the referent is determined in different ways. The referent of a definite description is the unique entity that satisfies the descriptive content, possibly enriched with pragmatic factors. Salience per se does not appear to be decisive factor in the identification of the unique referent of a definite description, although it may play a supporting role. Deictic and anaphoric demonstratives refer uniquely, but their referent is not identified on the basis of the descriptive content alone. We saw that a deictic demonstrative can refer to something that is demonstrated by the speaker or to something that is already salient in the context of utterance, while anaphoric demonstratives corefer with a salient antecedent.

If we assume that the function of a demonstration is to make an entity salient, then the referent of a deictic demonstrative must be a salient element of the context. This descriptive generalization can be extended to anaphoric demonstratives as well. Roberts (2002) suggests that anaphoric demonstratives should be viewed as an extension of deictic demonstratives; anaphoric demonstratives are "deictic" in the sense that they refer to something in the linguistic context rather than something in the physical context. Since it's not possible to literally point at an element of previous discourse, we won't find demonstrations accompanying anaphoric demonstratives. Therefore, the referent of an anaphoric demonstrative, unlike the referent of a deictic demonstrative, must be salient in the context prior to the utterance of the demonstrative description.

The scope of an anaphoric definite or demonstrative description is the scope of its antecedent. In (25)–(28) below, the antecedent of each anaphoric definite has narrow scope under an operator on the most plausible reading. Each anaphoric definite has narrow scope under the same operator. Examples (27)–(28) below involve modal subordination, a phenomenon in which a modal or attitude verb allows a sentence to be interpreted as if it were in the scope of a modal or attitude verb in the previous sentence. (See Roberts 1996 for discussion.) The phenomenon makes it easy to construct examples in which an anaphoric noun phrase and its antecedent are interpreted in the scope of the same operator.

(25)   The grant review board didn't return any proposal to the/that proposal's author.

(26)   Every dog in the neighborhood, even the meanest, has an owner who thinks the/that dog is a sweetie. (Roberts 2002)

(27)   Scott will pick a number. The/that number Scott picks could be odd. (King 2001)

(28)   Mary believes that a unicorn is in her garden. She believes that the/that unicorn is ruining her lawn.

If the antecedent of an anaphoric definite has wide scope, then the anaphoric definite also takes wide scope, as shown below.

(29)   A dog down the street barks a lot. Every cat in the neighborhood is afraid of the/that dog.

(30)   There is a unicorn in the yard. Mary believes the/that unicorn is ruining her lawn.

The conclusion that anaphoric definites have the scope of their antecedents is no more surprising than the conclusion that deictic demonstratives have widest scope. The referent of an anaphoric noun phrase depends on the referent of the antecedent; if the referent of the antecedent varies, so will the anaphoric noun phrase.

2.3   Semantically Unique Definite Descriptions

Some definite descriptions have descriptive content that determines a unique referent independently of any context. These definite descriptions, which Löbner (1985) calls *semantically unique*, include descriptions like *the smallest prime number*, *the center of the Solar System*, and *the mother of John Smith*. Semantically unique, nonanaphoric definite descriptions can take narrow scope under anything except negation.

(31)   a.   John didn't meet the governor of California.
        b.   John didn't meet a gubernatorial candidate.

(32)   Every dog in the neighborhood sleeps in the sunniest room in its house.

(33)   The next president of the United States could be from New England.

(34)   John believes that the king of France is bald.

One of the more interesting properties of semantically unique descriptions is that they seem to *require* definite determiners: out of context, indefinite and demonstrative determiners are unacceptable, as shown below. In other words, indefinite and demonstrative descriptions appear to be subject to a *non*uniqueness condition — their descriptive content must hold of more than one individual.

(35)   *a/that {smallest prime number, center of the Solar System, mother of John Smith}

Given the right contextual support, however, it turns out that semantically unique indefinite and demonstrative descriptions are sometimes acceptable. Hawkins (1991) observes that indefinite descriptions whose descriptive content determines a unique referent independently of the context are acceptable with a set of predicates including the *be* in existentials. For example, B's response below is grammatical, if mathematically naive.

(36)   A: There is no longest number in arithmetic.
        B: Oh, I don't know. I'm pretty sure that there is a longest number in arithmetic.
            (Hawkins 1991:435)

Hawkins concludes that the "nonuniqueness" condition on indefinite descriptions is a conversational implicature, since it can be canceled.
        Semantically unique demonstrative descriptions are possible with a special emotive use that Lakoff (1974) names "emotional deixis." Lakoff observes that some uses of demonstratives are strongly emotive; she argues that they express "emotional solidarity" between the speaker and addressee. For example, (37)–(38) suggest that the speaker and the addressee feel the same way about Kissinger. This use of the demonstrative doesn't appear to convey any particular feeling about Kissinger himself. Incidentally, it's also interesting that the emotive use of the demonstrative can occur with a proper name.

(37)   That Henry Kissinger sure is a great guy!

(38)   That Henry Kissinger sure is a crook!

2.4   Explicit Demonstratives

The construction that I will call the *explicit demonstrative* construction is illustrated below. It is found in formal registers, and consists of *that* (or *those*) followed by an NP complement, and a PP or CP in a separate intonational phrase. Below, capitals indicate accent and brackets indicate intonational phrases.

(39)   [THAT hero] [who KILLS the dragon] [will INHERIT half the kingdom.]

(40)   [THAT runner] [who comes in LAST] [will RECEIVE a consolation prize.]

The postnominal phrase is required in the construction. When the postnominal PP or CP is missing, as below, the phrase can only be interpreted as a standard demonstrative. Note that (41) below can only be used if there is another last runner who will not receive a consolation prize. No such requirement holds of (40) above.

(41)   That last runner will receive a consolation prize.

The construction is incompatible with canonical demonstrations. For example, (39) cannot be uttered while pointing at Sir George; this is perhaps not too surprising here, given that the explicit demonstrative is in the scope of a future modal, as shown by the simple present tense marking in the relative clause.

(42)   #(Pointing at Sir George)
        [THAT hero] [who KILLS the dragon] [will inHERit half the kingdom.]

Note, however, that explicit demonstratives can be used when the referent is known to the speaker, as shown below; explicit demonstratives do not require a modal context.

(43)   [THAT teacher of John's] [who had the GREATest impact on his life] (namely Mary Jones) was featured in his autobiography.

Even though modality is not required, (39)–(40) are interesting, because they show that explicit demonstratives can take scope under modals much more easily than standard demonstratives. Explicit demonstratives can also take narrow scope under a matrix past tense, as shown by the use of *would* in (44) below. This option is not available for deictic demonstratives, as shown in (45). The fact that explicit demonstratives but not deictic demonstratives show sequence-of-tense phenomena is a useful diagnostic for telling them apart.

(44)   [THAT teacher] [who would TEACH John in fifth grade] was hired in 1942.

(45)   #(Pointing at Mary Smith)
        [THAT teacher] [who would TEACH John in fifth grade] was hired in 1942.

At first glance, the explicit demonstrative construction looks quite similar to the "he-who" construction consisting of a pronoun followed by a relative clause. Both constructions appear to contain a DP followed by a CP, both occur in formal registers, and both have roughly the same interpretation. The two constructions are not quite identical, however, as evidenced by the contrast below.

(46)   He who eats an apple a day will live a long healthy life.

(47)   ?[THAT man] [who eats an APple a day] will live a long healthy life.

The explicit demonstrative construction has the same scopal possibilities as semantically unique definite descriptions. Explicit demonstratives cannot occur in the scope of negation, but we've seen that they easily occur in the scope of modals. Examples of explicit demonstratives in the scope of quantifiers and attitude verbs are given below.

(48)   Every student worked on [THAT problem] [which interested her MOST.]

(49)	Mary believes that [THAT unicorn] [with the LONGest horn] is digging up her lawn.

The explicit demonstrative construction has semantically unique descriptive content, but in a special way. While the descriptive content as a whole determines a unique referent, independently of the context of utterance, the NP alone must not. Semantically unique definite descriptions, on the other hand, do not necessarily have a subconstituent that is satisfied by more than one entity.

## 3.	The Interpretation of the Demonstrative Determiner

We have seen that the descriptive content alone does not serve to identify the referent of a demonstrative description, but that demonstrative descriptions nevertheless refer uniquely. We need to capture the extra factor that identifies the referent. The most straightforward assumption is that demonstrative determiners have two arguments: the NP complement, which contributes a domain, and a second argument, which identifies the unique referent within the domain.

The idea that a demonstrative determiner has one more argument than we might expect is not new. King (2001) argues that demonstrative descriptions are interpreted as generalized quantifiers once one or more extra arguments have been saturated. According to Roberts (2002), the representation of a demonstrative contains a familiar "demonstration." Even Kaplan (1989) suggests that demonstratives are "completed" by a demonstration, though he equivocates about the place of this in the analysis.

What is the nature of the second argument of a demonstrative determiner? Kaplan and Roberts link this second argument to a demonstration. In the case of deictic demonstratives accompanied by a demonstration, it makes sense to think of the the second argument as something that is literally supplied by an extralinguistic act. For other demonstratives, of course, the "demonstration" must be something more abstract. King identifies the second argument with a speaker intention to refer.

If explicit demonstratives and standard demonstrative descriptions are given a unified treatment, the view of the demonstrative determiner's second argument changes. In the explicit demonstrative construction, the second argument of the determiner is the postnominal phrase, which contributes a property. The demonstrative determiner in the explicit demonstrative construction therefore appears to denote a function from two properties to entities. (That is, it's of type $\langle\langle et\rangle, \langle\langle et\rangle, e\rangle\rangle$.) The NP complement contributes the first property and the postnominal phrase contributes the second property; the function returns the unique entity from the set denoted by the first property that has the second property. In other words, a demonstrative determiner finds the intersection of two sets and presupposes that the intersection will be a singleton set. It does something more complicated than the definite determiner, which takes only one property as an argument.

I have argued that the relevant extra factor for deictic and anaphoric demonstratives is contextual salience, and this suggests the implicit second argument of a deictic or anaphoric demonstrative is the property of being identical to a salient element of the context. If all we say about the second argument of a demonstrative is that it is a property, we'd expect to find other properties being used as well — any property that identifies a unique referent given the context and domain should do. But if this were the case, there would be no way for the interpreter to recover what property was meant to fill the second argument position of a deictic or anaphoric demonstrative. The limitation of properties that actually are available to a single property having to do with contextual salience shows us that when the second argument of a demonstrative determiner is implicit, it must be given.

The semantic type that I have proposed for the demonstrative determiner allows us to explain why demonstrative descriptions are similar both to uncontroversially quantificational noun phrases and to uncontroversially referring expressions. In the present analysis, demonstrative descriptions are referring expressions: ultimately, they contribute an entity to the semantics. Since demonstrative descriptions are referring expressions, we expect them to have the logical properties of referring expressions discussed by Löbner (1985) and to form a natural class with pronominal ("simple") demonstratives. We correctly predict that demonstrative descriptions are not as free to participate in scope ambiguities as uncontroversially quantificational noun phrases like *every dog*.

On the other hand, on the current proposal demonstrative descriptions are not directly referential. The account predicts that demonstrative descriptions will be able to take narrow scope, not freely, but just when they contain a subconstituent that depends on an operator or bound variable. Deictic demonstratives take widest scope because their content does not depend on operators or bound variables. Anaphoric demonstratives take narrow scope just when their second argument (the property of having the same value as the value of a salient discourse referent) depends on a discourse referent that varies. Explicit demonstratives take narrow scope when some part of the postnominal modifier depends on an operator or bound variable. The scope facts thus support the claim that demonstrative descriptions contribute their descriptive content to the semantics.

We are in a position to begin to explain what demonstrative and definite descriptions have in common and how they differ. Assuming a standard treatment of the demonstrative determiner as type $\langle\langle et\rangle, e\rangle$, definite and demonstrative descriptions are both referring expressions with substantive descriptive content. Both are subject to a uniqueness condition based on their *entire* content; the fact that the unique referent of a demonstrative description is not identified on the basis of the NP complement alone reflects the fact that the NP complement is not the entire content of a demonstrative description.

To characterize the difference between demonstrative and definite descriptions more precisely, and to account for their scopal possibilities, we need make some more concrete assumptions about the treatment of definiteness. In the next section, I adopt the "determined reference" approach to definiteness (Farkas 2002) and extend it to demonstratives. The determined reference approach allows for a very natural statement of the analysis I have suggested here. Furthermore, the approach already accounts for definite noun phrases in English other than demonstratives. If the approach can be extended to demonstrative descriptions, we'll have a complete picture of the range of definite noun phrases found in English. Note, however, that the analysis could be translated into other frameworks.

4.   Determined Reference and Demonstratives

The central claim of the determined reference approach is that the variable contributed by any definite noun phrase has determined reference. The definition of determined reference is given below. A variable has determined reference if, when an input assignment function is extended to that variable, there is no choice about the value of the variable. The variable associated with a semantically unique description will have determined reference because there is only one entity in the model that satisfies the descriptive content. The variable associated with an anaphoric noun phrase will have determined reference because, given an assignment function that is defined for the antecedent, there will be no choice about the value that function assigns to the variable associated with the anaphoric noun phrase.

(50)   Let K' be the DRS obtained by merging the input DRS K with the DRS K_e, and let x be in the universe of K_e but not in that of K.
The variable x has determined reference iff for every f that embeds K, it holds for every f', f'' that extend f and which satisfy the conditions in K_e, $f'(x) = f''(x)$.

Note that the definition assumes a version of Discourse Representation Theory (DRT) in which noun phrases are first translated into separate preliminary Discourse Representation Structures (DRSs), then merged one at a time with the input DRS. For discussion of this framework, see van der Sandt 1992, Kamp et al. forthcoming.

The variables associated with some definite noun phrases have determined reference in virtue of the conditions that the noun phrases contribute, while the variables associated with other noun phrases have determined reference only with contextual support. Names and pronouns have inherently determined reference, that is, their variables have determined reference regardless of the state of the input context. For example, pronouns are always anaphoric, as shown by the representation of a pronoun below.

(51)   *it*

x
$x = y$

Definite descriptions, unlike names and pronouns, do not have inherently determined reference. Whether the variable associated with a definite description has determined reference depends in part on the descriptive content and in part on the context. If the descriptive content happens to denote a singleton set, then the variable will have determined reference. Descriptive content like *cat* does not guarantee determined reference. The variable associated with a condition like *cat(x)* will have determined reference if the context provides enough additional information to fix its value. Relevant contextual support consists of information about anaphoric links and about pragmatic factors like salience and relevance. For example, an anaphoric definite description will have an additional condition, $x = y$, representing the anaphoric link.[3] The variable x will then have determined reference for the same reason that the variable associated with a pronoun does.

The representation of a definite description is shown in (52) below. The definite de-

---

[3] See Umbach (2002) for discussion of anaphoric definites in this framework.

terminer contributes a distinguishing mark on the associated variable, and variables marked with exclamation points are required to have determined reference. In essence, determined reference is a presupposition contributed by the definite determiner.

(52)   *the cat*

$x!$
$cat(x)$

   In the last section I proposed that a demonstrative determiner is interpreted as a function that takes two properties and returns the unique element of the set denoted by the first property that has the second property. In DRT terms, this is a claim that a demonstrative determiner contributes the following function:

(53) $x = \text{Intended-Referent}(P_1, P_2)$
   a. P_1: property contributed by the NP complement
   b. P_2: property contributed by the second argument of the demonstrative
   c.   *Intended-Referent*: a function from properties P_1 and P_2 to entities that returns the unique entity in $P_1 \cap P_2$.

(54)   *that cat*

x
$x = \text{Intended-Referent}(cat, P)$

The name of the Intended-Referent function is arbitrary. It's merely a reminder that the choice of referent of a demonstrative description is commonly thought to have something to do with a speaker intention to refer. It's important, however, that the function is a function, not merely the operation of set intersection, so that the demonstrative will refer uniquely.

   Nothing further needs to be said about the scope facts — they follow from standard assumptions about DRT and from the determined reference approach. Deictic demonstratives will have widest scope simply because they are deictic. If the variable contributed by a demonstrative is equated with an entity in the context of utterance, there will be no room for variation. Anaphoric demonstratives will have the same scope as their antecedents. If the the variable contributed by a demonstrative is required to take the value assigned to its antecedent, then the value of the variable contributed by the demonstrative will vary when its antecedent does, and at no other time. Finally, the scopal possibilities of explicit demonstratives, as well as the scopal possibilities of semantically unique definite descriptions, fall out of the determined reference condition. The generalization was that these descriptions cannot take narrow scope under negation, but freely take narrow scope under other operators. Farkas (2002) shows that the determined reference condition can be satisfied if a variable depends on a parameter introduced by a quantifier or other operator; negation induces variation without introducing specific parameters that vary, and this sort of variation is incompatible with determined reference.

   Demonstrative descriptions are like definite descriptions in that their reference depends on substantive descriptive content. But they are like names and pronouns in that they have inherently determined reference. The condition in (53) guarantees that the associated variable will have determined reference, because the *Intended-Referent* function is a function: once the properties are supplied, there will be only one choice of value for x.

In the picture of definite noun phrases that emerges from the determined reference approach, at least two subdivisions can be made within the class of definites. One distinction can be made between demonstrative and definite descriptions, which have descriptive content, and names and pronouns, which do not. Because descriptive content can contain elements that are dependent on other parts of the sentence, having descriptive content (or not) will affect scopal possibilities. The second distinction is between names, pronouns and demonstrative descriptions, which have inherently determined reference, and definite descriptions, which do not. This is a less obvious way to divide up the class of definites, and it is one that we might not have reached without the determined reference framework.

The latter subdivision in the class of definites can help us understand the crosslinguistic distribution of definite noun phrases. Definite noun phrases with inherently determined reference are found in all languages, while definite descriptions are not. This is not arbitrary. The definite determiner contributes only the determined reference condition to the semantic representation, while names, pronouns and demonstrative descriptions contribute something more. Whether a variable has determined reference is always recoverable from the context and the rest of the representation of the noun phrase. So, strictly speaking, a morphosyntactic marker of determined reference is redundant, and it's not surprising that some languages do without it. The extra contributions of names, pronouns, and demonstrative descriptions are not recoverable from the state of the context, so we expect to find that all languages have these types of definite noun phrases.

If the definite determiner marks determined reference, and all definites have determined reference, then there is no semantic reason that the definite determiner should not be used with definite noun phrases other than definite descriptions. This is exactly what we find— for example, definite articles cooccur with demonstratives in Romanian and with demonstratives and names in Modern Greek (Giusti 1997). These observations suggest that the analysis of the English demonstrative determiner *that* presented in this paper is relevant to the crosslinguistic semantics of definite noun phrases.

References

Abbott, Barbara. 2002. Donkey Demonstratives. *Natural Language Semantics* 10:285–298.
Farkas, Donka. 2002. Specificity Distinctions. *Journal of Semantics* 19:1–31.
Giusti, Giuliana. 1997. The Categorial Status of Determiners. In Liliane Haegeman, ed., *The New Comparative Syntax*. New York: Longman.
Hawkins, John A.. 1991. On (In)definite Articles: Implicatures and (Un)grammaticality Prediction. *Journal of Linguistics* 27:405–422.
Heim, Irene. 1982. *The Semantics of Definite and Indefinite Noun Phrases*. Ph.D. thesis, UMass-Amherst.
von Heusinger, Klaus. 1997a. Definite Descriptions and Choice Functions. In S. Akama, ed., *Logic, Language and Computation*, 61–91. Dordrecht: Kluwer.
von Heusinger, Klaus. 1997b. Salience and Definiteness. *The Prague Bulletin of Mathematical Linguistics* 67:5–23.

Kamp, Hans, Josef van Genabith, and Uwe Reyle. forthcoming. Discourse Representation Theory. In Dov M. Gabbay and F. Guenthner, eds., *Handbook of Philosophical Logic*. Dordrecht: Kluwer, 2nd edn. Draft at <http://www.ims.uni-stuttgart.de/~hans>.

Kaplan, David. 1989. Demonstratives. In J. Perry J. Almong and H. Wettstein, eds., *Themes from Kaplan*, 408–565. Oxford: Oxford University Press.

King, Jeffrey C.. 2001. *Complex Demonstratives*. Cambridge, MA: MIT Press.

Lakoff, Robin. 1974. Remarks on *This* and *That*. *CLS* 10:345–356.

Lewis, David. 1979. Score-keeping in a Language Game. In Rainer Bäurle, Urs Egli, and Arnim von Stechow, eds., *Semantics from Different Points fo View*. Springer-Verlag.

Löbner, Sebastian. 1985. Definites. *Journal of Semantics* 4:279–326.

Roberts, Craige. 1996. Anaphora in Intensional Contexts. In Shalom Lappin, ed., *The Handbook of Contemporary Semantic Theory*, 215–247. Oxford: Blackwell.

Roberts, Craige. 2002. Demonstratives as Definites. In Kees van Deemter and Roger Kibble, eds., *Information Sharing*. Stanford, CA: CSLI.

Russell, Bertrand. 1905. On Denoting. *Mind* 14:479–493. Reprinted in A. P. Martinich, ed. (2001). *The Philsophy of Language*. Oxford: Oxford UP.

van der Sandt, Rob A.. 1992. Presupposition Projection as Anaphoric Resolution. *Journal of Semantics* 9:333–377.

Umbach, Carla. 2002. (De)accenting Definite Descriptions. *Theoretical Linguistics* 27:251–280.

Department of Linguistics
University of California
Santa Cruz, CA 95064

lwolter@ucsc.edu

Reduplication in English Homeric Infixation

Alan C. L. Yu

University of Chicago

1.   Introduction

In the Base-Reduplicant Correspondence Theory (BRCT: McCarthy & Prince 1995) reduplication is induced by the presence of an abstract RED morpheme. The surface manifestation of this abstract RED morpheme is regulated by a set of faithfulness constraints (e.g., B(ase)-R(eduplicant) faithfulness, BR-anchoring etc.). However, recent work has suggested that purely phonologically-driven reduplication is also possible, that is, reduplication that has no semantic import (Kawahara 2001; Inkelas in press; Inkelas & Zoll 2000, Yu 2003, Zuraw 2002). I call such cases of non-morphological reduplication *Compensatory Reduplication*.[1] In this paper, I argue for one such case of Compensatory Reduplication (CR), triggered by the Homeric infix in English. A novel theory of CR is advanced, which derives CR through the interaction between constraints on faithfulness and surface segmental correspondence within Optimality Theory, without resorting to stipulating the existence of parochial constraints in the grammar that induce reduplication by brute force (i.e. Zuraw 2002). Section 1 describes the phenomenon of the Homeric infix in English. I introduce the issue of CR in section 2, arguing that the Homeric infix is a genuine infix and that CR is derivative of the conflicting demands imposed by the bidirectional subcategorization of this infix. In the course of the discussion, an analysis of the Homeric infix is presented. Section 4 focuses on the proper treatment of CR. I propose an emergent approach to CR where CR falls out naturally as the result of the interaction between constraints on segmental faithfulness and the correspondence of similar segments. Section 5 summarizes the findings of this study and offers some preliminary thoughts on a general theory of CR.

---

[1] I refrained from using the term 'phonological reduplication' since its interpretation differs depending on the framework of reduplication under discussion. Thus, the term 'compensatory reduplication' is designed to be theory-neutral.

© 2003 Alan C. L. Yu
Keir Moulton and Matthew Wolf (eds.): Proceedings of NELS 34,
Stony Brook University: 619 – 633. GLSA, Amherst.

2.   English Homeric infixation: The basic pattern[2]

Homeric infixation is a morphological construction that has recently gained currency in Vernacular American English. People who are familiar with this construction invariably credit the TV animation series, *The Simpsons*, particularly the speech of the main character Homer Simpson, for popularizing this construction. The basic pattern is best illustrated with words with stress on odd-numbered syllables. In words which bear input stress on the 1st and 3rd syllables only, the infix, *-ma-*, invariably appears after the unstressed second syllable, whether the main stress is on the first (1)a & b or the third syllable (1)c & d.

(1)   a.   ˈσσˌσ   ˈσσ-ma-ˌσ   c.   ˌσσˈσσ   ˌσσ-ma-ˈσσ
              saxophone   saxo-ma-phone   Mississippi   Missi-ma-ssippi
              telephone   tele-ma-phone   Alabama   Ala-ma-bama
              wonderful   wonder-ma-ful   dialectic   dia-ma-lectic
       b.   ˈσσˌσσ   ˈσσ-ma-ˌσσ   d.   ˌσσˈσσσ   ˌσσ-ma-ˈσσσ
              feudalism   feuda-ma-lism   hippopotamus   hippo-ma-potamus
              secretary   secre-ma-tary   hypothermia   hypo-ma-thermia
              territory   terri-ma-tory   Michaelangelo   Micha-ma-langelo

In odd-stressed words which are long enough to have stress on the 1st, 3rd and 5th syllables, infix placement varies; the infix can follow either the 2nd syllable or the 4th syllable. *-Ma-* may appear two trochaic feet away from the left edge of the word (see (2)a, & (2)c) also. Words with essentially the same syllable count and stress pattern, nonetheless, may have different infixation patterns (e.g., (2)a vs. (2)b).

(2)   a.   (ˌσσ)(ˈσσ)(ˌσ)   (ˌσσ)(ˈσσ)-ma-(ˌσ)[3]
              underestimate   underesti-ma-mate
       b.   (ˌσσ)(ˈσσ)(ˌσσ)   (ˌσσ)-ma-(ˈσσ)(ˌσσ)
              unsubstantiated   unsub-ma-stantiated
       c.   (ˌσσ)(ˌσσ)(ˈσσ)   (ˌσσ)(ˌσσ)-ma-(ˈσσ)
              onomatopoeia   onomato-ma-poeia

This distribution suggests that *-ma-* prefers to appear to the right of a disyllabic trochaic foot, as captured by the subcategorization constraint in (3).

(3)   Homeric ma-infixation (First attempt)
       ALIGN (L, *ma*, R, FT$_{σσ}$) = L-ALIGN
       'Align the left edge of *ma* to the right edge of a disyllabic trochee.'

---

[2] Thanks to David Peterson, Meg Grant, Emily Horner, Rachel Goulet and Jake Szamosi for sharing their intuitions on *ma*-infixation with me.
[3] Infixing after the initial foot, i.e. *under-ma-restimate*, is also possible here (i.e. *repa-ma-pellent* vs. *repella-ma-lent*), though with concomitant reduplication.

The analysis makes an interesting, though erroneous, prediction regarding the following forms, however:

(4)   σ̀σ̆σ̆σ́σ̆   σ̀σ̆σ̆-ma-σ́σ̆   *σ̀σ̆-ma-σ́σ̆σ̆

     multiplication   multipli-ma-cation   *multi-ma-plication
     Mediterranean   Mediter-ma-ranean   *Medi-ma-terranean
     delicacy   delica-ma-cy   *deli-ma-cacy

Here, the input contains a ternary pretonic string. Secondary stress is on the initial syllable. Since most theories of English stress do not admit ternary feet, a word like *multiplication* is often parsed as *(mul.ti)pli(ca.tion)* (e.g., Pater 2000). The problem with this foot-parse is that the current analysis would predict the infix to appear after the second syllable, rather than the third (e.g., **(mul.ti)-ma-pli.(ca.tion)*).

(5)   Evaluation of /multiplication, ma/

(mul.ti)pli(ca.tion), ma	L-ALIGN	R-ALIGN
a. ☞ *(mul.ti)pli-ma-(ca.tion)*	*!	
b. ☜* *(mul.ti)-ma-pli.(ca.tion)*		
c. *(mul.ti.pli)-ma-(ca.tion)*	*!	

Following Hayes 1982, McCarthy 1982, Ito & Mester 1992, and Jensen 1993 & 2000, the third syllable is assumed to be adjoined to the initial foot, giving the following structure:

(6)

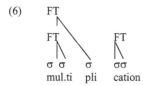

     σ σ   σ   σσ
    mul.ti   pli   cation

The advantage of assuming this foot representation is that the binary character of the pivot, that is, the unit to which an infix attach, can be maintained, which in turns allows the formulation of an alignment constraint that holds across the board without exception.

(7)   Revised L- ALIGN
     ALIGN (L, *ma*, R, FT_{max}) = L-ALIGN
     'Align the left edge of -*ma*- to the right edge of a maximal binary-branching syllabic foot.'

The notion of a *maximal foot* refers to a foot that is not dominated by another foot, which means that it must be directly dominated by a Prosodic Word. A *minimal foot*, on the other hand, refers to a foot that does not dominate another foot. By appealing to the notion of the maximal foot, the alignment constraint not only captures the infixation pattern in words like *multiplication*, but also excludes unattested patterns such as **multi-ma-plication*.[4]

Turning to the disyllabic stems, the analysis presented in (7) predicts that *ma-* should surface after the second syllable, giving the appearance of a suffix.

(8) oboe   *oboe-ma   purple   *purple-ma
     opus   *opus-ma   scramble   *scramble-ma
     party   *party-ma   stinky   *stinky-ma
     piggy   *piggy-ma   table   *table-ma

Curiously, this prediction is not borne out, as evidenced by the ungrammaticality of the examples in (8). Disyllabic stems must be expanded in order to host the Homeric infix. The nature of the expansion is described in the next section.

3.   Motivating Compensatory Reduplication

Two types of expansion patterns are found. When the stressed syllable is closed, a schwa is inserted to create a disyllabic stressed foot (9). This strategy is referred to as *schwa-epenthesis*. The epenthetic schwa is underlined below.

(9) careful   'kʰɛɹə̱-mə-fəl   lively   'lajvə̱-mə-lɪ
     grapefruit   'gɹejpə̱-mə-ˌfɹut   lonely   'lounə̱-mə-lɪ
     graveyard   'gɹejvə̱-mə-ˌjaɹd   Orwell   'ɔɹə̱-mə-wəl
     hairstyle   'hɛɹə̱-mə-ˌstajl

However, when the first syllable is open, in addition to schwa epenthesis, a consonant identical to the onset of the following syllable appears before the schwa (10). I refer to this as *partial reduplication*.

(10) oboe   oba-ma-boe   washing   washa-ma-shing
     opus   opa-ma-pus   water   wata-ma-ter
     party   parta-ma-ty   wonder   wonda-ma-der
     piggy   piga-ma-gy   aura   aura-ma-ra
     purple   purpa-ma-ple   music   musa-ma-sic
     scramble   scramba-ma-ble   Kieran   Kiera-ma-ran
     stinky   stinka-ma-ky   joking   joka-ma-king
     table   taba-ma-ble   listen   lisa-ma-sten
     tuba   tuba-ma-ba

---

[4] The main problem of this understanding of the prosodic organization of words like those in (6) is that it violates the Strict Layer Hypothesis (Selkirk 1984:26, Nespor & Vogel 1986:7). However, violations of the Strict Layer Hypothesis seem to be independently motivated regardless of the case discussed here (see Hayes 1982, Jensen 1993, Jensen 2000).

At this point, the question of why the Homeric infix cannot appear word-peripherally naturally presents itself. The non-peripherality of the Homeric infix cannot be attributed to general properties of infixation in English; expletive formation in English, for example, allows both infixing and 'prefixing' variants.

(11)   fantástic   *bloody* fantástic   fan-*bloody*-tástic
        Minnesóta   *bloody* Minnesóta   Minne-*bloody*-sóta
        Alabáma   *bloody* Alabáma   Ala-*bloody*-báma

Neither can non-peripherality be attributed to general rhythmic considerations of English. The rhythmic pattern of the illicit output **opus-ma* ['oʊpʰəsmə] (–∪∪), for example, is identical to that of *cinema* ['sɪnəmə] or *venomous* ['vɛnəməs]. Moreover, Homericized forms such as *Cána-ma-da* (–∪∪∪) and *véno-ma-mous* (–∪∪∪) are clearly acceptable to speakers despite the fact that there is a string of three unstressed syllables on the surface.

Some might argue that non-peripherality might be derivable from extrametricality in English. The final syllable of nouns and suffixed adjectives is said to be extrametrical, thus exempted from foot-parsing, hence stress assignment (Hayes 1982). Thus, a word such as *cinema* is parsed as ('cine)<*ma*>. Disyllabic words receive similar treatment. For example, *lively* is given the following foot parse: ('live)<*ly*>. Since the input to Homeric infixation is assumed to contain metrical information[5], the fact that -*ma*- cannot appear as a suffix falls out naturally from this assumption of foot assignment. Consider the following evaluation:

(12)   Evaluation of /lively, ma/

('lajv)lɪ, mə	L-ALIGN
a. ☞('lajv<u>ə</u>)-mə-lɪ	
b. ('lajv)lɪ-mə	*!

Here, candidate (12)b fails because -*ma*- is to the left of an unparsed syllable. This violates the dominating L-ALIGN constraint, which demands -*ma*- to appear after a maximal disyllabic foot. While such an analysis is appealing since one only has to invoke an independently-needed mechanism of English metrical phonology, namely,

---

[5] The input to Homeric infixation must already be parsed metrically. Consider, for example, the word 'Canada. Following the parametric approach to English stress assignment (cf. Hayes 1995), the main stress foot, which is trochaic, is built from right to left. The reason why this word has initial main stress, rather than penultimate, is due to the fact that the final syllable is extrametrical (e.g., ('Cana)<*da*>)). Now, consider the infixed version of this word 'Cana-ma-da. Primary stress remains initial. Yet, if stress placement occurs concomitant with infixation, antepenultimate stress (e.g., Ca('na-ma)-<*da*> similar to A'merica) is predicted. This illustration points to the fact that *ma*-infixation must have access to pre-existing foot structures. That is, the reason one finds 'Cana-ma-da, not *Ca'na-ma-da, is because the Homeric infix takes ('Cana)da as the input. The outcome of infixation is ('Cana)-ma-da.

extrametricality, it is unfortunately flawed. The above analysis relies on the fact that the final syllable is extrametrical, thus not footed in the input. Consider the following:

(13)   Evaluation of /listen, ma/

('lɪsn̩), mə	L-ALIGN
a. ☞ ('lɪsə)-mə-sn̩	
b. ●*('lɪsn̩)-mə	

The final syllable of underived verbs in English is generally not extrametrical. Words such as *listen* are parsed as a disyllabic foot. The extrametricality analysis erroneously predicts that the infix can appear both medially (13)a and finally (13)b since the final syllable is footed. Only (13)a is possible, however. In sum, the fact that -*ma*- never realizes as a suffix suggests that the proper placement of -*ma*- is contingent on its appearance as a ***genuine infix*** in the output; it must appear before *and* after something.[6]

The non-peripheral distribution of -*ma*- is derived here through the interaction of two phonological subcategorization constraints. The first constraint has already been introduced earlier; it requires the infix to appear to the right of a maximal disyllabic foot. The second constraint demands that the infix appear before a syllable. These constraints exert quite different, though not necessarily incompatible, demands on the Homeric word construction.

(14)   ALIGN (L, *ma*, R, FT_{max}) = L-ALIGN
        'Align the left edge of -*ma*- to the right edge of a maximal binary-branching syllabic foot.'

        ALIGN (R, *ma*, L, σ) a.k.a. R-ALIGN
        'Align the right edge of -*ma*- to the left edge of a syllable.'

Couched within Optimality Theory (Prince & Smolensky 1993, McCarthy & Prince 1993), these alignment constraints must be undominated and unranked with respect to each other. Their combined effect rules out any candidate with the improper placement of the -*ma*- infix (see (15)b & (15)c). The tableau below shows the evaluation of the Homeric word *tele-ma-phone*.

(15)   Evaluation of /telephone, ma/

('telə)(ˌfoʊn), mə	L-ALIGN	R-ALIGN
a. ☞ ('telə)-mə-(ˌfoʊn)		
b. ('te.-mə-)lə(ˌfoʊn)	*!	
c. ('telə)(ˌfoʊn)-mə		*!

---

[6] This property of the Homeric infixation is quite unique in comparison to the majority of infixes across the world's languages. 'Infixes' without a non-peripherality requirement are better analyzed as *phonological affixes*, that is, affixes that subcategorize for a phonological rather than a morphological constituent (see Yu 2003 for further discussions).

Candidate (15)b loses since it violates L-ALIGN due to the fact the material to the left of -*ma*- does not constitute a foot. Candidate (15)c fatally violates R-ALIGN since no syllable follows the 'infix'.

Let us now consider a disyllabic input. *Ma*- can never appear finally because it would fatally violate the R-ALIGN constraint ((16)b). It cannot appear prefixed since it fails to satisfy the L-ALIGN requirement ((16)d). Infixing -*ma*- without expansion would not work either since the L-ALIGN requirement ((16)c) is still not satisfied. Thus, this evaluation illustrates the fact that expanding the root through CR provides a means to satisfy both the L-ALIGN and the R-ALIGN requirements simultaneously.

(16)   Evaluation of /listen, ma/

(ˈlɪsn̩), mə	L-ALIGN	R-ALIGN
a. ☞ (ˈlɪsə)-mə-sn̩		
b. (ˈlɪsn̩)-mə		*!
c. (ˈlɪ-mə)-sn̩	*!	
d. mə-(ˈlɪsn̩)		

As illustrated in (17), however, root expansion may be accomplished by means of schwa-insertion as well. (17)b demonstrates the fact that -*ma*- cannot appear after a bimoraic foot in English because this infix left-subcategorizes for a *disyllabic* foot. The correct selection of *liva-ma-ly* is given below:

(17)   Evaluation of /lively, ma/

(ˈlajv)lɪ, mə	L-ALIGN	R-ALIGN
a. ☞(ˈlajvə)-mə-lɪ		
b. (ˈlajv)-mə-lɪ	*!	

The analysis presented thus far offers an account of *why* root expansion is needed to host the Homeric infix, namely, it is needed to satisfy the bidirectional subcategorization requirement of the infix. This analysis is silent, however, with respect to the question of why expansion is accomplished through CR with certain types of disyllabic roots but schwa-epenthesis with others. The answer to this question is explored in detail in the next section.

4.   The Nature of a Compensatory Reduplicant

As noted earlier, *ma*-infixation induces root expansion when it is necessary to satisfy its bidirectional subcategorization requirements. Two expansion strategies are possible: schwa-epenthesis and partial reduplication. This section focuses first on the nature of partial reduplication. As will be demonstrated in due course, the present analysis of reduplication has serious implications on the interpretation of schwa epenthesis as well.

Partial reduplication has two variants. Variant A shows the copying of the syllable following the infix; Variant B shows a similar pattern, though the vowel of the reduplicant is reduced to a schwa.

(18)   Variant A   Variant B
     piggy   pig<u>y</u>-ma-gy   pig[ə]-ma-gy
     table   tab<u>le</u>-ma-ble   tab[ə]-ma-ble
     listen   li[<u>sn</u>]-ma-[sn̩]   lis[ə]-ma-sten
     oboe   o<u>boe</u>-ma-boe   ob[ə]-ma-boe
     purple   pur<u>ple</u>-ma-ple   purp[ə]-ma-ple
     scramble   scram<u>ble</u>-ma-ble   scramb[ə]-ma-ble
     stinky   stin<u>ky</u>-ma-ky   stink[ə]-ma-ky
     party   par<u>ty</u>-ma-ty   part[ə]-ma-ty

When the stressed syllable is closed there is no variation in the realization of the reduplicant. Only schwa-epenthesis is allowed.

(19)   lively   ˈlajvə-mə-lɪ   *ˈlajvɪ-mə-lɪ
       lonely   ˈlounə-mə-lɪ   *ˈlounɪ-mə-lɪ
       grapefruit   ˈkɹejpə-mə-ˌfɹut   *ˈkɹejpu-mə-ˌfɹut
       graveyard   ˈkɹejvə-mə-ˌjaɪd   *ˈkɹejvaɪ-mə-ˌjaɪd
       hairstyle   ˈhɛɹə-mə-ˌstajl   *ˈhɛɹaj-mə-ˌstajl

Why is reduplication not possible without the copying of the onset consonant as well? Is the schwa that appears in the reduplicant of Variant A in (18) the "same" schwa that appears in (19)? To answer these questions, one must first answer a different question: why does the reduplicative copy always come from the syllable after the infix, rather than the one before? That is, why are there only examples such as *tuba-ma-ba*, but never *tuta-ma-ba*?

4.1. 'Copying' within RED

Compensatory Reduplication, by definition, affords no morphological representation in the underlying representation. This property of CR raises problems regarding the nature of the relationship between the 'duplicate' and the materials duplicated. Traditional theories of reduplication assume that a reduplicant copies from one of the edges of the stem or that of a stressed constituent (e.g., a stressed foot). Neither option is available here since the 'base' is neither morphologically nor prosodically coherent. Related is the issue of how identity between the reduplicant and the base is defined. Within BCRT, the direction of 'reduplicative copying' is regulated by the family of ANCHOR constraints that demand the edges of the reduplicant and the base correspond in a particular fashion. Such an analysis is not available here since there is no reduplicative morpheme in the usual sense.[7] To this end, I adopt the output segmental correspondence approach to CR, following the suggestions laid out in Bat-El 2002 and Inkelas In press. The idea behind this approach is that output identical segments stand in a correspondence relationship (Rose & Walker 2001; Hansson 2001). In particular, following Rose & Walker 2001 and Hansson 2001, I propose that directionality be stated as a correspondence relationship.[8] The particular constraint needed is defined below:

(20)   Correspondence-S_iS_j (SCORRI$_L$)
      'If S_i is a segment in the output and S_j a correspondent of S_i in the output, S_j must precede S_i in the sequence of segments in the output ($j > i$).'

The effect of SCORRI$_L$ is to rule out structures like (21)b where the copied material comes from the syllable before, rather than the one after the infix. The reduplicative copy is indicated with the subscript 'C'.

(21)

$(^{\prime}C_1V_1)C_2V_2C_3$, mə	SCORRI$_L$
a. ☞ $(^{\prime}C_1V_1C_{2C}V_{2C})$-mə-$C_2V_2C_3$	
b. $(^{\prime}C_1V_1C_{1C}V_{1C})$-mə-$C_2V_2C_3$	*!

Let us now return to the earlier dilemma. The fact that words like *lively* Homerize as ['lajvə-mə-lɪ], never *['lajvɪ-mə-lɪ] suggests that partial reduplication is not possible without the copying of the onset consonant as well. In light of the present analysis, a solution to this problem is now in sight, which I refer to as ***Surface Correspondence Percolation***.

(22)   Surface Correspondence Percolation
      'If syllable σ_i contains a segment S_i that is in surface correspondence with segment S_j in syllable σ_j, all segments in syllable σ_i must be in correspondence with segments in syllable σ_j.'

CR without the copying of an onset consonant is not possible in cases like *lively* because the syllable hosting any surface corresponding segments must also be in correspondence. That is, if syllable σ_i contains a segment S_i that is in surface correspondence with segment S_j in syllable σ_j, all segments in syllable σ_i must be in correspondence with segments in syllable σ_j. Such a correspondence relationship can be captured using the theory of Prosodic Anchoring advocated in McCarthy 2002. Two syllable-anchoring constraints are posited.

---

[7] Notice that the Morphological Doubling Theory of Reduplication (MDT; Inkelas and Zoll 2000) is also unavailable here since the reduplicant serves no morphological purpose, thus no morpho-semantic identity between the base and reduplicant (see also Inkelas In press).

[8] The idea that directionality is crucial in a correspondence relationship has been pointed out previously for the input-output relationship (i.e. IDEN-IO vs. IDEN-OI; Pater 1999) and in other applications of surface segmental correspondence, for example, in consonant harmony (Rose & Walker 2001, Hansson 2001).

(23)   L-ANCHOR$_\sigma$
        'The initial position of two syllables in a surface correspondence relationship must
        correspond.'
        R-ANCHOR$_\sigma$
        'The final position of two syllables in a surface correspondence relationship must
        correspond.'

The compliance of these two constraints is asymmetric; L-ANCHOR$_\sigma$ must dominate R-ANCHOR$_\sigma$. Below is an example of an infixed disyllabic input.[9] The analysis predicts the reduplicant to be a CV syllable when the pivot is expanded by reduplication. While the copying of the nucleus from the syllable after the infix would be sufficient to satisfy the disyllabic requirement of the pivot, as illustrated by (24)b, such a candidate fatally violates L-ANCHOR$_\sigma$, which demands the initial segments of the corresponding syllables to match.

(24) $['C_1V_1][C_2V_2]_j$, mə

	L-ALIGN	L-ANCHOR$_\sigma$	R-ANCHOR$_\sigma$	SCORRI$_L$
☞ a. $['C_1V_1][C_2V_2]_j$-mə-$[C_2V_2]_j$				
b. $['C_1V_1][V_2]_j$-mə-$[C_2V_2]_j$		*!		

This constraint hierarchy also predicts that no reduplication is possible when the initial syllable is closed. As illustrated below, (25)a is ruled out by virtue of the fact that the onsets of the corresponding syllables do not match. The syllables before and after the infix in (25)a are in correspondence due to the fact that the reduplicative vowel is in a correspondence relationship with the final vowel. (25)b prevails even though it contains an epenthetic schwa. The syllables before and after the infix are not in correspondence in this candidate since none of the segments of the respective syllables invoke surface correspondence.

(25) $['C_1V_1C_2][C_3V_3]_j$, mə

	L-ANCHOR$_\sigma$	R-ANCHOR$_\sigma$	SCORRI$_L$
a. $['C_1V_1][C_2V_{3C}]_j$ -mə-$[C_3V_3]_j$	*!		
b. ☞ $['C_1V_1][C_2ə]$-mə-$[C_3V_3]_j$			

So far, the discussion has concentrated on understanding the mechanism of 'reduplicative copying' in phonological reduplication. In the next section, I return to the issue of what motivates the reduplicative copying in the first place.

4.2.   Why reduplication?

Traditional theories of reduplication assume that reduplication happens only when it is called for by the presence of an abstract RED morpheme in the input (e.g., McCarthy & Prince 1995; Alderete et al 1999) or a COPY constraint in the constraint ranking (e.g., Yip 1998). These analytical devices are inadequate in dealing with cases where

---

[9] The angled brackets indicate syllable boundaries.

'reduplication' is required solely in order to satisfy the size requirement of the pivot and there is no evidence for positing an underlying RED morpheme in the input. What then motivates the recruitment of a reduplicative copy over fixed consonant epenthesis? Zuraw (2002) claims that reduplication without semantic import is a matter of Aggressive Reduplication, which is forced by the constraint, REDUP, in the grammar. In this section, I argue that no such constraint is needed since CR can be derived straightforwardly through the interaction of constraints that are already independently needed in the grammar. In particular, I argue for an emergent approach to CR where CR falls out naturally as the result of the interaction between constraints on segmental faithfulness and the correspondence of similar segments. CR is favored over default segment insertion because it does not introduce segments that are not already in the input. The impetus of this approach comes from the nature of epenthesis itself as it is understood within OT.

In OT, epenthesis is regulated by DEP, a constraint that requires a segment in the output to have a correspondent in the input. The constraint, * FISSION, penalizes output candidates that realize multiple exponents of an input string. Thus, a candidate with epenthesized fixed segments, such as (26)b, would fatally violate DEP_{IO} when DEP_{IO} is ranked above *FISSION. This allows the candidate with reduplicative epenthesis (26)a to emerge as the winner.

(26)

$(p^h\textrm{ɪ})g_i i_j$, mə	DEP_{IO}	*FISSION
a. ☞$(p^h\textrm{ɪ}.g_i i_j)$-mə-$g_i i_j$		**
b. $(p^h\textrm{ɪ}.\textrm{ʔə})$-mə-$g_i i_j$	*!*	

This analysis explains why the epenthetic syllable is a reduplicative copy rather than some fixed segments: reduplication does not introduce segments that are not already in the input. This analysis also illuminates the difference between the schwa of the partial reduplicant and that of schwa-epenthesis. As illustrated in (27), the schwa in the reduplicant must stand in correspondence with the final vowel, otherwise, the candidate would fatally violate R-ANCHOR$_\sigma$ (see (27)b).

(27)

$('p^h\textrm{ɪ})g_i i_j$, mə	L-ANCHOR$_\sigma$	R-ANCHOR$_\sigma$	DEP_{IO}	*FISSION
a. ☞$(['p^h\textrm{ɪ}][g_i\textrm{ə}_j]_k)$-mə-$[g_i i_j]_k$				**
b. $(['p^h\textrm{ɪ}][g_i\textrm{ə}]_k)$-mə-$[g_i i_j]_k$		*!	*	

On the other hand, when a schwa appears alone without an accompanying reduplicative onset, the ranking predicts that such a schwa must be genuinely epenthetic. The correspondence between the schwa and the final vowel would have required the respective syllables to stand in correspondence also.

(28)

$('lajv)l\textrm{ɪ}$, mə	L-ANCHOR$_\sigma$	R-ANCHOR$_\sigma$	DEP_{IO}	*FISSION
a. $(['laj][v\textrm{ə}_j]_k)$-mə-$[l_i \textrm{ɪ}_j]_k$	*!			*
b. ☞$(['laj][v\textrm{ə}])$-mə-$[l_i \textrm{ɪ}_j]_k$		*	*	

As illustrated by (28)a, such a candidate would fatally violate L-ANCHOR$_\sigma$ since the onsets of the corresponding syllables do not match. The remaining question is why the reduplicative vowel reduces some of the time but not others (see (18)).

4.3.   Variation in the reduplicant

The variation to be dealt with in this section concerns the vowel quality of a reduplicant. Such a vowel may appear as a full vowel or a reduced vowel, namely, schwa. This variation follows straightforwardly from the phonotactics of English. Full vowels in English are generally found in syllables with some degree of stress. The epenthesized syllable under infixation always occupies the weak position of a trochaic foot, thus must be stressless. Consequently, candidates such as (29)b can be ruled out by a dominating constraint against unstressed full vowels in English, called 'REDUCE'.

(29) $(p^h\text{I})$gi, mə

	REDUCE	DEP$_{IO}$
a. $(p^h\text{I}.g_1i_2)$-mə-g_1i_2	*!	
b. ☞ $(p^h\text{I}.g_1ə_2)$-mə-g_1i_2		

The introduction of REDUCE alone prevents any variation in output selection, however, as shown by the failure of (29)a, an attested output. Thus, some additional force must counteract the effect of REDUCE. The key is in the evaluation of (29)b. The partial reduplicant in (29)b contains a schwa that is in correspondence with the final syllable. However, the two nuclei are not identical, thus should not have entered into a surface correspondence relationship. Following Walker 2000, Rose & Walker 2001 and Hansson 2001, I amend the earlier analysis and propose that correspondence is established in terms of similarity, rather than absolute identity. The following correspondence constraints that hold of pairs of similar vowels are posited:

(30)   Similarity-based Surface Correspondence Hierarchy
        CORR- $V_i \leftrightarrow V_i$ >> CORR-$V \leftrightarrow ə$

The faithfulness between these corresponding segments is regulated by featural IDEN-VV constraints. In this case, I posit a IDEN-VV$_{[reduced]}$ which demands that surface corresponding vowels must have identical [reduced] specification.

(31)   a. $(p^h\text{I})$gi, mə

	REDUCE	IDEN-VV$_{[reduced]}$	DEP$_{IO}$
a. $(p^h\text{I}.g_1i_2)$-mə-g_1i_2	*!		
b. ☞ $(p^h\text{I}.g_1ə_2)$-mə-g_1i_2		*	

   b. $(p^h\text{I})$gi, mə

	IDEN-VV$_{[reduced]}$	REDUCE	DEP$_{IO}$
a. ☞ $(p^h\text{I}.g_1i_2)$-mə-g_1i_2		*	
b. $(p^h\text{I}.g_1ə_2)$-mə-g_1i_2	*!		

)

This IDEN-VV[reduced] constraint is assumed to be co-ranked with respect to the constraint, REDUCE (e.g., Anttila 1997). At the time of evaluation, a particular ranking permutation of these two constraints is selected, producing a unique winning output. The permutation of the two constraints produces, in this case, two possible outcomes, both of which are attested (see the winning candidates in (31)).

     In this section, I argue that, while the Homeric infix induces foot-expansion to provide a suitable pivot for infix alignment, CR is motivated by the constraint schema DEP$_{IO}$ >> *FISSION and by surface segment correspondence. The final constraint hierarchy of the co-phonology associated with the Homeric infix is given below:[10]

(32)   Summary of the Homeric Infixation Constraint Hierarchy
       R-ALIGN, L-ALIGN >> I-ANCHOR, SCORRI$_L$, L-ANCHOR$_\sigma$ >> {REDUCE
       <<>> IDEN-VV[reduced]} >> R-ANCHOR$_\sigma$, F- ANCHOR >> DEP$_{IO}$ >> *FISSION

5.   Conclusion

In this paper, I introduce the construction of Homeric infixation, arguing that *-ma-* is a genuine infix given its requirement of non-peripherality. This property of the Homeric infix gives rise to the situation of CR where it is employed to expand the base for the purpose of proper infixation. In the course of articulating the treatment of CR in Homeric infixation, a general theory of CR, schematized in (33), emerges.

(33)   A General Theory of Compensatory Reduplication

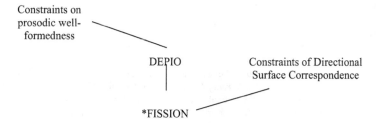

A theory of CR must consist of three major components: (i) the high ranking of some constraints demanding prosodic well-formedness of the output. They may be constraints

---

[10] The Homeric infixation construction is associated with its own co-phonology, given the fact that non-peripherality is an idiosyncratic and intrinsic property of the Homeric infix and that the Homeric infixation construction must take a metrically parsed input. To this end, I adopt a Sign-Based Morphology (henceforth SBM) approach to co-phonological phenomenon. SBM is a declarative, non-derivational theory of the morphology-phonology interface which utilizes the basic tools one finds in any constituent structure-based unificational approach to linguistics originally developed by Orgun (1996, 1998, 1999). It assumes that both terminal and non-terminal nodes bear features and that non-terminal nodes also include the phonological information along with the usual syntactic and semantic information (i.e. co-phonology: Orgun 1996, Inkelas, et. al 1997, Inkelas 1998, Inkelas & Zoll 2000, Yu 2000, Orgun & Inkelas 2002; similar co-phonological approaches: Antilla 2001, Kiparsky To appear).

on morpheme well-formedness (e.g., minimality, templatic constraints, or a phonological subcatgerization requirement) or constraints of prosody (e.g., *CODA, ONSET etc.). The high ranking of such a constraint creates scenarios where phonological compensation or expansion is needed; (ii) a directional surface correspondence constraint that specifies the 'source' of the reduplicated material; (iii) the constraint schema, DEP$_{IO}$ >> *FISSION, which favors CR over default segmental insertion when additional phonological materials are needed to satisfy some dominating prosodic requirement. All three components of the theory are independently motivated. This approach contrasts favorably with the Aggressive Reduplication model argued in Zuraw 2002 where CR is encoded in the grammar in the form of a constraint, called REDUP. I contend that no such constraint is needed since CR can be derived straightforwardly through the interaction of constraints that are already independently needed in the grammar.

References

Alderete, John, Jill Beckman, Laura Benua, Amalia Gnanadeskian, John McCarthy, and Suzane Urbanczyk. 1999. Reduplication with fixed segmentism. *LI* 30: 327-364.

Antilla, Arto. 1997. *Variation in Finnish Phonology and Morphology*. Ph.D. dissertation. Stanford University.

Antilla, Arto. 2002. Morphologically conditioned phonological alternations. *NLLT* 20: 1-42.

Bat-El, Outi. 2002. Hebrew reduplication: the interpretation of forms with identical consonants. Handout of a talk presented at UCSC, April 26.

Hansson, Gunnar. 2001. *Theoretical and typological issues in consonantal harmony*. Ph.D. dissertation, UC Berkeley.

Hayes, Bruce. 1982. Extrametricality and English stress. *LI* 13: 227-276.

Hayes, Bruce. 1995. *Metrical stress theory: Principles and case studies*. Chicago: University of Chicago Press.

Hyman, Larry M., Sharon Inkelas, and Galen Sibanda. 1999. *Morphosyntactic correspondence in Bantu reduplication*. Ms. University of California, Berkeley.

Inkelas, Sharon. 1998. The theoretical status of morphologically considered phonology: a case of dominance effects. *Yearbook of morphology* 1997: 121-155.

Inkelas, Sharon. 1999. Exceptional stress-attracting suffixes in Turkish: representations vs. the grammar. In H. van der Hulst, R. Kager, and Wim Zonneveld (eds.) *The Prosody-Morphology Interface*. Cambridge University Press. 134-187.

Inkelas, Sharon. In press. Morphological Doubling Theory I: Evidence for morphological doubling in reduplication. In Bernhart Hurch (ed.) *Studies in reduplication*. Mouton.

Inkelas, Sharon, and Cheryl Zoll. 2000. *Reduplication as morphological doubling*. Ms. UC Berkeley and MIT.

Inkelas, Sharon, Cemil Orhan Orgun and Cheryl Zoll. 1997. Implications of lexical exceptions for the nature of grammar. In Iggy Roca (ed.) Constraints and Derivations in Phonology. Oxford: Clarendon Press. 393-418.

Ito, Junko, and Armin Mester. 1992. Weak layering and word binarity. In Linguistic Research Center, LRC-92-09, University of California, Santa Cruz.

Jensen, John T. 1993. *English phonology*. Amsterdam: Benjamins.

Jenson, John T. 2000. Against ambisyllabicity. *Phonology* 17(3):187-235.

Kawahara, Shigeto. 2001. Reduplication not driven by a RED morpheme. Ms. University of Massachusetts, Amherst.

Kiparsky, Paul. To appear. Paradigm Effects and Opacity. CSLI monograph.

McCarthy, John J. 2000. Faithfulness and prosodic circumscription. In J. Dekkers, F. van der Leeuw, J. van de Weijer (eds.) *Optimality Theory: phonology, syntax, and acquisition.* 151-189. New York: Oxford University Press.

McCarthy, John J. and Alan Prince. 1993. Generalized alignment. In Geert Booij and Jaap van Marle (eds.) *Yearbook of morphology* 1993. 79-153. Dordrecht: Kluwer Academics.

McCarthy, John & Alan Prince. 1995. Faithfulness and reduplicative identity. *UMOP 18: Papers in Optimality Theory*. 249-384.

Orgun, C. Orhan. 1996. *Sign-based morphology: a declarative theory of phonology-morphology interleaving*. PhD dissertation, University of California, Berkeley.

Orgun, C. Orhan. 1998. Cyclic and noncyclic phonological effects in a declarative grammar. *Yearbook of morphology* 1997. 179-218.

Orgun, C. Orhan. 1999. Sign-Based Morphology: a declarative theory of phonology-morphology interleaving. In Ben Hermans & Marc van Oostendorp (eds.), The derivational residue in phonological Optimality Theory. Amsterdam: John Benjamins. 247-67.

Orgun, C. Orhan and Sharon Inkelas. 2002. Reconsidering Bracket Erasure. *Yearbook of morphology 2001*: 115-146.

Pater, Joe. 2000. Non-uniformity in English secondary stress: the role of ranked and lexically specific constraints. *Phonology* 17(3):237-274.

Prince, Alan, and Paul Smolensky. 1993. *Optimality Theory: Constraint interaction in Generative Grammar*. Ms. Rutgers University, New Brunswick, and University of Colorado, Boulder.

Rose, Sharon and Rachel Walker. 2001. A typology of consonant agreement as correspondence. Ms. UCSD & USC.

Walker, Rachel. 2000. Long distance consonant identity effects. *WCCFL* 19: 532-545.

Yip, Moira. 1998. Identity avoidance in phonology and morphology. In S. Lapointe, D. Brentari, and P. Farrell (eds.) *Morphology and its relation to phonology and syntax.* Stanford, CA: CSLI. 216-263.

Yu, Alan C. L. 2000. Stress assignment in Tohono O'odham. *Phonology* 17(1): 117-135.

Yu, Alan C. L. 2003. The morphology and phonology of infixation. PhD dissertation. UC Berkeley. http://home.uchicago.edu/~aclyu/dissertation.html

Zuraw, Kie. 2002. Aggressive reduplication. *Phonology* 19(3): 395-440.

Department of Linguistics
1010 E 59th Street
Chicago, IL 60637

aclyu@socrates.berkeley.edu

www.ingramcontent.com/pod-product-compliance
Lightning Source LLC
Chambersburg PA
CBHW071103050326
40690CB00008B/1090